SCREENING PARTY

SCREENING PARTY

DENNIS HENSLEY

MANUFACTURED IN THE UNITED STATES OF AMERICA.

THIS TRADE PAPERBACK ORIGINAL IS PUBLISHED BY ALYSON PUBLICATIONS,
P.O. BOX 4371, LOS ANGELES, CALIFORNIA 90078-4371.
DISTRIBUTION IN THE UNITED KINGDOM BY TURNAROUND PUBLISHER SERVICES LTD.,
UNIT 3, OLYMPIA TRADING ESTATE, COBURG ROAD, WOOD GREEN,
LONDON N22 6TZ ENGLAND.

FIRST EDITION: SEPTEMBER 2002

02 03 04 05 06 a 10 9 8 7 6 5 4 3 2 1

ISBN 1-55583-733-6

LIBRARY OF CONGRESS CATALOGING-IN-PUBLICATION DATA
HENSLEY, DENNIS.
SCREENING PARTY / DENNIS HENSLEY.—1ST ED.
ISBN 1-55583-733-6
1. HOLLYWOOD (LOS ANGELES, CALIF.)—FICTION.
2.MOTION PICTURE INDUSTRY—FICTION. I. TITLE.
PS3558.E543 S34 2002
813'.54—DC21 2002026050

CREDITS
- COVER DESIGN BY MATT SAMS.
- COVER AND INTERIOR PHOTOGRAPHY BY GREG HENRY, ASSISTED BY ART GRAY.
STYLING BY CLIFF HOPPUS, ASSISTED BY SAUL LYONS. HAIR AND MAKEUP BY BRETT FREEDMAN.

To Edward Margulies,
who loved talking about movies more than anyone

Contents

ACKNOWLEDGMENTS

For me, working on *Screening Party* was like being on a year-and-a-half-long scavenger hunt, in which I pilfered ideas, jokes, anecdotes, and entire story lines from wherever I could find them. By the end, I was practically going up to strangers and saying, "What happened to you this morning? Great, that'll close out my chapter." I was shameless.

The following individuals—and others I'm sure I'm forgetting—opened their minds, mouths, hearts, and, in some cases, junior high diaries to me, and I will always be grateful for their candor, enthusiasm, and trust.

Thank you, Judy Hopkins, for 15 years of friendship, laughter, encouragement, and hilarious celebrity rants. I know your participation in this book involved a good deal of time, technology, and postage. Thanks for always being game and delivering beyond my wildest expectations.

Thank you, Tony Tripoli, for allowing me to paint you as cattier than you really are, making me laugh more than anyone in the world, and giving me a home.

To Mark Salzberg: From treats in Tupperware to St. Olaf stories, you brought so much to the party. Thank you for your friendship and for talking me down from the ledge on more than one occasion.

To the Screening Party Regulars: Robert Abele, Alonso Duralde, Gabriel Goldberg, Kathy Griffin, Shane Jacobsen, Debra Praver, Erin Quill, Margy Rochlin, Paul Schneider, Tom Walsh, and Dave White. Thanks for continuing to haul your asses out to the Valley and being so hilarious, insightful, and fun to be around.

Thank you to following friends, who either popped by for a party or two or helped me out in some other significant way: Veronica Alicino, Norman Arnold, Scott Brassart, Andy Bruce, David Buik, John Cantwell, Clark Carlton, P.J. Castellaneta, Mike Cisneros, Karen Dyer, Jeffrey Epstein, Brett Freedman, Michael Fruehstorfer, Alex Kaufman, Shannon Kelley, Joe Kirkendall, Evan Koursh, George Lee, Clinton Leupp, Terrence McFarland, Mitch Moore, David Moreton, Haas Mroue, Jose Ortiz, Joelle Pezley, Laurie Pike, Jack Plotnick, Peter Ray, Phillip B. Roth, Jody Sakstrup, Bill Santoro, Red Savage, Geoff Schackert, Grant Shaffer, Eddie Shapiro, Dennis Smeal, Kate Smeal, Robert Smith, Thom Storr, Denise Taylor, David Todd, Ben Wexler, Gilles Wheeler, Scott Williams, and Mike Windt.

To Scott Brassart at Alyson: Thanks for saying yes to my pitch for a fun, fast novelty read and for being so patient and supportive when that original idea grew into the Book That Ate Cleveland. Thanks also to Angela Brown for getting me the rest of the way through the process, Dan Cullinane for helping to get the word out, and everyone at Alyson for their hard work and enthusiasm.

To the cover team: Thank you to Matt Sams at Alyson for your vision, energy, and style. Thanks also to Greg Henry and his assistant Art Gray for the terrific photographs, Cliff Hoppus and his assistant Saul Lyons for the perfect clothes, and Brett Freedman for making us all beautiful and giving me the best hair I've ever had.

Thank you to my agent, Bonnie Nadell; manager, Kassie Evashevski; and publicist, Henry Penner, for taking care of business with such energy, humor, and professionalism.

Thank you to my family for their love and support and for not disowning me for writing about some of the things I write about in this book.

To Matt Mueller, thank you for nurturing the original column and getting this whole thing rolling. This makes two books you helped inspire. Your check must have gotten lost in the mail.

Thank you to Felix Pire for saving my ass during the big final crunch, which ended up going on for months. I don't know what I would have done without you.

The folks at the Coffee Bean and Tea Leaf in Toluca Lake and the Starbucks in Studio City, for not charging me rent or utilities for all the hours I spent loitering in your establishments.

Finally, to all the dedicated, creative people who make movies for a living: Thank you for giving us all so much to talk, think, and laugh about.

INTO THE MOUTH OF MADNESS

If it's true that most of our adult hang-ups and predilections can be traced back to childhood, then I think I know the moment I became someone who loves to talk back to the television. I was 12 years old, watching an episode of my then-favorite show, *Charlie's Angels*, in my family's living room in Holbrook, Arizona, when I turned to my father and said, "Dad, what's prostitution?"

How I could enjoy that show week after week and not know what prostitution is seems absurd to me now, because wasn't every episode about prostitution? What did I think the ratty-haired day players in fish-nets were being arrested for, money laundering? In any event, I asked the question, and here's what my father replied:

" ."

That's right, folks. Absolutely nothing. Silence. Crickets. This could have been the jumping-off point for the birds and the bees talk I never got and really could have used, but no. He didn't even bother to make up a lie.

Since that fateful day, I've tried to populate my world with people who like to say things about what they see on television—people who ask questions, make observations, offer fashion commentary and occasionally crack wise. The MVP in this department is my roommate for the last seven years and best friend for 10, Tony Tripoli. From his end of the Comedy Couch (our friend Marcus's nickname for the well-traveled forest green sofa that faces our 26-inch screen), Tony can make sense of any confounding image or sound bite that might emanate forth from our beloved idiot box, except for maybe *Caroline in the City*. He's not a miracle worker.

At the moment, Tony and I are on our way to my favorite movie rental place, Video Master in Studio City. I love it for its colorful movie categorization system, the inventor of which, I figure, is either gay or seriously bi-curious. Who else would give John Waters and Gregg Araki their own kiosks? Or bother to stock multiple copies of *Ab Fab*? Let's say you wanted to rent *All About Eve*—you wouldn't find it under Drama, Comedy, or even Classics. You'd find it on the Legend of Bette Davis shelf, which is just above the shelf dedicated to The Scares of Stephen King. Think you'll find *Driving Miss Daisy* in Drama? Think again. It's under Oscar Winners You Never Want to See Again as Long as You Live, right between *Unforgiven* and *Gandhi*. OK, I made that last one up, but you get the idea.

"Why don't you just go to Blockbuster?" wonders Tony, who makes his living as a "singer who moves well" in theme parks, on cruise ships, and, for a brief time in the mid '90s, on ice in a Las Vegas casino. "It's closer to the house and they let you keep the tapes longer."

"I'm trying to give it up to the mom-and-pops," I say, turning into the parking lot.

Once inside, I head straight to the counter to ask directions, hoping to forgo the usual goose chase I usually go on whenever I try to find a movie here on my own. The clerk, Ross Fowler, according to his name tag, is a 35-ish, bushy-headed, tattooed fellow in Daria glasses and a seriously distressed Sex Pistols T-shirt. He's in the middle of a hushed but heated phone conversation that clearly has nothing to do with the fine art of video clerking. "Look, Julie," he says. "If you want it to be over, then consider it over." Noticing Tony and me, he shakes his head and mutters into the phone, "I know, I know, I know. You're right. Look, I can't talk about this now. I'll call you later."

He hangs up and gives me a "this better be good" look. I try to think of an obscure movie to ask for, something quirky enough to merit interrupting his important phone call, but the obscure movies I'm trying to think of are so obscure that I can't think of them. What is it about my personality that makes me want to apologize to people for wanting them to do their job?

"Where would I find *Jaws*?" I ask as cheerfully as possible. "The original."

"Horror," Ross says dryly, his subtext clearly smacking of *Duh*.

"Well, I don't know," I say playfully. "You guys have so many special categories. For all I know, Joan Crawford was the voice of the shark, which would put it in the Mad About Joan section."

This gets a chuckle out of Ross. Thank God.

"Here it is," says Tony, arriving at the Horror aisle before me. He grabs the tape from the shelf and meets me back at the counter.

"I'm sorry I was rude to you," Ross says, before taking my membership card and scanning it into the computer. "Girl trouble," he adds, gesturing to the phone.

"It's cool," I say.

Tony, uninterested in girl trouble in general and Ross's in particular, turns to me and says, "So, Dennis, do we have to be nice or can we be mean?"

"I want you to be whatever you feel," I say. "But from what I understand, *Jaws* is pretty great."

"Just wait till we do *The Bodyguard,*" Tony says menacingly. If my roommate were the type to sport a long curly mustache, he'd be twirling it right now.

"One opus at a time," I say. "We gotta make sure they like the first one."

"You guys doing some kind of show or something?" asks Ross.

"An article," I say. "For my job. I write for magazines—like profiles and essays and stuff—and my editor at *British Premiere* wants me to write something about *Jaws* for its 25th anniversary."

"It fucking rocks, dude," says Ross.

"So I hear," I say. "I've never seen it."

Ross looks at me as though I have three heads, two of which are connected by a long strand of earwax. "You don't know how bizarre that is to even imagine."

"I know, I suck," I admit.

"*Jaws* is number 3 on my all-time top 10," says Ross.

I can tell by the look on his face that he's dying for me to inquire as to what numbers 1 and 2 are, but I resist the temptation. "So because I've never seen it," I continue, "I said to my editor, 'How 'bout I invite some mouthy friends over and watch it for the first time and write about *that*?' And he said to go for it, believe it or not." I grab the worse-for-wear *Jaws* video box from the counter and stick it under my arm. "So now I have to do it," I say.

"You gonna put something in there about how *Jaws* wasn't the original title?" Ross inquires.

"I don't know," I say. "I didn't know that."

"It was a last minute decision of the part of the novelist, Peter Benchley, and his book editor," he says, his tone shifting smoothly away from Cheech and Chong land into Siskel and Ebert territory. "Benchley was considering titles like *A Stillness in the Water, Jaws of Leviathan,* and *Jaws of Death,* and he decided with his editor, like 20 minutes before the thing went to press, that the only word they even thought worked at all was *jaws,* so they were like, 'Fuck it, dude. Let's just call the thing *Jaws*.' "

"Really?" says Tony teasingly. "They said, 'Fuck it, dude?'"

"Or words to that effect," says Ross.

I pull one of the half-dozen Uni-ball pens I carry everywhere out of my pocket, ask Ross to repeat the passed-on titles, then scribble them on my receipt. "Thanks, man," I say, tucking the receipt into my wallet. "I guess you get to know a lot about movies working here."

"I guess," says Ross. "But I've always been obsessed with movies, and I know that *Jaws* story because someone was talking about it at school. I used to go to UCLA. Film school."

"I always thought it would be so cool to go to film school," I say.

"Since when?" wonders Tony.

"When I was in high school," I say defensively. "I still think it would be cool."

"Get a DVD player," says Ross. "Same difference."

"I've been telling him we should get a DVD player," says Tony, finally finding a common ground with our friend in the camouflage pants.

"It's a cash flow thing," I say.

"I said I'd split it with you," says Tony.

"You're unemployed," I say.

Tony hasn't worked since his last cruise ship gig ended two months ago. Though he managed to save a good deal of money over the six-month stint, it's going fast, and now he's starting to feel pressure to find his next source of income. What's more, he's burned out on performing and determined to stay in L.A. this time. So if you hear of anything…

"They're not that expensive," says Ross. "You can get a DVD player for, like, $200 now."

"Next big assignment I get, I'll buy one," I vow, before following Tony to the exit. I turn back to Ross and thank him for his help.

"Have fun at your little screening party," he says.

"We'll try," I reply as the door closes behind me. Tony and I climb into my Toyota 4Runner, but I don't close my door all the way.

"What?" questions Tony.

"He seems cool," I say. "And it seemed like he kind of wanted us to invite him. Did you get that?"

"He's creepy, Dennis," says Tony. "Those tattoos looked homemade. He's going to want to do beer bongs and shit, and I'm going to be making cracks about people's hair and stuff and I don't want to worry about *alienating the straight guy.*"

"Please, he works at the gayest video store ever," I say. "Besides, you heard him. *Jaws* is number 3 on his all-time top 10. I could use someone that actually knows stuff about the movie. We can't just make fun of people's hair."

"You haven't seen these people's hair," says Tony.

"He's probably going to say no anyway."

"It's your article. It's just that no one likes a know-it-all, Dennis. That's all I'm saying."

"I'll be right back," I say.

"Just remember," Tony says as I get out of the truck, "if he ends up being crazy, you're going to have to start going to Blockbuster, and you know what that means. No porn."

I dash back inside and wait while Ross finishes with another customer. Why does it suddenly seem like I'm asking the prettiest girl in the whole eighth grade to slow dance? I stammer through my invitation, then write the directions on a piece of scrap paper. Ross actually seems less enthused about the prospect than I thought he would be. Either that or he's playing hard to get. Still, he shoves the directions into his pocket and says he'll do his best.

•

Two hours later, with 15 minutes to go before our guests are scheduled to arrive, Tony and I return to our North Hollywood condo from the grocery store to find Ross waiting at our doorstep.

"Oh, great," says Tony under his breath. "He's already stalking us."

"Sorry I'm early, dude," Ross says as we greet him on the sidewalk.

Interesting. He said 'dude,' singular. He didn't say 'dudes,' plural, so I'm choosing to think that *I'm* the dude and Tony's just some nondude *with* the dude who wouldn't know true dudeness if it bit him in the ass.

"I came straight from work," Ross explains, before pulling a green and white box from behind his back and adding, "via Krispy Kreme."

"Rock on!" shouts Tony. Apparently, my roommate is only leery of people who are different from him when they don't show up with doughnuts.

"So who else is coming?" wonders Ross. "Any, you know, straight chicks?"

"Two, actually," I say, unlocking the front door. "But I thought you were seeing someone. The girl on the phone."

"We're considering that over," says Ross. "So are you two, like, together?" he asks, gesturing to the wanna-be-artsy black-and-white pictures of Tony and me over the couch.

"No," I say. "That's why we're still roommates after seven years."

I hear a car door slam outside and look out the window to see our friend Lauren O'Donovan trudging up the sidewalk, a bottle of vodka in one hand, a bottle of cranberry juice in the other. Quite an unusual cocktail herself, Ms. O'Donovan is a half-Irish, half-Chinese, born-in-Australia, raised-in-New York aerobics teacher and aspiring stand-up comic, the only one I know of in captivity.

"What's with the booze?" I ask, after she enters.

"They've found that it really comes in handy when you want to get drunk," she replies.

"Barry?" I ask.

Barry is Lauren's boyfriend of five years who, much to Lauren's dismay, seems to have taken up permanent residence on the square of linoleum that falls halfway between shitting and getting off the pot.

"I don't want to hear about your fucked-up lives. I'm kidding...OK, I'm not really." —Dr. Beaverman

Lauren doesn't respond, so I ask the question again. "Barry?"

"No, Rick Schroeder," she snaps. "Of course, Barry. But it's the same old story."

Before I even have time to introduce her to Ross, Lauren is in the kitchen mixing her first drink. Just as she returns, there's a knock on the front door followed by the words, "Land shark."

"Marcus is here," says Tony.

I open the door to greet Marcus Goldin, a junior entertainment lawyer and closet Betty Crocker I met doing the AIDS Ride in 1995. Our friendship was born when I, fed up with the official ride lunchables, made a detour to Taco Bell. Marcus was waiting in line at the next register and when the song "Dancing Queen" came on over the Muzak, we simultaneously began tapping our bike shoes. We've been friends ever since. "I've made Rice Krispie treats in the shape of severed limbs," he announces, holding up a plate covered in tinfoil. "Help yourself."

"Is this everyone?" asks Lauren impatiently.

"Almost," I say, before climbing onto the couch and knocking three times on the ceiling.

"Who are we missing, Tony Orlando?" asks Marcus.

"My neighbor," I explain. "I didn't think she'd say yes when I invited her. I just didn't want her to complain if we get loud and unruly, but she said yes so here we go. She's a psychiatrist or psychologist—whatever Bob Newhart was, I think. She has a practice in Sherman Oaks and teaches part-time at one of those schools-without-walls places. Anyway, if her comments at the yearly condo association meeting are any indication, she should have some interesting things to say."

"It's hard for me to remember what happens in *Jaws,* because the first porno I ever saw was called *Gums,* which was about a mermaid who sucked off guys in the ocean until their dicks fell off." —Tony

"Sorry I'm late, kids. I had to catch the end of *Poison: Behind the Music,*" says Dr. Beaverman when I open the door. While the rest of us figured jeans and T-shirts would suffice, my 40-something neighbor with the unnatural blond bob decided to dress for the occasion in a fitted charcoal coat and skirt that's either Chanel or wishes it was. A pair of black-framed half-glasses hangs from her neck atop enough gold chains to dress all the background actors in *A Night at the Roxbury.*

"Everyone, this is Dr. Beverly Beaverman," I say, resting a hand on her left shoulder pad. "She'll be giving us lots of psychological insights today."

"But just about the movie," she clarifies. "I don't want to hear about your fucked-up lives." With that, she plops down on the end of the couch that's closest to the door. "I'm kidding," she says, patting Ross's thigh playfully. "OK, I'm not really."

While I try to track down the various remotes we'll be needing, my guests settle into the viewing positions that they'll eventually make their own. Lauren, Ross, and Dr. Beaverman occupy, from left to right, our larger couch, while Marcus sprawls on the floor. Tony brings a chair in from the kitchen and sits backward on it like Chachi used to do on *Happy Days,* which leaves the love seat for me. Before I take my place on it, I slide *Jaws* into the VCR and then position my minicassette recorder on the coffee table between the doughnuts and the goldfish crackers.

"My family used to summer-vacation in Massachusetts, about a hundred miles from where this movie was filmed," says Marcus, just as Ross grabs the remote and starts the movie. "I was swimming in the ocean when I was 9, and I got, like, bumped or something by a shark. It was the most terrifying thing I had ever experienced, and I was hysterical about it for days. A few months later this movie came out and I watched the whole thing with my mouth hanging open. It was like it had been made solely to fuck with me. I swear to God, I wasn't able to go to the bathroom in the dark until that rolling blackout a few months ago."

"It's hard for me to remember what happens in *Jaws,*" admits Tony, "because the first porno I ever saw was called *Gums,* which was about a mermaid who sucked off guys in the ocean until their dicks fell off. My best friend's older brother had a tape of it. Every once in a while, an image will pop into my head and I won't know if it's *Jaws* or *Gums.*"

"I saw it first-run in the theater," recalls Dr. Beaverman, the lone baby boomer of our posse, "and all I remember is that I was wearing a halter top."

While we wait for the FBI warning to pass, I shove a doughnut into my mouth and listen intently as Ross dispenses more background info. "This movie was like the *Waterworld* of its day," he reports. "It was way over budget and way over schedule and getting bad-mouthed around Hollywood like crazy. And the mechanical shark never worked right. Dreyfuss tells this story about how all you could hear coming over the walkie-talkies was 'The shark isn't working, the shark isn't working.'"

If Lauren's glazed expression is any indication, the gang is not nearly as captivated by today's free film history lesson as I'd hoped they'd be. "I thought the red food coloring on these would keep me from indulging," she says, polishing off her first Rice Krispie foot. "Guess I was wrong."

At last, the film begins—with a tracking shot of a gaggle of hormonally- charged teens carrying on at a late night beach party. "Everyone's making out," I say, taken aback by the blatant promiscuity. "Not very Spielbergian."

"It was the '70s," says Dr. Beaverman wistfully. "The sexual revolution was in full swing."

"Without us," carps Tony.

I shush my friends so we can watch in silence as Chrissy, a leggy and carefree babe who even has '70s *breasts,* bounds off from the party for a moonlight swim.

"I skinny-dipped in the '70s," reveals Dr. Beaverman, "but I didn't have a shark after my white ass, just a bellhop."

We all look at her. This wasn't necessarily the kind of commentary I was expecting from my esteemed condo association secretary, but what the hell, bring it on.

"It was at a Holiday Inn in Monterey," she adds.

"Did he catch you?" I ask.

"I don't remember," she says, though she clearly does.

Just then, John Williams's indelible "Impending Shark Attack" music kicks in, signaling the fact that little Miss Chrissy is about to be punished—for her wanton ways, her underage boozing, and most importantly those tacky gold hoop earrings.

"Are we seeing her private parts?" I wonder, surprised by what looks to me like an underwater two-shot of Chrissy and the Beav.

"You're allowed to show bush as long as she dies a painful death," says Marcus.

"Why didn't that rule apply to *Showgirls*?" wonders Lauren.

"No rules applied to *Showgirls,*" I say. "That's what makes it such heaven."

Chrissy does indeed die a painful death, but not before being dragged about the

Atlantic, grabbing a buoy with one of her remaining extremities, and stating the obvious: "It hurts."

"That first moment when she gets pulled underwater," says Ross, "Spielberg actually did the pulling himself. Chrissy was hooked up to some kind of cable and he was the one who yanked it."

"Well, if you want something done right..." I say.

We laugh and scream through Chrissy's brutal final moments, but are soon brought to silence by the gruesome sight of her crab-covered fingers poking out of the sand like the table centerpiece at a hand model convention.

"Not the first case of crabs to be contracted on that beach," says Lauren.

"There was a moment just like this in *Gums,*" recalls Tony. "But the guy was still hard, which I always thought was weird."

Soon, Roy Scheider is introduced as Amity's new sheriff, Martin Brody, who is deathly afraid of the water even though he has never seen *Jaws* or even read the book.

"I don't like Roy Scheider," Tony decides after the actor has been on screen for maybe six seconds. "He looks like a wife beater."

"I think he's sort of hot," I admit, "in a leathery sort of way."

"Who thinks he's scary?" asks Dr. Beaverman, requesting a show of hands. Tony, Dr. Beaverman, Marcus, and Lauren all reach for the sky. Ross pretends to be preoccupied with breaking the toe off a piece of Rice Krispie foot so he doesn't have to vote. "It's four against one for scary," says Dr. Beaverman. "The tribe has spoken."

A few minutes later, when Brody returns to his office to do some typing, Tony initiates another survey. "Who in the room really believes he can type?" he asks. Silence. "It's like Demi Moore in *Disclosure* going on about the computer chips and megabytes. Uh-huh, right."

"I miss Demi," says Marcus with a faraway look in his eye. "I mean, how great could Idaho *be*?"

I'm this close to copping to my own Demi-related feelings of abandonment when a more worthy object of concern appears on the screen for the first time, Lorraine Gary as Brody's dutiful blond wife, Ellen. "What is she *wearing*?" I want to know.

"Bell-bottom sleeves," says Dr. Beaverman dryly. "I used to have a shirt just like that and I'd always end up losing my keys."

"Lorraine Gary was married to Sid Sheinberg, the head of the studio," Ross informs us. "She could probably wear whatever she wanted."

"Why don't they just stick her head in the water?" wonders Tony. "That shark would swim for Bermuda."

"OK, I have a theory," Dr. Beaverman announces, clasping her French-manicured hands together for effect. "Can we pause for a second, Dennis?"

I oblige.

"It is quite clear to me at this point that Scheider has a castration complex," Dr.

Beaverman says, taking on a more academic tone than before. "This would explain not only his fear of the shark but the fact that he all but cowers in terror every time Lorraine Gary enters the room."

"Anything else before I unpause?" I ask.

"No," she says. "Oh, wait, there is something else: Jaws is mommy."

We all nod dutifully at this unusual declaration, though none of us really know why. Before I restart the movie, I steal a glance at Ross to see how he's holding up. He catches me and grins like a person who's actually enjoying himself. All right, then.

A few scenes later we're granted an audience with the town's mayor, a husky good ol' boy and shark skeptic who belches out lines like, "The beaches *will* be open this weekend!"

"He just seems like a small-town, dim-witted, Boss Hogg cliché in a tacky blazer," I say. "Like he was supposed to be in *Smokey and the Bandit* and he wandered onto the wrong set."

"It's because we've seen so many people imitate this movie," reasons Ross. "In the mid '70s, the mayor wasn't considered over-the-top."

The question of how much is too much segues us smoothly into the next scene, which begins with a shot of a gigantic female extra in a straining-to-keep-it-all-in bathing suit walking along the beach.

"Jaws should just eat *her,*" says Tony. "He wouldn't be hungry again until the sequel."

"Now, who says the fitness craze of the '80s and '90s didn't do any good?" poses Lauren, who makes her living whipping such women into shape.

"It's certainly no *Baywatch,*" I say. "I mean, where's Yasmine Bleeth when you need her?"

"Fred Segal, I imagine," says Lauren.

"I was going to say Promises Malibu," says Tony.

"If you only have room for one of those lines, Dennis, go with Promises Malibu," says Lauren graciously. "It's edgier."

"May I remind you all that this is *Massachusetts,*" asserts Marcus, our East Coast expert. "There's nothing there but fat white people. Trust me, I've lived it."

"Brody's son has a pretty toned body," I inexplicably say out loud.

"For a 12-year-old," chides Lauren.

Suddenly, the "ISA" music is pumping again and Jaws is swimming around under a young boy on a raft named Alex, who was warned by his mother just minutes before to get out of the water because he was turning into a prune and who, for the record, doesn't have nearly as toned a body as Brody's kid. Around this same time, another beachgoer notices that his playful pup Pippin is missing in action.

"You know it's a bad sign when the dog disappears," says Lauren.

"And you knew Alex was a goner as soon as he was given a name and a couple of lines," figures Ross. "Jaws won't eat extras, but day players might as well have LUNCH tattooed on their rafts."

"What I love is that Jaws eats dogs," I say. "And kids! Kids and dogs never get eaten at the movies anymore because our culture can't handle it."

"I know I couldn't handle seeing a kid get eaten onscreen," says Dr. Beaverman. "It'd spoil me. I'd think, *Why not take 'em all?*"

"Didn't a kid get eaten in *Jurassic Park 2,*" asks Tony, "by all those yappy little motherfuckers?"

"Yes," says Ross. "But they didn't *show* it."

"The next *Jurassic* movie, every person in it should get eaten," I proclaim, as though I'm running for mayor of Hollywood. "Kids, girls, blonds, everybody."

"Starting with Téa Leoni," says Ross, holding up his beer bottle as if to toast. As he lowers it, Tony gives me a look that says, *OK, he can stay.*"

With Amity now in a panic, Scheider calls for backup, and soon we're introduced to a pair of spirited great white aficionados: rich kid–turned oceanographer Matt Hooper, played by Richard Dreyfuss, and been-there, harpooned-that shark hunter Quint, played by Robert Shaw. The mismatched pair may disagree on how best to properly deter the man-eating beast, but they're of one mind when it comes to sporting painfully unsightly facial hair.

"Dreyfuss looks so young," I marvel, "like a little elf with those muttonchops. I bet he lives in a hollow tree."

"What do you mean, 'little elf'?" bellows Tony. "He looks like a homeless person. If they had a freeway overpass on Nantucket, he'd be living under it in a cardboard box."

Tony's distaste for Dreyfuss prompts Ross to let loose with another little known fact about *Jaws*. In the novel, he explains, there's a sex scene between Dreyfuss's hotshot oceanographer and Lorraine Gary's frustrated wife that didn't make the movie.

"Spielberg must have taken one look at his cast and thought, *There are limits to what an audience can take,*" says Dr. Beaverman.

"I can either have Robert Shaw getting eaten alive or those two getting it on," says Tony, speaking for Spielberg, "but I can't have both."

Meanwhile, back in Amity, Alex's grieving mother puts a bounty on Jaws's head, causing every yahoo with a fishing pole and some unused sick days to head to the ocean and try to reel him in. It proves to be an effective ploy, for soon a shark is killed. But Dreyfuss suspects it's actually a Jaws Mini-Me and that Jaws Proper is still at large and getting hungrier by the second. So he heads to Brody's house to try and convince the sheriff to let him cut the fucker open.

"Lorraine Gary is so emasculating in this scene," observes Dr. Beaverman as Dreyfuss gets hammered while sitting with the Brodys at their dinner table. "I'm surprised she doesn't turn to Dreyfuss and say, 'Last night, Martin couldn't get aroused. More wine, Matt?'"

"I think my mother was up for her part," says Marcus.

After enduring all manner of marital woe subtext, Hooper finally gets Brody drunk enough to let him slice the dead shark open. The impromptu autopsy nets the pair a tin can, a license plate, and a bunch of shark guts, but, alas, no 10-year-old boy parts. "Wouldn't it be cool if they found one of those Farrah Fawcett makeup heads?" I say.

"Or that tacky necklace from *Titanic,*" says Tony.

"Or a six-pack of Billy Beer," says Ross.

"Maybe my fucking prom date that never showed up is in there," says Lauren before heading into the kitchen to refresh her drink.

"My 20s and 30s might be in there too," says Dr. Beaverman.

"Marcus?" I ask.

"It can be anything?" he asks. After about 10 seconds of careful consideration, he says, "OK, either a bunch of lost episodes of *Falcon Crest* or an effective and inexpensive AIDS vaccine."

"Glad to see you've got your priorities in order," says Dr. Beaverman.

"Can I change mine to world peace?" calls Lauren from the kitchen.

"What is this, Miss Teen USA?" wonders Ross.

"No, that's next week," I say. "You're welcome to come over. We'll be here."

"It's a national holiday in this house," says Tony, "like the running of the bulls in Pamplona."

Just then, something on the screen catches both the light and my attention. "Hold on a second," I say. "Is Lorraine Gary wearing the same gold hoop earrings that Chrissy got eaten in?"

"Looks like it," says Marcus.

"No wonder she's not very freaked out about the shark attacks," I say. "She's pilfering accessories from the dead."

Then, out of the clear blue sky, Ross groans as though he's just smashed his hand in a car door. "This fucking tape blows!" he carps. "I wasn't going to say anything, Dennis, but this pan-and-scan is bullshit. Why didn't you get the letterboxed copy?"

"You rented it to me," I remind him, and then pass the buck to Tony, "and *he* picked it out."

"Oh, no, I got the wrong tape," Tony says dryly. "How will I ever be able to live with myself?"

"OK, next time I'm in charge of the tape," declares Ross.

"So you'll be our special Video Master?" Tony says, teasingly.

"Sure, why not?" says Ross tentatively.

"We don't expect monogamy," I assure Ross. "You can see other parties. We just don't want to hear about it."

Though I've never given much thought to such matters, I see Ross's point about the drawbacks of pan-and-scan during a confrontation scene between Dreyfuss and Shaw, which, scaled down for video, looks like a spat between sideburns.

"Screw the letterboxing," says Dr. Beaverman. "What I need is subtitles. I can't understand a word Robert Shaw is saying. I think he's supposed to be Irish, but he sounds like he's got an entire mouthful of Lucky Charms."

Like the movie itself, my living room simmers down considerably when Dreyfuss, Scheider, and Shaw head out on the shark hunt that makes up the final third of the film.

"Love triangle alert!" chirps Dr. Beaverman. "Dreyfuss and Scheider are clearly competing for Shaw's affections in this scene. They need validation from Daddy, and you don't have to have a doctorate in psychology with an emphasis in Freudian theory to see that. Although it helps."

Shaw adds fuel to Dr. Beaverman's theory by giving Dreyfuss and Scheider such innuendo-laden orders as "Keep it steady, I've got something big here" and the ever-popular sex party favorite, "Get behind me!"

Spent from an afternoon of shark chasing and double entendres, the trio head down to the hold to have some grub and get loaded. When Shaw and Dreyfuss start playing "my scar's cooler than your scar" I realize what's missing from *Jaws* for me: someone to boff. "Oh, what I wouldn't give for a little Mel Gibson and Rene Russo right about now," I muse, referring to the photogenic twosome who ripped off this scene in the considerably less-enduring *Lethal Weapon* 3.

"This movie would never get made like this today," laments Ross. "You'd have Charlize Theron in a wet suit and Ben Affleck in glasses as the shark expert."

"Swapping scar stories with Jackie Chan," adds Marcus.

"This movie would never get made like this today. You'd have Charlize Theron in a wet suit and Ben Affleck in glasses as the shark expert." —Ross

"And it would *suck*!" concludes Lauren.

"I so want Dreyfuss to go, 'Speaking of scars, boys, when I was 8 days old, the rabbi cut me right here in my bathing suit area,'" says Tony. "'You can touch it if you want.'"

"Now that you mention it, I have a question," says Marcus. "How many Jews do you know who hunt? I'm related to tons of them and they only hunt for things that can't outrun them, usually at outlet malls."

Then Shaw starts into his monologue about how he survived the sinking of the USS *Indianapolis* in World War II but scores of his comrades were eaten by sharks. "Shaw was actually drunk when they shot most of this scene," Ross reports. "It's still one of the most incredible parts of the film for me. They actually give you character development in the middle of all this tension. You couldn't do that today because the producers would be going, 'The test audiences think this is boring. We can't have people *talking*. Someone needs to get eaten or laid every eight minutes.'"

"Starting with me," says Lauren, who's now on her third Absolut and cranberry.

Daylight comes, and after some embarrassingly obvious foreshadowing involving compressed air canisters—"You screw around with these tanks and they're going to explode!"—the three sharkbusters get serious with the toothy title character to the strains of some John Williams scoring that seems downright *happy*.

"I don't mean to be cranky," Tony says, "but this shark has eaten like 14 residents, and Pippin the dog, and they're giving us *The Nutcracker*? What *is* that?"

"They don't know whether to kill the shark or do a little ice dancing," says Lauren, who's starting to slur her words the way drunk people do in movies.

Which brings us to my favorite *Jaws* moment so far; when Brody is at the foot of the boat and Jaws, liberated for the first time from his theme music, just sort of pokes his head out at him as if to say, "Does this fin make me look fat?" and then disappears back under the water. I nearly choke on my Rice Krispie forearm.

"Spielberg can do those scare-the-shit-out-of-you moments like nobody else," maintains Ross. "In fact, remember that earlier scene where Dreyfuss goes underwater and finds that fisherman's boat and that dead guy's head pops up in his face? Well, that moment was a reshoot. They'd done a test screening without it and Spielberg realized he could get another scream out of the audience, so he reshot that moment at his own expense in the swimming pool at his editor's house." Pleased with himself, Ross takes a swig of his beer, then adds, "Watching this makes me realize how totally on autopilot he was for *Jurassic Park*."

Then, for some reason, Dreyfuss decides to climb in a cage and go underwater for a little one-on-one time with Jaws. Jaws, however, doesn't want to hear his bullshit stories about the making of *American Graffiti* and makes quick business of destroying the cage. "A lot of this footage is actually a real shark," says Ross as Jaws repeatedly tries to eat Dreyfuss through the bars. "But because the shark wasn't as big as Jaws is supposed to be, they used a smaller cage and stuck a midget in there. The same guy who doubled for Elizabeth Taylor in *National Velvet*."

"He must have figured if Liz didn't eat him, the shark wouldn't," says Tony.

"Actually, he was totally traumatized by the shark," says Ross. "He was hyperventilating and everything."

"Who wouldn't be?" I ask. "Could you imagine? One day, you're singing the "Oompa Loompa" song and snacking on M&Ms and the next, they're like, 'OK, put on that wet suit, climb into this cage, and act like a scared Jewish guy when the shark tries to eat you.'"

"Here's what I've always wondered about little people," mumbles Lauren. "If you don't want to go into showbiz, does your family pressure you?"

Suddenly, the room gets dead quiet so we can watch Robert Shaw get eaten alive. Four times, thanks to the magic of rewind. It's totally awesome, and I can't get enough of it. Lauren, however, is another story. By the fourth feasting, she's so queasy she has to cover her mouth and dash to the bathroom. Tony chases after her while I stay put and glance over to Ross, who's staring straight at the screen and trying not to look uncomfortable.

"She's actually very nice," I tell him. "It's rare that she throws up the first time she meets someone."

Back on the screen, Dreyfuss is still underwater hiding, so it becomes Jaws versus Brody in the final showdown. Before the hydrophobic sheriff recalls what we all learned earlier about those air canisters, he tries everything he can think of to deter the peckish predator, at one point even poking the animal with some kind of stick, a ploy I compare to attacking an elephant with a crayon. "Roy Scheider," Dr. Beaverman proclaims, "acupuncturist of the sea."

Air tank at the ready, Scheider is seconds away from eliminating his foe, but before he does, he first must deliver one of those crowd-pleasing, farewell fuck-you lines like "*Hasta la vista*, baby!" that has, in the years since this movie was released, become an adventure movie staple. *"Smile, you son of a bitch!"* Scheider screams, and then he blows Jaws up with the gas tank. Though it was probably in the script, I like to imagine Schneider nabbed that line from the photographer who did his last set of head shots.

"I heard they blew a cow up for that shot," says Marcus as shark guts rain down on the ocean, "but I don't know if that's true."

"That would never happen today," I say. "Alicia Silverstone wouldn't allow it."

"But if you were a cow, wouldn't you rather be blown up for *Jaws* than turned into a bunch of Big Macs and sandals?" poses Ross. "I mean, you'd live forever."

Tony returns from tending to Lauren just as Dreyfuss reemerges to join Scheider *Titanic*-style on a piece of floating boat. "How much you wanna bet there's an alternate take where they kiss?" says Marcus. "Because it looks like they're dying to."

"Rent *Gums,*" says Tony.

As the credits roll, I can't help but whine about the fact that I wasn't part of the original *Jaws* phenomenon. Hell, I wasn't even part of the *Gums* phenomenon. Sure, I did buy the novelty record "Mr. Jaws" by Dickie Goodman on 45, but that's not the same as screaming my head off in a crowded theater and not showering for months on end out of sheer terror. "I missed out," I say despondently.

"But if you hadn't missed out, we wouldn't have had today," says Marcus, the king of the positive spin.

"And I would have had to get drunk and throw up all by myself," groans Lauren, emerging from the bathroom.

We watch with a mixture of concern and disbelief as she staggers to the center of the room, drops to her knees, and then curls up on the floor in the fetal position. Ross literally has to step over her to retrieve the tape from the machine.

"I wonder if young people today will feel the same way about *The Blair Witch Project* in 25 years," I say, sitting on the floor and rubbing Lauren's back.

"Hell, no," Ross replies. "*Jaws* is one of the great entertainments ever made. It took a knife and just etched images into your brain that would always be there."

"Well, thanks for coming, Ross," I say, getting up to walk him out, "and for all your little nuggets of information."

"And the doughnuts," says Tony.

"Anytime," says Ross.

Maybe it's my imagination, but there seems to be a spring in Ross's step as he walks to his car. Suddenly I feel like the man who finally opened a bowling alley in the town where the world's most naturally gifted bowler had been living undiscovered for decades. It's a nice feeling.

•

The next time I see Ross, at our Miss Teen USA get-together a few days later, I confirm his knife-etching theory. "I can't get the image of Lorraine Gary in bell-bottom sleeves out of my head," I confess. "But that's the only thing close to a nightmare I've had. I feel so robbed."

Ross just laughs and says, "Just wait till the next time you go to the beach."

Turns out I don't have to. That very night I have the *Jaws* nightmare to end all *Jaws* nightmares.

I'm blaming it all on Marcus's sugar cookies. See, whenever we watch a pageant, he bakes 51 cookies, iced with the abbreviation of each state and the District of Columbia. Then, after the parade of states, we pick cookies based on which girls we think are the foxiest. The player whose cookies fare the best wins. Therefore you can't eat a specific cookie until that girl is out of the running. Well, none of my little ponies even cracked the top 10, so I ate all my cookies at once to punish myself. And boy, did I.

Anyway, my insanely far-fetched yet remarkably vivid sugar-induced *Jaws* nightmare goes like this: I've been sent to the movie's set in New England to interview Lorraine Gary for *Maxim*. (I told you it was far-fetched.) Anyway, the first thing she says is, "I heard you've been making fun of the way I look." Then I stammer some lame apology and start to fiddle with my cassette recorder when I suddenly realize I left my batteries back at the charming seaside bed-and-breakfast the magazine was nice enough to pay for. (Again, I told you it was far-fetched.)

A word about batteries: Over the years, I've noticed that whenever I dream about conducting an interview, there's some kind of battery problem. They're either missing or dead, and the rest of the dream devolves into a hunt for fresh batteries that never ends well.

Anyway, I leave Lorraine Gary's trailer to go find batteries, and I'm wandering the set, lost, when I hear a deep voice coming from behind me. I turn around to see the largest Star Wagon they make. The door is open.

Before I get to what happens next, I must confess that for years I've harbored a secret fantasy of having an affair with one of the actors I interview—after the story has come and gone, of course, for conflict-of-interest reasons. What would happen is I'd run into the actor at, like, the Virgin Megastore months after our first meeting. He'd pull the unwashed hair from of his unwashed face, stare into my eyes, and say something about how I really captured his true essence, blah, blah, blah. Cut to: Twenty minutes later, we're back in his suite at the Chateau Marmont sharing an experience that falls somewhere between cheap, meaningless sex and a mind meld. Whatever it is, it goes on for days. During one of our carbohydrate breaks, I run lines with him for an audition he has coming up with either Ridley or Tony Scott, he's not sure. During another, he lets me pick an item to take home from the boxes of free shit Nike sent over that afternoon. In short, it's bliss.

Our affair continues for weeks, and I have to say that during this time, if I were asked to list my occupation on a tax form or something, I would write "Dirty Little Secret." As time goes by, however, our rendezvouses grow shorter in duration and usually end with me being shoved onto a fire escape or into a closet when his starlet "girlfriend" pops by unexpectedly. I start to lose faith during this era, but my actor assures me we're still on. He even promises to stroke his cleft for me on Leno as a signal that he's thinking of me and my "hot little white ass," and then he does. In short, it's still bliss.

The Leno cleft stroke, as it turns out, is the last bit of communication I ever get from my actor. The next day he jets off to London to shoot the Scott movie, stopping in Vegas on the way to marry the girlfriend. I'm so devastated I lose 15 pounds, which is also sort of bliss.

Years later, my actor wins a Golden Globe for playing a sensitive gay guy with a sensitive gay guy kind of problem, and I'll be damned if during his tearful speech he doesn't revisit the Leno cleft stroke. I excuse myself from whatever Golden Globe party I'm at, go into the bathroom, and weep. It's not really bliss, but it's not bad either. It's like bliss-adjacent.

Anyway, that's my sick fantasy, and last night I experienced the whole fabulously fucked-up thing—pulled it right out of my subconscious like I was a dream jukebox. There's just one problem. The man in the Star Wagon with the deep voice is Roy Scheider. *It wasn't supposed to be Roy Scheider.* It was supposed to be Viggo Mortensen or Johnathon Schaech or Eric McCormack or Matt Damon or Eric Thal or Timothy Olyphant or Dylan McDermott or David Boreanaz or Justin Timberlake or Billy Baldwin or Mark Wahlberg or Antonio Sabato Jr. or Luke Wilson or Chayanne or fuck it, I'd take Jenna Elfman at this point. But I got Roy: dangling out from a hotel robe. Roy: playing footsie with me in the tub and rolling his eyes while he talks to Ann Reinking about "that bastard Bob" on the telephone. Roy: tracing the stripes on the cross-trainers he let me have with his tongue, for crying out loud. If this is what I get for voting that he wasn't scary, I demand a recount!

•

The next afternoon, I run into an uncharacteristically denim-clad Dr. Beaverman going through boxes in the two-car garage our units share, and I tell her about my crazy dream.

"Obviously," she says, "your greatest fear going up against these celebrities is that you're not good enough. Hence, your anxiety about being caught 'powerless,' or without batteries." Dr. Beaverman reaches into her pocket, pulls out a silver flask, takes a long, noisy pull from its contents, and continues. "You desperately seek validation, which this cheesy backdoor love affair with some cowardly closet case would purportedly give you. But, in actuality, it's horrible treatment. Treatment Dr. Beaverman cannot condone. Should this guy actually take you on Leno and introduce you as his lover, then *that* would be a healthy fantasy, but you probably don't want to fuck Harvey Fierstein."

Dr. B takes a break from analyzing long enough to walk over to a dusty wooden card table with a missing leg and say, "This needs to be thrown away. Grab the other end."

On our way to the dumpster, she starts in again. "On a Freudian level, the battery obviously represents a phallus," she says dryly, "a hard, cylindrical object, the source of all energy, looking only for the appropriate hole to slip into." With that, we dump the old table into the garbage bin, where it lands with a deafening thud.

"In your dream, however, you've left your batteries back at the charming seaside inn," she continues, as we make the trek back. "The word that jumps out at me is *seaside.* Fish plus Freud equals Mommy. Mommy represents safety, which is why you return to her as your source of power, but it's time to cross over into manhood, Dennis."

"Already?" I say.

"Perhaps you should take my course at SSW," she suggests. (SSW stands for School-Sans-Walls, an unconventional adult education facility in Encino where Dr. Beaverman teaches the odd workshop, and I do mean *odd* workshop.) "It's six weeks," she continues, "one night a week, and it's called 'Recharging Your Batteries: How to Fuck Like the Energizer Bunny.'"

"Seriously, there's a class called that?" I ask.

"There is now," she says. "In the meantime, Dr. Beaverman suggests that you quit sucking up to these unworthies and make them fear *you.* After all, you have the power to make them look like the boring, pampered, uneducated narcissists they really are." With that, the good doctor puts her arms on my shoulders like a football coach sending his third string quarterback into the game and says, "Bone up, son, for the pen is mightier than the love sword!"

I listen and nod, grateful that a trained professional is willing to expend so much mental energy on my ridiculous fantasy life. "Thank you," I say and turn to go into the house.

"And remember, Dennis," she calls after me, "it could have been worse."

"Yeah?" I say.

"It could have been Dreyfuss."

TOO COOL FOR SCHOOL

Two weeks after the *Jaws* mixer, I arrive at Lauren's 12 o'clock noon Tuesday–Thursday spin class at Crunch to find her in a much better mood, flashing both a smile and good-sized gold-and-sapphire ring.

"Barry proposed?" I ask.

"Hell, no," she carps. "It's not an engagement ring. It's like an 'I'm sorry' ring or whatever. But it's pretty, don't you think? And the makeup sex was great."

"So you guys are good?"

"Basically, we're in the same place that we were except I'm not pissed off anymore because I have a new ring," she says, while digging around in the Yugo-size backpack she carries with her everywhere. "You're gonna love the music I put together for class today," she says, pulling out a CD. "Not one song was recorded in the last 10 years."

Unlike most 21st-century fitness gurus, who traffic in either superbeats for queens on ecstasy or the mellow strains of Enya and her ilk, Lauren "Don't forget to breathe" O'Donovan likes her charges to sweat to tunes that you forgot existed and yet know every word to, like last week's cool-down number, "The Last Game of the Season" by David Geddes. By the time the blind man in the bleachers kicked the bucket and, as a result, got to see his son play football, there wasn't a dry bike in the house.

"My editor liked the *Jaws* story, thank God," I tell her while adjusting the seat on my usual bike in the second row. "It hits the stands in England in a couple of weeks."

"Did you put in that I barfed?" she asks. "Please tell me you didn't. The last thing I need is, like, Elizabeth Hurley thinking I can't hold my liquor."

"I didn't put it in," I say. That's a huge lie, but put yourself in my shoes. Robert Shaw is coughing up blood on-screen while getting eaten alive and one of my sample group pukes? How could I not put that in? "He wants us to do another one," I say.

"Seriously?" she says while slipping into her spinning shoes. "That's great. I'll try to be in a better mood this time. What's the movie?"

"Don't know yet," I say. "I'm supposed to call him tomorrow with some ideas."

"Can we do a Meg Ryan movie?" she suggests. "I've really had it with her cute-as-a-button bullshit."

With that, Lauren presses play on the stereo, hops on her bike, and starts pedaling. The opening track, "The Groove

Line" by Heatwave, kicks in and makes for a disco-fueled warm-up. But it's the fourth selection of the class, a climb set to John Parr's "Man in Motion," that really gets my blood pumping.

"This is it!" I holler to her over the music. "We should watch *St. Elmo's Fire*!"

Lauren takes her hands off her handlebars just long enough to give me a double thumbs-up sign. When the newcomers in class mimic her and nearly fall off their bikes, I pretend not to notice.

•

"I don't know," says Marcus, who meets us for a postspin burrito lunch at Baja Fresh on Sunset. "I thought we were supposed to do good movies."

"*St. Elmo's Fire* is a good movie," I assert.

Suddenly, the place gets so E.F Hutton commercial quiet that all you can hear is the distant sizzling of fajitas. "OK, it's not, but it's got so much nostalgia value," I say, bringing my volume down a few notches. "And, Marcus, you said yourself you miss Demi."

"I do miss Demi," Marcus says wistfully.

"Did you see her last movie, *Passion of Mind*, when it was at the Sunset 5?" asks Lauren, referring to the art-house theater next door to Crunch.

"I meant to," he claims.

"Then I don't want to hear it," snaps Lauren. "What you really mean is that you miss who you were when Demi was Demi."

"Precisely my point," I say. "We all do. That's why we should do *St. Elmo's Fire*. As Rob Lowe would say, 'You won't believe how out of hand it's going to be.'"

"I do have my law school reunion coming up," says Marcus, who grew up about an hour from where the film was set. "*St. Elmo's* would certainly put me in the mood."

"Can you believe it came out 15 years ago?" asks Lauren. "It doesn't seem that old."

What I suspect Lauren means is that *she* doesn't seem that old. But she is. We all are. Still, I'm not too senile to remember the night I experienced *St. Elmo's* for the first time. It was the summer of '85 and I saw it with a couple of friends at the brand-new Cornerstone Theater near the campus at Arizona State University, where I went to college. We had dinner afterward at Garcia's Mexican Restaurant, and I remember being really bummed out. And no, not because I was out two hours and six bucks. *St. Elmo's Fire* was a downer because I felt that my life, as a junior broadcasting major and sexual tenderfoot, was nowhere near as interesting or glamorous as Demi Moore's, Rob Lowe's, Judd Nelson's, Ally Sheedy's, Andrew McCarthy's, Mare Winningham's, and hell, even Emilio Estevez's. None of my friends did coke. None of my friends drove black Jeeps. None of my friends had Billy Idol murals on their walls. And I resented them for it. I want to say the situation has improved since then, but who can be sure?

•

I share my Brat Pack inferiority complex with the rest of the gang at the outset of our viewing—believe it or not, Matt, my U.K. editor, said have at it—and most of them have similar bittersweet recollections.

"This kid in my high school died in a car crash," recalls Lauren, "so we sang the David Foster theme song at graduation."

"There are words to it?" asks Tony.

"Oh, yeah," says Lauren before crooning, "We laughed until we had to cry...we loved right down to our last goodbye..."

"Pay attention to those lyrics, kids," says Dr. Beaverman. "If I keel over and die watching this today, you can sing it for me."

"I went out and had my ear pierced because of Rob Lowe," recalls Tony. "I was like 17 and I wasn't going to rest until I had a dagger earring just like Rob's. Around the same time, I was obsessed with this picture of him that was in the back of *People* magazine where he was taking a shower on the beach in a Speedo. He had the nipples of a 9-year-old and I wanted to pull on them until he screamed." This revelation merits accusatory looks from both Lauren and Marcus. "Not *because* they were the nipples of a 9-year-old," Tony stresses. "Because they were the nipples of Rob Lowe. Sheesh.!

"I had my picture taken in front of the bar that they used for *St. Elmo's,*" boasts Marcus on his way into the kitchen. "It's actually called the Third Edition." When he returns, he's carrying a plate of gingerbread cookies baked in the shape of graduation caps. "Dig in, kids."

Ross does just that. "I took this chick I'd had a few dates with who had a yeast infection at the time," he says, his mouth full of cookie.

"I told you it was a gay bar. Judd Nelson is kissing a guy. Oh, never mind, it's Ally Sheedy." —Tony

"So she actually had St. Elmo's Fire?" says Tony.

"Yeah, but it gets worse," says Ross. "While we were standing in line, she sort of absently read the line from the poster—'The passion burns deep'—out loud, and I said, 'Could you stop talking about your pussy for five seconds?' I was totally joking, but she walked home and never called me again."

The only one without a poignant memory to share is Dr. Beaverman. "I dragged this biker guy that I knew to see it," she recalls, "and he hated it so much, he made me watch Cher in *Mask* twice as recompense. It was the longest summer of my life."

As I slide the tape into the VCR, Ross pulls a small stack of index cards from his cargo pants. "I brought some little factoids," he explains. "My buddy Christopher from USC is working on the DVD of this that comes out next year. He told me some behind-the-scenes stuff over the phone, like how one day Judd Nelson was being such a pain in the ass that Joel Schumacher let him direct the rehearsal and that sort of solved the problem."

With that, I press play. As the film opens, the entire ensemble walks in their graduation gowns toward the camera.

"It's like Brat Pack red rover," I say.

"Red rover, red rover, send...Eric Stoltz right over!" chants Marcus.

With that, Tony gives Marcus what, in our house, is referred to as a Bea. A Bea is that two-beat look of incredulity that Bea Arthur gives the audience on *The Golden Girls* every time Betty White says something inane. Tony has turned Bea-ing into an art form.

"Or not," Marcus says.

"Interesting," I say, "Schumacher chose to have his directing credit appear over Emilio Estevez."

"He knew the audience would cherish anything else that appeared in the frame," says Tony.

The film's first sequence is set at a hospital, where the gang have gathered because hammered bad boy Rob Lowe had an accident while driving Mare Winningham's new car. When they discover him, he's blithely wailing away on his sax in the back of an ambulance. Apparently, after an exhilarating evening of drunken driving, Rob loves nothing more than to wind down with a little jam session.

"I can just imagine the press junket for this movie," says Tony. "Rob sitting in front of the poster in a 'Let's Get Physical' headband talking about how he bonded with his sax teacher during their daily eight-hour sessions and how he got to sit in with Toto at the Hollywood Bowl."

"Rob was shooting *Youngblood* when he was learning the sax," says Ross. "He used to practice in his hockey gear."

"Is that what it says on your little card?" asks Marcus.

"Uh-huh," says Ross. "Just a little Fun Fact."

"I interviewed Rob just before *The West Wing,"* I say, "and he told me he went as himself in *St. Elmo's* to a Halloween party at his kids' school and he wore that same sleeveless yellow shirt and had the original sax and everything."

"And then he fucked the school nurse," says Tony.

"What is it with sax players being pussy hounds?" says Dr. Beaverman. "There's Rob, President Clinton, Kenny G..."

"Kenny G's not a sax player," says Marcus.

"I rest my case," replies Dr. Beaverman.

The clique leaves the hospital and heads straight to St. Elmo's Bar, where Rob takes to the stage for more sax synching. When the camera pulls away from him, Tony notices something peculiar about our gang's cherished watering hole.

"All the customers are men," he says. "St. Elmo's is a gay bar!"

"St. Homo's Fire," mutters Lauren, who's had so many straight things turn out gay in her life, she's not even fazed anymore.

"Not so fast," says Marcus, pointing at the upper left corner of the screen. "There's a couple of chicks at the bar."

"Indigo Girls," says Dr. Beaverman.

When Bawdy Demi tells Dowdy Mare that she should get over Rob and pronto, Mare rationalizes her crush by saying, "Well, that's life in the fat lane," to which Demi replies, "You're not fat." This causes Tony to leap on the pause button and deliver the longest Bea of his life, a SuperBea if ever there was one.

Meanwhile, in another part of the bar, up-and-coming politico Judd learns that perennial fuck-up Rob lost yet another of the jobs he keeps getting for him, so he drags the pretty boy into the bathroom and shoves his head in the toilet. When Rob emerges, the pair, joined by tortured writer Andrew and busboy Emilio, do something I've never seen any mammal do in my entire life: They execute identical arm movements while chanting, "Yuggadah, yuggaduh, yuggaduh, ha-ha-ha!"

"I hated that in 1985 and I hate it now," I admit. "I never buy those phony, here's-our-inside-joke moments in movies."

"I was about to suggest the six of us come up with a secret Screening Party handshake," says Marcus, "but I guess not."

"I told you it was a gay bar," says Tony when the boys leave the bathroom and return to the bar. "Judd Nelson is kissing a guy." We look closer. "Oh, never mind, it's Ally Sheedy."

Judd and Ally continue to suck face at their glamorously stark apartment, but they're interrupted by Demi, who bursts in looking so her-name-is-Rio-and-she-dances-on-the-sand that I expect Simon Le Bon to pop up from behind the wall of glass blocks.

"Oh, I almost forgot," says Ross, before hitting the pause button. He reaches into his jacket pocket and tosses an old copy of *Spy* magazine on the coffee table. "There's a nude shot in here of Demi from the early '80s I thought you might enjoy."

Lauren's closest to the magazine and therefore gets first gander. "Oh, my God," she gasps. "They should have called this movie 'St. Elmo's Brushfire.'"

"Careful," I say. "You don't want to lose your new ring in there."

Having seen the designer digs of Ally and Judd, we're next treated to the scrappy bachelor pad that Andrew McCarthy and Emilio Estevez share. Andrew's indulging in a little pre–Matthew McConaughey bongo playing while lip-synching to Aretha Franklin's "Respect" because, according to Dr. Beaverman, "he's the most deep and soulful of the group and therefore down with Motown." Meanwhile, Emilio, whose subplot involving his obsession with woman doctor Andie MacDowell has always bored me silly, scores a few points for sporting a sprightly package in his tight mid-'80s jeans.

"I've never noticed that before." I say, pointing it out to the room.

"Too bad Paula Abdul took half of it in the divorce," says Dr. Beaverman.

Schumacher soon proves his cast can look good in natural light as they drive down a picturesque Georgetown street in Demi's jeep. As the gang ride, everyone's hair flows beautifully in the wind except for Ally's. It's like she's the lone disciple of some kooky D.C. helmet law. "Judd's giving the best hair movement in the whole Jeep," I decide.

"And that's just in his nose," adds Tony.

"A lot of the campus stuff is actually the University of Maryland," says Ross, pulling another Fun Fact from his cards. "Georgetown wouldn't let them shoot there because there was too much sex and drugs in the script. They said that kind of stuff didn't go on there."

"But didn't they shoot *The Exorcist* at Georgetown?" asks Marcus.

"Yes, they did," says Ross. "Schumacher actually said to them, 'Isn't this campus where a prepubescent girl masturbates with a cross and says, "Your mother sucks cocks in hell?' " And they said, 'Yes, but in that film, God wins out over the devil.'"

"And at the end of *St. Elmo's Fire,* Judd Nelson is still alive," says Tony.

Next, we're taken to Demi's Pepto-Bismol pink homestead, complete with a giant Billy Idol mural, for a scene in which she suspects Andrew to be gay simply because he's "the only guy in school who never made a pass at me."

"The only guy at Georgetown?" wonders Marcus. "No wonder she's so tired at 22."

"Andrew was totally my favorite back then," I announce, "because I really wanted to believe that just because you were creative and sensitive and musical, that didn't necessarily mean you were gay. Of course, now I know that's a big crock."

Andrew beats it out of there before he has time to get to know Demi's gay decorator, played by Matthew Laurance, who swishes over from next door in what amounts to a firestorm of Hollywood fairy dust. "I'm sorry, I've been gay 32 years," scoffs Tony, "and I've never come to the door in a pair of lime-green pants with a frou-frou drink in my hand."

Ross attempts his first Bea. It's actually not half bad—much better than my first.

"I might do one or the other," Tony clarifies, "but never both at the same time."

Later that night, Ally and Judd are awakened by a frantic phone call from Demi, who's snorting coke with a gaggle of Arabs and needs rescuing. "I think I just heard the words for gang bang," she gasps. This turns out to be untrue, but should Demi ever actually wish to hear the words for gang bang, might I suggest hanging out at a political convention with Rob Lowe.

Daylight comes and brings with it a scene where social worker Mare, dressed as though she's come straight from her shift at the Cracker Barrel, gets verbally abused by a welfare mother. "Just give me my check," the haggard woman groans as though she's speaking not only for herself and her unkempt brood but for everyone in the film as well.

"Have you ever seen a character more in need of a makeover montage than Mare?" wonders Lauren, referring to Mare's frumpy sweater and peasant skirt. "She looks like something out of *Little Women.*"

"Little?" says Tony.

"She reminds me of someone, but I can't put my finger on who," says Marcus. "It'll come to me."

Marcus is still wracking his brain when the welfare mom delivers my favorite line in the film. It's a line that has crossed my mind repeatedly over the last 15 years, usually during moments of extreme social frustration, like when I'm at a club and the two guys I've been checking out all night start hitting on each other. Or when I'm trying to cruise-direct an evening of large-group recreation and my friends either show up late or don't get along with each other or somehow manage to be a pain in my ass. "You get yourself some hot clothes and get yourself a man and you won't have to worry about all this shit," the woman says.

Amen, welfare mom. I should get a refrigerator magnet made.

Rob arrives on the scene just as the woman is leaving. His first words to Mare are not "Hello" or "Sorry I wrecked your car the other night" or even "How are things at the Barrel?" No, our boy Rob chooses to strut in with the observation, "Welfare recipients are getting better-looking."

Until this point, Dr. Beaverman has kept the shrink rap to a minimum, but now she can no longer hold back. "Rob is a garden-variety narcissist, and as such he's going to fuck everyone in his sphere," she explains, making a circle in the air with her index fingers. "If they're homeless with snot-nosed kids, fine. If they wear support hose and bad sweaters, fine. It doesn't matter. Narcissists are going to keep all their options open. Plus, with Mare, Rob can smell daddy's checkbook, and like most narcissists, he wants to be taken care of."

When Mare takes Rob home to meet her family in the next scene, Marcus literally leaps from the floor and exclaims, "Mrs. Doubtfire! That's who she looks like!" He plops back down with the blissful exhaustion of a spent honeymooner. "Once I saw her next to the banister, it was so clear. Mrs. Doubtfire."

We give Marcus's epiphany a round of applause and finish just in time to hear Mare confess to Rob that she's a virgin. When Rob expresses disbelief and assumes that she gave it up to her dweeby former boyfriend, Stewie Newman, Mare says, "Would *you* do it with Stewie Newman?"

"Yes, I think he would," I say. "If the price was right."

"Very good, Dennis," Dr. Beaverman says. "Narcissists don't always go after the most attractive girl at the dance. They'll take anyone as long as they can see themselves reflected in the other person's eyes, or, in some cases, their Coke-bottle glasses. I'd also like to point out that Mare's character's name is Wendy. Now, in *Peter Pan,* who was in love with the boy who wouldn't grow up?"

"Wendy," the rest of us say in unison.

"Very good, class," says Dr. B.

Mare's just minutes away from kissing that hymen goodbye when Rob does something so insensitive it shatters the mood. While reaching up her skirt, he snaps her girdle onto her thigh and quips, "It's your scuba suit."

"That moment was painful in the '80s, and it's still painful today," I say.

"The only difference now is the other moments in the movie have caught up to it," says Dr. Beaverman.

"I swear, you guys, I started a diet and joined a gym the day after I saw this," says Lauren. "I promised myself if a sax player who looked like Rob Lowe was ever going to go up my skirt, he was *not* going to find a girdle."

"So let me get this straight," I say. "If you'd never seen this movie, you might not have become a fitness instructor, which means my ass wouldn't be sore right now from yesterday's class?"

"Demi, whose newly crimped hair makes her look like a Pointer Sister whose father was white, is compelled to dry-hump the jukebox."

"It's the way of the universe, Dennis," says Dr. Beaverman, nodding. "If Mare Winningham flaps her arms in China, we feel it here in North Hollywood."

"And it's no picnic," says Tony.

Mare is still pissed at Rob in the next scene, in which the gang shows up at St. Elmo's on Halloween night sporting Groucho Marx–style nose glasses.

"This is the one night a year where Judd Nelson feels normal," says Tony.

In this scene, Rob's sax synching is so powerhouse that Demi, whose newly crimped hairdo makes her look like a Pointer Sister whose father was white, is compelled to dry-hump the jukebox.

"I'm obsessed with this moment coming up," says Marcus, "where Rob starts clapping and says, 'Let's rock!' I think he looks so awkward."

"Gwyneth Paltrow's obsessed with it too," I report. "I interviewed her years ago and we spent 20 minutes talking about that moment and how was the one crack in his super-cool veneer."

"Tell them about shitheap," urges Tony.

"You know how we call bad movies shitheaps?" I ask. "Well, I got that from Ms. Paltrow when I interviewed her in like '95 or '96. Shitheap was her and Brad's pet name for a bad movie."

"Let me guess," says Ross. "*Hush*?"

"I can't remember if it was one they were in or not," I say. "In any event, that's where shitheap comes from. Use it with pride."

Just then, Lauren takes her first bite of cookie and nearly gags. "Oh, my God," she says, before spitting into a napkin. "So gross."

"I didn't bake them, all right," Marcus barks. "I didn't have time to bake, so I bought them at Ralphs. You can say they suck if they suck."

"They suck," say the rest of us.

We watch Rob blow on his sax for a while, and then suddenly, apropos of nothing, Dr. Beaverman says, "I'm not really a doctor."

"What?" I say.

"I'm not really a doctor," she repeats, staring at her shoes.

I pause the movie and let her continue.

"As long as we're coming clean about things, I lied about being a doctor, OK? I completed all the coursework years ago, but I hadn't finished my thesis until recently."

"So when will you be a doctor?" I ask.

"This week," she says. "I graduate this week."

"Can I come to the ceremony?" I ask.

"Let me think about it," she says, before reaching over and unpausing the movie. "It's really not a big deal."

"I think it's a huge deal," says Marcus.

The rest of us offer Dr. Beaverman our kudos, then turn our attention back to the screen, where Rob takes a break from rocking long enough to play a little tonsil hockey with Demi. Just then, his wife traipses in looking like she just escaped from Pat Benatar's "Love Is a Battlefield" video. When Rob notices she's with another man, all hell breaks loose.

"Get your hands off of my wife!" threatens Rob.

"With narcissists," explains Dr. Beaverman, "everything *belongs* to them. They see everything as an extension of themselves. They are not independent objects." Dr. B takes a sip of her margarita and adds, "Unlike whatever Demi's got stuffed into her bra, which seems to have a mind of it's own."

"And check out that metallic lip gloss," says Tony. "It looks like she just went down on C-3PO in the bathroom."

Which brings us to Andrew McCarthy's encounter with Naomi, a streetwalker in a red "Beat It" leather jacket, played by Anna Maria Horsford. When Naomi grabs Andy's tie in an attempt to seduce him, Dr. Beaverman introduces a theory on the neckwear of *St. Elmo's* that's so complex we should tell Ross's friend to give it its own audio track on the DVD.

"It's the way of the universe.... If Mare Winningham flaps her arms in China, we feel it here in North Hollywood." —Dr. Beaverman

"Look to the neckwear for sexual symbolism," she instructs. "Notice, Andrew's tie is completely flaccid, whereas Rob's is always going every which way, completely untamable and out of control."

"And Judd Nelson seems to favor the primary-colored power tie," says Marcus.

"Read that as no foreplay, my friends," says Dr. Beaverman.

"Does the sexual neckwear theory also apply to women?" I ask, during the next scene, when the three gals do lunch at Mare's soup kitchen.

"Well, Mare's wearing a turtleneck," Dr. Beaverman points out, "indicating that her hymen is up to her throat. I wouldn't be surprised if it were built into the girdle."

"What about Ally with that Ralph Lauren lace doily thing around her neck?" wonders Tony. "She looks like she came straight from a wardrobe fitting for *Maid to Order.*"

"It indicates that Ally is not only old-fashioned but frigid," says Dr. Beaverman. "The Barbara Bush pearls underline this point."

By this time, we've forgotten that Emilio Estevez is even in the movie. He makes his reappearance in a scene in which he follows Andie MacDowell, as Dr. Dale Beaverman—no relation—to a fancy party. When the former cover girl steps out of a red Volkswagen, Ross says, "If there's one thing Andie MacDowell doesn't have, it's Farfegnugen."

Then, as the rain-drenched Emilio watches Andie through the window while she chats up a handsome fellow doctor, Dr. Beaverman offers her take on the Emilio/Andie relationship. "Notice, there's no tie on Emilio," she says. "He's completely castrated seeing Mommy with Daddy. And that rain on his face? Amniotic fluid. He's wet from the womb and upset because he's not a part of Mommy and Daddy's primal union."

When Emilio makes a scene at the party, Andie takes him back to her apartment and, in an attempt to convince him to get over her, starts listing her flaws. "I'm a slob," she asserts. "I can't even make a bed straight. I steal *People* magazine from my dentist's office. I rarely take out the garbage."

"I so want her to bend over and go, 'And look, Kirby, dingleberries,'" says Tony.

"Check out that metallic lip gloss. It looks like she just went down on C3PO in the bathroom."
–Tony

Berries or no, Emilio's not about to give up. A few days later, he throws a huge party in Andie's honor, which she doesn't even attend. The soiree reaches its climax when Judd throws Andrew to the ground because he believes it was Andy who told Ally he was cheating. For my money, however, the highlight of the sequence is when Demi is seen spinning à la Cyndi Lauper in the "Girls Just Want to Do Coke" video.

On a hunch, I grab the remote control and hit super slo-mo.

"Oh, God," Tony says as Demi rotates one frame at a time, "Are we going to see what's going on under that dress?"

"With any luck," I say.

"Is that shadow what I think it is?" asks Marcus.

"Wait a minute!" gasps Lauren. "She's got no underwear on."

Ross grabs his *Spy* magazine off the coffee table and shouts, "You saw it here first!"

Meanwhile, more obsessed than ever, Emilio chases Andie up to some ski lodge in

Mare's Chrysler Le Baron. "The snow indicates that it's going to be a cold, frigid outing," says Dr. Beaverman, "because having sex with Mommy is taboo."

When the car gets stuck in the snow, Emilio tries to get it out but fails. Andie shouts, "Come inside."

"Mixed messages from Mommy," says Dr. Beaverman with a sigh.

Emilio goes into the cabin, where he ends up crashing overnight. The next morning, Andie's beau comes outside to see Emilio off.

"Look," says Marcus. "The top button on that guy's jeans has totally popped open."

"It's his way of showing Emilio who's Daddy," says Dr. Beaverman as Emilio grabs Andie and plants one on her.

"Ooh, I have a Fun Fact," says Ross, holding up a note card.

"Ross has a Fun Fact," says Lauren.

"The studio executive in charge of this film hated the relationship between Emilio Estevez and Andie MacDowell," he explains. "He was embarrassed by Emilio's desperation and he wanted the whole subplot cut. But then they test-screened it and the audience cheered when Emilio grabbed Andie and kissed her, so Schumacher got to keep it in."

Which brings us to my favorite scene in the film, where Andrew proclaims his love to Ally and they do it in a coffin.

"I adored Andrew in this scene," I say, unwilling to underplay my fervent McCarthyism any longer. "I thought this was the best acting in the movie."

"Me too," says Lauren. "But I never understood why he'd want to seduce a woman who was dressed like that. It's like fucking an armchair."

"Ally's leaving the pearls on?" wonders Tony. "Who is she, Seka?"

"Just wait," says Ross. "She's going to have an extra set in a few minutes."

Andrew, Ally, and the pearls go at it, at one point, boffing with such gusto that they break Andy's shower door. They're basking in the afterglow when Judd stumbles in wearing a black suit and brown shoes.

"All those years in a gay bar," laments Tony, "and he still can't dress."

Andrew tries to tell Judd that the mystery woman in his bedroom is Ally and not the fat chick from the party as Judd suspects, but he can't find the words.

"I wish Andrew had said, 'Judd, I've got something to tell you: Smell my hand,' " I say.

When Ally emerges, pearls all aglow, and says, "It's not the fat chick," Judd's nostrils literally become bigger than his eyes. He's still fuming when Ally returns to their designer pad to pack her stuff. "I didn't just *fuck* Kevin," Ally whines.

"I sucked his cock and popped a couple of zits on his back too," says Tony.

"I was confused and angry and I care about him," continues Ally.

"Why didn't she just say, 'I was drunk,' like a normal person?" wonders Lauren.

"Or she could have said, 'I broke his shower and I didn't have my checkbook. How else was I supposed to pay for it?' " offers Marcus.

The pair argue over custody of albums by Bruce Springsteen, Billy Joel, and Carly Simon, and things get pretty heated. Thank God the battle for Juice Newton and Scandal happened off camera. The next time Ally and Judd speak is when Ally shows up at Judd's office to report that Demi, in the throes of a major meltdown, has blocked the door to her apartment with a curtain rod and opened all the windows.

"Apparently, her creditors repossessed everything but the wind machine," I observe.

"This is what I've never gotten about this movie," says Lauren. "How exactly is she in grave danger?"

"I agree," says Dr. Beaverman. "All the drugs in that house and she picks hypothermia as a means of suicide? It's not even that cold."

"Apparently, Schumacher knew someone who tried to kill themselves that way," says Ross, serving up yet another Fun Fact.

"She's not even naked," says Marcus.

"Demi wanted to be naked," says Ross. "She was willing to do it for the sake of realism, but Schumacher didn't know how he'd shoot it."

"So she decided to be naked in every other movie," says Lauren.

The gang pound on Demi's door to no avail. Finally, Rob shows up looking like a pump-boy dancer from Billy Joel's "Uptown Girl" video wearing a jumpsuit and either leg warmers or scrunch socks, we can't tell. Demi lets him in, and while she rocks back and forth pathetically, Rob regales her with the legend of St. Elmo, using some spectacular spur-of-the-moment pyrotechnics, that, given the amount of hair products on that set, could have had the whole lot of them boffing in coffins.

Mare gets to hear about it all later from Rob, who pops by her new place before leaving for New York to sponge more money off her and star as the meat in a Winningham sandwich.

"I bet you could hear that cherry pop clear back at the frat house," I say as Mare surrenders herself to Rob.

"OK, class, let's see if you've learned anything," says Dr. Beaverman as Rob and Mare make sweet, tender love. "The narcissist only lays his hopes and dreams on the overweight Holly Hobbie one. Why?"

"Because you can always count on the overweight Holly Hobbie one?" I say.

"Exactly, Dennis," replies Dr. B. "Would he ever ask Demi for money?"

"I'm going to say no," says Marcus.

"That's correct," says Dr. Beaverman. "Ms. Moore's strictly a pleasure diddle."

While a freshly deflowered Mare and the rest of the gang bid adieu to Rob at the bus station, Ally voices-over something about not remembering who boffed who first or who became friends first. Then, in an ending Ross says was changed several times, Ally tells Judd and Andrew, who both are still hot to couple with her, "I just want to be by myself for a while."

"Boy, did she get her wish or what?" says Tony.

•

The next day, I get an E-mail from Dr. Beaverman inviting me to her graduation ceremony that Friday afternoon. I forward it on to the rest of the posse, and remarkably, we're all able to make it. Dressed in the most presentable outfits we've probably ever seen each other in, we arrive separately at the designated address at roughly the same time.

"She must have typed the street number wrong," I say, trying to explain why we've all ended up at a strip mall in Van Nuys.

"What's the name of the college again?" asks Lauren.

"Ivy-by-the-Pacific," I say. "Let me try her cell."

I'm about to press send when I hear Dr. Beaverman call out from behind me, "In here, kids!"

We turn around to see her disappear into a Mail Boxes Etc.–type establishment called Postal Depot. We follow, and the second we're inside the muted musical strains of "Pomp and Circumstance" begin to play.

"Is that everyone?" the clerk, a bespectacled young man of Middle Eastern descent, asks me.

I nod. Then, suddenly, from behind a row of post office boxes emerges Dr. Beaverman, wearing one of her nicest suits and a mortarboard. She step-touches her way to the counter, then reaches over and presses stop on her pocket-size tape recorder. The music stops.

"In honor of your years of hard work and other kinds of things, I present you with this," says the clerk, before bringing the envelope to his face and reading, "from Ivy-by-the-Pacific University, established 1997."

"Thank you, Hasid," says Dr. Beaverman.

Dr. B takes the envelope from Hasid, slips one of her perfect nails under the seal, and slices it open. Then, as Hasid aims a disposable camera at her, she slowly pulls a pristine sheet of cream-colored paper from the envelope; it's her diploma. She has Hasid take two pictures—one with her glasses, one without. As Hasid continues to snap away, she takes the gold tassel from her cap and deliberately moves it from the student side to the graduate side. Then she closes her eyes for a spell, as if to take in the moment. When she opens them, she looks over to us and says, "Who's hungry? Lauren, I know you are."

After hugs all around, Dr. Beaverman explains that the only downside to furthering your education over the Internet is that there's no ceremony. "So I improvised," she says.

We cross the street *St. Elmo's*-style in a big red rover line and settle into an oversized booth at Ye Olde Spaghetti Company, the kind of dive I would have eaten at regularly in college because on Sundays they have two-for-one dinner specials.

As we silently peruse the menu, I reflect on my friendships in 1985 versus now, and I'm pleased to report that I'm no longer jealous of the Brat Pack. Sure, they made good money and had lots of sex, and a few of them have careers still, but I'm happy with the friends I've got, thank you very much.

My friends never dress like people from music videos and they pretty much always wear underwear. They'd never borrow my car to chase after Andie McDowell unless their intent was to scare her, and they only say stuff like "Yuggadah, yuggaduh, yuggaduh, ha-ha-ha!" when making fun of people who say stuff like "Yuggadah, yuggaduh, yuggaduh, ha-ha-ha!" And, unlike Rob Lowe's pretty-to-look-at mooch in *St. Elmo's,* my friends always bring something to the party. If it happens to be a pre-Tallulah Belle beaver shot of Demi Moore, well, so much the better.

"We're still going shopping for my reunion outfit next week, right?" Marcus asks me outside the restaurant.

"Call me," I say.

"I'd stay away from the pink sweaters and doily necklines," suggests Tony. "Assuming you want to get laid."

"And remember," says Dr. Beaverman, tapping Marcus's chest with her doggie bag for emphasis. "Never underestimate the power of the right necktie."

THE METER'S RUNNING

As moods go, I'm feeling pretty fancy free when I saunter into Marcus's law office in Century City a few weeks after *Elmo's*-palooza. My countenance takes a dramatic downshift, however, when my junior entertainment lawyer friend intercepts me at the elevator and grunts, "Did you bring it?"

"It's right here," I say, indicating the manila envelope under my arm. I start to slide something from it when Marcus practically goes into cardiac arrest. "No, no, no, not here," he gasps. "Follow me."

My uncharacteristically jittery friend leads me through a maze of offices and cubicles, most of whose occupants are gone for the day, to the copy room in the back.

"There it is," he says reverently, using his chin to indicate his firm's state-of-the-art color Xerox machine. "Find the page before we even go near it," he instructs, shifting his gaze nervously.

"Look, if this is a problem, I can just go to Kinko's," I whisper. "I don't want any trouble."

"It's fine, it's fine, it's fine," he says. "It's just that one of the partners here is a total prick. No one else would care." Marcus cranes his neck to look around the office, then gasps, "His door's closed. Go! Go! Go!" and shoves me into the copy room.

While Marcus stands guard outside and pretends to peruse a brief, I slide my just-arrived copy of *British Premiere* from the envelope and prepare to make five copies of my *Jaws at 25* article, one for each of the loveable loudmouths who inspired it. Though the Xeroxing itself seems to last longer than the average Drew Barrymore marriage, I manage to copy, collate, and staple without getting busted by the office asshole, who I've chosen to believe looks and acts just like Dabney Coleman in *9 to 5*.

"Next time, remind me to wear my black unitard," I tell Marcus on our way to the mall across the street, "and I'll dangle from the ceiling like Tom Cruise in *Mission: Impossible.*"

"Believe it or not, our little escapade was the most fun I've had all day," he says.

"So, where do you want to go first, Macy's?" I ask. "I think they actually have a line of clothes named Reunion."

"I'm not going," says Marcus. "Let's go eat."

Over pizza slices and Caesar salads in the food court, my "casual Friday"–clad friend explains his reasoning for playing hooky from his law school reunion. "When I first got the invitation, I thought, *I* have *to go because I might not be around for the next one,*" explains Marcus, who learned he was HIV-positive in the fall of 1994. "And then I decided I'm not going to let HIV make my decisions for me. I didn't particularly want to go. My friends from school that I like I talk to all the time. It might be nice to see some other folks, but I don't *need* to. Besides, I *will* make it to the next one, so I can see them then. So I'm not going to go. That's where I'm at now. Do you want to split a Mrs. Fields' cookie?"

"So you could still change your mind?" I ask.

"No," he says. "I cashed in my ticket." I follow my friend's gaze across the dining area to a table in the corner where a pair of teenagers, who are clearly immersed in that kind of puppy love that comes complete with orgasms, make out. "So when's the next Screening Party?" he asks.

"I guess we can have it next weekend," I say. "If you're going to be in town."

"Something upbeat, I hope," he says.

"Well, that all depends."

"On what?" he asks.

"On how you feel about child prostitution."

•

"All the animals come out at night," says Robert De Niro's cabbie character, Travis Bickle, near the outset of Martin Scorsese's classic 1976 stalker drama *Taxi Driver.* "Whores, scum pussies, buggers, queens, fairies, dopers, junkies..."

"And me!" chirps Dr. Beaverman.

"Whaddaya know," I say to the usual suspects positioned in their usual spots in my front room. "He's welcoming us!"

"I can't decide which slur suits me better, bugger or scum pussy," says Tony. "I think bugger."

In the aftermath of *St. Elmo's,* my U.K. editor, Matt, figured it might be nice, for our third outing, to showcase a film that, in his words, "isn't shite." And since the magazine was already running a Q&A with actor Albert Brooks, Matt suggested we take a fresh look at the film that gave us not only Mr. Brooks in an Afro but Jodie Foster in hot pants and Robert De Niro in an ever-deteriorating state of sanity. And like *Jaws* before it, here was another classic that for some reason I'd never seen, most likely because when it came out it was all I could do to keep up with the Disney comedies starring Kurt Russell as Dexter Riley. The last thing I needed in 1976 was another genre.

"It's so nice to know other people decorate as I do," says Dr. Beaverman when we get our first look at Bickle's shit-hole New York apartment.

"Can you pause for a second, Dennis?" asks Ross. "If we don't get that flashing 12:00 off your VCR, I'm going to shave my head into a Mohawk and shoot someone."

My visibly agitated friend squats in front of the VCR and in 10 seconds flat programs not only the correct time, 2:17 P.M., but the day and date as well. Given that I can't remember the last time those settings have been accurate, I half expect the machine to open its cassette flap and belch, "Thanks, I needed that."

When we restart the movie, Bickle is driving his cab back to the garage while accompanied by the jazzy, atmospheric score by composer Bernard Herrmann, the genius behind the music for *Psycho, Vertigo,* and countless other classics.

"Herrmann completed this score the day he died," says the perpetually in-the-know Ross, who informed me when I called to invite him that he wouldn't need note cards this time out, as *Taxi Driver* is number 7 on his all-time top 10. I still haven't asked what number 1 is and probably won't unless we decide to go parachuting together and there's a chance that one of us may die. "It's a great score in a film that's widely considered to be one of the seminal films of the '70s."

I'm about to ask Ross what exactly he means by *seminal* when I get my answer from De Niro's voice-over. "Each night when I return the cab to the garage," he says, "I have to clean the come off the backseat."

"He should just be glad he wasn't working on *Can't Stop the Music,*" says Marcus as Bickle returns his cab to taxi headquarters.

Though the garage is suitably grimy and altogether believable, something's missing from the scene for me. But I can't put my finger on what it is.

Tony, however, has no such trouble. "I so want Marilu Henner to come walking in wearing one of those nasty spandex tops," he says, "pissing and moaning about how Latka forgot to change her transmission fluid."

De Niro leaves the garage and before heading home pops by his local porn theater for a little after-work entertainment.

"I didn't know porno theaters had concession stands," says Lauren as De Niro picks up some snacks for the movie.

"I'd like a small popcorn and a medium Pocket Pussy, please," says Tony.

"Would you like a large for a quarter more?" asks Marcus.

Back on screen, De Niro says via voice-over, "I don't believe that one should devote his life to morbid self-attention."

"Why is he starting every sentence with *I* then?" wonders Dr. Beaverman, clearly gearing up for an afternoon of serious armchair analyzing. "This is starting to sound like an Alanis Morissette record." Though Dr. Beaverman admits she hasn't been in a record store since the days of vinyl, she's a devoted MTV, VH1, BET, and CMT viewer and as such knows more about current music acts than anyone in the room.

In the next scene we're introduced to campaign office workers Cybill Shepherd and Albert Brooks, who manage to find time to exchange flirtatious banter while working to get their man elected.

"I'm not proud of this," says Dr. Beaverman, gesturing to Brooks's Brillo do, "but I have a thing against non–African-Americans wearing Afros. I think it started with Barbra Streisand and the Brady boys, and then *The Greatest American Hero* just sent me over the edge."

"She appeared like an angel," the infatuated De Niro says as we get our first close-up of Cybill, who in her colorful poly-blend ensemble would look exactly like a cashier from Sambo's were it not for her long flowing scarf. "Why couldn't she go riding in a convertible with that scarf on?" pleads Tony. "We could chop an hour out of this film."

"I have a thing against non–African-Americans wearing Afros. I think it started with Barbra Streisand and the Brady boys, and then *The Greatest American Hero* just sent me over the edge." —Dr. Beaverman

Cybill skips the convertible ride and instead accompanies Albert to a diner where he attempts to charm her with his theory on why Mafia men leave dead canaries on their victims. Though some women might be turned off by small talk about dead birds, Cybill just smiles.

I grab the remote and freeze on Cybill's oft-photographed face, then announce that it's time for a special Screening Party bonus. While Marcus distributes his special *Taxi Driver* lemon squares, I go to the stereo and play for my guests a snippet from one of my prized possessions, Cybill Shepherd's 1979 jazz album, *Vanilla.* It's the music I put on whenever I need to feel better about me, and when I play it for other people, they always ask me the same question.

"Was she drunk?" asks Marcus as Cybill belts and riffs her way through "Ain't Misbehavin.'"

"I wasn't there," I say. "Unfortunately. She had all these major jazz cats playing with her and I think she did every song in one take."

"Clearly," says Tony.

I stop the music, unpause the movie, and watch as Albert and Cybill return to their office. A few moments later, De Niro, now fully obsessed with the vivacious blond, comes in to volunteer.

"I think that you are the most beautiful woman I've ever seen," he tells her.

"Dr. Beaverman worries that women can easily fall for such shallow, sleepy-time foreplay," says Dr. B., who, as you've probably noticed, ofte refers to herself in the third person. "She's fallen for Albert Brooks's dead canary shtick and now this, a man in a maroon corduroy jacket."

"That looks like the kind of jacket that if you go to a nice restaurant and you don't have one, they give to you," remarks Marcus.

"And her dress is a total LSD hallucination," says Tony. "I mean, Shirley Jones looked at that and went, 'No fucking way.'"

I tear myself away from the fashions just in time to notice something peculiar about De Niro. "He just looked right into the camera," I say before scanning back a few frames. "Watch, it's right after Cybill's goofy laugh."

"Maybe he's just rolling his eyes," says Lauren.

"Maybe he did it on purpose," says Tony. "Like he thought, 'If I look right at the camera, maybe Marty'll let her try it again.' "

In spite of De Niro's ticking-time-bomb demeanor, Cybill agrees to meet him later at a diner. While he attempts to woo the onetime hair color queen, the four of us try to solve the real mystery of the scene. "Do you think that's three separate necklaces," asks Lauren, pointing to Cybill's cleavage, "or does it have one clasp in the back?"

"One clasp," say the rest of us.

Unlike all of us, De Niro sees Cybill as more than just a necklace stand. He reflects on his diner dream date in voice-over in the next scene. "I called Betsy again in her office," he says wistfully, "and she said maybe we'd go to a movie together...Betsy, Betsy, oh no, Betsy what? I forgot to ask her last name..."

"Wetsy," says Dr. Beaverman. "That was too easy."

"Miss Wetsy if you're nasty," says Lauren.

As fate would have it, the next passenger we see step into De Niro's cab is the very politician Cybill and Albert are trying to get elected.

"Let me tell you something," says the candidate, who, unlike Ms. Shepherd, doesn't need a brick to fall on his head with a note from God attached to it that says, "The cabbie's cracked, watch your ass," to realize De Niro's nuttier than Almond Joy. "I've learned more about America from riding in taxi cabs than in all the limos in the country."

"Well, you're sitting in come right now, sir," Dr. Beaverman says before gasping and slapping a hand over her mouth. "Put that line in someone else's mouth, Dennis," she says regretfully, "like Tony's."

"You'll name it," chides Tony, "but you won't claim it."

"I have my reputation to think about," she replies. "I really shouldn't say 'come' unless it's in a professional context."

"Like you could say, 'Tell me more about your come phobia, Mrs. Peterson?' " I suggest.

"Yes," says Dr. Beaverman, "and have on occasion."

Back in mad cabbie land, Cybill shocks us all by agreeing to let De Niro take her to his favorite porn palace to sample the latest in Swedish erotica. "He's so fucked-up that he doesn't know how to go on a real date," says Ross, "so he figures he'll take her to a dirty movie."

"Welcome to the world of men," says Lauren.

"Cybill actually looks like this is her first time seeing a dirty movie," says Marcus.

"That she's not in," clarifies Tony.

"The last guy I dated actually put a porn movie on as we were about to sleep together for the first time," I say.

"You never told me that," says Tony.

"Red flag much?" says Lauren.

"This was like a month in and I think he just wanted it to go well," I say. "He was trying to set the mood or something. It didn't bother me at the time, but looking back it seems like kind of an odd tactic."

Before you can say, "Hey Travis, what's that in your popcorn box?" a seriously grossed-out Cybill ditches her lovesick suitor and runs from the theater in a huff.

"Is there supposed to be any pathos for Bickle?" Dr. Beaverman wonders.

"Don't think I'm a psycho, but I've always identified with his loneliness," offers Ross. "A lot of the stuff he says, like 'You're as healthy as you feel,' are things we've all felt, but when they're combined in this particular guy, the results are psychotic."

"The film seems to be saying, 'You can't really tell a psychotic from a normal person because we're all so alienated,' " says Dr. Beaverman.

"I get it," says Tony. "But if you're using De Niro as the wacko and Cybill Shepherd as the control side of the experiment..."

"How's a person to know?" says Dr. Beaverman.

Having suffered more ribbing that even a model-turned-actress should have to, Cybill pretty much takes herself out of the picture. Without her to push around, we bide our time until the film's other hot tamale, Jodie Foster, Oscar-nominated as a 12½-year-old hooker named Iris, sashays onto the scene.

"How does she not get busted?" wonders Tony. "It seems to me that anyone could see Jodie Foster wearing a hat like that and immediately make a citizen's arrest. She looks like Rose Kennedy in the Hamptons."

"Is it Friday? 'Cause this sure is Freaky," says Marcus.

"Those white bell-bottoms threw me for a sec," claims Lauren. "I thought we had switched movies and were in *On the Town*."

"It seems to me that anyone could see Jodie Foster wearing a hat like that and immediately make a citizen's arrest. She looks like Rose Kennedy in the Hamptons." —Tony

"Is it just my MTV generation attention deficit disorder, or do these scenes go on forever?" I ask.

"The movie's designed to be like a trance, a hypnotic slow-burn," says Ross. "If you surrender to it, it can really get under your skin."

"You know what it is?" says Tony. "I just don't think we've ever seen De Niro with bangs before and we're transfixed. It's like, 'Goddamn it, De Niro's got bangs!' "

Which brings us, finally, to the famous scene in which Bickle, in full-tilt vigilante mode, riles himself up by looking in the mirror and saying, "You talkin' to me?" over and over in various inflections.

"That line was never actually in the script," says Ross. "De Niro improvised it."

"He's taking every primitive macho metaphor and distorting it," observes Dr. Beaverman. "A guy like this is not going to be happy with a pizza, a football game, and a little hair pie. With Travis Bickle, there is no gray area."

"Except for that skin," says Tony. "He's taking all this time to get in shape and he won't take a few minutes to go to the fake-and-bake? I could give him a coupon."

Suddenly, just as we've sampled Bickle's last interpretation of "You talking to me?" the tape Ross brought from work starts to snap, crackle, and pop in my VCR. As for the picture, it looks like it's being shot through a snow globe.

"You know what it is," figures Lauren. "Every wanna-be actor in town has rented this tape and watched this scene over and over again for their scene study class."

"Maybe it was John Hinckley," I suggest.

"Is Hinckley the guy who tried to shoot Jodie Foster?" asks Tony.

"He didn't try to shoot Jodie," lectures Ross without taking his eyes from the screen. "Hinckley was in love with Jodie Foster and he tried to assassinate President Reagan to get her attention by imitating Travis Bickle's actions in this movie. It wasn't about killing Jodie Foster. It was about saving Jodie Foster."

"Then why didn't he do anything about *Anna and the King*?" wonders Tony.

"The music is so distorted it sounds like Della Reese's stomach," says Dr. Beaverman. "No wonder the composer died the next day."

"The picture's not much better," says Lauren.

"Just try to blink along with it like Tammy Faye Bakker," suggests Marcus.

"Speaking of weird blinkers," I say, "does anyone else think Madonna has a blinking problem, like she blinks at weird times? I've been waiting for years for someone to blow the lid off that phenomenon."

"Shut the fuck up about Madonna!" Ross bellows.

I decide not to take Ross's Madonna malice personally, as he's clearly preoccupied with our tape dilemma and probably feels somewhat responsible for it. What he doesn't seem to understand is that the rest of us aren't particularly bothered one way or the other.

"You should get your money back, Dennis," says Lauren. "Just say the movie was unwatchable."

"Well, they know that already," says Tony. "Cybill Shepherd's in it."

"I didn't pay for it," I remind everyone. "Ross brought it from work. Hold on, I have an idea." I disappear into my bedroom and return a few minutes later with my second VCR. "This one's used to cranky videotapes," I say as I start hooking it up.

"It's trained in porn from 20 years ago," clarifies Tony. "Of course, it's never had to play for more than seven or eight minutes at a time, so this should be interesting."

Ross, ever the video technician, unhooks VCR 1, connects its replacement, and once again sets the time and date.

I'm happy to report that VCR 2, despite its seedy pedigree, rises to the occasion and delivers a perfectly adequate picture and not a single Della Reese rumbling. It's a good thing too because we've come to the scene where De Niro rents Jodie from her pimp, played by a buffed-out Harvey Keitel.

"You know, if Harvey worked out a little, he could play Tina Turner," says Tony.

Jodie leads De Niro to a candlelit room where, presumably, the curly-headed junior ho will go about the business of putting out. "Jodie Foster playing a hooker is like Tommy Tune playing *American Gigolo,*" I say. "She's not hot to trot at all."

"She's 12," Marcus reminds us.

"I'm with you, Dennis," says Ross. "Jodie's never struck me as remotely sexy. If I had a thing for 12-year-olds, I would *not* have a thing for Jodie Foster."

"She gives child prostitution a bad name," concludes Dr. Beaverman.

"Let me get this straight," says Lauren, clearly a little creeped out. "If you were so inclined to do a 12-year-old, you'd still want it to be a *hot* 12-year-old?"

"Yes," Ross and I say in unison. "With some back," adds Ross. "Jodie don't have back."

"She had a nice set of hot rollers, though," says Dr. Beaverman. "You gotta give her points for that bouncin' and behavin' hair."

"In a few of these shots, it's not even her," Ross informs us. "The board of education wouldn't allow Jodie to do some of the more adult stuff like unzipping De Niro's pants, so they used a double."

"So who is it?" wonders Lauren.

"It's actually kind of interesting and surprising," teases Ross.

"Jimmy McNichol," guesses Tony.

"Billy Barty in a wig," I say.

"Cybill Shepherd in knee pads," says Dr. Beaverman.

"It's Jodie's sister," says Ross, "who is actually eight years older than Jodie."

Whoever it is, De Niro refuses to diddle her, leaving Jodie with an unexpected window of free time, which I like to imagine she used to think up names for her production company and to start a list of possible sperm donors. Though he opts not to defile her, Bickle's far from done with Ms. Foster. He makes a diner date with her for the next day.

"What's with all the diner scenes in '70s movies?" I say. "It must have been impossible to get a decent patty melt back then without having to jump over cables and sign a release."

"And those sunglasses on Jodie," groans Tony. "She looks like she's going to burst into 'Crocodile Rock' any second."

"This is a classic case of reversal," deduces Dr. Beaverman. "Travis wants to help her because he sees himself in this girl." We all nod agreeably, and then Dr. Beaverman, unable to stop herself, adds, "Except with a better ass."

The next thing you know, De Niro's doing a swan dive right off the deep end, voicing-over foreboding lines like "My whole life is pointed in one direction" and "There never has been any choice for me." To complete his menace to society makeover, he razors his head into an eye-catching Mohawk. Then he heads off to shoot Cybill's candidate.

"You could see with the Mohawk," says Marcus, "how he really wanted to blend in. He didn't want to give security any reason to be suspicious."

"He actually didn't shave his head," says Ross, whose sense of humor seems to have gone the way of VCR 1. "It's a bald cap that they had to do over every day."

"That surprises me," I say. "I mean, De Niro always seems to go the extra mile."

"He did actually get a cab driver's license, though," says Ross, "and he would drive around for research and pick people up."

Not surprisingly, Travis's tragic hair-don't and crazy-motherfucker demeanor are not lost on the Secret Service men on the scene, who promptly put the kibosh on his assassination plans. So the wacky cabbie, determined to knock off somebody, *anybody,* heads Keitel's way.

"Now we come to one of the most famous sequences in movies," announces Ross.

"The dance at the gym?" says Marcus hopefully.

"You know who Keitel looks like in that wig?" asks Tony, just as De Niro takes Keitel out. "Doug Henning. Maybe Travis Bickle just doesn't like magic."

"I know I've never cared for it," says Dr. Beaverman.

"And that's why he's so pissed off," Tony continues. "He's like, 'Try levitating with a bullet in your ass, you one-armed, unitard-wearing piece of shit!' "

Travis continues his shooting spree by blowing off the hand of a gruff character actor in a loud-patterned jacket. It's all a bit much for Dr. B., who buried her face in her hands back at Keitel. "Dr. Beaverman doesn't like blood," she explains, peeking out from between her fingers. "It did improve the plaid, though."

"Every once in a while, you just need a little splash of color," says Lauren.

"Speaking of color," says Ross. "The ratings board made them desaturate the colors in this scene in order to get an R rating because it was too graphic the way it was."

"Please let Cybill come walking in," Tony pleads as the carnage continues. "Couldn't she go down in friendly fire?"

"Tony, why do you hate Cybill so much?" I ask, finally sticking up for the singer-actress-pitchwoman.

"I hate anyone who insists on singing their own sitcom theme song," he states simply, as if it's the most logical explanation in the world. "If Kelsey Grammer and Linda Lavin were in this movie, I'd be gunning for them too."

Speaking of gunning, De Niro's still firing off bullets like crazy on screen. "This is every psychopath's wet dream," says Dr. Beaverman as the gunplay makes it's way to Jodie's room, where the curly-headed prostitute scurries about dodging bullets. "Look at those curls just bouncing away," she adds. "I'm so jealous."

"Even when *you* can't hold up any longer..." I say.

The scene reaches its blood-soaked climax when Travis turns the gun on himself, but, wouldn't you know it, he's fresh out of bullets so he calls it a day and heads home. In the aftermath of the massacre, Bickle is credited with reuniting Jodie with her parents, and he becomes a veritable folk hero as a result. Even Cybill, whom he runs into one day by chance, sees him in a new and improved light.

"I read about you in the paper," she purrs.

"Just like a woman," mutters Dr. Beaverman.

As the credits roll and my guests dry off from the bloodbath, I do a little stock-taking and decide that it's true what they say about *Taxi Driver.* Scorsese's grimy masterpiece painted a chillingly accurate and indelible picture of a certain kind of white male pathology, one that seems to rear its head regularly on school playgrounds, in parking lots next to government buildings, and in movies with Ed Norton. That said, however, for my money the film doesn't hold a candle to that *other* Martin Scorsese meditation on urban decay and the human psyche. I'm referring, of course, to Michael Jackson's "Bad" video. "Now, *that* painted an accurate picture of New York City," I say and begin rewinding the movie. "I think it's a question we've all asked ourselves at one point or another: 'Who's bad?' "

"I think the problem with Travis Bickle was his name," says Marcus. "I think if he had had a better name, like Travis Winterbottom III, his whole life would have been different."

"Obviously, he was thinking with his Bickle a little too much," says Dr. Beaverman.

Dr. Beaverman's line seems the perfect bon mot to end our evening. But just as it lands, VCR 2 begins to rattle and hum in a way that made VCR 1's overtures earlier seem like a lullaby.

"Now it *really* sounds like Della Reese's stomach," says Lauren.

"Can I put on more Cybill?" asks Marcus, walking over to the stereo. "Maybe we can drown it out."

"Knock yourself out," I tell him.

"Just eject it, Dennis," says Ross before plopping down next to me in front of the VCR. "I'll rewind it back at the store."

I press stop, then eject. Ross goes to withdraw the movie but a portion of the tape itself seems to be stuck inside. No stranger to such half-inch hiccups, Ross tries to gingerly coax the tape out without doing irreparable damage to the movie or his masculinity. This strategy seems to be working until the woeful moment when one of Ross's love taps inexplicably causes the device to revert to its normal resting state: with 12:00 flashing in the display window.

It's at this point that Ross does what can only be described as losing one's shit.

"Motherfuck!" he screams while yanking the cassette out in one violent motion, leaving two strands of tape connected to the inside of the machine. He pulls on the strands but they don't budge. By this time Marcus has restarted the music, so Ross looks as though he's doing a rhythmic gymnastics routine to Cybill Shepherd's scat-tastic version of "A Foggy Day in London Town."

"Straight rage, ladies and gentlemen," declares Tony.

This doesn't help the situation.

By the time Ross cools his wayward jets a chorus or so later, there are streams of exposed *Taxi Driver* all over the room. "Fuck it, fuck it, fuck it," he rants, and starts wadding the tape into a huge ball.

Dr. Beaverman slips a business card in his shirt pocket and says, "First session's on me."

Marcus stops the stereo and the room falls silent. We freeze where we are and look at the floor, like individual meatballs in a giant discomfort stew.

It takes me a while to think of a subject to change it to. "Oh, I almost forgot," I say finally, jumping up to retrieve the Xeroxes of my *Jaws* article from under the coffee table. "There's a copy for everyone," I say as I pass them out. "I also made you all a cassette of Cybill's *Vanilla* because keeping it to myself just feels wrong."

Ross takes his copy of the article but doesn't look up. "Check it out, there's my name," he says.

"You put in that I puked," says Lauren.

"I wanted to sort of heighten the drama," I admit. "I can change the names next time if you want."

"No," says everyone but me.

"Puking's nothing compared to the shit I just pulled," says Ross, moving toward the door. "I *wish* I had puked."

By now, Tony has gathered what's left of *Taxi Driver* and stuffed it into a discarded bag from El Pollo Loco.

"We should save those strips," says Marcus. "Mariah Carey might need an outfit for the Soul Train Awards."

"Do you want to take it back to the store, or should we just throw it away?" Tony asks Ross.

"Throw it away," says Ross. "I'm sorry, you guys."

After everyone leaves, Tony and I get into a debate over whether Ross had a Shit Fit, as I maintain, or a Conniption Fit, as Tony maintains. Since there's nothing on TV, we spend the next hour breaking down four different varieties of fits so the next time something like this happens we'll have some guideposts. They are, in ascending order of fury:

1. Tizzy: More an act of clumsiness than an act of anger, the Tizzy Fit involves the thrower fumbling a physical act, getting frustrated with himself, and then losing control

for a spell, resulting in a brief burst of unfocused energy. A Tizzy thrower might call himself a "spaz" or refer to what they just did as "spazzing out." Though tizzies are ultimately harmless, they can be quite entertaining to watch. Witness Beth Howland as Vera accidentally hurling straws about the diner in the opening credits of TV's *Alice*. A classic TV Land Tizzy.

2. Hissy: Unlike a Tizzy, the Hissy Fit is brought on because the thrower believes he or she has been wronged. It has elements of a Tizzy, in that it contains physical movements that the thrower cannot control. However, in the case of the Hissy these movements can often be quite effeminate, which is why a Hissy thrower will never refer to the outburst afterward as a Hissy, though everyone who witnessed it will. Hissy throwers often have an overgrown sense of entitlement. They want what they want when they want it, but they don't like to get their hands dirty. They'd rather just bitch and twitter. A Hissy thrower is unlikely to ask you to step outside to rumble. They will, however, speak to your manager and have you fired. For several examples of classic Hissies, I suggest you rent the Elton John documentary *Tantrums and Tiaras* or get a job as a personal assistant for one of the Velvet Mafia.

3. Conniption: The dictionary defines conniption as "a fit of violent emotion." Indeed. Though there is a good deal of violence in the Conniption Fit, it is by far the most focused and justified of the fits. The Conniption thrower is not unreasonable, he's just had enough and he's not going to take it anymore. He might "blow a gasket" or "rip someone a new one," but he's usually right and in complete control. Angela Bassett setting her cheating husband's car on fire in *Waiting to Exhale* is a conniption, albeit a simmering, tightly wound one.

4. Shit: Look the fuck out. Shit Fit throwers are not just reacting to the perceived injustice of the moment. No, a lifetime of disappointment and rage bubble to surface as well. The Shit Fit thrower is out of control, dangerous, and probably a little bit crazy. Jack Nicholson smashing someone's car with a golf club, and the "no wire hangers" scene in *Mommy Dearest* would fall under the category of Shit Fit.

There is nothing remotely scientific about the above classifications. They just work for us. Feel free to adapt them to meet your own needs. That's half the fun.

•

The next day, Ross calls to apologize for his Shit Fit—he actually used those words, so there, Tony--and report that he's considering dropping *Taxi Driver* from his all-time Top Ten out of sheer embarrassment. I tell him that's not necessary. I still don't ask what number 1 is.

"I just wanted you to like it," Ross says

"I do like it," I say.

"I think that's why I lost my shit," he says.

"Look, I had a meltdown just like that at the DMV this morning," I tell him, though I haven't been to the DMV in years. "The movie's right," I conclude. "There's a little bit of Bickle in all of us."

BEVERLY HILLS CROCK

"They couldn't have come up with three more diverse vaginas if they *tried*," remarks Dr. Beaverman as she, Lauren, and I stand in line to pick up our tickets for *The Vagina Monologues* at the Canon Theater in Beverly Hills. Though countless A-, B-, and C-level actresses have turned up in the show worldwide, I don't think I'd trade the cast we'll be seeing tonight—Katherine "*Soap*" Helmond, Daphne "*Melrose Place*" Zuniga, and Naomi "My album *Babywoman* was very popular in Japan" Campbell—for all the tea in China.

"You know what I want to see?" I say as we take our seats. "Katherine interviewed on *Extra* going, 'Well, I've always wanted to work with Daphne Zuniga and Naomi Campbell, but the right project never came along.'"

"My fantasy is the veteran, Katherine, was reluctant to share the stage with the untrained Naomi," theorizes Lauren, "but then the producers said, 'What if we sweeten the pot a bit with Daphne Zuniga?' and she said, 'Where do I sign?'"

I've brought my lady friends to the theater tonight to celebrate their birthdays. Lauren turned 31 two days ago and Dr. B will be 40-some-odd years old tomorrow, though she's not too keen on reveling in it. In fact, the only reason I know it's her birthday is that a postcard from her dentist reading "Happy Birthday Tooth You" landed in my mailbox instead of hers.

"When I was an undergrad at Berkeley, I started to write something similar to this, but I was too busy chasing after rock stars to get very far," says Dr. Beaverman. "It was like *The Vagina Paragraph*."

"Wait a second," Lauren says. "You were a groupie?"

"Oh, yeah, but I never cared for that term," says Dr. B. "I prefer slut. Someday I'll tell you about what I got up to backstage at Live Aid, but suffice it to say that Huey Lewis is not the happy-go-lucky guy he pretends to be in videos. There's a dark side."

"You and Huey?" I say, pantomiming a dirty act with my fingers.

"No," she says. "But I had a couple of the News, so I was around, you know."

Lauren and I take a moment to consider this latest wrinkle in the tapestry of my neighbor's life. I'm about to ask for more details when the lights dim. I pull my cell phone from my coat pocket and explain to the girls how I promised Marcus I'd call him during the show. "He wants to hear Naomi Campbell say vagina with an R at the end," I whisper, dialing his number. "But he doesn't want to pay for it."

"Oh, he's going to pay for it," maintains Dr. B. "We all are."

Just then, our ladies take the stage, the stage lights come up and the show begins...but there's no Zuniga. What the fuck? Oh, great. Looks like we've got ourselves a no-name understudy who I bet has never even auditioned for an Aaron Spelling show, let alone headlined one.

My disappointment is obliterated, however, when Naomi starts into a Vagina Monologue in which she repeatedly uses the term "coochie-snorcher." Dr. Beaverman looks over to my lap and nods. I press the green send button on my phone, then aim the mouthpiece at Naomi who, I'm happy to report, still has a good five coochie-snorchers left in her. At the end of the monologue, Lauren leans over and says, "I'll be right back," then disappears up the aisle.

We don't see her again until 10 minutes after the show when she emerges from the ladies' room, her brow furrowed in frustration.

"Are you OK?" I ask.

"Now I am," she mutters. "Let's get out of here."

The second we're outside, Lauren rants, "Leave it to me to get my period during *The Vagina Monologues*. And not one of the women who came in during the show had a tampon, though one woman thought they might have some for sale at the souvenir stand."

"I didn't see any," I say. "They just had key rings and T-shirts and bright red coin holders that you squeeze."

"At least you're not pregnant," says Dr. Beaverman. Based on her just-revealed groupie past, I can't help but wonder if "At least you're not pregnant" has been her mantra over the years—a catch-all rationalization good for anything that ails you. Getting audited by the IRS? Having your house burn to the ground? Dentist says they have to come out? Well, at least you're not pregnant.

"I ended up getting something from Naomi's publicist," Lauren continues. "I ought to send him a thank-you note."

"Him?" I ask.

"He was holding Naomi's purse," she explains.

"Marcus is going to love this story," says Dr. Beaverman.

"Oh, my God," I gasp. "I never hung up with him." I pull the phone from my pocket and discover that I've just left Marcus a barely audible, 45-minute message, all about pussy. He'll be thrilled.

"Well, I'm glad someone got to enjoy the show," says Lauren.

•

I don't see the girls again until a week later at our Screening Party for *Pretty Woman,* a film my U.K. editor Matt chose because, with *Erin Brockovich* just out in England,

Miss Julia is hotter than ever. Matt figured a look back at the movie where we first fell in love with her would be in order. And make no mistake, I am in love with her and her inimitable Julia-osity, no matter what transpires in my living room today.

"I wonder if Erin Brockovich saw this when it came out and thought, *I should dress like that whore,*" I say, looking down at the miniskirted, rubber-booted Julia on the video box.

"It could be a whole vicious circle those two have going," says Dr. Beaverman.

Marcus is the last guest to arrive, and when I open the door I can see why. He's gone to the considerable trouble of not only baking a chocolate cake—with white polka dots in honor of Julia's dress in the polo scene—but also tracking down a publicity photo of Daphne Zuniga and taping it over his face with Daphne's cut-out mouth replaced by his own. He steps into the living room and presses play on a mini boom box, then lip-synchs to one of the many Vagina Monologues left on his machine by Daphne's understudy and her cohorts. "I felt bad that Daphne didn't appear and that Lauren missed most of the show," he explains after shutting off the tape. "So I made a copy of my answering machine tape. If you listen closely, you can hear someone pass gas just before the curtain call."

"It was the chair," says Dr. Beaverman.

While I pop the *Pretty Woman* tape into the VCR, Marcus takes his usual position on the floor and says, "I owe my law career to this movie."

"Here we go," says Tony. "Another St. Olaf story."

Because of their long-winded similarity to Betty White's hometown reminiscences on *The Golden Girls,* Tony and I have taken to calling Marcus's recollections of his movie-going history St. Olaf stories.

"I was studying for my Corporations final one afternoon," he begins, "and my friend Janet calls and says, 'We're all going to see *Pretty Woman.* Wanna go?' And I say, 'I'm studying.' She's like, 'Come on, it'll relax you. Plus there's all this law-related stuff in it like corporate raiding and white knights.'"

"There is?" I ask.

"Yes," says Ross. "But no one in the audience cared. People just wanted to see Julia and Richard fall in love."

"*I* cared," insists Marcus. "So anyway, I'm like, 'OK, Janet, you sold me,' and I go to the movie. Next day, 'white knight' is on the final and I ace it."

I try to grab the remote before Marcus can continue, but it's nowhere to be found.

"Fast-forward to the bar exam," Marcus says, diving back in. "The night before the test, you're supposed to do something relaxing, so I see *Pretty Woman* again. Next day, 'corporate raiding' is one of the essay questions. I nail it and pass the bar. All because of *Pretty Woman.*"

After a smattering of applause from the peanut gallery, I finally find the remote—in my hand, of all places—and press play.

"I knew a theater manager in Dallas," says Ross as we zoom through the previews of coming attractions, "and he said there was this one little old lady who saw the Wednesday matinee of *Pretty Woman* every week for a year."

"That's what I've never understood," I say, "why women love this movie so much. I mean, Julia's fabulous, but she's a whore. Ladies, any thoughts?"

"Every time you fuck a guy, you might as well be a whore," says Lauren flatly. "So this is like our ultimate movie. And Julia gets to shop." Lauren takes a breath and then dives into her own *Pretty Woman* memory. "The first time I saw this movie, I was with my brother who lived in the Bronx. We came out of the theater behind these two Italian chicks with big hair, Guidettes, my brother called them. Then, as they were crossing the street to get into their white Camaro, one of them stopped dead in her tracks and said to the other, 'Oh my God, that movie was my life.' And I thought to myself, *No, it wasn't.*"

"The original script was much darker," Ross informs us. "It ended with Richard's character saying, 'I'm not in love with you. You're a hooker!' and then hitting her and dumping her back in the gutter. And then she drags herself up to her apartment only to discover that her roommate has overdosed. Then Garry Marshall was brought in to lighten it up."

"Garry's the king of we-need-a-joke-here," says Tony, who has held my hand through such past Marshall yuckfests as *Exit to Eden* and *The Other Sister.* "You could say to him, 'But Garry, it's the rape of the crippled child's mother?' and he'd be like, '*What if before the guy rapes her he says, "Pull my finger?" How'd that test?*'"

My roommate's straight-outta-Brooklyn deez-dem-doze Garry Marshall impression is so spot-on that I decide to ask my editor if it can have its own font, a nice Fairfield italic perhaps.

"The original script was much darker. It ended with Richard's character saying, 'I'm not in love with you. You're a hooker!' and then hitting her and dumping her back in the gutter." —Ross

The movie begins with a hoity-toity Hollywood party, at which a magician does sleight-of-hand tricks with gold coins. "This is supposed to symbolize that Richard is a whore for money," explains Dr. Beaverman as we're introduced to Gere's superslick corporate raider, Edward Lewis. "He's a whore for business with no feeling, whereas Julia's a sticky, gooey, all-feeling person who happens to be a whore. She's got the heart of gold. He's got the heart of the gold standard."

Fed up with the stuffy bash, Richard borrows a Porsche Lotus from his skeevy lawyer, Jason Alexander, and speeds down the hill. Before long, he finds himself lost in Divine Brown territory so he pulls over to ask the nearest hooker, who happens to be Julia Roberts, dolled up in a blond pageboy wig and sailor's cap, how to get to Beverly Hills.

"She looks like the Captain and Tennille rolled into one unfortunate person," says Lauren.

"What every john wants," says Tony, "a theme skank."

"Men don't ask women for directions," says Dr. Beaverman. "That's one of our first indications that this is a fantasy."

"And I'm sorry," says Ross, "but there are no whores on Hollywood Boulevard who look like Julia Roberts."

"Sure there are," argues Tony. "But they're men."

Julia hops in Richard's borrowed car and tells him that her name is Vivian. "From the French root *viver,* meaning 'to live,'" notes Dr. Beaverman. "So she's lively. She's got life in her, whereas he's dead Edward, as dead inside as..." Dr. Beaverman struggles to complete her comparison.

"Marie Osmond?" offers Tony.

"Thank you," says Dr. B. "Yes, that's it."

The deep-pocketed Gere gives Julia 20 bucks to get him where he's going. Julia must figure he wants a little entertainment with his directions, because once she's in the car, she jabbers nonstop about her hourly rate, the size of her feet, and the boys back home in Georgia that she grew up with.

"She's the only hooker in history who seems to have had an OK home life," observes Lauren. "No major abuse or dysfunction going on. It's like she just moved to L.A. and had a really bad month."

"It seems like I saw an interview with Garry Marshall somewhere," recalls Ross, "where he said Vivian had only been hooking for a couple of weeks, so it's still fun for her."

"She's so new," says Tony as Garry, *"no one's even come on her back yet."*

"That, my friends, is why men like this movie," says Dr. Beaverman. "Because they all want a whore, but they want her the first day on the job."

As Julia and Richard roll through Tinseltown, Julia expresses her admiration for the borrowed Lotus, cooing, "This baby must corner like it's on rails."

"She sounds as convincing talking about cars as I would," says Tony, before pausing the movie and regaling us with a story he swears is related, about the time he was playing Danny Zuko in a cruise ship version of *Grease.* "One night, the guy who played Kenickie was sick so I had to cover the song 'Greased Lightning,'" he explains. "Well, you know I don't know shit about car parts, so all I did was sing gibberish and say 'palomino dashboard' about 10 times. The audience thought I was having some kind of fit."

"Most probably a Tizzy," I add.

We restart the movie in time to see Dick and Julia swap places so she can take the wheel. "It's *Driving Miss Daisy Chain,*" I remark.

Soon, our toothy twosome arrives at the swanky Regent Beverly Wilshire Hotel in Beverly Hills. According to Ross, it's the only first-rate hotel in the zip code that would allow the filmmakers to shoot there. "The rest claimed that no one ever brought hookers to their hotels," says Ross. "Then the movie turned out to be a huge hit, and the Regent Beverly Wilshire got all kinds of business from it. I think there's even a *Pretty Woman* package you can get with strawberries and cream and the whole bit."

"Does it come with a body double for all the stuff you don't want to do?" wonders Lauren.

While Julia waits on the curb to catch a cab back to Hookerville, Richard approaches and says, "If you don't have any prior engagements, I would be very pleased if you would accompany me into the hotel."

"Well, I'm going to miss the free needle exchange, but what the hell," I say, speaking for Julia.

Richard tries to make her look less like a hooker by draping his trench coat over her. Now she looks like a hooker with a trench coat draped over her.

"In addition to the sexual perversion level that this movie can be read on, there's also a good deal of class warfare at work," says Dr. Beaverman. "Here's where we get our first glimpse of the uptight, repressed, conventional class of society who stare down their noses at our spunky American heroine, Vivian. But Vivian will fight against them and we'll eat it up, because Americans like scrappy little fighters that stick their noses up at the elite, horsey set. She might be a whore, but she's still an American. And that should be pronounced Ameri-*can* because she is, at heart, a good ol' capitalist. She's Norma Rae in a G-string, basically."

"So, take away the thigh-high rubber boots and it's actually *The Beverly Hillbillies*?" I suggest.

"Exactly," replies Dr. Beaverman. "*The Beverly Whorebillies,* you could call it. This movie is Frank Capra on Hollywood Boulevard, as populist as *Mr. Smith Goes to Washington*. When it comes to class warfare, Americans will always side with the lowest rung, even when it's a skanky whore. In fantasy, anyway. Real life is another matter."

Whore in tow, Gere approaches the front desk and says, "Can you send up some champagne and strawberries?"

"And some extra-strength disinfectant and a two-pack of Brillo pads," adds Ross, "because someone is getting a *Silkwood* shower."

Richard and Julia arrive at his suite, and we're treated the first penetration shot of the evening when Richard inserts his key card into the designated slot.

"*Richard, can you jack the card in the lock?*" says Tony as Garry. "*Yeah! Fuck her with the key in the lock. Make that light just light right up. Ha ha ha ha ha ha.*"

Once inside, Julia proceeds to make playful small talk with Richard, though if I were her, I'd be casing the joint for valuables and fretting about which ones this john's going to want to stick in me. When Richard asks if she's known many lawyers, Julia replies, "I've known a lot of everybody."

"Even though I've only been doing this for a week," says Lauren.

"I want her to whip out a price list she's had laminated at Kinko's," I say.

Instead, Julia whips out an assortment of multi-colored condoms. Then, within minutes of announcing, "I'm a safety gal," she proceeds to floss her teeth, something any whore or circuit boy worth his or her salt would know is an unwise thing to do before blowing a stranger.

Then, before servicing Richard, Julia once again demonstrates her carefree, goofy side by plopping down on the floor and guffawing through an episode of *I Love Lucy*. "She's probably wondering why a swanky hotel like this doesn't have color TV," figures Ross.

Then she blows him.

The next morning, over breakfast, our lady of the evening peppers Richard with questions about his work life and says insightful things like, "You must be really smart, huh?"

"I want him to be like, 'How 'bout if you just fuck me and I give you money and you don't give me career advice?'" says Tony indignantly. "'How 'bout that?'"

"Blooper alert!" says Marcus. "Watch her hand, you guys. Julia's going to miraculously switch from a croissant to a pancake."

Lo and behold, she does. Then comes the famous sequence in the bathtub where Julia belts her carefree heart out while listening to Prince's "Kiss" on her Walkman. Though many Juliaphiles cite this as the moment she captured their hearts, I feel like she could have brought the goofiness down a notch or 10 and still been in a Garry Marshall film.

"Notice this whore's entrepreneurial spirit. Like Rockefeller and Carnegie, she cuts her own deals. She's a self-contained muff mogul and she doesn't deal with a middleman. Unless she's making a john sandwich with Laura San Giacomo."

—Dr. Beaverman

"Notice she's singing, 'All I want is your extra time and your kiss,'" Dr. Beaverman points out. "Yet both of those things are no-no's in her profession. She never kisses on the mouth, and, let's face it, extra time is not in your vocabulary if you're a whore. Time and a half, maybe."

After a little haggling, Richard convinces Julia to be his companion for the week for the tidy sum of $3,000. "The film's original title was *3,000,*" says Ross, "but they thought it sounded too sci-fi."

"Notice this whore's entrepreneurial spirit," says Dr. Beaverman. "Like Rockefeller and Carnegie, she cuts her own deals. She's a self-contained muff mogul and she doesn't deal with a middleman. Unless she's making a john sandwich with Laura San Giacomo."

"Which is 10 bucks extra," figures Tony. "It's like supersizing it."

They seal the deal, and as soon as Richard leaves, Julia lets out a girlish scream, runs into the bedroom, and flops onto the bed. "I think the idea of lounging around all day is just as alluring as shopping and having sex with Richard Gere," I remark. "I think people see Julia hanging out in that hotel robe and think, 'Yes, that!'"

In his absence, Richard has instructed Julia to buy a cocktail dress for a business dinner he plans to take her to later that night. So Julia heads to a Rodeo Drive boutique staffed by a gaggle of women who haven't had an orgasm since the first moon landing. "You're obviously in the wrong place," drones one of the women, whose CAA agent husband probably left her for a bim just like Julia. "Please leave."

"I've never bought the way the movie acts as though you'd never see anyone who dresses like a whore in Beverly Hills," says Ross.

"I've seen oil princesses on Rodeo Drive who make Julia seem positively demure," agrees Lauren.

"And doesn't Goldie Hawn hang out there?" I ask.

A demoralized Julia heads back to the hotel, where she gets interrogated by the hotel's manager, played by Garry Marshall's MVP, Hector Elizondo, who, coincidentally, questioned Richard Gere in his breakout turn as a sex worker in *American Gigolo.* "Hector should have a musical number," I say before bursting into the *Dr. Dolittle* theme. "If I could talk to the prostitutes...talk to the prostitutes..."

Hector takes Julia into his office, where she bitches to him about her shopping misadventure while fumbling with a big wad of cash.

"She's like, 'I'm such a whore that I don't know from ones, fives, and tens,'" says Tony. " 'I've just got a big ball of green. I don't even own a purse or a fanny pack!' "

" 'Though my fanny has been packed' ," I say. " 'Earlier today, in fact.' "

" 'As a matter of fact, that's where I keep this giant wad of cash!' " says Tony.

"There's some very obvious Freudian symbolism at work here," says Dr. Beaverman as Hector pours water onto a plant that is clearly not long for this earth. "Nothing grows in that stifling atmosphere of status and money. There's no life there. It's all desiccated and dried-up, whereas Vivian the whore, with that hair sprouting all over, is nothing but life and passion and orgasms waiting to happen."

With Hector's help, Julia solves her cocktail dress dilemma, settling on a black number with western fringe that looks like something out of Disneyland's Diamond Whoreshoe Revue. "That's a cocktail dress only in the sense that it's what Miss Kitty would serve them in," says Lauren.

"What you can't see is that she actually has on spurs," adds Tony. "That jingle jangle jingle."

"Another 10 bucks extra," says Ross.

Richard returns from work and walks in that supersexy way that only Richard can through the lobby. "I want him to be like, 'I'm looking for my whore,'" says Ross. "'Has anybody seen my whore?'"

Richard spots Julia, looking resplendent at the bar, then escorts her to the hotel restaurant where they dine with Ralph Bellamy, whose company Richard plans to steal.

"I had my first snails recently," announces Lauren as Julia tries to figure out how to use the escargot fork. "Delicious."

"Anything soaked in garlic butter is awesome," agrees Tony. "You could take a cat turd and soak it in garlic butter and I'd probably eat it."

"I'll remember that for next time," says Marcus.

"Here's a whore who can untangle any kind of sex toy ever invented," says Dr. Beaverman, "but she can't at least mimic Ralph Bellamy as he's negotiating with the little snail tool. Not likely."

After Bellamy leaves in a huff, Julia tells Richard she thought the old man was nice. Not that Richard asked.

"I want her to be like, 'That geezer seems like he'd come quick,'" says Tony. "Just rating everyone based on what kind of john they'd be. 'And that bellhop? I bet he precomes like nobody's business.'"

Back in their suite, Julia and Richard's relationship continues to deepen when Richard opens up about his fear of heights and hints that he may have a few issues with his father.

"Do you want to talk about it?" Julia asks.

"No," says Richard.

"Do you want to fuck my tits, then?" says Tony.

"As this scene shows, their edges are softening," says Dr. Beaverman. "Which means she's no longer going to sit on his important faxes without wearing a panty liner and he's no longer going to ask her to jam a ferret up his back door. They're moving toward the center."

Later that night, Julia wakes up to find Richard missing in action, so she grabs the phone and calls the front desk.

"Do you have Prince Albert in a can?" says Marcus.

"Is your elevator running?" wonders Lauren.

Wearing just a robe, Julia ventures downstairs to find Richard tickling the ivories in the hotel's deserted banquet room. Before you can say, "Play that funky music, white boy," he's hoisting her onto the keyboard and slipping her the metronome.

"FYI, her ass has perfect pitch," says Tony, who's done enough musicals to know.

"I do think this is a sexy scene," I admit. "I bet Garry Marshall was losing his mind when he shot it."

"He's like, *'Hey Richard, once you're inside her, can you play 'Chopsticks' with your balls*!'" says Tony. *"Ha ha ha ha ha ha."*

The next morning, Richard takes some time off to do a little shopping with his whore. While they stride down Rodeo, Julia spits out her gum and Richard says, "I can't believe you did that."

"Excuse me?" says Tony incredulously. "I mean, she swallows strangers' come for money and he's shocked she's a litterbug?"

They arrive at a swanky boutique where Richard is greeted by Larry Miller, the veteran character actor and comedian who was anally penetrated by a giant gerbil in *Nutty Professor II*. Coincidence? You decide. Then, while Roy Orbison's title song plays in the background, we experience what I consider to be the cinematic equivalent of a sugar rush. Yes, folks, it's time for the "Julia tries on clothes" montage.

"I think for certain women, this sequence is like mainlining," says Ross.

"If *Mary Reilly* had had a 'Julia tries on clothes' montage, it would have been a hit," figures Lauren. "Of course, she would have tried on 20 of the same frumpy black frock."

"But this scene also appeals to men," adds Dr. Beaverman, gesturing to Marcus, who is literally clapping like a seal. "And not just gay men prepping for the bar exam. Straight men like it because *he* is controlling the purchasing. And notice there are a lot of shots of Julia from just the neck to the pelvic bone, a disembodied object. Pretty woman, walkin' down the street..." Dr. B. recites. "Pretty woman...just a piece of meat..."

"I want her to get in the mirror and pantomime sex acts as she shops," says Tony, "like getting down on all fours. She's like, 'These pants really give at the knee. I'll take 'em.' "

Then, in a moment that was cheered in theaters, Julia stops back by the Bitch Boutique to get her revenge on the hags who wouldn't serve her the previous day. "You work on commission, right?" she taunts, her arms full of bags from other stores. "Big mistake. Huge."

"People went crazy for this moment, but I think the revenge is kind of weak," I say.

"The real revenge would have been to try on a bunch of outfits and then go, 'I don't want any of that. Bye,' " says Lauren.

"And leave skid marks in the clothes," says Tony.

After a romantic bathtub scene, which I spend the entirety of fixated on Richard Gere's amazing Buddhist nipples, we're off to the polo match, where Julia wears the brown polka-dot outfit that, according to Lauren, looks good on no one on the planet but Julia Roberts.

"If *Mary Reilly* had had a 'Julia tries on clothes' montage, it would have been a hit. Of course, she would have tried on 20 of the same frumpy black frock." —Lauren

After the match proper, our lovers take part in the traditional stomping-of-the-divots ritual. "One word of advice," bellows the polo announcer, "avoid the steaming divot!"

"Garry Marshall," Ross and I say in unison.

"*Can you say something about divots with corn in them?*" says Tony as Garry.

Then Jason Alexander, a.k.a. Señor Smarm, starts grilling Richard about the mystery babe in the polka dots, suggesting that Julia might be a corporate spy. "She's not a spy," Richard shoots back. "She's a hooker."

"She's a hooker, standing in front of a boy, leaning against a horse, asking him to love her," I clarify.

Armed with this new bit of information, Jason crosses the field to Julia and says, "Quite a nice change from Hollywood Boulevard. Maybe you and I could get together?"

This pisses Julia off to no end, though none of us can figure out why. "All of a sudden she's sensitive about her hookerness?" says Ross.

"She should be giving out business cards," says Lauren. "This crowd is the networking opportunity of a lifetime."

Later, back at the Reg Bev Wil, Julia rips into Richard for telling Jason she's a hooker. "I hate to point out the obvious," Richard spits back, "but you are, in fact, a hooker."

My living room, save Marcus who's cutting the cake, erupts in applause. "I'm so glad that he calls her on her shit here," I say.

"Totally," says Tony. "I'd be like, 'Did my check bounce, Vivian? OK then, shut the fuck up.'"

"I've never had anyone make me feel as cheap as you did today," Julia whines.

"Except for the guy that peed on me, but that was by accident," says Ross.

"Ten bucks extra," says half the room.

In spite of their spat, Richard soon admits that he's starting to have feelings for Julia and that seeing her talk to another man at the polo match made him jealous.

"You're *more* than a whore," says Marcus. "You're *my* whore."

Somehow the two of them make up. I'm not really sure how because Tony and I are too busy fantasizing about what Julia's conferences with her high school guidance counselor must have been like.

"Your aptitude test shows that you'd be good at rimming," says Tony, taking on the tone of my fourth-grade teacher, Mrs. Grandstaff.

"But stay away from triple penetrations because you scored low on multitasking," I add.

Before long the couple ends up back in the sack, which I have no problem with because I find Gere's bedroom body language a total turn-on. There's something supple and almost feminine about it that makes me long to be in Julia's shoes. I can't imagine some macho action star like Kevin Costner or Bruce Willis being one-tenth as cuddly.

All of which brings us, happily, to Julia's Opera Dream Date. The evening begins with the untamed redhead sauntering out of the hotel room in a red velvet dress looking super gorgeous but also a tad like Barbara Mandrell at the Country Music Association Awards in 1983 with white gloves that don't match her dress.

Our mega-dapper Richard presents Julia with a $250,000 necklace he borrowed for the night. Then, just as she reaches to take it, he snaps the red velvet box lid down on her fingers. "Tell me that doesn't signify a vagina with teeth," says Dr. Beaverman as Julia laughs with abandon. "Which is exactly what he fears so very much."

"That box trick was actually an ad-lib on Gere's part," says Marcus. "Julia was sleepy and he did it to keep her awake."

"Couldn't she just do crystal like everyone else in Hollywood?" I ask.

Then it's off to San Francisco on a private jet for a performance of *La Traviata.* Julia appears to be riveted to the onstage goings-on, but I don't buy it. I can't help but think she wishes she'd thought to bring the Jumble from that day's paper or a piece of string so she could regale her fellow box-sitters with her renditions of "Jacob's Ladder" and "Grandma's Bra."

"Why is crying at the opera always a sign that someone has crossed the line and is now sophisticated?" wonders Lauren as Julia dabs at her eyes.

"As a season ticket holder to the L.A. Opera," says Ross, "I can tell you that people actually cry."

"You like opera?" says Tony.

"What do you think," says Ross, "that I leave here and go to Hooters before returning to my cave?"

"I'm just surprised, that's all," says Tony.

So am I, frankly, but I'm glad I wasn't the one to say it out loud.

"Let me remind you of the famous quote, 'Sex is the poor man's opera,'" says Dr. Beaverman. "But Vivian doesn't have to revert to sex anymore. She's not a poor man anymore. She's a lady. She's a bleedin' loverly lady."

The lovers continue their Dream Date back in Los Angeles by playing chess.

"I want her to grab the king and the queen and go, 'Look, they're sixty-nining,'" I say.

"Or get him to look away and then pull a bishop out of her snatch," says Tony.

The next day, Julia talks Richard into blowing off work so they can take part in a woo-pitching montage replete with horseback riding, adoring glances, and barefoot picnics in the park.

"This sequence is troubling," says Dr. Beaverman. "And not just because Julia uses the expression, 'Cop a squat.' It was the belief of Dr. Freud that women, like children, drain men's energy and impede their progress in the world. Which is exactly what Julia's doing to Richard by encouraging him to play hooky."

Dr. Beaverman's point is borne out in the next scene, which finds Richard passed out cold, worn out from all the canoodling. Julia looks at him lovingly while he sleeps. "It would be so funny if she put his hand in a bucket of warm water," says Marcus.

"And then let him pee on her," adds Tony.

"Ten bucks extra," we all say.

"She's been nickel-and-diming him all week anyway," says Lauren. "You know she's emptying the minibar every day, sending Toblerones to Laura San Giacomo."

When Richard wakes, they kiss on the lips for the first time and then get it on again. This time, it's so mind-blowing that the next morning Richard tells Julia he wants to get her off the street. He's basically offering to make her the Fresh Princess of Bel Air, but Julia gets all uppity and stomps out onto the fake balcony. It's here that she lets fly with the fantasy she had as a young girl where a white knight would come and rescue her from a tower.

"What do you want?" Richard finally asks her.

"I want the fairy tale," says Julia.

"The very words that men hate to hear," says Dr. Beaverman with a sigh. "Men don't want Rapunzel. They want a whore, and here she is turning out to be just like every other damn woman he's ever met."

"Does anyone else think she's not holding up her end of the fairy tale by being a whore?" I ask.

"Precisely, Dennis," says Dr. Beaverman. "Julia has no initiative. She doesn't want to go to school or open her own Color Me Mine franchise or become a businessperson. She just wants to be rescued."

Unable to strike a deal, Richard, whose business attire has been getting lighter the more love-struck he becomes, tries to get some work done but ends up walking barefoot in the park instead. It's a wonder Garry Marshall didn't have him literally stop and smell the roses. Meanwhile, Julia, dressed in a Fergie-style jacket and shorts set from Talbot's, lunches with Laura San Giacomo, who calls her on her fairy tale delusions, saying the only person it's ever worked out for is "Cindefuckingrella."

"I heard that reference was a huge deal with Disney," says Tony. "They were like, 'You will *not* put a dirty word in the middle of Cinderella.' "

"How 'bout Pocafuckinghontas then?" poses Marcus.

We spend the next few minutes inserting the word "fucking" into the names of well-loved Disney characters. Our top laugh-getters: Tinkerfuckingbell, Cruella DeFuckingVille. Mufuckinglan, and my personal favorite, Annette Funifuckingcello.

Back on the screen, Julia returns to her suite just in time to receive a surprise smarm delivery from Jason Alexander. "What is she working on?" asks Lauren, in reference to the notebook Julia's scribbling in.

"Garry Marshall asked her to write down any place in the script where she thought she could put in a fart joke," figures Tony.

"It's actually her gratitude journal," I say. "She's been reading *Chicken Soup for the Hooker's Soul.*"

When Richard returns, he has to literally throw Jason off of Julia.

"Get your own whore!" shouts Ross.

"If they do end up getting married, can you imagine her at the PTA meetings?" I say. "She'd be like, 'Bake sales can be fun, kids, but if you really want those new band uniforms, I suggest you start thinking outside the box.' "

"Better yet, 'Think inside the box,' " adds Tony. " 'Start thinking *with* your box,' that's what I say."

Julia and Richard rid themselves of Jason but still, sadly, decide to go their separate ways. Julia heads downstairs to say goodbye to Hector the Fairy Godfather. Then, later, Richard pops by Hector's desk to return the $250,000 necklace.

"I heard that one of the reasons Garry Marshall uses Hector Elizondo in all of his movies is that he's not a pain in the ass," says Marcus. "Like he's on time and knows his lines and Garry hopes everyone else will try to emulate him."

"That explains why I've never worked for the same employer more than once," admits Tony.

"Well, Hector's subtexting me to death in this scene," I say, as the well-heeled actor tells Richard re: the necklace, "It must be hard to let go of something so beautiful."

"You're right, Dennis," agrees Ross. "His inner monologue is deafening."

"He's got a secret that he's not telling the audience," says Lauren, who's no stranger to such acting class tricks. "Like maybe he's wearing panties under his suit."

Having passed on her chance for a life of luxury, Julia rides back to Hookerland in a white limo while the Roxette song "It Must Have Been Love" plays in the background.

"That limo was actually auctioned off for charity," Marcus informs us. "A plastic surgeon bought it, and now it's the limo that picks you up if you're going to have work done."

"Like I needed more incentive," says Dr. Beaverman.

"And Roxette actually sings that song to you live," says Ross. "They keep them in the trunk."

"I was wondering what happened to them," says Lauren.

Returning to her dumpy apartment, Julia tells Laura San Giacomo that she's throwing in the G-string and giving up hooking. She's not terribly specific about what she'll do instead, but then she doesn't have to be because Richard, who's now a changed man, is going to come and rescue her. First, though, he saves Ralph Bellamy's company instead of destroying it. Then he hops into his own limo—which Marcus has no idea what happened to—and sets off to Hollywood Boulevard. As opera music blares from the sunroof, he shimmies up Julia's fire escape, conquering his fear of heights, and rescues her.

"So what happened after he climbed up the tower and rescued her?" Richard asks Julia as they embrace.

"She gave him a disease," says Tony.

"She rescues him right back," coos Julia.

"This is the epitome of a '90s dysfunctional relationship," says Dr. Beaverman. "They fit together because they're both dysfunctional. Their dysfunctions match, even if the pancake shots don't."

As the credits roll, I have to admit that I still don't get why chicks love this movie so much.

"It's because we all want to be rescued," says Lauren matter-of-factly. "And the fact that it's Richard Gere helps, because most of us think we can get rich or sexy but that we can't land both in one package."

"I think the movie inspires people," adds Marcus, "because it says no matter how bad my current circumstances are and no matter what bad Toni Tennille wig I'm wearing, someone will see past all that and take me away to a life of luxury."

"And defend us against their jerk friends like Jason Alexander when they hit on us," adds Lauren while stuffing the *Vagina* tape and Daphne mask into her bag, "instead of telling us it's *our* fault that Jason's hands are on our ass because Jason would never do a thing *to them*."

•

The next night, I go see *La Traviata* with Ross at the Dorothy Chandler Pavilion. His normal opera date, Perry from Video Master, is sick, so Ross offered me the ticket. I cried like a baby clear through it, and now I'm better than you because of it. Next week: chess.

When I get home, there's an E-mail from Dr. Beaverman.

Dennis,

Thank you again for the *Vagina* outing. I had a lovely time in spite of the Daphne Zuniga no-show and the rest of it.

Couldn't sleep last night so I expanded on my *Beverly Whorebillies* parallel and wrote a new *Pretty Woman* theme song which is actually twice as long as "The Vagina Paragraph." It's meant to be sung to the tune of *The Beverly Hillbillies,* but I'm not going to sing it. Dr. Beaverman does not sing.

Come and listen to a story about a whore named Viv,
a poor streetwalker who had to screw to live.
Then one day she was scoutin' for a trick,
and up to the curb pulls a Lotus and a dick.
Richard, that is, Dick Gere, cash cow.

Well, the first thing you know old Viv's a millionaire,
street folk said, "Viv, move away from here."
Said the Regent Wilshire is the place you oughta be,
so she loaded up her lube and moved to Beverly.
Hills, that is, twisted men, movie stars.

(INSTRUMENTAL BREAK)

Well, now it's time to press rewind and say so long to Viv,
and don't forget this fairy tale is leaky as a sieve.
You know in truth poor Viv is in her old locality,
still sellin' heapin' helpins of her hospitality.
Sex, that is, what the hell, take your pants off,
y'all come now,
ya hear.

SEX AND THE SHITTY

"This is the first movie I ever reviewed in my college paper," recalls Ross while removing today's movie from its Video Master bag and standing it upright atop my entertainment center. "I couldn't say enough bad things about it."

"Well, now you can," I say.

So begins our Screening Party honoring that 1985 classic of bondage and back-lighting, director Adrian Lyne's *9½ Weeks*. Matt in London is putting together the magazine's annual "More Sex Than You Can Shake a Stick At" issue and figured that a look back at the days when Mickey Rourke could get Kim Basinger to return his calls, not to mention crawl across the floor and beg to be spanked, would be in order.

"Are any of us even getting laid?" ponders Marcus as he gathers the ingredients for Jell-O à la Basinger on the kitchen counter. "Maybe the article can end with all of us sticking our head in the oven."

"The oven's broken," says Tony, dragging in from a long morning of trying to convince shoppers at the Third Street Promenade to sign up for the AIDS Walk. Last week he landed a temporary position as an assistant to the organization's volunteer coordinator, and so far, knock Elijah Wood, it's going well.

"The oven's fixed," Marcus says. "I fixed it back at *Taxi Driver.*"

"Let's not do that thing where we talk about how long it's been since we've had sex," I beg. Not that I don't know: six months and change, Stephen Pool, his place, not bad considering I ultimately wasn't into him.

"I thought you gay guys where supposed to get it all the time," says Ross.

"I'm afraid we're not very representative," I say. "Most gays are sluttier than we are."

"I *can* be slutty," Marcus reminds us. "I have slutty phases. Right now I'm holding out for a hero. But I feel a slutty phase coming on." Marcus dumps the Jell-O powder into a mixing bowl, then says to no one in particular, "We should do *Footloose*."

"Are *you* getting laid?" Tony asks Ross.

"Define getting laid," says Ross. "'Cause I got plenty during the summer."

"OK, here's the criteria," I say. "Could you pick up the phone right now and call someone and arrange a booty call without drastically lowering your standards or having to write a check?"

"I could," chirps Marcus. "Oh, wait, I accidentally washed the guy's number. Never mind."

"Ross?" asks Tony.

Ross ponders the question for a moment, then scoffs, "Would I be sitting here if I could do that?"

"I suspect yes," says Tony, patting him on the shoulder. "I think you secretly love hanging out with us."

"Something's wrong with the color of this Jell-O," frets Marcus. "It's supposed to be fire-engine red, but this looks more like Cher's hair from the cover of the *Heart of Stone* CD."

"For moments just like that," Tony says to Ross.

Just then, Dr. Beaverman makes her first-ever entrance without knocking.

Tony and I have been in the market for a Kramer for years. At last we have one.

"I'm bringing in the heavy artillery today, boys," she says, indicating the stack of self-help books under her arm. "I can't handle this shitheap without some serious backup."

"Dennis wants to know if you're getting laid," Ross says to Dr. Beaverman.

"No, he doesn't," I say.

"Something's wrong with the color of this Jell-O. It's supposed to be fire-engine red, but this looks more like Cher's hair from the cover of the *Heart of Stone* CD." —Marcus

"*No habla español,*" replies Dr. Beaverman.

"That makes none of us," says Tony, who recently pulled the plug on a long-distance thing he had going with a Welsh dancer he worked with on his last cruise ship.

"Oh, wait, Lauren's getting laid," remembers Marcus. "She's in a relationship."

Dr. Beaverman shoots him a withering look.

"That just slipped out," says Marcus. "Of course I know it's possible to be in a relationship and not have sex. If my parents taught me anything..."

"But Lauren could pick up the phone and call what's-his-face, right?" says Ross. "If that's the criteria."

"Barry," says Marcus.

I shake my head from side to side spastically, then signal for everyone to come in for a huddle. "They had a big fight last night," I whisper, spitting out the information as quickly as possible, "so she's staying here. That's her in the shower. So to answer your question, even if she could call him, I don't think she wants to."

"Call who?"

We turn around to discover Lauren standing in the doorway in Tony's robe. "I told them why you were staying here," I say. "I hope that's OK."

"Fine," Lauren says, taking her usual seat on the couch. "And *I* left *him,* by the way, so you don't need to tiptoe around me." Then she turns to Dr. Beaverman and says, "Can I get your opinion about something?"

Dr. Beaverman nods, and I immediately suspect it will be a good 30 minutes before we even put Mickey and Kim in the VCR and at least an hour before he starts inserting things into her.

Lauren combs through her wet hair and recounts the fight that sent her packing. It all started, she insists, because of a Gap billboard. "You know that giant ad they have on Sunset that's, like, the whole side of a building?" Lauren asks. "Well, you can see it from our bedroom, and it is my belief, doctor, that the image on that billboard consciously or unconsciously informs the way Barry relates to me."

"I need examples," says Dr. Beaverman, while scribbling notes on the back of our *TV Guide* from three weeks ago.

"OK," says Lauren. "If it's some scruffy actor guy up there, like Giovanni Ribisi, he can't get enough of me."

"Vince Vaughn?" I suggest. "Heath Ledger?"

"Oh, my God," gushes Lauren. "The Heath Ledger month was heaven. When the hot actor guys are up, Barry's attentive and affectionate and he wants to talk about the future. He's the perfect boyfriend."

"But when Julia Stiles goes up..." suggests Tony.

"He won't even touch you," guesses Marcus.

"No," counters Ross. "He screws you silly."

"He screws me silly and *then* he won't touch me," says Lauren, touching her nose affirmatively as if she's playing Charades. "Outside of the bedroom, cold and aloof and doesn't want to talk about anything, let alone getting married. It's like he's thinking, *Why should I settle for Lauren when the whores from* American Pie *with their ribbed tanks and fake boobs are still on the market?*"

"Isn't Breckin Meyer up there now?" I ask. "He seems harmless enough."

"They took him down Wednesday," says Lauren. "And now it's Joan Allen, who you would think would work in my favor, but she looks, like, 20 in this picture in her cute little low-waisted khakis. I mean, *I'd* fuck her."

"What did Barry say when you confronted him?" asks Dr. Beaverman.

"He said he thought I was crazy," says Lauren. "But I could see in his eyes that I wasn't totally off-base. He claimed that the reason he seemed distracted was he was just preoccupied with trying to get his business off the ground."

Barry is a studio musician, a keyboard player more specifically, who recently put together a six-piece combo in the hopes of cashing in on the convention–private party market.

"He assured me he wasn't going anywhere," Lauren says, "and I said, 'Prove it, then. Marry me.'"

"What did he say to that?" asks Dr. Beaverman.

"He said he wasn't ready," replies Lauren. "He's been saying that for two years."

"Why do you want him to marry you so badly?" asks Dr. Beaverman.

"Because I love him," says Lauren.

"Why else?" says Dr. Beaverman.

"I don't know," says Lauren, an edge of defensiveness creeping into her voice. "Anyway, this isn't about me," she says. "It's about him."

"See, I think that's where you're wrong," says Dr. Beaverman. With that, she tosses the *TV Guide* back onto the coffee table, as if to say, "This session's over; see you next week." Lauren sits silently for a moment while Dr. B. stifles a yawn. "I also think if we don't start the movie soon, I'll be in a coma by week 3."

In one fluid movement, Ross sticks the tape in the VCR, grabs the remote, and presses play. "I worked at the campus cinema when I was at SMU," he says, zooming through the previews and warnings. "And whenever we would screen this, the theater would be packed. College kids are horny, as it turns out."

"I always expect to see Dustin Hoffman as *Tootsie* pop up in scenes like this," I say as we get our first gander at Kim Basinger, playing a sexually repressed art dealer named Elizabeth, striding down a bustling Manhattan street.

"Dustin Hoffman could teach her a thing or two about makeup," asserts Tony. "Who makes her eyeliner, Sharpie?"

"I forgot that Kim was ever this winsome," I remark. "She's got ingenue written all over her."

"Of course, it's spelled wrong," says Lauren. "I'm going to be cranky today, you guys," she warns. "I can already feel it coming on."

Tony is clearly thrilled by this news.

An atmospheric shot of a flopping fish appears on the screen and Dr. Beaverman is off: "Our own flopping fish is, of course, Kim Basinger," she says, "who is ready to start loosening up those repressed genes of hers."

Kim disappears into a Korean deli with her frizzy-haired roommate, Molly, who tells the counter person to give her "half a dozen of those little birds, please."

"And a small Georgia town for me," adds Dr. Beaverman, speaking for Kim.

Later, in a dinner party scene, we're treated to the only party trick in the film that doesn't require lube: bit player Christine Baranski balancing a spoon on the end of her schnoz.

"I'm so impressed that she can do that," I say.

"Of course she can do that," spits Tony. "That's the craziest rhinoplasty in Hollywood. You could store a service for eight on that nose."

The next scene takes us back to the busy street, where a reggae band plays while Kim peruses the offerings of various vendors. She's particularly charmed by a wooden chicken knickknack that emits small brown eggs from its behind. "Not the last poo to be taken on screen today," predicts Tony.

Kim falls in love with a colorful, fruit-patterned scarf but decides not to buy it when the seller tells her the price: $300. The next time she sees it, a few minutes later, it's being presented to her by Mickey Rourke, the man who will later plumb her most private of areas with enough food to stock a Sizzler.

"It's for you," says Mickey, who plays a mysterious businessman named John.

"To cover up those roots with," says Lauren.

"Mickey Rourke is hot!" I blurt.

"There was a moment when he looked good," confirms Ross, "and it was during this movie. I saw him the other day at the grocery store and he looked like Rue McClanahan on a bender."

Mickey's charm assault on Kim does the trick, and before you know it he's taking her out for a sumptuous Italian dinner. Afterward, they go to a place on the water that Mickey claims belongs to a friend for a little dessert and what have you.

"Are you going to follow a man you just met to a wharf?" wonders Dr. Beaverman.

The rest of us ponder the question for a moment. "Who are you asking?" says Marcus.

"You, I guess," says Dr. Beaverman.

"Depends on whether or not I'm in a slutty phase," Marcus replies.

Soon after they arrive, Mickey puts Billie Holiday's "Strange Fruit" on the turntable, a song title with far too many heavy-handed metaphors to list here.

"One major theme at work here is that ethnic people are the only groups able to enjoy a free sexuality, an unencumbered libido," says Dr. Beaverman. "It's this simple: White men can't hump, not without help from their ethnic brothers and sisters."

By this point, it seems, Kim and Mickey have each settled on a dominant personality trait that will define their entire performance: She's twitchy and he's mumbly.

"Dr. Beaverman can't understand a word Mickey's saying," says Dr. Beaverman. "He's so whispery, it's amazing we're not seeing a boom mike."

"Maybe she's sitting on it," I say.

"I bet if we pressed the closed captioning button, it would say, 'We have no idea, folks. Be glad you're deaf,' " figures Tony.

Remarkably, Mickey and Kim don't make any whoopee quite yet. Mr. Rourke's plan is to reel her in slowly. He starts by sending her flowers the next day at work, which really sets her atwitter.

"Kim's such an easy mark for this kind of guy," I remark. "She'd bring out the sadist in anyone with that twitchiness. Mickey's probably, like, a substitute algebra teacher by day and he saw her twitching on the street and thought, *Fuck it, I'll be a perv for a while. I've got 9½ weeks to kill before the fall semester.*"

Sensing their budding love affair could benefit from a little rama-lama-lama-ka-dinga-da-dinga-dong, Mickey takes Kim to a carnival for date number 2. There, he instructs the Ferris wheel operator to leave her stranded at the top of the ride. This gets a bloodcurdling scream out of Kim.

"She's just seen the dailies," figures Ross.

"Beware of a woman in a bowler hat," cautions Dr. Beaverman, pointing to Kim, "whether it's Liza Minnelli in *Cabaret* or Lena Olin in *The Unbearable Lightness of Being*. It denotes that something carefree and a little bit perverse is about to happen. In point of fact, you don't ever see Liz Smith or Barbara Walters in a bowler."

After a few tense minutes, Kim's finally returned to earth, where she forgives Mickey for his sick joke by sticking her tongue down his throat.

"This is like an Amy Grant video gone wrong," groans Tony.

On their way home from the carnival, Kim and Mickey encounter a rainbow-colored gaggle of street kids, one of whom boasts that he can fart the theme from *Jaws,* provided Mickey forks over $5. Kim giggles girlishly at the suggestion and leans into Mickey and whispers something. "What do you suppose she's saying?" I ask.

"I'll queef the *Star Wars* theme for 10," says Dr. Beaverman. Then she giggles along with the rest of us at her crude quip. "You know, Dennis," she adds, "there was a time when I would have begged you not to attribute a queef comment to me. That time has passed."

"Does this excite you?" Mickey asks Kim.
"Yes," says Kim.
"No," say the rest of us.

Fart serenades must really get Kim sexed up, because in the next scene, back at her place, she finally lets Mickey have his way with her. He starts by blindfolding her with a white scarf.

"Sales of white scarves went up, like, 80% after this came out," says Lauren as Kim closes her eyes and accepts the blindfold.

"She's closing her eyes and thinking of England Dan and John Ford Coley," I say. "That was a stupid joke, you guys. Sorry."

"That he didn't put it over her mouth is the biggest crime of this movie," figures Tony. "So far."

"*We've replaced Kim's regular cock with Folger's Crystals,*" says Ross in his best announcer's voice. "*Let's see if she can tell the difference.*"

Then Mickey starts swirling some ice cubes around in a glass, getting them warmed up for their trip to Nipple Island.

"Wouldn't it be funny if it were his teeth in that glass?" says Tony.

"The ice is a metaphor," says Dr. B. as Mickey rubs a cube over Kim's naked torso, "Mickey is the catalyst for the dissolution of this solid block of Puritan repression. Hence, the melting ice."

"Does this excite you?" Mickey asks Kim.

"Yes," says Kim.

"No," say the rest of us.

At this point, my mind wanders and I envision a world where Mickey does blindfolded therapeutic ice rubbings for a living. I decide to share this notion with the room. "If his mission in life was to loosen up solid blocks of Puritan repression," I suggest, "who do you suppose would be his 2:15, Helen Hunt?"

"You," says Tony. "Oh, did I say you?" he backtracks. "I meant Jill Eikenberry."

"Mrs. Fields, the cookie lady," says Lauren. "I'm telling you, I've watched her show and I think every dirty thing she's ever wanted to do goes right into those cookies. If she got laid proper, she'd never bake again."

"Meryl Streep," says Marcus on his way to the bathroom.

"Nuh-uh," says Ross, shaking his head. "I bet Meryl Streep fucks good."

"Totally," agrees Tony. "Even if she were bored, she could act the hell out of it, like, 'You want a Dutch hooker today, Daddy? Just press play.' "

We turn our attention back to the screen to find Mickey and Kim making goo-goo eyes at each other in Mickey's ultramonochromatic, Sharper Image–stocked apartment. There, Mickey presents Kim with a red box, like she doesn't already have one of those.

"Save the paper!" shouts Marcus as Kim unwraps the gift—a beautiful gold wrist-watch, which, Mickey tells her, she's to look at each day a 12 o'clock and imagine him touching her.

"There's actually an inscription," says Dr. Beaverman. "*It'll keep on ticking when you take a kicking.*"

The next day at work, Kim dutifully observes her noontime Touch Break, and, before you know it, she's pleasuring herself while watching a slide show of erotic paintings.

"This is one actor-director conference I would've loved to have been a fly on the wall for," says Ross, as Kim, back arched, plants her feet on a nearby sculpture and frigs away.

"Don't worry about the fact that that sculpture is 700 years old, Kim," says Tony. "Just go ahead and put your feet right up on it."

"Do you suppose this is what they mean by 'Expose yourself to art'?" wonders Lauren as Kim uses her ass to operate the slide show remote.

"The thing about having a roommate is sometimes you *have* to masturbate at work," I say in Kim's defense.

"Don't I know it," says Tony.

Dr. Beaverman starts rifling through her books and says, "This scene is saying that if you get a woman sexed up, she can't concentrate. It exploits the very unsubstantiated opinion some men have that women's essence is nothing but childlike and animalistic." Dr. Beaverman settles on a book, then opens it to show us a few pages with paintings on them. "I refer you to the artwork of the 19th century, in which women were portrayed as these languid creatures who were always hanging out naked twirling garlands in their hair, contributing nothing. Ironically, it's the same kind of art that Kim seems to enjoy wanking to."

"What week are we in?" asks Marcus, returning from the can.

"It's day 2," groans Ross.

"We're like the hostages in Iran," says Lauren. "There's going to be camera crews out front any minute now."

Things are looking up, however, as we've come to what is arguably the film's most famous scene. Send the kiddies to bed because Kim's just brought Mickey home and now she's going to let him rub and insert various foodstuffs onto and into her body while her roommate, Molly, sleeps blissfully down the hall. It's a sequence best described as a cross between the *Girls Gone Wild* and *Supermarket Sweep*.

"This brings to mind the age-old question: Which came first, the chicken or Kim Basinger?" I say as Mickey kicks off the buffet by cracking a couple of eggs.

"Open wide, Kimmy," coos Tony as Mickey grabs a handful of strawberries. "Here comes the airplane!"

"I was dating a chick in the late '80s and we based our food sex-play on this movie," reveals Ross.

Normally, I'd file that comment under Too Much Information, but this is *9½ Weeks,* not *Old Yeller.* What did I expect people to talk about? "Was it fun?" I ask.

"Yeah," Ross replies, "but it gets real messy real fast, and then after a while you just don't want to work through whipped cream to get to what you want."

"Tell me about it," says Lauren. "I did this once with what's-his-face."

"Barry," says Marcus.

"I know his name," snaps Lauren. "Anyway, it sounded like a really sexy idea at first, but after two foods I was like, 'This is absolutely disgusting. Can I have a doggie bag?'"

As Mickey starts to dollop honey on Kim's tongue and Tony predicts that Kim's going to have "a honey of an O," I can't help but wish there were more clever product placement. "Like why can't she touch up her bikini wax with a Chiquita label?" I suggest.

"I bet I know what she'd do for a Klondike bar," says Tony. "But where the hell are you gonna find a goat in Manhattan?"

"There's always room for Jell-O," says Ross, "in my snatch."

Though easy to make fun of, this scene is not without its charms. Ross admits to being turned on when Mumbly douses Twitchy's breasts with milk—it does a body good, after all—and I give high marks to the ravenous way Mickey kisses.

"Why doesn't her roommate respond to her screaming?" wonders Lauren.

Dr. Beaverman just stares at the screen with her mouth agape. While I'm sure all sorts of psychosexual theories are colliding in her beautiful mind, she instead chooses to focus on questions of refrigerator realism. "Who keeps that much fresh food in the house?" she asks incredulously. "I've had a frizzy-haired roommate, and I'd come home from Mrs. Gooches and that stuff would be gone in an hour, and you're telling me there could be an untainted Jell-O mold in that refrigerator? I beg to differ."

"You don't have to beg," I tell her. "But Kim does."

"I was a bulimic when I saw this, and this scene totally traumatized me," says Lauren.

What?

I pause the tape and look at her as if to say, *I never knew you were fucking bulimic.* Everyone else opts to look at me instead of Lauren.

"One of my friends in junior high was very overweight," Lauren starts. "She ate all the time and I would go with her after school, like to the pizza parlor, and I didn't know how to tell my mother that I was basically having dinner before I got home. I'd eat four or five meals a day and I put on an enormous amount of weight, like I was 40 or 50 pounds heavier than I am now. So I started making myself throw up. I was pretty good at it, actually. This went on for a few years, and then one day my mother totally called me on it. She said, 'I found vomit in the bathroom. I don't know whose it is, but I know it better stop or that person is going to the hospital.' So I stopped."

"Just like that?" asks Dr. Beaverman.

"Just like that," says Lauren.

"And this movie reminds you of that?" I ask.

"Totally," says Lauren. "I was still bingeing and purging when I saw it—it was on cable at a friend's house—and when he tied her up and he fed her all the food, I got freaked out because I thought, 'How is she going to get to the bathroom in time to throw it up before it all starts being digested?' I totally panicked and had to leave the room."

I'm not sure how to proceed at this point. It seems insensitive to just say, "That's interesting," and then go back to the movie. Luckily, Lauren changes the subject herself. "Of course, Mickey Rourke's thumbs didn't help matters much."

"Excuse me?" I ask.

"He has hammer thumbs," says Lauren. "Haven't you noticed? I thought he was cute for a while and then I saw the thumbs and it was over."

We restart the movie to find Kim, more sex-addled and lethargic than ever, lounging on Mickey's bed with a remote control in her hand.

"She's looking at that thing going, 'I haven't had sex with one of *these* before,' " says Ross.

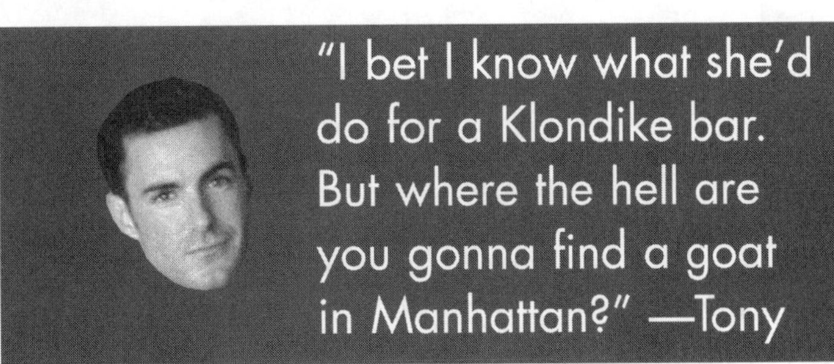

"Her world will forever be divided into two parts," I say. "Objects she can have sex with, and objects she can't."

"Will Fit and Won't Fit," simplifies Tony.

Like any good girlfriend, Kim decides the time has come to rifle through Mickey's possessions. When Mickey returns he busts her on her snooping and vows to punish her. "Face the wall and lift your skirt because I'm going to spank you," he commands.

"I thought 'Spanking' was week 7," I say, rifling through the pages of my notepad like it's a class syllabus. "Are we switching that with 'Fun With Shame' from week 5?"

"Any boyfriend worth his salt should try to spank you at least once," proclaims Marcus.

This comment raises a few eyebrows. Unfortunately, the only question I can seem to formulate is totally inane: "What does it mean to be worth your salt?"

"It means your personality is worth more than what they could get for boiling you down to carbon and selling you," says Ross.

"Really?" I say.

"I don't know," says Ross.

When Mickey skips the appetizer and goes right to the main course, so to speak, Lauren throws her hands into the air and barks, "Give me a break, she wasn't even wet! But, of course, since a man directed this, she *loved* it."

"This music selection is called 'Unsafe Sex in E Minor,'" says Tony. "In case anyone's interested."

"You bring up a good point," says Ross. "This movie, while not that good, was to the first wave of the AIDS crisis what screwball comedies were to the Depression. It was all about vicarious thrills."

When Marcus suggests we play hooky for a week or two and adjourn to the kitchen for some coffee cake and Jell-O à la Basinger, none of us can resist.

"I get how the Jell-O goes with the movie," Lauren says, "but why the coffee cake?"

"Because everything's in the box," replies Marcus. "Cake, frosting, even the pan."

"That makes sense," says Ross, his mouth full of cake.

We take our treats and return to the front room just in time to see Kim toss her beloved bowler into the air, Mary Tyler Moore–style. "She's going to make it fit after all," says Tony.

Which brings us to a sex montage set to Bryan Ferry's infectious and sexy "Slave to Love" in which Kim and Mickey rub uglies in a giant clock tower.

"What time is it," I say, speaking for Kim, "when the big hand is on the 12 and the little hand is in my cleavage?"

"There are limits to lust," proclaims Dr. Beaverman, savoring the alliteration, "particularly if you're a white woman. That's what all these timepieces represent. And time is running out on Ms. Basinger. She's got herself 9½ weeks, and then it's back to Abstinence Avenue."

"I thought 9½ weeks is how long she's going to have to be on the penicillin after they break up," says Tony.

"No," says Ross. "You're thinking of *Another 9½ Weeks.*"

Then we return to Kim's office for a scene that's notable only because it introduces the film's B-story: Molly, the sound-sleeping, frizzy-haired roommate, is knitting something.

"We're a bustling, pretentious art gallery," I can imagine her boss saying, "but feel free to bring handicrafts from home."

"Or to masturbate in the slide room," adds Marcus.

Kim takes up a new hobby of her own—cross-dressing—in a subsequent scene set at the Algonquin Hotel, in which she dines with Mickey while sporting a faux mustache and Charlie Chaplin suit. "She's like the Little Tramp in this scene," I say.

"As opposed to the rest of the movie where she's a big tramp," says Lauren.

"A woman would be very suspicious of a man who wanted her to dress like another man," says Dr. Beaverman. "That's all I'm saying."

"I stayed at the Algonquin when I was on my book tour for *Misadventures,*" I say, referring to my '98 novel, *Misadventures in the (213).* Available now in paperback! "If you're an author on tour, you get to stay for free for one night. It's their way of keeping the literary tradition of the place alive, I guess. Anyway, I have a picture of me sitting at the famous round table."

"I'd say it's a Won't Fit," says Tony.

"Definitely," I confirm.

"Did you stick your gum under it?" asks Ross.

"No, but I jacked off in the slide room," I reply.

Mickey and Kim leave the restaurant only to get chased down the street by some lowlifes. We're meant to think the thugs attack because they don't like the idea of two men together, but I wouldn't rule out the possibility that they're just fed up with Twitchy and Mumbly's cavalcade of bullshit. Mickey and Kim ward off their foes, then proceed to rut like rabbits in a rat-infested gutter while dirty New York water pours down on them.

"Nothing like a good gay bashing to get a girl in the mood," says Lauren.

Though I half expect Kim to spend the rest of the movie nursing hepatitis, she survives the gutter fuck unharmed. In fact, she's practically glowing in the next scene, in which the pair visits a department store to shoplift a little jewelry.

"Kleptomania has its own chapter is this book, *Female Perversity in the 21st Century,*" says Dr. Beaverman, passing a giant leather-bound tome down the couch to Lauren. "I've highlighted some key passages."

"Wait, this is from the Burbank Public Library," says Lauren, looking inside the front cover.

"You stole it?" asks Ross.

Dr. Beaverman shrugs.

"Next on *Ricki,*" I say in my deepest announcer's voice, "women who steal books about kleptomaniacs and the gays who love them."

Still in the department store, Twitchy and Mumbly leave the jewelry area to go shop for mattresses. Though the saleslady doesn't have a handle or a spout, she bears a striking resemblance to Mrs. Potts, the animated teakettle Angela Lansbury voiced in *Beauty and the Beast.* Not surprisingly, Tony can serve up Angie's Cockney brogue on the spot.

"*Are you going to do it in the bad hole, sweetheart?*" Tony says as Mrs. Potts.

"Get out the Garry Marshall font," says Marcus.

"Would you like to open up a Macy's charge account after you come, love?" says Tony. *"You could save 10% on that bed you just soiled."*

"This scene is where I learned what ticking is," says Ross, "so something good did come out of this movie."

"Ticking?" I repeat. "Is that where you take someone's balls and—"

"No, no, no," says Ross, cutting me off. "Ticking's the cloth on the outside of the mattress."

"You're thinking of the Filthy Sanchez, Dennis," says Tony.

"I'm always hearing about the Filthy Sanchez," asks Lauren. "What is it?"

Though Tony has no trouble saying such things as *"Put one of our new goose down pillows under her ass and you'll drill deeper, dearie"*—as Angela Lansbury, no less—he can't bring himself to describe the Filthy Sanchez out loud. So he scribbles the definition on my notepad and passes it to Lauren.

"That's beyond disgusting," says Lauren.

"That's not even what it is," says Ross, looking over her shoulder. "Give me your pen, Dennis."

Ross writes down his definition of the Filthy Sanchez and hands it back to Lauren. Judging by her dry heaves, it's *beyond* beyond disgusting. We pass the sheet around the room and split on which definition we think is accurate. I stick the sheet on my refrigerator so I can ask future visitors for their opinion, and then get back to the movie where we find Kim, back at the gallery, so catatonic and sex-obsessed she'd sell Michelangelo's *David* for $5 and queef the theme from *Close Encounters* for no extra charge. She must be conserving her energy for the next scene, in which she does a striptease to Joe Cocker's "You Can Leave Your Hat On" while Mickey eats popcorn and guffaws inappropriately. It's almost like he's watching something else entirely, like *Airplane!* or *Eddie Murphy Raw.*

"Where's Jennifer Beals's dance double when you need her?" asks Lauren as Kim does the best bumping and grinding she can muster.

"The unemployment office," says Tony. "In France."

"I think Kim's OK in this," I say. "I mean, I've done this number in this very room and it's trickier than it looks."

When, halfway through her dance, Kim spontaneously picks up the kitchen telephone, we can't resist imagining what she might say into it.

"I'm happy with my long distance carrier, but thanks," says Lauren.

"It's Loni Anderson," I holler, as if I'm addressing Mickey in the next room. "She wants to know if she can change her Thursday to Friday."

"She wants to switch with Sally Field," adds Tony. "Isn't that ironic?"

"She says she hasn't gotten off since Burt," says Ross.

"Parks," says Dr. Beaverman.

Kim finally starts to suspect that there's something unsavory about her beau when he insists that she crawl across the floor of his apartment for money.

"I don't want to crawl," she tells him.

"I'm saving all fours for my *Maxim* cover," I say.

"And she was too highbrow to do *Boxing Helena*?" wonders Ross.

"Can't we go back to the old days," pleads Marcus, "when you shoved rutabagas in me and left me on the Ferris wheel overnight? God, we were so happy then."

As Kim relents and starts crawling across the floor, I decide I've had about all I can take of Mickey's colorless apartment. "He's like Mr. Monochrome Man," I complain. "If she showed up in a yellow sundress, I bet he'd beat the shit out of her."

"Maybe color could be her weapon," proposes Lauren. "Like she could go, 'I've got a lime-green handkerchief in my purse, asshole, and I'm not afraid to use it.' "

"Or drop a half-pound bag of M&Ms on the floor," says Tony. "Mickey would literally just melt like the Wicked Witch of the West."

The final straw in this so-called relationship comes when Mickey lures Kim to a hotel room and tries to make her knock boots with a hooker who looks like Rita Moreno, only younger and more strung out. "Isn't Rita Moreno one of the only performers to win an Oscar, a Tony, a Grammy, and an Emmy?" I ask.

"I think so," says Marcus, "and they're all Will Fits except the Emmy."

"I love that Kim's shocked that he'd want to have a three-way," says Tony. "It's like, 'You can stick strawberries up my ass, but what's with the crazy foreigners?' "

"Mickey's so bored with her in this scene," observes Ross as Kim runs, "Justify My Love"–style, from the hotel room.

"He totally phones it in that last half a week," agrees Tony. "He's like, 'Mumble, mumble, scarf, pussy, I'll be in my trailer.' "

Then, after coming to blows *Jerry Springer*–style, Mickey chases Kim into a nearby porno theater. By this point, Mickey's shown himself to be such a sleazebag that I half expect the *Cheers* theme to start playing and the extras to greet him by name.

Mickey finally catches up with Kim, who by now is so miffed at him she can't help but kiss him some more. He lures her back to his place, but Kim stops in the name of love and tells him it's over. Mickey tries to persuade her to stay. He even tries showing a softer side by revealing to her that his mom was a supermarket checker. Like we couldn't have guessed that from the way he maneuvered that kumquat over her pubic mound.

"This is the only real conversation they have in the whole movie and it's so arbitrary," marvels Ross.

Mickey's newfound humanity is too little, too late, and too mumbly for Kim to bear, so she leaves.

"I love you," says Mickey after Kim walks out for the final time.

"And if you see Bernadette Peters in the foyer, tell her to give me two minutes," hollers Ross.

"Take her this scarf," adds Tony, "and tell her to go ahead and blindfold herself and take off her panties."

Alas, Mickey's confession of love has no effect, and the next time we see Kim the credits are rolling and she's back on the street, alone, knowing she'll never wear a bowler hat again.

"The film should have ended with a shot of Kim hanging a sign on her panties that says Closed for Renovations," I say.

"Pardon our mess," says Tony.

"Gone fishin'," says Dr. Beaverman.

"So, what's she going to with the other half of week 10?" wonders Marcus.

"Take up knitting," says Lauren.

"That's right," I protest. "They never show us what became of Molly's knitting."

"She made a nice tea cozy that doubles as a cock warmer," says Ross. "But you have to rent the unrated version to see it."

"I don't like this bastard Adrian Lyne," rants Dr. Beaverman, of the British-born director who will go on to give us *Fatal Attraction, Indecent Proposal,* and *Lolita.* "He makes it out like men can be unfeeling and compartmentalized, but hey, there's always another chick around the corner. But Kim's been educated the hard way and now she'll go back to work and behave herself, numb furthermore to the brutes in her future. That's her punishment. Don't you get out of line again, my dear: That's the message here, and I'm really fed up."

"I read an interview with Adrian Lyne once," says Ross, "where he said that in test screenings men were way more bent out of shape over this movie than women, even though it's the female character who suffers all the degradation."

"That doesn't surprise me," mutters Lauren. "It probably hit too close to home."

"How about you guys?" I ask everyone else. "Is anyone even remotely turned on?"

"Actually, I feel kinda sick," says Tony, unbuttoning the top button of his jeans.

"Red Shoe Diarrhea," figures Ross.

"Scratch what I said about a slutty phase coming on," says Marcus. "I may never have sex again."

•

The next time I see Marcus, at the AIDS Walk office, three nights days later, the first thing he says is, "Remember when I said I felt a slutty phase coming on and then after watching the movie I said, 'Scratch that?'" he asks. "Well, scratch that."

"Scratch the scratching?" I ask.

"Yes," he says. "I went to the Factory last night and met someone."

Marcus proceeds to give Tony and I the lowdown on his latest nocturnal companion, an architect named Kyle, while the three of us stuff fliers into envelopes that say "I Walk Because..." on them. The AIDS Walk has a massive mailing that has to go out tomorrow, and as part of his new job, Tony was in charge of corralling volunteers to make sure that happened. When the high school kids he'd lined up at the mall failed to show, he called us in a panic.

After a while, Marcus runs out of scintillating details about his fling so he asks how the *9½ Weeks* article is coming along.

"I spent all day transcribing the tape," I explain. "As much as it wasn't a very good movie, it's sort of stayed with me, and I have to say, as someone on the low end of the slut scale, there's something really exciting about the idea of someone coming along and totally rocking your world that way."

"Yeah, but one-night stands can do that," reasons Marcus. "No reason for it to drag on for 9½ weeks."

"But it has to be more than a onetime thing," I argue, "because anticipating the next time is half the fun. You have to be driven to distraction, miss deadlines, blow off all your friends and be really irresponsible for, like, six weeks."

"OK, two weeks," says Marcus.

"Four," I say.

"Three," says Marcus.

"Three and a half," I say.

"Sold!" declares Tony. "To the man in the bootleg Britney Spears concert T-shirt." (That would be me.)

"Good, you guys are still here," says a voice from behind us. We turn to see Lauren, fresh from her Pilates class, standing in the doorway. "I got your message after class and came right over."

Lauren joins us at the table and immediately seizes the floor, explaining that she's had a post–*9½ Weeks* epiphany that she needs to share with the group. "First of all," she starts, before grabbing a stack of fliers and envelopes. "I realized at the end of the movie that I could do a hell of a lot worse. I mean, Barry has his quirks, but at least he doesn't make me fuck him in a gutter."

Judging by their faces, our fellow stuffers, a trio of middle-aged Latinas, find this remark curious. But they say nothing.

"Plus," continues Lauren, "what Dr. Beaverman said about it really being about me got me thinking. And she's totally right, the bitch."

"Well, she graduated from Ivy-by-the-Pacific," says Tony. "What do you expect?"

"Barry ain't going nowhere, I know that," Lauren continues. "I think the reason I wanted to get married so badly was so I could rationalize not going after my career the way I need to if anything's ever going to happen. I could be like, 'I know I wanted to be a comic, but being a wife takes so much time and energy.' I'd be off the hook if I were married."

"Do you want to be off the hook?" asks Marcus.

"You can be off the hook," I add. "It's not a crime."

"No," insists Lauren. "No, I don't. That's what I just realized. And I told Barry, too. I said, 'I love you and I totally want to be with you, but right now I've got to focus more on my career and less on you,' and he was cool with it." Lauren reaches across the table for more envelopes to stuff, then adds, "So you guys better come and laugh when I do sets around town."

"Of course," I say.

Two hours later, we're still stuffing. To help pass the time, we've invented a guessing game called "I Walk Because…" It's inspired by the envelopes we're stuffing and the AIDS Walk posters plastered all over the office (and the city at large) featuring celebrities and their reasons for walking. For example, one has a photo of Madonna and the quote, "I walk because AIDS is a disease that still kills people." To play the game, one person tosses out a reason for walking and the other players must guess the celebrity behind the reason.

"I walk because I just married my grandpa and it's the only way I can get out of the house," says Tony.

Celine Dion's too obvious, though both Tony and I adore her. I want to say Anna Nicole Smith, but since Grandpa's dead and Tony knows he's dead—he's been following the Anna case closer than anyone—I just shrug.

"C.Z. Jones," says Tony. That's what we call Catherine Zeta-Jones in our house.

"I should have gotten that," says Lauren.

"My turn," I say. "I walk because I miss Alec and I've had a celery stalk stuck in my ass for the last 15 years and it hurts to sit."

"Kim Basinger," Marcus, Tony, and Lauren say all at once. And just as I stuff the last envelope too.

On the elevator ride downstairs, Lauren turns the conversation back to Barry. "You know the cutest thing he did?" she asks, practically blushing. "While I was staying at your place, he switched our bedroom with his studio. He moved all the furniture and everything. So the Gap whore of the month doesn't get to watch us screw anymore."

"That's love," says Tony.

"Wait, I've got one," I announce. "I walk because I was in *Pleasantville* and ever since Barry moved the furniture I've been bored out of my skull."

Judging by their faces, Marcus and Tony both know the answer, but they opt to let Lauren field this one. "Joan fucking Allen," she says.

I touch my nose.

THE SPY WHO LOVED ME BUT WASN'T *IN* LOVE WITH ME

"Does this shirt make my ass look big?" Tony wonders while painstakingly rolling up the sleeves of his Lycra-cotton, short-sleeved, button-down shirt.

"How can a shirt make your ass look big?" asks Ross. "It doesn't even touch your ass."

"You know nothing about fashion," says Tony.

"Were we supposed to try and pull it together?" asks Lauren, tugging at the drawstring of her distressed Old Navy sweat jacket for emphasis. "I thought it was supposed to be a casual shot. I didn't even wash my hair."

"It is supposed to be a casual shot," I assure her.

"If we're not being fussy, why is Marcus in the bathroom plucking his eyebrows?" she asks.

"Because *he's* fussy," I say. "The enterprise as a whole is not meant to be fussy."

"Sorry I'm late, kids," says a freshly frosted Dr. Beaverman, screeching up 15 minutes after the designated meeting time in her '92 Honda Accord. "My hair appointment ran long, though I guess I shouldn't bitch because Rudy opened the salon early just to do me."

"Fussy," reiterates Lauren, rolling her eyes.

"Oh, my God," squeals Tony as Dr. Beaverman, sporting a white silk blouse and short gray tweed skirt along with her eye-catching new do, saunters up the sidewalk where the rest of us are gathered. "You look like a fucking sex bomb!"

"Stop it," says Dr. Beaverman, giving him a big hug and lipstick-preserving air kiss.

The reason we're here this Sunday morning, in front of both Video Master and God, is that Matt in London wants a photo of the six of us for the magazine's contributor's page. "Your adoring public demands it," he said in his E-mail. He's just being silly, of course. As far as I know, our adoring public consists of two people: Matt and a woman who works in the accounting department named Fiona who included a complimentary note about our *Pretty Woman* outing with my last check.

"Smiles, everybody, smiles!" hollers Ross's Video Master colleague, Perry, emerging from the store with my 15-year-old Nikon 35mm camera hanging around his neck. Though Perry sports dome of chrome and has clearly never met a tattoo needle he didn't like, I have a hunch he's the man behind the store's delightfully gay-skewed categorization system. He also seems more than capable of snapping my shutter, or anyone else's for that matter.

He proves quite authoritative when it comes to placing us in front of the store's poster-filled windows, as though he's done this countless times. "About my camera," I tell him, "push it halfway down and it focuses."

"I got it, sport," he replies before grabbing me by the shoulders, positioning me front and center, and fiddling artfully with my shirt collar. "Just leave it to the artiste."

Perry's mock pretentious retort propels me into a daydream that I'd have Dr. Beaverman analyze if there were any possible meaning to infer other than that I'm a showbiz obsessed media whore wanna-be. In any event, as Perry snaps away, coaching us along by saying things like, "Hello, gorgeous," and, "That's it, beautiful," my fantasy unfolds like this: The six of us are indeed being photographed, but not for a postage stamp–size shot for the inside page of a magazine that doesn't even come out in my native land. No, in my daydream our likeness is being captured for the cover of *Vanity Fair*—by Annie Leibovitz, no less. Naturally, it's the annual Hollywood Issue. You know, the really thick one where the town's sexiest up-and-comers, in outfits calculated to look uncalculated, pose en masse in front of a neutral background that won't compete with their staggering natural beauty. I'm sporting a half smirk, my best hair ever, and that Hugo Boss leather jacket I tried on at the Beverly Center last week that the clerk literally had to rip off me so she could close. The rest of the gang wears equally nifty clothes along with facial expressions that seem to say, "We're just a little bit better than you and we know it, but if you call us on it, we'll deny it."

At one point, I suggest to Annie—she insists that I call her Annie—that maybe I could be holding a remote control for some shots, and she adores the idea. Oh, my God, she's so nice. While I'm on a roll, I also ask if we can make sure that I'm on the front cover and Tony's not. "I have enough trouble getting dates as it is," I explain. Annie smiles warmly and positions us accordingly.

"That's 24," says Perry, breaking my reverie. "Everybody grab a movie for the last 12 shots."

In his E-mail, Matt requested that in addition to the just-stand-there-and-smile pose, we shoot a setup where everyone, except me as Screening Party ringleader, holds one of the five James Bond movies we're going to be watching later today as part of our Who's the Better Bond Film Festival.

Lauren rifles through the stack first and takes *Live and Let Die* starring Roger Moore. Moore, she explains, was her first Bond. "And when you pop your Bond cherry," she asserts, "it stays popped."

Ross chooses *On Her Majesty's Secret Service* with one-shot Bond George Lazenby. "People say that if Connery had made this movie, it would have been the best of all of them because the rest of the movie is so good," says Ross. "But I don't think Connery could have pulled off the love story the way Lazenby did."

The World Is Not Enough with Pierce Brosnan as 007 is Marcus's choice for three reasons: 1. He loves Garbage, who sing the theme song; 2. It's the only Bond movie where the number 1 villain, the mastermind behind the mayhem, is actually a villain-*ess*, and he's all about girl power; and 3. the blue background on the video box goes great with his Kenneth Cole top.

Though Dr. Beaverman, like myself, has never sat through an actual Bond movie, she seems pleased with the movie she's going to be holding, *The Living Daylights* with Timothy Dalton as Bond. "This college professor I had a little fling with had a dimple in his chin just like Dalton's," she recalls fondly. "It was as though God gave him a little poke."

"I'm not touching that," says Perry, who's clearly getting a kick out of this whole ridiculous dog and pony show.

"I hate chin dimples," mutters Tony. "I've hated them ever since I went out with this guy who literally Naired inside his because he couldn't shave in there."

"This is yours, then," I say, handing Tony the box for *Goldfinger,* with Sean Connery as Bond.

"Seriously, I get Connery?" he says incredulously. "That's awesome because everyone knows he's the best. And I love the gadgets in those early movies because they *look* like they actually do what they're supposed to do. They're not all digital and shit."

With Perry coaching us on how to make sure our video boxes don't cause a glare, we finish off the roll and then head to the condo for Bondfest 2000. Since Tony and I drove separately—he wanted to hit the tanning booth before the shoot—I send him to have the film developed at Rite Aid while I pick up some tasty treats at Dairy Queen.

•

When we reconvene, I remind my guests that our mission, aside from polishing off two packages of Dilly Bars and making fun of *Live and Let Die* ingenue Jane Seymour, is to evaluate the five dashing actors who have filled the tux pants of 007 over the last 35-plus years. "I've divided the judging into three categories," I explain, while passing out small stacks of index cards and Sharpies to each of my panelists. "The first category is Swimsuit. This includes physique, fitness level, chest hair, agility in fight scenes and stunt sequences, and anything else you might want to lump under swimsuit."

"Like how lumpy his swimsuit is?" suggests Tony.

"Sure," I say. "OK, category 2 is Interview. This covers anything that comes out of Bond's mouth."

"Like the way he says, 'My name is Bond, James Bond,'" offers Marcus.

"Exactly," I say. "Is he charming, self-deprecating, articulate? As dry as the martini he sips?"

"We get it," says Dr. Beaverman, stealing a glance at her watch.

"OK, OK," I say. "Finally, we have Evening Gown. Does he clean up well? Is he dashing? Sophisticated?"

"How he looks in a tux," adds Lauren.

"You got it," I say, taking my seat. "So let us begin with Sean Connery in 1964's *Goldfinger.*"

I've barely pressed play when Ross serves up his first Fun Fact of the day. "Originally the producers wanted Cary Grant," he informs us. "But Grant would only agree to do one movie. So then they offered it to James Mason, who would only do *two* movies. They wanted someone to hang around for more movies so they screen-tested Connery, who was an unknown at the time, along with a few other nobodies, and settled on Connery even though Ian Fleming, the author of the books, didn't like him. He called him the great snorting lorry driver."

"I'm so stoked this movie is my selection," says Tony about 10 minutes in, when a tuxedo-clad Connery bursts in on a buxom babe in a bubble bath. "We haven't even gotten to the credits and we've already had a major explosion, the tux under the wet suit, Sean's basket in a swimsuit, and a hot bim in a bathtub. You guys are never gonna top that."

"Who's the girl?" I ask, wanting to stay on top of every detail of my Bond baptism.

"It doesn't matter," says Lauren. "The key to understanding Bond is, it doesn't matter who the girl is."

Before the couple can couple, they're interrupted by a thug whom Connery sees reflected in the eye of his love doll. A rough-and-tumble fight ensues. "This is the kind of scene that Roger Moore would never do well," declares Ross, "because he doesn't get mussy and dirty. He would have had a stunt double step in immediately."

The action-packed scene leads us into the opening credits, which feature Shirley Bassey's seriously screechy interpretation of the title song. "Can I tell you how heady it was, as a child, to hear this on the radio interspersed with the Beatles?" says Dr. Beaverman. "I still have the scars."

> "Room service, can you send up some turpentine? I have a golden whore in my room."
> —Ross

A small case of Bassey damage, however, is nothing compared to the fate that befalls Jill Masterson, a perky blond, who, after boffing Connery silly, winds up facedown and dead on a hotel bed. She's painted gold from head to toe, so it's clearly the work of the movie's supervillain, Goldfinger.

"Room service, can you send up some turpentine," says Ross into a pantomimed phone. "I have a golden whore in my room."

"No, not Susan Anton," I say.

"No, not Rue McClanahan," says Tony.

"You not only objectify a woman as an art object," says Dr. Beaverman distastefully, "but you make her into a fetish. It's like having sex with an Oscar."

"Speaking of which," says Tony, "when are we going to do a Kevin Spacey movie?"

"Why is there no paint anywhere but on her?" I ask. "Was she painted somewhere else and brought there, like O.J.'s bloody glove?"

Bond says that Miss Masterson died from skin suffocation, but Marcus begs to differ. "When I was in fourth grade I asked my biology teacher about it," recalls Marcus. "And he said that when you paint someone, there's no release for the body heat so your enzymes denature and that's how you die, not skin suffocation. Thank you, Mr. Widmer."

"Thank you, Mr. Widmer," I echo.

In the next scene we're introduced to Miss Moneypenny, the dutiful, bullet-bra–wearing secretary Connery sexually harasses but never slips it to. "The most lethal weapon in this whole movie are her tits," maintains Dr. Beaverman. "Look at those things. They should be registered with the Pentagon."

"Moneypenny is like one of your high school friends' hot mom," says Ross.

"She is a little *Harper Valley PTA,*" agrees Tony. "But they should call her Moldypussy because, let's face it, Bond's never going to give it to her."

Character actor Desmond Llewelyn turns up next as Q, the agency's in-house inventor, whose job it is to demonstrate for 007—and the audience—the various high-tech gizmos we'll be seeing throughout the remainder of the film. "The scenes with Q are where Bond is at his most quippy," remarks Ross after Sean jokes with Q about "stopping off for a quick one."

"So Q dedicates his life to inventing expensive gadgets and Bond just traipses in and makes sex jokes?" I ask.

"Exactly," says Ross. "And then he returns those expensive gadgets in shambles."

"Are you picking up on the repressed homoeroticism?" asks Dr. Beaverman.

"On the screen?" I ask. "Or between me and this Dilly Bar?"

"I said 'repressed,'" replies Dr. Beaverman. "Q is clearly in love with Connery. Just look at the way he's manhandling that stick shift."

Speaking of stick shifts, our party gets a screen grab–worthy dose of Connery's in a subsequent scene, when the Scottish stud saunters across a putting green to remove his golf ball from the hole.

"Is this in 3-D?" wonders Tony, before rewinding the tape and showing us the moment again.

"He's dressing left," observes Marcus.

An impromptu circumcision debate ensues with uncut winning out 5 to 1. "He's circumcised, I tell you," wails Ross, the lone holdout. "Run it back again if you don't believe me."

Tony obliges.

"OK, freeze it there," commands Ross. "See, Orca's definitely coming to the surface."

With the evidence staring us in the face, we concede to Ross, who will hereafter be regarded as the Jessica Fletcher of foreskin.

We don't get rowdy again until the next babe turns up. This one, who turns out to be the golden girl's sister, gets starry-eyed for Bond after he intentionally punctures one of the tires on her convertible with a Q-issued car gadget just so he can get in her pants.

"He could have killed her," gripes Dr. Beaverman. "James Bond is such a bastard."

"That's the key to his appeal," says Lauren.

"But aren't you afraid he might have a few too many martinis and beat you up?" I ask.

"That's why it's sexy," Lauren admits. "It's not sexy if there's no danger."

Unfortunately, before Connery can finish the poking his car gadget started, Convertible Girl gets decapitated by a razor-brimmed derby thrown by one of Goldfinger's henchmen, Odd Job. "I don't get how a hat decapitates someone," I say, "even if the brim is a blade. It seems like the top of the hat would keep the blade from going all the way through."

"Dennis, in a few movies you've got Denise Richards as a nuclear physicist," says Ross. "I suggest you start suspending your disbelief now."

"Can you imagine having to call these girls' parents?" poses Marcus before retrieving the imaginary phone Ross discarded earlier. "Mr. Masterson, one of your daughters is dead in a Miami hotel room. She's been gold-painted to death. And your other daughter, well, she's in Europe and she's been decapitated by a hat."

Tony grabs his own phony phone and picks up where Marcus left off. "Gold-*painted*, not gold-plated," he says. "Miami, uh-huh. No, just a hat, like on your head. It was coming at her pretty fast, like a Frisbee. The other girl? Gold-painted, yes. I don't really know, sir, if it was an enamel or a latex. I suppose it could have been spray paint. But I think you're missing the big picture here, sir. The point is your daughters are dead and I don't think open caskets are going to be an option. Yes, I suppose it could have been Sherwin-Williams. Now you're going back to the hat. You know what? Is *Mrs.* Masterson home? Can you put her on the phone? No, it wasn't a magic hat, sir. It was just a derby..."

Soon, Connery gets captured and taken to Goldfinger's lair, where the baddie ties him spread-eagle to a metal platform and aims a deadly laser beam at his crotch.

"I've always wondered how laser vaginal rejuvenation works," remarks Tony as the laser inches closer to Sean's family jewels. "The ads in the *L.A. Weekly* are so vague."

"Let Dr. Beaverman adjust her glasses," says Dr. Beaverman. "Now, Goldfinger says the laser *cuts through solid metal*, which is meant to imply that Bond's dick is solid metal."

"Yes," I say, "and getting more solid by the second."

"Of course he's getting turned on," says Dr. Beaverman. "He's got a spotlight aimed at his crotch. This skirt-chasing spy is so able to mix death and sex that the two are interchangeable to him. For men like Bond, the threat of violence is a total turn-on."

By now, I'm starting to realize that Bond girls are like lizards' tails. If one dies—and according to Marcus, the first girl per film to sleep with Bond *always* dies—another one grows back in her place. Enter Pussy Galore, Mr. Goldfinger's personal pilot, who Bond first encounters when he wakes up from a bout of stun gun–induced unconsciousness to find himself on an airplane bound for America.

"What the hell is her shiny, happy suit made of?" Tony asks.

"Velour," says Dr. Beaverman. "Pussy Velour."

When James asks Pussy where in the world they are, she purrs, "Ninety-five thousand feet, flying southwest over Newfoundland."

"God, I hate flying Southwest," I moan, speaking for James. "The last time I did, they lost my luggage."

When the curiously butch Ms. Galore resists Bond's advances, Marcus explains her thought process this way: "I have to hold off for a couple more scenes. If I'm a slut now, I might get killed by a derby."

A bunch of other terrifically exciting things happen in *Goldfinger,* I'm sure. I just can't tell you what they are, though, because this is where we eject Sean Connery in order to evaluate his successors. Besides, let's face it, no one watches Bond movies for the story. "I've seen some of these movies a dozen times," relates Ross, "and I couldn't tell you what the plot is. The fun is, what's the next action scene, who's the next babe, what's the next wisecrack."

"Do we get a little techno theme music while we enter our scores like on Miss Teen USA?" asks Tony, marker at the ready.

"We're not that high-tech, I'm afraid," I say.

"We could rewind to Shirley Bassey," suggests Marcus.

"That's OK," says Dr. Beaverman. And with that, we score.

SEAN CONNERY

	SWIMSUIT	INTERVIEW	EVENING GOWN	TOTAL
BEAVERMAN	9.85	9.78	9.56	29.19
ROSS	8.83	8.95	9.17	26.95
MARCUS	9.63	9.85	9.73	29.21
DENNIS	9.64	9.81	9.52	28.97
LAUREN	8.94	8.52	9.92	27.38
TONY	9.92	10.00	9.89	29.81

George Lazenby's sole shot at Bond-dom, 1969's *On Her Majesty's Secret Service,* is next and opens with the token 007 iris shot, which we all agree Lazenby does with particular finesse. "I love how he does a little shoulder roll and then drops to one knee," coos Tony. "It's so *All That Jazz.*"

George is equally agile in the film's fight scenes, the first of which takes place on the beach where a caftan-clad Diana Rigg is committing suicide and fashion hara-kiri simultaneously. "Why is Stevie Nicks walking into the ocean?" wonders Marcus.

"Lazenby's the best in the fight scenes," says Ross as George pummels one of several attackers right in the kisser. "He doesn't just punch the guy once. He has to beat the fuck out of him and drown him."

"But look at that broad, horizontal ass," laments Lauren. "Lazenby got back."

"He looks great in a tux, though," I say during the next scene where James saunters through a casino. "He's like the Aramis Bond."

"He's got the right frame," agrees Marcus. "But Connery's got the attitude. Lazenby can't deliver the wisecracks. He's taking himself way too seriously."

"I can never get past that Kirk Douglas chin and those big ears," admits Dr. Beaverman.

"And that hair is so Student Night at Vidal Sassoon," says Tony.

"In defense of Lazenby, he could be a prick, but he could also be romantic, and this movie requires that," says Ross. "Connery, you could tell, was emotionally disengaged at some level, so it's just as well that he didn't make this one."

Even though Lazenby's Bond falls in love, he refuses to let the fairer sex walk all over him. In fact, in a later scene in which Diana Rigg refuses to reveal what she knows, George smacks her across the face. "What year could you not slap a woman anymore?" I wonder.

"Probably like 1972 or '73," says Ross. "Once the bras started burning, the party was over."

"So we didn't even get a few good licks in on Anita Bryant?" I gripe. "That's a crying shame."

Worn out from all the chick smacking, Lazenby takes a moment to go through his desk, where he discovers cherished mementos from the previous Bond movies even though he wasn't in them. It's quick but poignant, though I'm sure if George looked a little harder, he would find less sentimental artifacts too, like soiled panties, prescriptions for penicillin written in Swahili, and a dog-eared copy of *Frommer's International Directory of Abortion Doctors.*

Aside from a scene at a bullfight that makes me miss Selena, things don't really heat up again until George dons a kilt for a dinner party thrown by a group of Manson-era superbabes.

"This looks like the green room at *Shindig,*" says Dr. Beaverman as Bond lounges on a sofa surrounded by a few of the leggier members of the harem. "They're pooped from doing the watusi."

> "I was supposed to see *Diamonds Are Forever* with my father. But I didn't want to go because the Shirley Jones episode of *This is Your Life* was on TV." —Marcus

Later, during dinner, one of the ladies reaches under Bond's skirt and writes something in lipstick. "It's the old lipstick up the kilt trick," says Lauren.

"I never thought I'd say it, but he looks hot in the kilt," says Marcus.

"If Roger Moore had worn a kilt, it would have been for laughs," says Ross, who's turning into the world's biggest George Lazenby fan right before our eyes. "But Lazenby really means it."

Lazenby even gets lucky in the kilt, but by this point we've seen enough. Once that kilt hits the floor, I hit the stop button and reach for a fresh note card.

"Are you guys including the kilt under evening gown?" asks Lauren.

"Totally," says Marcus, jotting down his score.

GEORGE LAZENBY

	SWIMSUIT	INTERVIEW	EVENING GOWN	TOTAL
BEAVERMAN	9.53	3.21	9.43	22.17
ROSS	9.42	9.15	9.79	28.36
MARCUS	9.72	9.67	9.78	29.17
DENNIS	9.81	7.94	9.62	27.37
LAUREN	8.76	7.19	8.92	24.87
TONY	9.38	9.73	9.68	28.79

Next up is Roger Moore in 1973's *Live and Let Die*. While I'm ejecting George and inserting Roger, Marcus takes a swig of water, sits up straight, and clears his throat, which can only mean one thing: It's St. Olaf time. "This was the first Bond movie I ever saw," he recalls. "My older brother saw it first and said I would love it. Well, I'm terrified of snakes and my brother *knew* I was terrified of snakes and he didn't bother to mention that there are tons of snakes in the movie. He totally set me up. I literally spent half the movie cowering behind my father."

"The first one I saw was *Diamonds Are Forever,*" remembers Ross. "My dad took me right after my parents divorced. It was so great, because when they were married my sister and I could only see G-rated movies, and then after they got divorced we could see PG and sometimes R. I think their thinking was like, 'We've already damaged you irreparably by splitting up, so a few boobs and dirty words ain't gonna kill you.' It's like the rules for everything changed overnight."

"That's weird because I was *supposed* to see *Diamonds Are Forever* with my father," remembers Marcus. "But I didn't want to go because the Shirley Jones episode of *This is Your Life* was on TV."

"Are you two done?" asks Tony.

"Almost," says Marcus. "David Cassidy wasn't on. He didn't show up. I thought that was weird."

"Is that it?" wonders Tony.

"For now," says Marcus.

"Good, because I just remembered a good story," says Tony. "I sang in this male strip show in Europe a couple of years ago and we did a James Bond number where one of the strippers picks a woman out of the audience and brings her up onto this giant bed and humps her. One night the guy was so high or drunk or dumb that he picked a transvestite and didn't realize it. At one point, the music segues from the James Bond theme into Sheena Easton's "For Your Eyes Only." Well, this drag queen starts lip-synching her ass off. The stripper was unzipping his pants and looking at her like, 'What the *fuck*?' She could not have been less interested in him. She felt the lights on her skin, and it was showtime! He just sort of stood there, helpless, while she put the show in her purse and went home with it. I kinda felt sorry for him."

"Dr. Beaverman is fascinated," says Dr. Beaverman.

Tony promises to regale her with all the male stripper stories she can stomach on a day when we don't have five movies to get through. "I have pictures too," he teases.

We start the movie and after a phoned-in iris pose from Moore, we get to watch our super spy unzip his latest sex slave's dress with one of Q's magnetic gadgets while commenting on her "sheer magnetism." As droll line readings go, it's about the best we've heard all day.

"If you like your Bond funny, then Moore's your man," says Ross.

"Yeah, but I have to say, I don't like a sandy-blond Bond," I admit.

"Moore himself admitted that he was a pussy," says Ross. "I saw this interview where he said that the directors used to get mad at him whenever he had to shoot a gun because he would blink right before he did it."

"That's probably why I connect to him," says Marcus. "I blink at the thought of shooting a gun. I also love the fact that Moore can go an entire movie without breaking a sweat."

"I bet he's like that in bed too," asserts Dr. Beaverman. "Where the big-boned Connery could really deliver in the orgasm department, Roger's more likely to sit back and let Jane Seymour do all the work."

Ms. Seymour, who plays the beautiful tarot reader Solitaire, will have to wait, though, as Bond is currently preoccupied with a conniving soul sister with an Angela Bassett hard body named Rosie Carver, who works the counter at a charming Afrocentric New Orleans voodoo boutique. "Welcome to Bed, Bath, and Beyoncé," says Tony.

"The woman who plays Rosie Carver, Gloria Hendry, was a secretary at my first law firm in L.A. like 10 years ago," boasts Marcus. "She never mentioned being an actress, and then one day I saw this again on TV and I was like, 'Was that you, Glo?' And she was like, 'Oh, yeah,' just like totally blasé about it."

"Did she have lots of Bond-like gadgets on her desk?" I ask.

"None that you could see," says Marcus. "But I liked to imagine that her pencil sharpener shot poisoned darts. I would always be careful where I stood when I visited her cubicle."

Marcus's former office mate is but one of a cavalcade of '70s African-American actors who turn up in *Live and Let Die*. "This movie came out at the height of blaxploitation," explains Ross. "I think it's the only Bond film with the lines 'Right on, brother' and 'Take this honky out and waste him,' although I'm hopeful for the next Brosnan flick."

"This was like mid '70s, right?" I ask.

Ross nods.

"I wonder if everyone was talking about their *Roots* audition between takes," I say.

"Or the *Good Times* pilot," says Tony.

"Oh, that reminds me," says Marcus. "Guess who I saw at Ikea the other day?"

"Jimmie 'J.J.' Walker," I say, going for the obvious.

"No, but you're close," says Marcus. "This guy also starred on a sitcom in the 1970s."

"John Ritter," guesses Tony.

"John Ritter's not black," says Lauren.

"How do we know the guy's black?" asks Tony.

"Because *Good Times* is what reminded him about it," argues Lauren.

"That means nothing," scoffs Tony. "You've seen how his mind works with the St. Olaf stories. He could have easily made the mental leap from *Good Times* to the show he switched to when *Good Times* got canceled, which, more than likely, had tons of non-black actors like Anson Williams, for example. Is it Anson Williams, Marcus?"

"It's Gary Coleman," answers Marcus.

"I told you he was black," says Lauren, before dodging the first of several speeding note cards.

"*Anyway,*" Marcus bellows, "Gary Coleman was at Ikea. He was dressed in full fatigues and going up to entertainment centers and shaking them to see if they would topple in an earthquake. I kept looking around for his parents to come and chastise him, but then I realized he's like 50."

Marcus's surreal star sighting properly acknowledged, we turn our attention back to the movie just in time to see Moore encounter Jane Seymour, whom he discovers playing with her cards behind a secret revolving wall. "I love walls and bookshelves that turn around," I say.

"Of course you do," says Tony, "because it's like a game show. It's like, 'He's a spy who loves martinis and pussy! Please give a big *Match Game* welcome to...Roger Moore!'"

Proving, irrefutably, that he's the Calgon, Take Me Away Bond, Moore concludes his long day of spying by drawing himself a hot bath. His beauty soak is interrupted, however, by yet a pesky snake. Moore wards the slithering critter off with hair spray—I suspect it was the Dry Look, though I didn't get a good peek at the label—then tells Rosie Carver, when she turns up later, "You should never go in there without a mongoose."

"He's very supercilious," pronounces Lauren.

I don't know what that word means at all, and I say so.

"It means haughty, disdainful, arrogant," says Dr. Beaverman.

"She said superciliously," says Ross.

"Thank you," I say. "One of the things that I like about myself is that if I don't know what something means, I just say it right out loud."

Once Bassett-body buys it, Bond surprises Jane Seymour by taking over her bejeweled card-reading chair while she's out of the room. "Connery would never have gotten in that gay chair," says Ross. "I mean, that fucker looks like it's on loan from the Liberace Museum."

Then Moore seduces the psychic by tricking her into choosing a card from a deck he's switched with hers, one made up entirely of lover cards. "Don't you wish it was that easy to get someone to sleep with you," muses Tony, "by just having them pick the right card?"

"Essentially it is," says Lauren. "It just has to say ICM on it."

With that, Moore seals the deal, finally giving Solitaire something to fiddle with besides her cards, namely his so-so torso. The next morning finds the couple basking in the afterglow. "They obviously didn't have a very good time," says Dr. Beaverman. "They're two feet apart in bed."

"It's the wet spot," says Tony.

Soon, in one of the film's major set pieces, the couple get chased through the Caribbean boondocks in a double decker bus driven by an African-American actor whose intensity here may be informed by the fact that he just lost the lead in *Roots*. "What do you mean they went with LeVar Burton?" barks Tony as the bus driver. "Goddamn it, Benny. You're fired. I'm going to steal that ICM card from Jane Seymour."

When a low bridge appears in the distance, I can't help but do a little armchair looping for Roger. "Jane, can you go upstairs and get my jacket?" I say.

"Then she really would have been like Jane Seymour," says Lauren.

Tony gets a quizzical look on his face, but I'm the one who says, "Huh?"

"Jane Seymour was Henry the VIII's wife who got beheaded," Lauren explains. "Jane Seymour is not Dr. Quinn's real name. When she decided to go from ballet to acting, she picked the name Jane Seymour because she felt sorry for the *real* Jane Seymour, who was labeled a witch and beheaded."

"And Pink was taken," says Marcus.

"Glad you explained that, Lauren," says Tony. "Unlike Dennis, when I don't understand something, I just pretend I do."

We stick with Roger and Jane long enough to get our couple back to New Orleans. As they stride out of the airport, Marcus says, "Wow, that's a gay shirt," in regard to Roger's tight shiny black short-sleeved button-down.

"Oh, my God, I'm wearing that shirt right now," Tony points out just before I stop the tape. "That shirt is so gay, I'm wearing it. But don't worry, that won't affect my scoring."

ROGER MOORE

	SWIMSUIT	INTERVIEW	EVENING GOWN	TOTAL
BEAVERMAN	6.54	9.01	9.98	25.53
ROSS	7.16	8.15	8.27	23.58
MARCUS	8.97	9.03	9.24	27.24
DENNIS	8.42	9.25	9.62	27.29
LAUREN	8.31	9.78	9.45	27.54
TONY	6.54	2.10	3.84	12.48

Timothy Dalton, whose résumé includes a shitload of Shakespeare as well as the Brooke Shields cult fave *Brenda Starr,* is up next with 1987's *The Living Daylights.* Despite a lame opening theme by A-Ha that makes me long for the soothing tones of Shirley Bassey, Dalton starts things off with some pretty impressive stunts set on the exotic island of Gibraltar.

"I've been to Gibraltar," I boast. "They have these monkeys running around that you can hang out with and have your picture taken with."

"It's like an O-Town meet and greet," says Ross.

"Do not disparage O-Town in this house," cautions Tony. "I won't have it."

Back on the screen, Dalton tries to prove who wears the pants in this franchise by riding on the roof of a careening Jeep, head-butting the driver, then parachuting onto the yacht of a hot-to-trot no-name babe. "They wanted a more physical Bond after Moore," reasons Ross. "Moore could hardly unzip his tux pants without having to break for a martini."

Unfortunately, it doesn't take long to see the effect of late-'80s political correctness on the Bond franchise. Where the other 007s treated their spying duties as something to do between lays, Dalton's Bond is a spy first, a lover second. Tim's 007 doesn't even sexually harass Moneypenny. Where Lazenby might have smacked his woman around a bit, Dalton takes her to a carnival and wins her a freaking stuffed animal. In short, he's just not a hell of a lot of fun.

"He tries to be ironic," says Ross, charitably, "but it's just not in him."

"He lacks a light touch," agrees Dr. Beaverman. "That kind of seriousness usually means one thing: premature ejaculator."

"He always looks like he's slumming," I say, "like he'd rather be doing Heathcliff in *Wuthering Heights* opposite one of the Richardson sisters."

"Timothy played Bond like he was having a career crisis," agrees Ross, "like, 'I hate this fucking job.'"

"As opposed to Roger Moore," says Lauren, "who always looked like he was thinking about getting a manicure-pedicure."

There are a few laughs to be had in Dalton's getting-to-know-the-gadgets scene with Q, however, if only because the beleaguered inventor's getting a bit long in the tooth. "Can you believe he turns up in *The World Is Not Enough* eight years later?" remarks Ross.

"His next invention's going to be a bedpan that converts into a helicopter," remarks Tony as Q demonstrates a key ring that emits a deadly gas when its user whistles "Rule Britannia."

"I don't want to know what that thing does to 'Gypsies, Tramps, and Thieves,' " says Dr. Beaverman.

"You guys know Q's dead, right?" says Ross. "He died last year and it wasn't even of old age. He died in a car crash. He was driving. How do you like them apples?"

"It's a verse Alanis Morissette forgot to write," says Marcus, sadly.

Bond's girl in *The Living Daylights* is Miriam D'Abo, a former model with a wedge haircut, as mysterious cellist Kara Milovy, a name that doesn't make anyone think of pussy. "Roger Moore would never carry some chick's cello," scoffs Ross as the chivalrous Dalton totes her enormous instrument down the street.

"He'd be blowing on his nails, going, 'Carry your own damn cello, I don't want to fuck up my topcoat,' " adds Tony.

Of course, the cello comes in handy when the lovers, on the run from the baddies, are able to use the instrument's case as a makeshift luge. "Good thing she didn't play the triangle," says Marcus as the couple coasts down the mountain to safety.

Having seen all we need to of the earnest-to-a-fault Dalton and the doe-eyed D'Abo, we stop the movie and write down our scores.

TIMOTHY DALTON

	SWIMSUIT	INTERVIEW	EVENING WEAR	TOTAL
BEAVERMAN	8.42	6.57	8.82	23.81
ROSS	7.85	7.15	9.14	24.14
MARCUS	9.01	9.31	9.43	27.75
DENNIS	9.53	8.62	9.27	27.42
LAUREN	9.67	8.26	9.27	27.20
TONY	3.88	7.39	5.91	17.18

Which brings us, finally, to our current Bond, Pierce Brosnan, and *The World Is Not Enough*. I've chosen this film, Brosnan's third outing, for three simple reasons: Denise Richards and her breasts. I've been a Denise Richards booster since *Starship Troopers,* in which she piloted a spaceship while driving Patrick Muldoon wild with desire. I'm not saying she's good or bad. What I *am* saying is, I can't get enough of her.

"Anyone need a seventh-inning snack?" asks Marcus, emerging from the kitchen with a large cube of tin foil. "These are blond brownies," he says, before unveiling them. "When I was at the store, something about the packaging caught my eye and I did a little Denise Richards eyebrow arch, right there in the dessert aisle. It seemed like a sign."

"Mmm, do I taste chocolate?" asks Dr. Beaverman, enjoying her first bite.

"There's a layer of chocolate on the bottom," says Marcus. "You can't make Denise Richards Blondies without brown roots."

As I start the movie, Ross informs us that *The World Is Not Enough* is not, in fact, the title of an Ian Fleming novel. "They used up all the Fleming titles a while back," he explains. "*Goldeneye* was actually the name of Fleming's estate in Jamaica, and *The World Is Not Enough* is mentioned briefly in *On Her Majesty's Secret Service* as the motto of the Bond family."

"I think the next movie should be called *Beating the Living Daylights Out of a Dead Horse Again,*" says Dr. Beaverman.

Pierce makes his first appearance with the traditional opening iris shot, but we're unimpressed with his technique. "I think that would be hard to do, because how can you make it yours?" says Tony, rising to Pierce's defense.

"But you take the job knowing that's part of it," says Lauren. "It's not like they sprung it on him at the last minute. He's had 35 years to bring Debbie Allen in to give him a little shoulder flourish or something."

After an action-packed opening in which Pierce repels from a skyscraper using just a miniblind chord, our hero finds himself in an extended speedboat chase on the Thames with a purple jumpsuit–wearing woman who looks like Catherine Zeta-Jones.

"That's right around the place where the Spice Girls fell into the Thames in *Spice World,*" says Marcus, pointing to the screen.

"Explains the color of that water," mutters Dr. Beaverman.

After eliminating the C.Z. Jones clone, Pierce gets busy with his doctor, played by Serena Scott Thomas. "I'd like to know what HMO he's got," carps Tony, "because I can't get my doctor to spend 20 minutes with me, let alone get me off."

Soon, Dame Judi Dench arrives on the scene as Bond's pixie-haired boss, M. "She's going to hold on to that haircut until we all just cry uncle," says Tony. "She looks like Anne Heche's grandmother."

"Celestia the first," says Dr. Beaverman.

"Does anyone want to hear my Judi Dench fantasy?" I ask. I take my cohorts' unanimous silence as a yes and venture forth. "My Judi Dench fantasy is that she does popcorn movies like this one because she needs furniture and she spends her two months on the set shoplifting everything she can."

"And it's not discussed," injects Tony gleefully. "You know the first AD's going up to the director like, 'Excuse me, sir, but Miss Dench seems to have pocketed the...' and the director's like, 'MHHHHnnnnnBBbb,' just plugging his ears and singing 'Mary Had a Little Lamb.'"

When Lauren jumps into the game, I realize that I'm going to have to ask Matt if Judi can have her own typeface. Is there a such a font as Dame Chancery?

"I got paid only 14 pounds for Mrs. Brown," complains Lauren as Judi. *"I'm taking that divan with me when I leave today and you can all just kiss my ass."*

As amusing as this Dame Sticky Fingers business is, Dame Judi is *not* Denise Richards, so we zoom ahead in search of Neecy. We're sidetracked briefly by a scene in which Pierce and Sophie Marceau, as the duplicitous daughter of an oil tycoon, go skiing together. Their dream date is soon thwarted when a flock of skiing baddies in parachutes descend from the sky and begin chasing after them. Midway through the pursuit, Pierce slides on a pair of mod sunglasses that you just know MGM merchandised the fuck out of, right along with that silver Beemer.

"Judi Dench has about a hundred pairs of those at home," I say. "They were her stocking stuffers that year."

"Along with a large assortment of *Chocolat,*" adds Ross.

When an avalanche hits, Pierce thinks fast and inflates a giant inhabitable ball that Q bestowed on him earlier. He and Sophie jump inside and weather the downfall. The bad guys aren't so lucky. "Connery would never have let her in the bubble with him," scoffs Tony as Sophie, a.k.a. French Slut Barbie, yammers on hysterically. "He'd keep the bubble for himself then fuck her dead frozen body."

Instead, Pierce gives it to her live hot body at Sophie's beautifully appointed chateau.

"Best chest wig so far," proclaims Dr. Beaverman, who I feared had nodded off back at Dalton. "Right up there with Jon Bon Jovi."

"Pierce is a little too cuddly and vulnerable for my taste," I say. "He looks like he's thinking, *Gosh, I hope Sophie likes me.*"

"My Judi Dench fantasy is that she does popcorn movies like this one because she needs furniture and she spends her two months on the set shoplifting everything she can." —Dennis

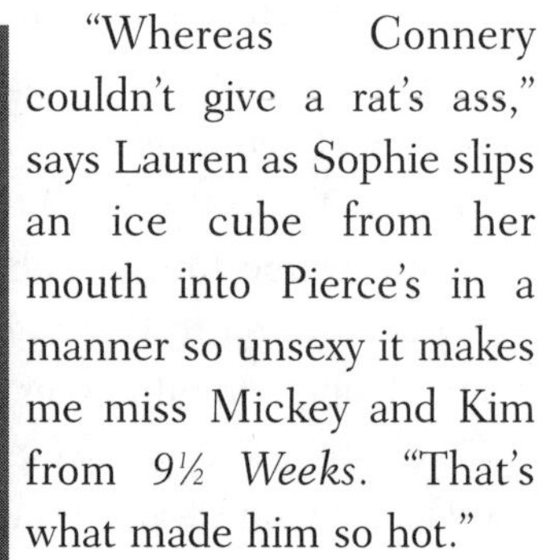

"Whereas Connery couldn't give a rat's ass," says Lauren as Sophie slips an ice cube from her mouth into Pierce's in a manner so unsexy it makes me miss Mickey and Kim from *9½ Weeks*. "That's what made him so hot."

"I want Judi Dench to come in and take that candelabra from the back of the shot," says Tony. *"Don't mind me, love. I have company coming for the weekend."*

"Excuse me, Sophie, I'm going to need your robe, please," says Lauren. *"I know you're in the middle of a scene, but my car is here."*

"I drew Emma Thompson for my Secret Santa this year," I say, *"and she would adore those earrings."*

"Does anyone know who I'd talk to about a guest spot on Friends?" asks Ross. *"I'm in the market for a foosball table."*

Unable to control my jones for Denise Richards any longer, I grab the remote and zoom to the scene where she makes her first appearance, as nuclear physicist–sex bomb Christmas Jones.

"It's beginning to look a lot like Christmas," I announce.

By this point, I've waited over four hours for some words from Denise, and her first line doesn't disappoint. "I pulled the plutonium out of the one inside," she tells her scientist colleagues. "You can detonate the triggers now."

"She's literally talking about plutonium," marvels Tony.

"I bet there's all kind of outtakes with her saying 'nucular,'" says Marcus.

"Nothing says, 'Take me seriously as a scientist' like coochie cutters and a crop top," says Tony as Denise strips down to coochie cutters and a crop top.

"I could watch her all day long," I gush.

"Denise Richards is great when she's in on the joke, like *Wild Things,*" assesses Ross. "The problem is when they try to make her the ingenue when they need to make her the slutty bitch. She's the Gen-X Morgan Fairchild."

Soon, Denise introduces herself to Pierce with a stern, "I'm Dr. Jones, Christmas Jones, and don't make any jokes because I've heard them all."

"Besides, I don't get them," adds Dr. Beaverman.

Then Pierce and Denise outrun more baddies in a plutonium mine skirmish, after which Pierce learns that his beloved Sophie has been kidnapped. He joins Judi in a subsequent scene where they watch Sophie plead for help on a TV monitor.

"Sophie, love," says Tony, his Judi getting snootier by the quip. *"Could you ask the kidnappers to go wide. I'd love to see a larger shot of that chair you're sitting in."*

"Bollocks, it's got cream cushions!" fumes Lauren. *"I'm looking for olive."*

"Where's Christmas?" I shout, unable to endure one more second of this marathon without Denise.

"It's in our hearts," Marcus reminds me.

After zooming through a scene in which Denise wears a supersnug purple dress—"She looks like a slut sausage," decides Dr. Beaverman—we make it to the climax of the film, where Pierce outfoxes some of those giant-pizza-cutter-rotating-vertical-blade-like things that only exist in movies like this one. "These Bond movies are like one big David Copperfield special," mutters Tony.

"Pierce doesn't look like he's having much fun," says Ross, as Pierce dodges the blades. "With Connery, you always get the feeling that he *wants* it to be a close call. He gets off on cheating death."

Our Who's the Better Bond Film Festival limps to a close when Pierce, basking in the afterglow with a dewy Denise, deadpans, "I was wrong about you. I thought Christmas only comes once a year."

"That's just gross," says Tony, before uncapping his marker and jotting down his scores.

PIERCE BROSNAN				
	SWIMSUIT	INTERVIEW	EVENING GOWN	TOTAL
BEAVERMAN	5.32	9.54	8.65	23.51
ROSS	7.35	8.27	8.85	24.47
MARCUS	9.52	9.58	9.81	28.91
DENNIS	9.66	9.25	9.70	28.61
LAUREN	8.94	9.63	8.46	27.03
TONY	9.18	9.77	9.81	28.76

While Tony and I feverishly tally the final scores, Dr. Beaverman and Marcus start clearing away the used plates and glasses. "James Bond is a straight white man's fantasy," says Dr. B. "There's nothing in these movies to capture the attention of a girl. He's just talking too much man talk. He's not pulling his pants down or anything."

"James Bond is completely offensive," agrees Lauren. "But his overriding charm is that even within the sexism, he loves women, which is different from a Bruce Willis or Jean Claude Van Damme movie where the women are still ornaments but there's no love."

"I like Bond because he's self-created," says Marcus. "Maybe it's a gay thing, but I like people who just say, you know, 'Screw it, I'm going to be extraordinary if it kills me.' "

"It's the lack of a sense of danger that appeals to me," says Ross. "There's no sense of jeopardy with anything he does. He's like Cary Grant with a mean streak and he gets everything he wants. It's a teenage boy thing."

"I think mine is a teenage boy thing too," adds Marcus.

Once we finish compiling the scores, I stand in front of the TV, the five Bond videos propped atop the entertainment center, awaiting their fate. If they weren't inanimate plastic boxes, they would surely be holding hands right now. "The fourth runner-up," I announce, "is Roger Moore, with an average composite score of 23.94!"

Tony picks up the Moore box like a hand puppet and waddles him sadly to the back of the entertainment center.

"The third runner-up," I continue, "is Timothy Dalton, with a total average score of 24.58!"

Tony bops Tim offstage, then moves Brosnan in closer to Lazenby and Connery.

"The second runner up," I say, "is George Lazenby, with an average score of 26.78."

As Ross applauds wildly, Tony walks George off, then moves Pierce and Sean, who are, by now, both vibrating with nervous energy, center stage.

"Now, the first runner-up is a very important position," I remind everyone, "because if the Best Bond can't fulfill his duties because he's just too old or because he gets arrested for statutory rape in Singapore, the first runner-up will assume the mantle of Best Bond."

"We get it, we get it," says Dr. Beaverman testily.

"The first runner-up, with an average score of 26.88 is Pierce Brosnan!" I proclaim. "The Best Bond is Sean Connery, with a whopping score of 28.58!"

As the rest of us applaud, Tony wraps up his makeshift Muppet Show by giving Sean a short victory stroll which culminates with the other four video boxes doing a dog pile on our winner.

"So the upshot of all this is, if we can't have Connery, we could do a lot worse than Brosnan," I surmise.

"Amen," says Lauren.

Having had their fill of teenage boys and their things for the next century, the ladies head home, leaving the four of us guys spent but also insanely hungry for some main courses after a full day of desserts. I suggest we hit City Wok, the Chinese place next to the Rite Aid where our photos from earlier are being developed.

While Marcus and Ross grab a table, Tony and I run over and pick up the pictures, vowing not to view them until we get back to the Wok. When we do, Ross snatches the envelope out of my hand and begins looking through the shots. "I've got to lay off the Krispy Kremes," he groans, before passing the photos one at a time to Marcus. Of course, in my fantasy world, this scene is unfolding at Annie Leibovitz's superminimalist loft–studio and J. Lo was on her way out when we were on our way in. "I've said it before and I'll say it again," says Ross. "Beaverman's got nice legs."

"When did you say it before?" says Tony.

"OK, maybe I didn't say it before, but I thought it," says Ross.

"I should have gotten a haircut," frets Marcus. "I didn't want it to look like I just got a haircut, but now, looking at them, I would rather look like I just got a haircut than all poufy."

"You don't look poufy," Tony assures him.

"Maybe we can fix it in post," offers Ross.

As the first of the pictures make it to me, I smile with relief that they're usable and, truth be told, pretty good. The light is even, the shots are well-framed, and the store window in the background more than delivers in the local color department. Thank you, Perry.

"I think they gave us someone else's pictures," says Ross, holding up one of the shots for Marcus to see.

As Marcus glances over, a look of resigned discomfort passes over his face. "No, they didn't," he says, sighing.

"What?" I ask.

"There's three of them," continues Ross, handing two other photos to Marcus.

Marcus reluctantly hands me the first picture. There, in a shot that's just a hair out of focus, is Stephen Pool, the event planner I went out with for a few months earlier this year. In the photo, he's holding the camera away from himself with one hand and pointing at his left eye with the other. The blue striped shirt he's wearing is the same one he had on the night I decided our relationship was done and put a fork in it. I was running late when he came to pick me up to go to a play. He must have taken it when I was in the shower.

I slide my soda back and set the picture on the table in front of me.

"Oh, shit," says Tony.

Ross places the other two pictures—one of Stephen pointing at the camera, one of him touching his heart—next to the "eye" picture, considers them for a moment, then switches the order of the second and third picture. "I love you," he says.

This clearly confuses the busboy, but none of us care. I scoop the three pictures up like playing cards and put them back in the envelope. Then, over dinner, I try to get Ross up to speed on the Saga of Stephen Pool as quickly and succinctly as possible so as not to drive Marcus and Tony to madness. They were there for the real deal, after all: talking it out with me ad nauseum and getting their shoulders soaked when I'd start crying in places like Jerry's Deli and the food court at the Burbank mall.

"If you did the dumping, why was it so upsetting?" asks Ross.

It's a perfectly valid question.

"Guilt?" he suggests.

"Some, but not really," I say. "I don't know."

"I know," says Marcus after a moment or two. "Can I say?"

"Please," I say.

"Because someone finally was into you the way you wanted someone to be into you for all the reasons you wanted them to be into you and you weren't into it," he says.

I just nod. Indeed, Mr. Pool stepped up to the plate in a way that no one has before or since and I said, "No, thank you," and did a tap dance on his heart on my way out the door. I just didn't love him and I told him so. And it was agony for everyone involved.

"Why weren't you into him?" asks Ross.

"It was just instinctual at the time," I say. "I just knew it wasn't right. But looking back, I see that there are legitimate reasons, like he resented my friends for starters."

"Unacceptable," says Ross, who I'm pleased to say is now one of them.

•

Though I'm not going to have them framed any time soon, I opt not to throw away Stephen's three-panel mash note from the past. Instead, I tuck the pictures in a box with other stuff I want to save but don't want to look at every day, like prom photos and tax returns.

You'd think that after a full day of ski chases, gadget lessons, and heterosexual sex, I'd nod right off, but I can't fall asleep. I pad out into the front room, pop in *Goldfinger,* and pick up where we left off earlier. The teenage boy in me finds himself quite entertained, and I stay up until 6:30 in the morning watching back-to-back Bond. (Ross tossed two of his other Connery favorites, *Thunderball* and *You Only Live Twice,* into my bag before we left Video Master earlier today.)

What intrigues me most about the Bond films in my post-Stephen state of mind is that Bond ends each movie in a romantic clinch with that movie's hottest babe, and she is invariably gone and forgotten by the next movie. Are their partings ever ugly, or painful? Does Bond give them the Talk or does he just stop calling? Does Jane Seymour ever blubber into her soup at Jerry's Deli? Does Denise Richards ever egg 007's Beemer as a way to deal with her shattered heart? Does Miriam D'Abo use Bond's secret Q-issued spy cam to take "I love you" pictures of herself while curled naked around her cello? Or is it just a zipless fuck for her too? And then I wonder, Does James Bond ever feel lonely?

I wonder about these things, but I don't want the answers.

They don't call it escapism for nothing.

NUNNIER BUSINESS

The first movie I remember seeing in a theater was Robert Wise's 1965 Best Picture Oscar–winner, *The Sound of Music*. I was 6 or 7 and my mother took me to see it in Snowflake, Ariz., a one-stoplight town 30 miles away from Holbrook, Ariz., the one-stoplight town I grew up in. I think the theater I saw it in used to be a church, though I could be mistaken. Maybe it just *felt* like a church because I was having a glued-to-my-seat, eyes-big-as-saucers religious experience. For the first time, I wanted to pack my bags and move into a movie.

Though I had no significant beefs with my family, we didn't exactly do production numbers on the steps of City Hall. And that—if the Von Trapps were any indication—was clearly the way to live. High-tech marionette shows, rainy night sleepovers, narrow escapes from oppressive political parties—that was the life for me. Why couldn't I be a Von Trapp? My family wouldn't miss me that much and if they did, maybe I could just be a Von Trapp for the summers. That's when all the fun stuff went down anyway. Besides, the V.T. Family Singers could use another strong voice to drown out Brigitta. Not to be catty, but that girl's got worse pitch problems than Faith Hill on Oscar night.

And I was a natural blond at the time too. What's more, I loved to sing and dance, though I never did much of either publicly as it wasn't particularly encouraged in my corner of the world. Some of us didn't have a mother like Lynne Spears, dragging us to jazz class while we were still in diapers and buying us *You Sing the Hits of Whitney Houston* karaoke tapes so we could develop our stage presence at the annual Kentwood Peach Festival. Some of us had to do the groundwork for our future career as showbiz triple threats on our own, in our imaginations.

Still, I desperately wanted it, and that, I've come to believe, counts more than anything. Character is more important than talent, as my high school choir teacher used to say. Maybe I wasn't as photogenic as Friedrich or as precocious as Kurt, but I could kiss governess ass with the best of them. I'd wear my curtain-made play clothes with pride, never uttering a peep about how itchy they were. I'd do my choreography full-out every time, no marking like that half-assed tagalong Marta. And I wouldn't give Julie Andrews any lip.

Today, at our 35th Anniversary Screening Party, I doubt I'll be so well behaved.

We're having this month's soiree two weeks earlier than usual because Tony's leaving town for a month. He's been summoned overseas to serve his country as the lead singer in *Man-O-Man*, an all-male Chippendales-style review that tours Germany, England, and Switzerland. He's shaken his moneymaker for the company before, a few years ago, but swore he'd hung up his sequined hot shorts for good at the end of his last tour. His plan as of last year was to leave the showbiz gypsy life behind, stay in L.A., and get a real job. However, the closest he's come to that so far was his two-month stint at the AIDS Walk, which, fulfilling as it was, ended a week after the event. So when Man-O-Man Inc. came a-callin', offering him double his usual money to replace a singer who overdosed on God knows what in Amsterdam, Tony couldn't say no.

The timing of Tony's Tour of Doody—his term, not mine—has coincided rather unfortunately with Marcus having to undergo an emergency tonsillectomy. A week ago we went to see Garbage in concert, screamed our guts out, and then stayed out dancing till the crack of ass. When Marcus awoke the following afternoon, his tonsils were the size of punching bags. After three days, they still hadn't returned to normal, so his doctor told him they'd have to come out—and that the ordeal, from surgery to recovery, would take roughly two weeks. So Marcus scheduled the procedure for the next day, exactly two weeks from his 38th birthday, hoping he'd be chipper enough to celebrate when the big day rolled around.

The operation was four days ago, and according to Marcus's E-mails, his throat still smarts so badly he can hardly groan, let alone come over and chatter through a three-hour movie. When I E-mailed Matt in London to tell him we'd have to do without either Tony or Marcus for this month's installment, his replay consisted of just four words: "Keep the evil queen." I didn't say anything about Matt's directive to Tony or Marcus, and I don't plan to.

So we're having the *Sound of Music* Screening Party today, before Tony flies out tomorrow. When Ross, Lauren, and Dr. Beaverman arrive, I explain to them why Marcus won't be joining us. "According to his last E-mail," I say, calling from the kitchen where I'm fetching drinks, "he's been so hopped up on painkillers that he spends all his time either passed out or ordering shit off QVC."

"Can we call him?" asks Dr. Beaverman.

"Let's wait till after the movie," I suggest. "Then we can tell him how much he was missed."

"Speaking of Marcus," says Ross. "I don't suppose anyone thought to bake us a tasty treat."

"I have a yeast infection. Does that count?" asks Lauren.

"I bought cookie dough," I announce.

"I'm just kidding, I don't have a yeast infection," clarifies Lauren. "I have to be smart-alecky now because I'm going to be useless during the movie. *The Sound of Music* meant everything to me when I was a kid."

"Same here," I say excitedly, then recall for my guests my childhood fantasy of being a Von Trapp child. "I'd be to them what Cousin Oliver was to the Bradys," I add while delivering Dr. Beaverman a Coke with enough room to add a little something else should she choose to, "a supernaturally gifted long-lost relative brought in to boost ratings and be adorable."

"My reaction to the movie was different from yours," says Lauren. "I didn't want to be a Von Trapp because my family was already sort of like that."

"Rub it in my face," I whine.

"Or as much like that as you can be in Westbury, Long Island," she adds. "My mother had been a dancer when she was younger and was still kind of bohemian and artsy, so we never fit in that whole suburban what-will-the-neighbors-think world. And this movie was the first time I saw people like us, who actually expressed themselves and did creative things, and it was so reassuring, like, 'OK, you're not a freak.' I mean, I thought people *should* skip down the streets of Düsseldorf or wherever and dance around fountains and put on puppet shows. That's the way life should be."

"That's totally the way life should be," agrees Ross.

"Oh, shit, are you a fan too, Ross?" Tony groans.

"It's number 4 on my all-time top 10," he says with a shrug. "The entire five hours or however long it is are so nostalgic and comforting to me, I don't even think I can look at it ironically."

"Did you go to the sing-along version they had at the Hollywood Bowl?" Lauren asks him. "I was so mad I missed it."

"Fuck no," says Ross. "The last place I want to be to watch that movie is in an amphitheater with 3,000 queens dressed up as nuns and shouting shit at the screen." He shoots a sidelong glance at Tony. "No offense."

"None taken," says Tony. "That's about the last place I'd want to be, too."

"My ideal setting for watching *The Sound of Music* is Christmastime, with a mug of cocoa, under a big quilt that my mom made," says Ross. "Maybe it was because I just had one sister and I've always wanted a big family like the Von Trapps."

"I was in a big family, and let me tell you, we didn't sing," says Dr. Beaverman.

"*The Sound of Music,* to me, is this perfect family," declares Ross, "where every moment is a moment for singing. I know it's corny, coming from a guy who pulled a total Travis Bickle right here in this room, but it's true. I feel the same way about *White Christmas,* which is my number 9."

During Ross's *Sound of Music* mash note, I watch Dr. Beaverman and Tony survey the faces around the room, searching for looks of dissent. Finally, they settle on each other. "It's you and me against the world," says Dr. Beaverman with such steely determination that I don't think she even realizes she's just quoted Helen Reddy.

"I'd say it's a pretty even match," says Tony cockily.

"Oh, that reminds me," I say, standing in front of the TV and facing my guests.

"Before we start the movie, I have a little dramatic reading to perform. Matt in London forwarded this to me yesterday. I think you'll find it pretty interesting."

Just as I pull the printout from my pocket, there's a knock at the door. I open it to discover Marcus. At least, I *think* it's Marcus. Our visitor's face is blocked by a notebook-size dry-erase board with a picture of George Michael from the "Faith" era in one corner. On it, in purple marker, someone's written, "Can't talk. Had to get out of house."

Marcus lowers the George board and smiles dizzily. "Are you OK?" I ask. "Did you drive here? Are you on painkillers?"

Marcus smacks his forehead with the dry-erase board, as if to monitor how the painkillers are doing, then nods affirmatively. Once inside, he takes his usual place on the floor, with his George board on his lap and his markers, eraser, and Big Gulp within arm's reach. Once he's gotten situated, I explain that I was about to perform a dramatic reading when he arrived, then clear my throat and begin:

Dear British Premiere,

As a longtime fan of Martin Scorsese, I devour any articles on his masterful work that I can find. I love to read about my favorite artist, and even when the writer disagrees with me, I usually find something of value to take away. Dennis Hensley's piece on Taxi Driver, *however, turned my stomach. I don't know who this pratt and his cadre of wankers think they are but I can't believe a major magazine has given them a forum in which to spew their venom. Particularly distressing were the petty criticisms leveled at the wonderful Cybill Shepherd, who, in addition to being one of the most beautiful women of our time, has undeniable acting talent and the awards to prove it.*

Hensley likes to position himself a champion of movies and those that make them, but his shallow, potty-mouthed commentaries do nothing but degrade everyone involved. What's more, they're not nearly as funny as he seems to think they are. In fact, they're not funny at all. Hensley is obviously a man who is so unsatisfied with his own achievements that he has to put down the contributions of others.

I, for one, have had more than my fill of it. As of today, I'm canceling my subscription. I'd rather receive a turd in my mailbox than another issue of British Premiere.

Ungratefully Yours,
Rutherford Shelton III
Leicester, England

Dr. Beaverman is the first to speak. "We've arrived," she says, smiling blissfully.

"Oh, man, I've got goose bumps," says Ross.

"Are you going to frame it?" asks Lauren. "You should."

"Framing an E-mail isn't as cool as framing a real letter," argues Ross. "It's too virtual."

"Cybill Shepherd's a sacred cow," ponders Dr. Beaverman. "Who knew?"

"I didn't know about the sacred part," says Tony, before yanking the printout out of my hand and having a closer look. "I love that he thinks she's 'of our time.' That's my favorite part."

"What did he call us, a 'cadre of wankers'?" asks Ross. "Don't you have to have a witch to be considered a cadre?"

"Present," says Tony.

"Any thoughts, Marcus?" I ask.

My tender-throated friend turns his board around to reveal a charmingly adolescent picture of a cow with a halo over its head. He's operating on a 20-second delay, apparently. "Very pretty, Marcus," says Dr. Beaverman dotingly. "You get a gold star for today."

"How do you feel about it, Dennis?" Lauren asks.

"I feel sort of guilty about it, but I'm trying not to," I admit. "I mean, we clearly ruined this guy's day."

"And yet, he *made* ours," declares Tony. "That's what's so beautiful about it." With that, Tony leaps up, grabs the *Sound of Music* video box from the coffee table, and hoists it over his head like it's the World Cup. "I say we go for a whole bag of hate mail today!" he proclaims. "Who's with me? C'mon, you cadre of wankers, it's time to separate the men from the boys!"

Dr. Beaverman is the only one who makes a sound, a short but passionate high-pitched whoop. Marcus is, as we've established, mute, and Lauren and Ross are Von Trapp groupies from way back. As for me, I'm too distracted by the video box itself to focus on Tony's rallying efforts. "Does anyone else think the *Sound of Music* typeface is a lot more swinging than the subject matter would indicate?" I ask, before taking the movie from Tony. "It's like *Sound of Music: The Nun Who Shagged Me* or something."

I slide the tape into the VCR and I'm about to press play when I realize I'm forgetting an important portion of our monthly ritual. "Marcus," I say, "do you have a St. Olaf story for this movie?"

He shakes his head no and writes, "Never seen it."

"Excuse me?" says Lauren. "You've got *Pretty Woman* memorized, but you've never seen *The Sound of Music*?"

"He likes sex workers better than nuns," says Tony. "Is that so hard to understand?"

"You're going to love it," promises Ross.

"You're going to hate it," warns Tony.

"Love it," says Lauren.

"Hate it," repeats Tony.

Marcus's head goes back and forth like he's watching a tennis match, finally settling on Dr. Beaverman. "Join us, Marcus," she beckons ominously. "Come to the dark side."

"Tell you what, Marcus," I suggest. "In order to properly gauge your enjoyment of the film, I suggest you wag your eraser every time you're moved or delighted."

"And if you're bored," says Tony, "feel free to draw more crazy facial hair on George Michael."

"Or give him handcuffs," adds Lauren.

With that, I start the movie.

The opening, which features the overture being played over scenic shots of Austria, goes on longer than I remember. It's pretty, in a jigsaw puzzle sort of way, but also a little boring. "Yawn," writes Marcus, offering his first movie-related comment of the day.

"Attaboy," says Tony.

As Marcus erases his board, Dr. Beaverman offers a tip. "Maybe you should write 'Yawn' again, kind of small in the corner," she suggests. "That way you can just point to it throughout the film instead of having to rewrite it every 15 seconds."

Soon, the camera zooms in on our protagonist—free-spirited nun Maria, playing hooky from the nunnery atop a hillside near Salzburg.

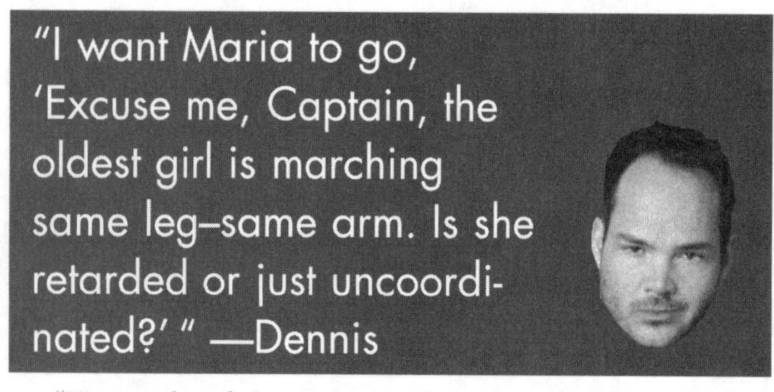

"How many nuns do you know who do this?" poses Dr. Beaverman as Ms. Andrews belts out the title song. "I mean, there are people dying in hospitals who Maria's supposed to be administering to, and she's up on a mountain lip-synching."

"Every take of that opening shot, the wind from the helicopter would literally knock Julie Andrews down," says Ross, "but she'd get back up and do it again."

Marcus holds up his board. "Weeble," it says. The rest of us just look at him blankly.

"Oh, because Weebles wobble but they don't fall down," says Tony, finally. "I get it."

"But she *did* fall down," says Lauren.

"Fuck me, then," writes Marcus, before grabbing his Big Gulp cup and spitting what appear to be ribbons of blood into it.

"When stitches come out," he scribbles, "U need 2 spit."

"He speaks Prince," says Dr. Beaverman.

Back on the screen, Maria finishes her song, then gets a panicky look on her face and dashes off. "That's what you get for giving your pager number to God," I say.

Meanwhile, back at the abbey, the rest of the nuns are engaged in that most Christian of pastimes, idle gossip. When the head nun floats the topic of Maria and her unabashed Maria-ness, the rest of the nuns can't wait to start in with the dissing.

"Here's my question," says Dr. Beaverman. "Why do those nuns bother wearing habits when their faces are already their chaperones? The vow of chastity is just a formality."

"The nun on the right is Marni Nixon," says Lauren, as the sisters begin singing,

"How do you solve a problem like Maria?" "Marni was the voice of Audrey Hepburn in *My Fair Lady* and Natalie Wood in *West Side Story*."

"She finally gets to actually appear on-screen," says Tony, "and what do they do? Stick her in a penguin suit and deny her moisturizer."

"Why does Maria show bangs in her habit and the other women don't?" I wonder.

"The bangs represent a blossoming sexuality that the other nuns have either never possessed or lost long ago," says Dr. Beaverman. "Maria *has* bangs because she is going *to* bang."

"Are nuns allowed to dance?" I ask, when the ladies break into a fit of synchronized sister-ography while referring to Maria as both a "whirling dervish" and a "flibbertigibet."

"Yes," says Lauren, "as long as they don't use jazz hands."

"Rules are rules," writes Marcus.

As the number builds to a climax, Dr. Beaverman pauses the remote and gets uncharacteristically existential. "I've got know," she implores. "Where was God? Would he have allowed this?"

When the song ends, Maria makes her entrance into the Abbey in a manner so bumbling I'm surprised Marni Nixon doesn't do a holy water spit take. "Julie Andrews is more slap-sticky than I remember," I admit.

"She's lobbying to do the next *Pink Panther*," says Tony.

Then the Mother Abbess, a Julia Child–Yoda hybrid with the voice of a Monty Python character, takes Maria into her office and springs the Von Trapp governess assignment on her. Before you can say, "Use the force, Maria," our heroine, looking very *El Mariachi* with her guitar case in tow, is on her way to the Von Trapp mansion. "I love in movies when people move and all they take with them is one small bag, a guitar, and a giant hat," says Tony.

"Can't you see Robert Wise taking Julie Andrews aside and going, 'You're *indomitable* at this point'?" Dr. Beaverman muses as Maria bell-kicks her way through town singing "I Have Confidence" and inspiring horse fountains to spit up in adulation as she passes.

"Correct me if I'm wrong," I say, "but I'm getting that Maria's unconventional. She moves to her own drummer, no?"

"She's a nun-conformist," says Ross.

It's a groaner of a pun, but I'm happy to have it, for it means our resident film geek may come out and play today after all.

"Watch for the real Maria Von Trapp behind Julie Andrews," advises Lauren, before rushing up to the TV and pointing to a woman in a kerchief in the background. "That's her right there walking."

"She's on her way to the bank," I figure.

Soon Maria arrives at the Von Trapp mansion where she's greeted by Franz, the family's stoic, gray-haired butler. "We did this play in high school, and that was my role," recalls Ross. "I was Franz."

"Then what would you say is going through his mind right now?" I ask.

"He's wondering who the comedian is," Ross says. "He's thinking, 'Did the Captain hire a clown? Is there a birthday party no one told me about?' "

"I thought you weren't going to be silly," I say.

"Ah, well, I cracked," says Ross, bemusedly. "But I could turn on a dime and start crying. I'm warning you now."

Franz ushers Maria inside, where she comes face to face with Captain Von Trapp, a retired naval officer played by Christopher Plummer, who, incidentally, used to refer to the movie as *The Sound of Mucus,* so it's not just us who like to be mischievous. When Plummer blows his whistle, his seven children march downstairs and stand at attention. "Because his own penis is so flaccid," starts Dr. Beaverman, "and has been ever since his wife died, he needs to see seven rigid penises in front of him at all times."

"I want Maria to go, 'Excuse me, Captain, the oldest girl is marching same leg–same arm. Is she retarded or just uncoordinated?' " I say.

After asking Maria to do a 360 so he can check out her hot nun ass, the Captain has his children step forward and introduce themselves one at a time. When the coquettish Louisa takes her turn, Ross informs us that the actress portraying Louisa, Heather Menzies, later posed for *Playboy.* This tidbit of trivia is the inspiration behind Marcus's most ambitious creation so far; a stick figure woman with two circles for boobs and a squiggly triangle for a vagina, standing in front of a pair snowcapped mountains. As we watch, Marcus writes *Playboy* across the top of the drawing, then points to a white space next to the girl. Clearly, he's waiting for a headline.

"Heather and the Hills," suggests Lauren.

"Very good, Lauren," says Dr. Beaverman.

"Is 'How Do You Solve a Problem Like Gonorrhea' too wordy?" I wonder.

"Edel-pussy," says Tony.

We have a winner, folks!

On her way upstairs to change for dinner, Maria discovers that one of the rascally tykes has put a frog in her pocket. Not surprisingly, she hurls the scaly creature to the ground in horror, though I'm not exactly sure if she's afraid of the frog or the embarrassing wah-wah sitcom music that accompanies the frog-throwing moment. It could easily be either. "Remind me to look for a disclaimer in the credits that says, 'No frogs were harmed in the making of this film,' " I say, " 'but we did have to beat the shit out of Gretl a few times.' "

" 'And Liesl wasn't allowed to eat solid food after the first week,' " adds Lauren.

The pranks continue at the dinner table when Maria learns, the hard way, that one of the brats put a pinecone on her chair. "All this time she's been saving herself for God," says Tony, as Julie removes the prickly annoyance and takes her seat, "and she loses her cherry to a pinecone."

After dinner, Liesl, the oldest daughter, sneaks outside to rendezvous with her telegram-boy beau, Rolf. If I were at that dinner table, I would have sneaked out after her and spied on them from a distance. This is because I love Rolf. I've always loved Rolf and the way his delivery-boy uniform pants hug his bicycle-riding, ballet-dancing, Nazi-sympathizing ass. If this were my junior high notebook and not a document for publication, I would be writing "Rolf Rolf Rolf Rolf Rolf Rolf" right now. Though I have to say, looking at him today for the first time in years, he's more Kiefer Sutherland–ish than I remember him being, which is a little bit of a bummer but not a total deal breaker.

"Liesl sprained her ankle doing this scene," Lauren tells us, as the couple flit and flirt their way into the jailbait anthem "Sixteen Going on Seventeen."

"Maybe she tripped over a big pile of phony," says Tony.

As the starry-eyed teen lovers pirouette into the dance break, Dr. Beaverman introduces a theory on the Von Trapps' stately gazebo. It's quite a humdinger, even for her. "Gazebo equals Vagina," she says firmly.

Marcus jots G = V on his board as though he may be quizzed on it later.

"The rain beating down upon the gazebo," Dr. B. continues, "represents Liesl's hormonal juices. She's primed, she's ready, she could go all night. Rolf, however, is another story. He has major intimacy issues and refuses to get close. Once the cymbals crash and the song climaxes, he's out of there."

Meanwhile, back upstairs, Maria receives a visit from the family housekeeper, Frau Schmidt, who, as of today, is my new favorite character in *The Sound of Music* and here's why: because she knows there's some seriously fucked-up parenting going on here at Casa Von Trapp and she says nothing. In fact, when Maria tells her she thinks the militaristic manner in which the Captain runs his house is "so wrong," Frau Schmidt just sighs and says, "Ah, well." "Frau Schmidt is so 'not my department,'" I say, "and I love her for it."

"Totally," says Tony. "The Captain could be shooting porn movies with the kids, a few goats, and his wife's dead body and she'd dodder in and be like 'Would anyone care for some tea?'"

A short time after Frau Schmidt leaves, Liesl comes shimmying through Maria's window soaking wet, in more ways than one. "I always thought it was cool that Maria was so understanding when Liesl was out tramping around," admits Lauren. "The baby-sitters I had would either tell on you or try to molest you. There was no middle ground."

A deafening thunderstorm soon causes the rest of the brood to head, one by one, to Maria's room for comfort. "Just another night at Neverland Ranch," says Tony.

Maria sings "My Favorite Things" to them, which gets the first significant eraser wag from Marcus. Truth be told, this number has always set my own eraser wagging, metaphorically speaking. But now I find myself taking issue with the lyrics. "If you got bit by a dog or stung by a bee," I suggest, "would it really do any good to think of, like, a brown paper package tied up with string?"

"Sure," says Tony, "if there was a first aid kit inside."

When the song concludes, Marcus drops his eraser, grabs his Big Gulp cup and spits out more blood—a *lot* more blood—and it looks like a few stitches too.

"Can he not do that?" asks Dr. Beaverman.

"Sitting right here," scrawls Marcus.

Maria continues to win the children over in the next sequence, in which the Wondernun, having fashioned the brats play clothes out of the curtains from her room, takes the gaggle on a series of day trips around the city. This, of course, is the "Do-Re-Mi" number I longed to be a part of as a child. As an adult, I'm still charmed by it, but it seems to go on for *days*. At one point, I half expect somebody to pass the suddenly folksy Maria a joint as she strums her guitar a la Jewel on the mountainside. At another, I'm shocked when she pulls a Frau Schmidt and says nothing when one of her charges tosses her apple core to the ground while shouting out, "Fa!"

"She should have stopped playing and said, 'Sorry kids, we're going back to the mansion because *Brigitta* is a litterbug,'" I argue.

"I just feel sorry for that buggy driver," says Ross, later in the number, when Maria and the kids take a carriage ride. "You know he's thinking, *Ah, fuck, not that nun again. She's the shittiest tipper ever.*"

Meanwhile, the Captain Von Trapp is making his way back from Vienna with his alleged love interest, the filthy rich Baroness Schrader, and her "outrageous" music impresario friend, Max.

"Outrageous," figures Dr. Beaverman, "is how you told an audience in 1965 that someone was gay as a goose."

"Totally," concurs Ross. "When I did this show in school, Max was played by the campus closet case."

"I bet that was true in high schools all over America," I say, then ask Dr. Beaverman for her take on the Baroness.

"Let's just say her gazebo's been locked for years," says Dr. Beaverman.

"And that hair came right out of a box with Eva Gabor's picture on it," adds Tony. "She didn't even shake it out."

As a child, I never gave much thought to the Baroness, except to be glad that someone so chilly wasn't in charge of my upbringing. As an adult, I'm practically obsessed with her.

"The Baroness was every woman in my hometown, except for my mother," says Lauren. "They were all perfectly coiffed Stepford Wives who said and did everything right just like the Baroness. That's why I loved it when she lost in the end."

My Baroness Barometer gets a good workout in the next scene, in which the Queen of the Icy Blond Head Tilt attempts to woo the Captain in front of the family lake. "Where we had neckwear in *St. Elmo's Fire,* water is the sexuality symbol in this movie," Dr. Beaverman asserts. "Notice the water around the Baroness—it's so still it's stagnant. Maria, on the other hand, makes fountains come to life, she's so damn fertile."

Dr. Beaverman's water theory continues to be borne out a few minutes later, when Maria and the kids wind up drenched after the rowboat they sail up in tips over. "Notice Maria is sexually sopping while the Baroness is dry as a bone," points out Dr. Beaverman. "The Captain is secretly so turned on by Maria here that he can hardly speak."

"And how is that manifesting itself?" I ask. "The neckwear?"

"In his pants, if you look carefully," says Dr. B.

"The littlest girl, Gretl, couldn't swim," Ross informs us. "That's why that other girl had to carry her out. Julie Andrews was supposed to grab Gretl, but she kept falling on the opposite side of the boat. Apparently, there was one take where the girl didn't come up and one of the assistant directors literally had to jump in and save her.

"I was furious when I learned about that," recalls Lauren, "because I was a really good swimmer as a kid. I thought, *Well, why didn't they just get me?* The fact that I wasn't born at the time didn't occur to me until years later."

Foregoing his desire to drag the wet-chested Catholic to the nearest gazebo, the Captain instead rips Maria a new one, which, in a refreshing display of nun-conformity, Maria doesn't take lying down. As Maria rages back at him about how he doesn't know his children, recalling each by name and saying something sweet and specific about each of their personalities, I find myself oddly moved, even a little teary-eyed.

I'm not alone. "Great closing argument," writes Marcus.

"She'll never talk back to him once he shoves his tongue down her throat," predicts Dr. Beaverman.

The pair's heated argument is soon interrupted by the sound of the music coming from inside.

"What's that?" barks the Captain.

"It's six-part harmony, you ass," say Tony.

"Wait till you hear the Thunderpuss 2000 club mix," I add.

The Captain's anger seems to dissipate as he makes his way inside, toward the source of the music, and discovers his children singing for the Baroness. "I'm about to say something complimentary," Dr. Beaverman announces. "My favorite thing about this whole movie is the Captain's transformation. He goes from cold and unfeeling to loving and musical in half a song and makes you believe it. I think Christopher Plummer did a very subtle job with it."

"Traitor," mutters Tony.

Now that dad is in on the act, it's going to be virtually impossible to get the rugrats to stop singing. No one knows this more than the Baroness. During the next showstopper, "The Lonely Goatherd," in which the kids and Maria present an elaborate puppet show about goats, we all chime in with what we think the Viennese Ice Queen must be thinking at this point.

"Just drop a fucking armoire on me now, because it's over," I suggest.

"Am I at fucking Euro Disney? What *is* this?" says Tony.

"I was Miss Edelweiss 1932," offers Lauren. "I shouldn't have to put up with this shit."

"I came here to get laid, not see an Up With People reunion," adds Ross.

"You'd think the nunnery was a finishing school, everything she knows," says Dr. Beaverman.

"How's that cancer vaccine coming along, Maria?" hollers Ross.

Marcus holds up his board. It says "Wayland Flowers and Madame." I'm not sure what gag he's going for exactly, but it's definitely puppet-related and it makes me laugh.

As Maria staggers exhausted out from behind the puppet proscenium, I bounce a theory about the nanny's subtext in this scene off Dr. Beaverman. "Would you say that she's basically letting the Captain know that she's willing to be his puppet in the relationship?" I query.

"Exactly, Dennis. Congratulations," says Dr. Beaverman. "She's also saying she's horny as a goat."

Though the kids seem thrilled with their newfound theatricality, I like to imagine that petty jealousies are starting to bubble up, as they often do in showbiz families. For starters, I'm sure everyone resents the fact that Maria hogged all the good parts in the puppet show for herself. I can also just hear Brigitta saying shit to Louisa like, "When Maria goes for that high C, I want to fucking *kill* her." Liesl's spastic marching technique also must generate a few whispers. Then there's Gretl's chronic pants-wetting, Kurt's ADD, and Brigitta's aforementioned pitch problems. If things keep going like this, I won't be surprised if Friedrich runs away to America and shows up on Lou Pearlman's doorstep.

"This song always makes me think of my mother," says Ross, as the Captain and Liesl duet on "Edelweiss" a few scenes later. "The first time I watched this movie on TV, my parents were still together. The next year when it was on, they weren't, and I remember we were halfway through watching it when my dad came to pick me and my sister up to take us for a few days."

"What's Adalvise?" writes Marcus.

"It's that drug you're on right now," says Tony.

"It's a flower," says Lauren.

We listen quietly to the sweet flower song for a stanza or two, then Ross says, "I have my cell phone programmed to play this song whenever my mom or sister calls me."

"I have that feature too," says Tony. "But my family ring is 'Roll Out the Barrel.'"

Marcus holds up his sign. "'You're No Good,'" it reads.

Maria and the Baroness continue to compete for the Captain's affections at a party in the family mansion a few scenes later. Watching the three of them interact is like happening upon a really juicy episode of *Temptation Island,* only more civilized. It makes me long to see the ladies *really* duke it out on *Celebrity Deathmatch.* I can just see it: Maria sideswiping the Baroness into the ropes with her guitar case, the Baroness crawling across the ring in her evening gown and shoving a marionette up Maria's claymation ass. Someone, quick, get MTV on the horn!

While the party rages inside, Liesl and Friedrich dance together in the courtyard and dream of the future when they can attend stuffy parties. When Maria happens upon them, she says, "Why didn't you tell me you could dance?" It's the most bullshitty moment in the movie, if you ask me. "She doesn't know they can *dance*?" I say, incredulously. "She's been teaching them numbers for weeks. As a matter of fact, they've got another one coming up in a few minutes."

That number is, of course, the enchanting bedtime roundelay "So Long, Farewell," which goes over great with the stuffy crowd, despite a laughably lame moment of looping during Kurt's solo. "That's Marni Nixon again singing the high note on Kurt's 'Goodbye,'" Lauren tells us.

"Apparently Marni's testicles haven't dropped either," says Tony, before insisting we rewind to see the glaringly obvious overdub again and again.

The song concludes with the littlest Von Trapp, a.k.a. the Girl Who Can't Swim, saying her good nights and scooting her wee ass upstairs one step at a time. "This move is called Gretl's Carpet Bum Scooch," I explain. "It's a little trick she picked up from the Baroness."

Speaking of which, having interrupted the Captain and Maria sharing a dance earlier on the patio, our favorite blond zillionaire is now at her wit's end. "I half expect her to just taking a flying leap off the balcony," I say, "like, 'If you're not going to marry me, asshole, you're going to clean my blood of the statues!' "

"She's too resilient for that," figures Tony. "I want her to walk into the middle of that party and scream, 'Someone put it in me *right now*! I'll even take Max. Kitty needs to be *scratched*!' "

Instead, the tiara-wearing temptress tries to guilt Maria into forfeiting the game by getting her alone and telling her, "There's nothing more irresistible to a man than a woman who's in love with him." This strikes me as a big lie, so I look to Dr. Beaverman for clarification.

"That line should have read, 'an intact hymen,'" she says.

Maria, traumatized by her overwhelming desire to have this particular Plummer lay some pipe, hightails it back to the Abbey where the Mother Abbess encourages her to follow her whirling dervish of a heart and return to the Captain. "Do you know how much stained glass they must go through in a week?" I ask as the golden-throated soprano bursts into "Climb Ev'ry Mountain."

When Maria returns to the Von Trapp mansion, the first thing she learns is that the Captain and the Baroness are engaged. "She's thinking, *Wait a minute! I broke up with* God *for* this?" says Tony.

"Meanwhile, the Baroness must want to say, 'Maria, isn't it about time for your reprise of "So Long, Farewell"?'" says Lauren.

"Totally," agrees Tony. "She's looking into the orchestra pit going, 'Take it from the coda, boys. Five, six, seven, eight…' "

"I want there to be a shot of her putting on brass knuckles and saying, 'I know how to solve a problem like Maria,'" I say.

Instead, after trotting out her final fuck-me frock—a snazzy bolero-jacketed red number with sequins—the Baroness sends up the white flag, a piece of material that, if it weren't metaphoric, Maria would surely insist on turning into more play-clothes.

"No woman is this gracious throwing in the towel," says Lauren.

Left to their own libidinous devices, Maria and the Captain head to the gazebo, where else, to sing "Something Good," a number Ross claims was shot largely in silhouette because the two actors had the giggles and couldn't get through it without smirking. "I always loved this lyric," says Lauren, "because I was a holy terror as a child and I liked the idea that I might have had one redeemable moment."

Just then, I notice that Marcus has drifted into dreamland. We decide unanimously to let him snooze.

"Notice Maria now," gripes Dr. Beaverman, turning her attention back to the screen. "She's become a dishrag. She's submissive, self-effacing. The kicks in the air are gone. She can't sing 'I Have Confidence' anymore because she doesn't. He'll make her do power ballads for the rest of the movie."

"I wonder if God was at the wedding, getting drunk at the reception and telling people, 'I've had her.' " —Tony

"I'm telling you, God was absent from the whole production." —Dr. Beaverman

From the gazebo love match, we cut directly to the couple's wedding where a chorus of nuns sing a reprise of "Maria."

"What?" says Dr. Beaverman. "Was the sheet music for 'We've Only Just Begun' not available in Austria?"

"Can you imagine Maria at the wedding rehearsal?" I say. "She's like, 'OK, my nun friends, I'd really like you to sing a song that makes fun of me at my own wedding, preferably something that calls me a flibbertigibet. Any suggestions?'"

"I wonder if God was at the wedding," muses Tony, "getting drunk at the reception and telling people, 'I've had her.'"

"I'm telling you, He was absent from the whole production," insists Dr. Beaverman.

A month later, the Captain and Maria return from their honeymoon to find a Nazi flag hanging in front of their mansion. The Captain, who has always taken issue with swastikas and those who sport them, tears it in half angrily. "You know Maria's pissed," says Tony. "She could have made Uncle Max a nice caftan with that flag."

"She's become so matronly," laments Dr. Beaverman as Maria, in a moment straight out of a Judds holiday special, sits down with Liesl to sing a reprise of "Sixteen Going on Seventeen." "The message here is 'Give a woman a little of the love sword and it'll calm her right down.'"

A few scenes later, the Captain decides he doesn't want to serve the Third Reich, so he tries to take his family and flee the country. This causes Ross to let out an audible huff. "You're upset because they're leaving the butler behind, aren't you?" I ask.

Ross nods affirmatively and says, "I always like to imagine that Franz went off and became that guy who sold a button so Oskar Schindler could check three more people off his list or something," says Ross.

"And Rolf helped," I add.

After the family's first attempt to flee the country is foiled, the Captain fibs and tells the Nazis that they're all on their way to perform at an Austrian music festival. So they proceed to do just that, regaling the crowd with slow and boring *Unplugged* versions of practically every song we've heard so far. "The Nazis have got to be thinking, *Would it kill 'em to do something up-tempo?*" figures Tony, as the family segues into a curiously repetitive portion of their program that I like to call "The Jam and Bread Breakdown."

"Maybe their idea is to bore the audience to sleep, then escape before they wake up," I suggest.

Just then, Marcus stirs from his slumber, retrieves his board and writes, "I miss anything good?"

"No," says Lauren. "But you missed 'Something Good.'"

This clearly makes no sense to Marcus, but then not much has today.

The family finishes their set, then Max, so outrageous by this point he could be on *Frasier,* takes the stage and tries to buy the family some time by dragging out the announcement of the winners. "I want him to be like, 'Would the owner of a BMW license number C13 72Z please go turn off their lights,'" says Ross.

Finally, he can stall no more and declares the Family Von Trapp the evening's victors. Marcus shakes his head angrily and scribbles something. "Ace of Base were robbed," reads his board.

Much to the Nazis' chagrin, our winners are nowhere to be found. Turns out they've already flown the coop and are on their way to the abbey graveyard. There, they hide out from their flashlight toting pursuers in a suspense-filled scene that, as a child, nearly caused me to schnitzel with noodle in my pants.

"Are those dead nuns buried in those graves or all kinds of people?" Tony wonders.

"I think it's the audience," groans Dr. Beaverman, spent and cranky after three hours of commentary. "Next time, can we do something shorter, Dennis, like *It's Pat*?"

"When this originally played in Germany, they didn't show the third act," Lauren informs us.

"Is it too late to hop a plane?" asks Dr. Beaverman. "When I get out of here, there's going to be a Social Security check in my mailbox."

"Then you can buy the treats," says Ross.

"Oh, my God, the cookies," I yelp, then jump up and run into the kitchen. With only a few minutes left in the movie, I plop the log of raw cookie dough on a cutting board and take the whole thing into the front room with five forks.

No one complains.

The film reaches its climax when Liesl spots her alleged boyfriend Rolf and gasps, blowing the family's cover. Luckily, the nuns know more about car engines than one might expect, and are able to disable the Nazis' vehicles so the Von Trapps can get away.

"This never happened," says Ross as the family scales the Alps into Switzerland to the triumphant strains of "Climb Ev'ry Mountain." "In reality, the Von Trapps took a train to Italy the day before the borders closed."

"But who wants to hear a song about that?" says Lauren.

"I do," claims Tony. "And it's called 'Midnight Train to Georgia.' Hit it!"

As the credits roll, I'm happy to say that I'm pretty sure I still want to be a Von Trapp child, if only so I could spy on Liesl and Rolf when they make out. The singing and dancing still looks pretty fun too. I must admit, though, that I can't imagine 7-year-old Cousin Dennis being much of a trooper on that treacherous hike to freedom. I have a feeling I'd piss and moan the whole way and be booted out of the group by the time we got to Switzerland.

"A charming postscript," says Tony, as the tape rewinds. "A few days later, the Nazis came back, burned down the abbey, and raped all the nuns."

"While Liesl was making notes for her tell-all book in a five-star hotel in Zurich," says Dr. Beaverman.

"I'm guessing she already has a title in mind," I say.

"Uh-huh," says Dr. Beaverman. I can practically hear the gears in her brain crank into action. "It's called *I Let a Nazi in My Gazebo.*"

•

A week and a half later, we're gathered at Golf 'n' Games in Sherman Oaks in honor of Marcus's birthday. Tony, of course, is in Europe swinging another kind of putter. We're nine holes into an 18-hole game of putt-putt golf and I'm in the lead—not for nothing did I put in four years on the Holbrook High School golf team—though I must say, I'm rather disappointed with the course. I thought that since I didn't recognize a single video game on the way in (wherefore art thou, Centipede?) perhaps the tradition of miniature golf would have moved into the 21st century as well, with all sorts of newfangled variations.

If it has, they didn't get the memo here at Golf 'n' Games. "These holes are a snooze," I gripe, preparing to tee off on hole 10, which is basically a straight flat shot to the green, with a wooden V blocking the hole. "I mean, would it kill them to have a battery-operated windmill or something?"

"Someone should open up a kick-ass miniature golf place like at Universal Studios," suggests Ross, "and have all the holes be tied to different movies like they do with pinball machines. How cool would that be?"

"I'd just stay on my favorites and never finish the round," I say. "You'd have to drag me away from the *Showgirls* hole."

"How would you know which hole to aim for?" poses Dr. Beaverman, who's trailing me by only two strokes. Remarkable, considering she's in four-inch heels.

We spend the next 10 minutes imagining theme holes, like a hole based on *The Exorcist* where the player has to jump a moat full of green vomit and get their ball into Linda Blair's mouth while her head spins around maniacally. Then there's the *JFK* hole where you swing your club "back and to the left, back and to left," then traverse the mysterious grassy knoll, while not paying nearly enough attention to your wife, Sissy Spacek. Sounds challenging, sure, but it's a cakewalk compared with the hole inspired by Elisabeth Shue's *Molly*.

"What would the *Sound of Music* hole be?" says Lauren.

"Me, lying right here on the ground," says Dr. Beaverman, "while the rest of you beat me to death with your putters."

"I picture lots of papier-mâché alps," I say, "a lake, maybe a few fountains, 'Do-Re-Mi' on an endless loop."

"Same difference," declares Dr. Beaverman.

Suddenly, out nowhere, the melody of "Edelweiss" begins to play, like it's being noodled on a low-end Casio keyboard that happens to be underwater. "What the hell?" bristles Dr. Beaverman, before turning her gaze heavenward and saying, "Am I being punished?"

Ross pulls his cell phone from his jacket pocket and says, "Hello." He listens for a moment, then steps behind a nearby castle to talk more privately. From where I'm standing, I can hear him say, "Oh, my God," about seven times.

When he returns, the color is totally gone from his face. "That was my sister," he says. "My mom's in the hospital. They don't know what it is."

THE BASKET DIARIES

A week or so after our Golf n' Games adventure, Tony calls in the middle of the night. "Sorry to wake you up," he says breathlessly, "but this couldn't wait."

"Where are you?" I ask, fumbling to turn on the light.

"Nottingham, England," says Tony. "I found him."

"Found who?" I ask.

"Rutherford Shelton."

"Who?"

"Rutherford Shelton," Tony repeats forcefully. "The man who thinks that you're a total loser and your friends are a bunch of wankers."

"Oh, my God," I gasp.

"There was one Rutherford Shelton in the phone book," Tony explains. "So I went by his address and saw a *GoodFellas* poster through the window, so I figured it was him."

"Are you *crazy*?" I squeal.

"He's about 40," Tony continues, opting to gloss over the question of crazy for now. "And he's not as geeky as you would think. He's actually kind of handsome in a Stanley Tucci sort of way."

"You confronted him?" I ask.

"No, no, no," says Tony. "I just watched him from across the street for a while. He's a total asshole, though. At one point, he came out of his house just to bark at these kids who were just, like, riding their bikes, not hurting anyone."

"How long were you there?" I ask.

"About four hours," says Tony. "It was like a total stakeout, and I was an undercover agent. No wait, what's that other word I like better? Operative."

"You didn't have anything better to do?"

"Please," says Tony. "It was my day off, and what was I going to do, go look at another castle? I hate that tourist shit."

"So did you end up getting together with Matt?" I ask. Tony and my editor, Matt, had planned to hook up for a drink when the *Man-O-Man* tour hit London.

"Yes, and he's so cool," says Tony. "But wait, I'm not finished with my Rutherford Shelton story." Tony lowers his voice to a scarcely audible whisper—he's an operative, after all—and continues, "OK, remember how Shelton said he'd rather get a turd in his mailbox than another issue of *British Premiere*?"

"You didn't?" I groan, my stomach instantaneously constricting, as if I'd just imbibed a giant bowl of dread.

"No," says Tony. "You know it takes an act of Parliament to get a decent poo out of me."

I do know this, and you will too if you ever spend more than five minutes in conversation with Tony. It comes up a lot.

"I got one of the strippers to do it," he tells me. "Blaze."

"Blaze?" I say. "There's a person called Blaze?"

"Yeah. He was really into it, too. We sort of bonded right there in the alley in Leicester and now he's one of my best friends on the tour. It was a perfect coiler too. You should have seen it. Oh wait, you will."

"I will?" I say, helping myself to a second bowl of dread.

"I took pictures," Tony says.

•

Those very pictures are the first item of business at our next Screening Party three weeks later, and the less I describe them here, the better. Suffice it to say that it's a good thing Tony has a friendly rapport with the one-hour photo guy at Rite Aid, because printing your scat photos is not a task you want to trust a total stranger to do.

"Don't separate them from the stack yet," cautions Tony, before pulling the photos out from their envelope and handing them to Ross. "If you flip through 'em really fast, it's like you're right there with us."

"How many pictures did you *take*?" says Ross, using both hands to cradle the sizable stack of prints.

"I wanted to get every angle," says Tony. "Plus, there are doubles in there so it makes it seem like more."

"You got *doubles*?" says a clearly mortified Marcus.

"I always get doubles," replies Tony.

"Like any of us are going to want a copy," mutters Marcus.

"I want a copy," says Ross.

"I want a copy," says Lauren.

"I want a copy," says Dr. Beaverman. "At least I think I do. I may change my mind when I actually see the goods."

"I want a copy too," I say. "And we should send a few shots to Blaze."

"He took some with his own camera," says Tony. "It was hilarious how proud he was of it. Like somehow in his head he managed to make it about his sex appeal and virility. Like, 'Look, there on the ground, more proof that I'm a stud!'"

As the pictures make their way from person to person, the room fills with groans, shudders, and laughter, in that order. "The guy in this picture is sort of hot," says Lauren, sizing up a particular photo. "Is that Blaze?"

"No, Blaze has platinum hair and a crazy fake tan," replies Tony. "That's actually Rutherford Shelton taking out his trash. I used my zoom."

Lauren raises her eyebrows and purrs, "Hello, Mr. Shelton."

"Putting the poo in the fish and chips container is a nice touch," says Dr. Beaverman, tapping a fingernail on one of the prints. "It's always good to have a little local color."

"Even if that color is brown," I add.

"This is so weird, you guys," says Ross, while scrutinizing the dozen or so photos he's spread out on the coffee table. "Twenty-four hours ago I was in Texas taking my mother to her radiation treatment, and today I'm sitting on your couch trying to decide which turd picture I want."

We all stop what we're doing and look over to Ross.

"Take as many was you want," Tony says, finally, smiling warmly. "I can always get more made."

The day after Ross got the Golf 'n' Games call from his sister, his mother was diagnosed with stage 2 breast cancer. A few days after that, he flew home to Texas to be with her. He stayed until this morning. Before Tony got back from Rite Aid with the pictures, Ross gave the rest of us the latest update: that she's doing quite well, considering, and that the doctor thinks her chances for a full recovery are excellent.

"I can't decide," he says finally, throwing up his hands, "so I'm just going to take this top view and this side view and this other top view for Perry's bulletin board at work. Is that OK?"

Tony just waves his hands at Ross, Jewish mother–style, as if to say, "Take all you want. Eat! *Eat*!"

"You can have my share, too," offers Marcus.

"You don't want *any,* Marcus?" Tony says, a trace of vulnerability slipping into his voice, as though he might be irreparably heartbroken if everyone doesn't leave here today with at least one of his magnificent English alley still lifes.

"OK, put one aside for me," says Marcus. "The farther away it was taken, the better. Like from a helicopter would be good."

Then Ross, looking suddenly preoccupied, goes into the kitchen and refills his water glass.

I follow him. "Ross, if you don't want to be here today, it's totally cool," I say. "We can trash these movies without you."

"Nah, I've been looking forward to this all week," he says, then walks back into the front room, takes his seat, and declares, "A little mindless entertainment will do me good."

"It'll definitely be mindless," says Dr. Beaverman. "I'm not so sure about entertainment."

"I remember the night this was originally on TV," recalls Tony excitedly, before retrieving a beat-up videotape from atop our entertainment center and turning it around to inspect the back. "My mom was watching it in the front room and I hid behind the sofa and tried to see as much as I could."

"I wanted to watch it *so bad,*" remembers Marcus. "But my family was so uptight that I knew that I couldn't even *suggest* it. Luckily, we got a new TV in our basement that same week and I was able to watch it, uninterrupted, all by myself."

No, my pals are not referring to *Helter Skelter* or the abortion episode of *Maude*. What got their pubescent blood pumping, and mine as well, was *For Ladies Only,* a 1981 TV movie starring *Trapper John, M.D.*'s Gregory Harrison as a studly farm boy from Iowa who moves to the Big Apple with dreams of acting on Broadway, but ends up working as an exotic dancer. We're dissecting that little gem, along with the similarly themed *A Night in Heaven* starring *The Blue Lagoon*'s Christopher Atkins, as part of our Screening Party Double Dip Salute to the Phenomenon of Male Strippers.

You're probably wondering what on earth a purportedly classy outfit like *British Premiere* would want with a Screening Party Double Dip Salute to the Phenomenon of Male Strippers. Well, we're not doing it for them. We're doing it for *GayZone,* a splashy British homo rag whose readers are practically salivating for a Screening Party Double Dip Salute to the Phenomenon of Male Strippers. OK, they're not really salivating, but they do seem to like anything that has to do with hot guys taking off their clothes. "But not that *Full Monty* crap," the magazine's editor, Simon Foster, instructed in his last E-mail. "Write about guys you'd actually want to shag."

Tony's the one to thank for our new connection. He met Mr. Foster a few weeks ago in London when he was out having cocktails with Matt from *Premiere,* who, it so happens, is a friend of Simon's from their college days.

When Simon learned why Tony was in town, he insisted my roommate pen a tell-all, behind-the-scenes exposé about the oft misunderstood world of male stripping for *GayZone*.

"Then why didn't you just write a tell-all piece?" Ross asks Tony. "Then I wouldn't have to catch shit from Perry for taking home goofy gay shitheaps like this."

"Because I signed a contract that says I wouldn't trash the company," explains Tony.

"But it didn't say anything about trashing Gregory Harrison," I point out. "So, using these two movies as touchstones," I continue, standing up to face my guests, "we're going to try to debunk some of the myths about the world of male stripping."

"You mean a male stripper isn't just a really sensitive guy who can't get a break who's going to take me away and make everything better," says Lauren, pleadingly, "particularly if I'm a bored housewife with a high-collared shirt and a husband I feel is ignoring me?"

Tony shakes his head and says, "Fasten your seat belt, sweetheart. You've got a lot to learn."

While I slide the tape in, Marcus seizes the floor and regales us with his latest *histoire de St. Olaf*. "Just after this aired, I was flying for the first time by myself to Florida," he says spiritedly, clearly reinvigorated after taking last month off, "and there was a copy of *Us* on the plane with a full-page, color picture of Gregory Harrison in the Zorro Speedo. At the time, it didn't strike me as sexual attraction so much as '*That's* the body I want to have when I grow up.' So I took the magazine into the bathroom with me, tore the page out, and stuffed it in my pocket." With that, Marcus picks up the manila folder he brought with him, stands, and adds, "I've kept it ever since." He opens the folder to reveal his precious, threadbare magazine page, then escorts it from person to person protectively.

"Look how hot he was," I say, during my 10 seconds with the photo. "That body is *off the hook,* even by today's standards." I tilt the photo toward Tony and say, "How *hot* is he?"

"You can have him," says Tony dismissively. "I'm saving myself for a little blond bit of sugar by the name of Christopher Atkins."

"Is that the whole story, Marcus?" asks Dr. Beaverman after taking her window of time with the photo and complimenting Mr. Harrison on his exemplary goody trail. "Sometimes there's a part 2."

"Cut to Cornell University a few years later," says Marcus, diving back in. "My friend Molly was doing a scavenger hunt for her sorority, Alpha Phi, and there was a 25-point bonus that could be anything. I don't know where I got the idea from, but I was like, 'How 'bout I strip for you like Gregory Harrison?' and she was like, 'You'd do that for us?' and I said, 'Anything for Alpha Phi.' So I showed up at the sorority house in my little track suit, put Olivia's 'Physical' on the ghetto blaster, and stripped down to my Speedo. And then, as if that weren't enough, I poured suntan lotion all over me and sat on the president's lap."

"The president of the sorority?" I ask, wanting to get my facts right for the article.

"No, the president of the United States," says Ross.

"That's when Reagan started losing his memory," adds Tony.

"So that's what I did," says Marcus, folding his arms proudly. "And they got all 25 points."

On that triumphant note, I start the movie.

"I love this '70s brushstroke font," says Ross as the opening credits unfurl over shots of Gregory Harrison, fresh off the bus from Iowa, strutting down the streets of Manhattan like a hillbilly Tony Manero.

"Hold on a second," I interrupt, when Harrison's credit as a coproducer appears. "You mean he wasn't *forced* to do this?"

"He cowrote it and sings three songs too," Marcus informs us.

"This movie was like his *Citizen Kane,*" says Ross.

After finding a dumpy apartment, Gregory hits the town looking for acting work. Enter former first daughter Patti Davis as Sandy Green, prissy assistant to a major New York casting director. After talking her ear off about his passion for the theater, he turns the tables on her and asks, "Did you ever study acting?"

"Uh, no," Patti replies.

"Clearly," mutters Lauren.

"Let us examine Patti Davis," says Dr. Beaverman. "Her barrettes symbolize repression, of course. I predict everything she wears is going to be tight around the neck. If there's not a bow, there's some kind of busy, frilly thing going on. All are metaphorical chastity belts. Let's refer to Patti as the pre-Oedipal mommy. She's Gregory's safe, non-sexual wife type and she'll remain sexually unfulfilled because sex and genuine affection are separated and compartmentalized in this hustler's mind."

One of the multitude of women who will *not* be deprived of Gregory's love sword is Dinah Manoff, who plays a mouthy aspiring actress named Mary Louise. Our hero picks her up at a bar and, without even asking her name, bangs her silly—at least I think he does, she could have been silly going in. "God, I miss the man-whores of the '80s," I say wistfully.

"Eighties, shit," scoffs Tony. "Go on the road with me for a week if you want man-whores."

We all look to Tony expectantly. Suddenly it's like he's holding a bag of Big Macs and we haven't eaten in weeks.

"OK," he starts. "It was not uncommon on my tour for the stripper guys, if they had hooked up with a particularly naughty lady, to call us gay singers and be like, 'Get to room 312 right now.' And we'd put on our robes and slippers and go stand in the doorway and watch five guys on one woman or something crazy like that. It was so matter of fact, like, 'OK, we'll be right down.'"

"And you chose to take pictures of poo," mutters Marcus.

Back on the screen, Gregory, who's beautifully lit, and Dinah, who's practically in darkness, bask in the afterglow. "I'm smelling some nasty over-the-counter Brut," Lauren says, waving her hand in front of her face, "and I'm not sure if it's coming from him or her."

"I would think her," says Dr. Beaverman. "Manoff's tough and far too much of a man for him. He's willing to service her, but the relationship won't go anywhere because he can't handle an equal. He needs a mommy."

After a montage chronicling Gregory's struggles as a would-be Brando—dance classes, auditions, lame day jobs—our heartland transplant accompanies Manoff to acting class. "What's with that fedora on Dinah?" wonders Lauren. "Does she have a sax solo coming up?"

Gregory tries to wow the class with his interpretation of Stanley Kowalski, but his peers—the cruelest collection of classmates this side of *Heathers*—rip him a new one, saying pretentious things like, "I feel degraded by your interpretation." The afternoon's not a total wash, though, as Greg is soon befriended by Marc Singer as Stan, a fellow actor and Vietnam vet with a weakness for nose candy. In fact, it's Marc who suggests that Greg could supplement his income by working alongside him at the male strip mecca Club Max. "Oh, this is *completely* true," groans Tony. "Strippers are always trying to recruit younger, better-looking guys to come and strip with them."

Gregory agrees to sling cocktails at Max for *one night only,* and soon Marc is ushering our corn-fed cutie into the club, past a queue of screaming, clawing, sexed-up groupies. "OK, let's discuss strip clubs and women," drones Dr. Beaverman, as we head inside and discover that the Club Max waiters even do their side work shirtless. "Research has shown that women are not particularly voyeuristic. I think this is basically a man's fantasy—Gregory Harrison's fantasy—of what a woman's fantasy is. And why do all the women either look like the Duchess of Windsor or QVC shoppers?"

Before long, Gregory's loitering around backstage like Anne Baxter with a gym membership, bonding with the club's roller-skating emcee and his dumbbell-toting, oily-chested troupe of strippers. In addition to the camo-clad Marc Singer, there's "The Sheik," an Arabian-themed fantasy man who insists on mixing two different animal prints (even though he's bitchy and gay and therefore should know better), and a boyishly cute blond law student-by-day who wears a bag over his head and goes by the moniker "The Unknown Stripper."

"Oh, my God," gasps Marcus, when the bag comes off. "I *know* that guy. He goes to my gym. I just saw him on stage in this gay musical at the Celebration Theater."

"So we've already got one homo in the dressing room," I proclaim proudly, wishing I had a light-up tote board I could gesture toward.

"The conception is that most male strippers are gay," says Tony. "But almost all of the ones I've worked with are straight, narcissistic assholes."

"Except Blaze," I interject.

"No, Blaze is pretty much a straight, narcissistic asshole," admits Tony. "But he's *my* straight, narcissistic asshole."

"Speaking of straight, narcissistic assholes," grumbles Dr. Beaverman, as Marc Singer takes to the stage and begins yanking the zipper of his camouflage jumpsuit up and down. "I don't know about you all, but the last person I want to see strip is a commando from Vietnam having a flashback. What's next, Chip from Chernobyl?"

After another boring acting class scene, we return to the Club Max dressing room to find the strippers in a complete tizzy. Seems they're one dancer short for tonight's extravaganza. When the boss asks Gregory to fill in, our hero argues that he's a serious thespian and therefore above stripping, though we all know he's secretly dying to and is probably having a practice pole installed in his apartment as we speak.

"This scene is so, 'Come to the dark side, Luke,'" observes Marcus, as Marc Singer gives Gregory the hard sell, claiming that since he's been stripping he's made buckets of money, scored primo dope, and gotten into all the best restaurants.

"I'm sure that's true," mutters Ross. "They want the strippers right up front at Spago."

After much disingenuous hemming and hawing, Gregory finally agrees to fulfill his destiny and take it off. He psyches himself up backstage by taking a few big swigs of hooch straight out of the bottle. "See, they're getting him drunk," says Tony. "That's true. On my tour, before every show, the strippers would pass around a bottle of Johnnie Walker Red and everyone except me would take a hit of ecstasy."

Then, dressed like Tom Wopat at his debut cotillion, Gregory takes to the stage and, after an awkward deer in headlights moment, proceeds to remove his hillbilly duds one piece at a time. "You'd never see a stripper in jeans," says Tony, shaking his head, "because you can't get them over your feet. And you always wear boots that are three sizes too big so you can just kick them off."

"The baskets in this movie are very disappointing," remarks Dr. Beaverman, when Gregory gets down to his bikini briefs. "We need some cat toys stuck in their pants because the baskets are definitely lacking."

"A-tisket, a-tasket, where the hell's the basket?" echoes Lauren.

We get a little more face time with the basket in question when Gregory starts to work the room for tips. "They're putting dollar bills in his bikini," remarks Dr. Beaverman, "and I've got to wonder if it gives change. Do those Speedos give change?"

Stripping apparently agrees with Gregory, for, after another dull scene about how tough it is to be an actor in New York, we return to Club Max for a sequence I consider the centerpiece of the film. I'm referring, of course, to the Zorro Strip, in which Mr. Harrison, employing a mask, some flamenco music, and the chug step from dance class, serves up the salsa big-time.

"I think he's so hot in this scene," I confess, as Gregory swings in shirtless from a trapeze and strips down to the black bikini with the white Z that got Marcus through puberty.

"Do strippers really open-mouth kiss that long?" Lauren asks as Gregory plays tonsil hockey with a character whose name on the cast list is probably Hag #72.

"Oh, completely," confirms Tony. "Every single stripper has a giant bottle of Listerine backstage because they don't want to get herpes from somebody, even though they all already have herpes."

"Would *you* kiss the women?" poses Ross.

"Only on the cheek and even that was rare," says Tony. "As singers, we weren't really expected to do that. Thank God."

After the show, Gregory sticks around to bask in his Zorro triumph. Soon, he approaches Louise Lasser—whose character would have been dubbed Hag #73 were it not for the fact that she has lines, albeit lines that are not well synchronized with the movements of her mouth—and asks her to dance. "I never done anything like this before," she coos to him as they boogie.

"What, looping?" wonders Ross.

Next thing we know, Gregory's being called a "sweet little dancing person" by the newly orgasmic Louise as he reclines naked in her bed post-fuck. "You gotta love a movie where the men are naked and the woman are fully clothed," Lauren says, referring to fact that Louise has already gotten redressed. "She's like, 'I just fucked a Chippendale, now let me put my June Cleaver dress back on.'"

"He can't even drink her pretty," mutters Ross.

"That's what I don't get," I say. "All the women in this movie are so dowdy. What? Were the Landers sisters busy?"

"I'm sure that was a conscious choice," remarks Tony. "In my show, if there was an audience participation number, you were always supposed to pick a homely woman. You'd get yelled at by the producer if you brought up a hot woman. The idea behind it is that every woman in the audience needs to believe that if she played her cards right, it could be *her* going home with you. Then, after the show, your tips go through the roof because all the other women think, *God, if he picked THAT COW, then I must have a chance. I'm hotter than HER.* So that's an extra five bucks times 200 women."

Then it's back to acting class, where, in spite of the "trust exercises" they were seen doing together in an earlier montage, Gregory's acting classmates haven't really warmed to him at all. When they start in again about how much he sucks as an actor, he spits back, "This isn't working for me," and storms out.

It's clear from these class scenes that Harrison intended the movie to be a valentine to struggling thespians everywhere as well as a primer for such classics as *A Streetcar Named Desire, Richard III,* and *Picnic,* but the truth is, we just want to see him naked. And he probably knew it.

Given that Gregory's already slipped it to Louise Lasser and Dinah Manoff, none of us are particularly shocked when he spends the weekend servicing Lee Grant on her beautiful estate. "Her hat is killing me," cries Marcus, in regard to Lee's flower-laden derby. "I swear to God, I just lost 30 T cells."

Later, at the gym, his drugged-out pal Marc suggests they take their show on the road and strip at a private party thrown by matronly magazine editor Lee Grant. "Marc's weird hand motions are a common thing among strippers," says Tony, referring to Singer's herky-jerky style, which blurs the line between interpretive dance and a seizure. "The only way some of these straight guys can dance is to make really angry faces and violent motions. They're terrified of looking graceful or feminine, so instead they choose to look spastic and constipated."

Given that Gregory's already slipped it to Louise Lasser and Dinah Manoff, none of us are particularly shocked when he spends the weekend servicing Lee Grant on her beautiful estate. "Her hat is *killing* me," cries Marcus, in regard to Lee's flower-laden derby. "I swear to God, I just lost 30 T cells."

"The jaunty hat is supposed to cover up the fact that she's an old whore," says Dr. Beaverman as Lee and Gregory make eyes at each other over a picnic blanket. "But I don't care how many *Blossom* hats and petticoats and Martha Stewart fixings she's sporting, she's still an old whore."

Later on, in Lee's candlelit bedroom, the robe-clad career woman hovers over the bath and tenderly washes her nude stallion. "I love your body," she purrs while Gregory pours wine on her menopausal foot and licks it off. You read that right, folks. Gregory pours wine on her menopausal foot and *licks it off*. "All day long," she continues, "I work with flabby men who work with nothing but their mind..."

"Thank God you don't have one," mutters Ross. "In real life, Lee Grant and Dinah Manoff are mother and daughter. And he bangs them both."

"It was two-for-one day at the temple," figures Marcus.

When Lee offers to make Gregory her kept boy, he refuses because he has integrity. Then it's back to Club Max for the big Mr. New York Exotic contest! But by now, I'm afraid, we're all ready for this shaky allegory to come to a climax. Hell, if Louise Lasser can do it...

"Marc Singer needs to die and then the movie needs to end," decrees Lauren.

Not surprisingly, Gregory chugs off with the trophy by impersonating a cop and then humping the fuck out of his motorcycle seat, a coupling I insist on rewinding and watching again and again.

"He's having more fun mounting that bike than any woman he's tossed a leg over the whole movie," asserts Dr. Beaverman.

Gregory's triumph leads to a slew of magazine covers and talk-show appearances—I believe his agent mentions *60 Minutes* as a possibility. All this exposure, however, brings with it a chastising from mommy figure Patti Davis, who tells him he's "turned into someone I can't really understand." This from a woman who would later bare her former first-daughter beaver in *Playboy*. Twice.

After way more plot than any of us can endure—Gregory discovers that his credibility as an actor is shot, Dinah Manoff does summer stock, Marc Singer overdoses and gets carried off in a body bag, which, incidentally, is more fabric than he's worn the entire film—we finally arrive at the movie's final scene, in which Patti the pre-Oedipal Mommy claps wildly for Gregory's one-line turn as a Western Union man in an off-off-off-off-Broadway play.

"It must have been a big adjustment for him performing on a stage that doesn't light up," I figure.

"He originally wanted to make his entrance on a trapeze," reports Tony, "but the director said it would draw focus."

As Gregory himself croons the closing theme, a song he cowrote about 'dreams that shine their magic light,' Dr. Beaverman sums up the movie. "Though this film is called *For Ladies Only*, and many ladies appear in it, it's not about them at all," she remarks. "It's about Mr. Harrison's picaresque journey and how he has to fight back a world of screaming, cloying, dependent, needy, unfulfilled, childlike, primitive women in order to fulfill his transcendent, artistic soul. In a way, it's not unlike Ulysses encountering the sirens in Greek mythology."

While I remove *For Ladies Only* from the VCR and replace it with *Rocky* director John

Avildsen's 1983 groaner *A Night in Heaven,* Marcus serves us each an intermission treat: two mini cinnamon buns with white-frosted Z's on them.

"Ultimately, however," summarizes Dr. Beaverman between bites, "Gregory fails. In the end, he's still a delivery boy. *I will deliver* is the message."

"Deliver Christopher Atkins!" barks Tony, before trying to snatch the remote from me. "He's the reason I got out of bed today, and the reason that I'm going to have to go back early, for about eight minutes."

"I'll play the movie," I promise, hiding the remote behind my back. "But only if you tell the Mentos story."

"It's ChapStick," corrects Tony. "It just seems like Mentos because we were in Norway." Tony looks at the faces of our guests, then back at me. "Are you sure, Dennis? It's so gross."

"Don't want anything gross here today," says Marcus. "No sirree."

Tony waits for Lauren and me to polish off our second buns, then starts. "There was this stripper on the tour named Roman," he explains. "And Roman's particular kink was to pick up a woman after the show and convince her to let him put a ChapStick in her butt."

With this, Ross nearly chortles himself into a seizure.

Tony gives Ross a few moments to regain his composure, but it doesn't look like he's going to, so Tony trudges onward. "So Roman would take off the cap, insert the ChapStick, then unscrew the bottom and let the heat of the woman's ass, like, bite it off."

"Oh, my God, that's so-o-o *gross*!" screams Lauren.

"And then he would screw her in the ass," says Tony.

"Ah, good, a happy ending," says Dr. Beaverman.

"Afterward, he'd keep the empty Chapstick tube like a trophy," says Tony. "By the time I joined the tour, he already had a whole toiletry bag full of empty Chapstick tubes."

"Dr. Beaverman is speechless," says Dr. Beaverman.

"Did he have a favorite flavor?" I wonder.

"Bonne Bell Root Beer," says Lauren. "With the rope, because you don't want that thing getting away from you."

"You know why I like that story?" says Marcus. "Because everybody thinks gays are the biggest pervs."

"Believe me," says Dr. Beaverman, "big pervs come in all shapes and sizes, colors and flavors."

"Christopher Atkins!" demands Tony.

I toss him the remote and let him do the honors himself. Soon, we're watching Christopher Atkins as charm monster Rick Monroe presenting an unprepared oral presentation to his college speech class.

"Was 1983 the year of the postperm?" wonders Dr. Beaverman as Chris's classmates look on with various levels of interest. "It looks like everyone ran out and got a perm after the 'You Don't Bring Me Flowers' Grammy telecast, and now they were growing them out."

"This actually makes me uncomfortable to watch because I remember how badly I wanted him," recalls Tony. "I mean, it *hurt.* I used to watch *Dallas* with my family and that's when I fell in love with him. When they showed *The Blue Lagoon* on HBO, I would literally stand with my face pressed against the TV—hoping my mom wouldn't come in—and I could *not breathe.* That period of time was like my season of Christopher Atkins. Oh, my God, hold on a second."

Tony jumps up and rushes into his room. While he's gone, we unanimously vote to zoom ahead to the scene where Christopher, futuristically clad in what looks like Elroy Jetson's underwear, doffs his kit in front of a club full of squealing Floridians.

"March 24, 1984," Tony says, returning from his room with a small three-ring notebook. "Dear Diary, I can't get C.A. out of my mind, not that I would want to." Tony looks up from his notebook and explains that C.A. stands for Christopher Atkins, then resumes reading. "He is so perfect. Today I got my perm. It looks OK. When it grows in, it'll look better. Ron is sort of dry and boring. I think I may switch hairdressers."

"Oh, my God! Old diaries, the best!" declares Lauren. "I've been going through mine lately, looking for material for my act. I'll be right back."

While Lauren runs out to her car, I ask Dr. Beaverman if the Lawrence Welk bubbles floating through the strip club have any symbolic meaning.

"They're looking to be popped," she says wearily. "Do I have to spell *everything* out for you?"

Though C.A. has the entire audience eating out of his sweaty hand, he saves his best bumps and grinds for the face of his sexually frustrated, hard-ass speech teacher, Faye, played with high-collared frigidity by Lesley Ann Warren. "I love how he really singles her out and they make a connection," says Lauren, who has returned from her car with two little padlocked journals. "I'm sure that's very realistic."

"I interviewed Lesley Ann Warren for *Out* a few years ago," I report. "And she told me she was drunk when they shot this scene."

"Would that I were," groans Dr. Beaverman. "I'm just not getting the frenzy these women are experiencing. As if I'm going to be turned on by a boy with flat hair sticking that silver *Plan 9 From Outer Space* poly-blend diaper in my face. It's not a sexual fantasy, it's an Ed Wood movie."

"I had to do a caveman number that was even more degrading than this," confesses Tony. "We were all in these hideous sequined G-strings, and, let me tell you, those sequins cut your butt hole and it don't feel good."

"Tell me about it," deadpans Ross.

"The most embarrassing part, though, was later in the show," Tony continues. "There was this 'Jungle Love' number that featured the Tropical God, played by Carlos the long-haired guy, because there's always one long-haired guy. He'd come out with this giant plastic banana and then lie down on the ground and stroke it until it squirted Nivea lotion really high into the air. All the women would go apeshit and the curtain would close. Then I'd have to come out in front of the curtain and sing 'I'll Make Love To You' by Boyz II Men like I fucking meant it. Well, inevitably, Carlos would do his banana bit too far downstage. So while I'm doing my song, you could see this hand reaching out from under the curtain with a rag, you know, to wipe up the fake jizz I'm standing in. And I'm trying to be *serious*! Every night after the show I'd be like, 'Carlos, can you do your jizz further upstage? *Please?*' And he never took the fucking hint."

Back on the screen, we cut away from Christopher's *Plan 9* homage to meet the other man in Lesley Ann's life, her beleaguered aeronautical engineer husband, Whitney. "So, we go straight from these antifemale scenes of frivolous, screeching, *Urban Cowboy* extras in the bar to Whitney slaving away at the factory," remarks Dr. Beaverman. "Here is a man who is carrying the weight of the world on his shoulders. He's all lines and angles—he even has a pocket protector—whereas his shallow little wife is just looking for a little flesh and fantasy."

When we return to Chris at the club, he's doing his Deney Terrio–choreographed pelvic thrusts right in Lesley Ann's face. At the same time, he gazes into the eyes of his Fergie-esque girlfriend, proving that unlike Gregory Harrison, who wanted us to feel his artistic struggle, Christopher's not only going to jiggle his prick but *be* a prick.

"April 2, 1984," says Tony, treating us to another entry. "Yesterday there was a *People* magazine at my dentist's with C.A. on the cover and I took it! I'm so bad, Diary, but he's too perfect to resist. Today, I got up at 8 o'clock and got to school at 8:30. Wow! I just wash-and-go with my hair. I love this disheveled-type lifestyle."

"The lamp is a symbol, of course, a solidified, frigid, Georgia O'Keeffe labia metaphor. It's as hard and ossified as Lesley Ann's own labia and as big a distraction in the kitchen as her broken-down sexuality is in her life."
—Dr. Beaverman

"What day was that, April 2?" asks Lauren, thumbing through one of her journals and settling on a page. "While you were obsessed with Christopher Atkins and your new perm in Phoenix, this is what I was going through on Long Island: Dear Diary, No gorgeous guy has ever liked me. I know I'm ugly, but I didn't think it would turn off guys. Mom won't let me wear makeup until I'm 15, and then I'll have to buy it myself. I'll show her and wear it now! Then I have to get a perm to give body to my hair and buy new sexy clothes even though I don't have anything sexy to show off. I thought I was sociable and outgoing but since the guys don't like me, maybe I'm not. Bummer!"

We "a-a-aw" sympathetically at Lauren's schoolgirl vulnerability, then turn back to the

TV in time to see Christopher proposition Lesley Ann at a school reception. "I was wondering if I could retake the final," he suggests flirtatiously.

"In your pussy," adds Ross.

"She's even twitchier than Kim Basinger," laments Marcus.

"She's on an erotic journey," I say in Lesley's defense. "Give her a break."

Later, back in Lesley Ann's kitchen, she connives with her sister on the phone while Whitney sits nearby, under the most obnoxious, unsettling lighting fixture I've seen since *The Phantom of the Opera* came through town. "The lamp is a symbol, of course," asserts Dr. Beaverman. "A solidified, frigid, Georgia O'Keeffe labia metaphor. It's as hard and ossified as Lesley Ann's own labia and as big a distraction in the kitchen as her broken-down sexuality is in her life."

Bored senseless with the kitchen-sink dramatics, we fast-forward to the scene where Christopher and Lesley finally get it on, stopping only once to take in a rain-drenched montage set to Bryan Adams's "The Best Is Yet to Come."

"They got the 'yet to come' part right," says Marcus.

"April 16, 1984," reads Tony. "Today was OK. I'm not sure what to do about my hair. It's too curly. I hate my hair this curly. I'm going to keep washing it so it loosens. I looked at the C.A. picture 11 times today. Diary, I'm in the mood for love. I finally got my life all together, now I need a boyfriend. Who knows?"

"I don't think I can top that," says Lauren. "But I'll try. April 16, I'm so sick of Cynthia and the way she brags about everything she owns. She gets a purse for no special occasion. We live in a world of designer jeans, designer shoes, even designer socks, yet my parents haven't even bought me one single item of designer clothing. It doesn't seem fair. All of my friends have Calvin Klein jeans or Gloria Vanderbilt shirts. Why can't I look like them? Laura has everything, including clothes, money, and late hours. She's the perfect girl. I hope the play turns out good. That'll show her. I think I want to paint my room lavender. What do you think?"

After sharing with Lauren our divergent takes on lavender, we finally get to a scene in a cheap hotel room where C.A.'s going to not only solve Lesley Ann's twitching problem, but hopefully raise his letter grade for the semester. We all fall silent as Lesley kneels down and undoes his pants. "Do you see his *penis*?" I ask with breathless anticipation. "Oh, my God, you *do* see it."

"It's small," chides Lauren.

"It's perfect," gushes Tony.

"It's limp," says Ross.

"Of course it's limp, it's Lesley Ann Warren," bristles Dr. Beaverman, who was clearly ready for this marathon to be over ages ago.

"He's not even doing anything," I complain, after Christopher carries the still-dressed Lesley Ann to the bed and positions her on top of him.

"This is not at all a woman's version of erotica," Dr. Beaverman grumbles, as Lesley

Ann shudders and comes. "Women need *men*. This is a little boy. A good book would be so much better for her. I could recommend so many good books."

A few scenes later, Lesley Ann catches Christopher banging his hot Fergie girlfriend in the hotel shower. Then she has to pretend not to be a sobbing mess when Whitney calls five seconds later. Next thing you know, Whitney kidnaps Christopher, takes him to a boat on a remote lake, and forces him at gunpoint to strip and act at the same time. "Please, don't kill me," Chris blubbers pathetically.

"Where do you get off fucking my wife?" Whitney screams.

"Usually on her chest," I say, speaking for Chris. "But sometimes, on her back. We like to mix it up."

Whitney finds it in his heart to spare Christopher's life, much to Tony's relief, then goes home to reconnect with his apologetic wife under the labia lamp. "It's time for some Wild Turkey," Tony announces as Lesley Ann pours herself a drink from Whitney's bottle.

"There's no marriage that some good booze can't salvage," Ross says.

"I was actually referring to her hair," says Tony.

"For all the bumping and grinding, this movie is ultimately about Whitney," concludes Dr. Beaverman as the credits roll. "Here's a man who is completely tired of being the working man, and his wife's this big maw of overarching needs who's slapped back into her place at the end, once Whitney is again erect and potent by way of packing a piece. This movie proves that the only place for frivolous, needy women is in the kitchen under an ossified vulva lamp, and the only place for little boys is naked on a boat in a blue lagoon."

"On the plus side," says Tony, "I got over Chris pretty fast. I found someone else," he proclaims, looking at his diary. "May 16. Last night I went to a party at Justin's house. John Straffin was there. God, I was flirting with him so bad, giving him alluring glances, complimenting him. This girl, Alyssa, was showing us sign language, and I made an L and said to him, 'L is for lust.' He didn't bite, though. I'm so sad because he looks just like C.A. but taller and not as perfect. I guess I'm lonely. Tomorrow I'm going shopping." Tony closes his diary and says, "Maybe I didn't get over C.A. after all."

"But you did quit talking about your hair," says Dr. Beaverman, standing up to stretch, "which is a vital step on the road toward self-actualization."

"Here's my May 16," says Lauren. "I'm the most popular girl in school right now because of *Birdie*. Cynthia is so jealous of me. We did our last show last night. I'm kind of sad but also happy. My biggest problem right now is who to talk to at lunch." Lauren closes and locks her diary, then smiles with satisfaction.

"Fuck you," says Tony.

On her way out, Dr. Beaverman tries to summarize her observations from today like Jerry Springer giving his Final Thought. "The moral of both of these stories is that you can take a cheesy hustler out of his Zorro outfit but you can't ever make him legit," she says, moving toward the door. "Once a hustler, always a hustler. Be happy with who you are, in other words. Don't aspire to be more because your true self is going to ooze out like pubes from a Speedo."

Marcus is the last to leave, and, before he does, we share another look at his cherished, time-honored picture of Gregory. Before you know it, we've caught Harrison Fever again and I'm typing the superhunk's name into the eBay search engine. When a *For Ladies Only* iron-on decal comes up, with the option to "Buy It Now" for $9.95, I jump out of my skin, jump back in, and do just that. I promise Marcus I'll ask the seller if there's another available for purchase. If there's not, we agree, we'll just have to share custody.

•

April 30 , 2001

Dear Diary,

The iron-ons arrived today from eBay and they're so cool. Now we have to find the perfect shirts to put them on. I think I want gray or black. I don't know what Marcus wants. I hope I don't screw it up when I apply it.

Lauren called yesterday to say she can't use ChapStick anymore and that she hopes Tony's happy.

I finished the article for *GayZone* today. Whew. I hope they like it. Diary, I'm in the mood for love. I finally got my life all together, now I need a boyfriend. Who knows?

BEALS LIKE THE FIRST TIME

"I can't believe it took this shitheap to make you cave in and take the plunge," says Ross.

"I love that you call movies shitheaps now," I say.

"If the shoe fits," he mutters.

Ross and I are standing in the checkout line at Costco. He's perusing the list of special features on the back of the *Coyote Ugly* DVD while I prepare to purchase, at long last, a DVD player. That's right, folks, I'm finally venturing forth into the post-millennial universe of interactive menus, commentary tracks, and alternate endings. I've been beholden to the half-inch world for too long. Besides, when I discovered that the *Coyote Ugly* DVD included a commentary track with the Coyotes (the film's bootylicious quintet of lead actresses) and a "Coyote 101: How to Be a Coyote" featurette, resistance became impossible.

I brought Ross along today not only because he's good with gadgets but also because I was hoping I could get him to say "shitheap" a lot.

"Wait here," I say. "I want to run back and pick up *You've Got Mail.*"

"Seriously?" he says. "Talk about a shitheap."

"I'm kidding," I reply. "I just wanted to hear you say it."

About an hour ago, I picked Ross up at LAX—wow, I guess we are friends now—and we came straight here from there. On the way, he caught me up on the situation with his mother. Yesterday was her last radiation treatment and though her doctors are optimistic, they won't know for a few weeks how well it took.

"We're not doing this for Screening Party, are we?" Ross asks, before placing *Coyote Ugly* on top of my third item, a 24-pack of Costco-brand two-ply toilet paper.

"No," I say. "I begged Matt to let us do it, and he said it wasn't big enough over there." I ignore Ross's unnecessarily loud sigh of relief and continue. "He said we could do *Flashdance* instead, though, which is basically the same movie. They're both produced by Jerry Bruckheimer, they both have lots of red lettering, and they both feature girls with big dreams who look like whores and act like whores but aren't really whores."

"I suppose I can sit through *Flashdance,*" Ross says.

"How can you not love *Coyote Ugly*?" I

ask. "It's like the movie version of *Maxim.* And it has my favorite line of dialogue from any movie in years."

"Which is?"

"Let's have a big coyote welcome for Leann Rimes."

"Membership card?" says the clerk.

While I dig for my card, the clerk notices the *Coyote* disc on top of the toilet paper and smiles. "Can't have one without the other," Ross explains.

Before dropping Ross at his place, the two of us stop at the Coffee Bean in Toluca Lake for a little ice-blended pick-me-up. We're about to head inside when he pulls a large manila envelope from his overnight bag and places it on my dashboard. "I want you to read this and tell me what you think," he says. "It's a script for short film. I got sort of inspired when I was home."

"Way to go, man," I say, picking it up.

"I really want to make it too," he says. "I went on the Web and there's this short fiction filmmaking course at UCLA that looks perfect. You go through the whole process in five months, and at the end of it you have a movie."

"That's great, but I thought you already went to film school."

"I never said I finished," he clarifies. "I freaked out and quit after half a semester."

When I slide the script from the envelope, the first words I see are "*Shitheap: The Musical* by Ross Fowler."

"I don't have a title yet," he explains before jumping out of the truck. "I just put that on there to amuse you."

We go inside, order our usuals, then grab a table on the patio. "So what's it about, *Shitheap: The Musical*?" I ask.

"It's about this 12-year-old kid who wants to be in a Renaissance fair," says Ross.

"Is it autobiographical?" I ask.

"Sort of," says Ross. "I never wanted to be in a Renaissance fair, but I wanted to learn how to do sword fighting. This was right after I saw *The Empire Strikes Back,* which is by far the best of the *Star Wars* movies..."

"Top 10?" I ask.

"Two," he says. "Anyway, after I saw *Empire* I became obsessed with sword fighting because of the light sabers. That's all I wanted to do. It was during the summer, and there was a class offered in stage combat at the local college that teenagers could take. I got all the information. I was going to pay for it with my own money. I even talked to the teacher and everything. And then my parents wouldn't let me do it. My mom thought it was too dangerous, and my dad thought it was a sissy thing because it was in the theater department or something stupid like that. I think the truth is, they were in that phase of their divorce where they were both trying to be more strict and forbidding than the other. The honeymoon phase, where they spoiled us rotten, was over."

"That sucks," I say.

"Well, when I was just home, my mom and I did a lot of talking while I was driving her to her treatments, and one day I asked her about it, like why she didn't let me do it."

"What did she say?" I ask.

"She said she didn't remember," says Ross, "not just that she didn't remember *why* she wouldn't let me do it, but that she didn't remember it all, the whole thing. It was the most important thing in the world to me that summer, and she doesn't even remember it."

"Maybe she was just out of it from the treatments," I offer.

"Maybe, but I don't think so," says Ross. "She remembers other things. Then, this morning before I flew out, I had breakfast with my dad and asked him about it, and he didn't remember it either."

"I'm sorry," I say.

"I'm not," says Ross emphatically, "because I realized something. That it's crazy to live your life worrying what other people might think, because they *don't care*. I mean, they care about your happiness and health and stuff like that, but they don't care about your dreams, not the way you do. They've got their own problems and their own shit to deal with."

"Makes sense," I say.

"It's like, say, that girl behind the counter doesn't like your shirt. She probably doesn't like it *this* much," he says taking a single blue packet of Equal from the sugar caddy and putting in on the table in front of me, "like one packet worth. But if *you* really *love* your shirt," he continues picking up the entire container, "then you probably feel like *this* about it." With that, he dumps all the Equals and Sugars and Sweet'nLows over the original Equal packet. A few packets slide off the table and onto the floor. "So I'm going to make a movie because I've always wanted to," he says, while I start to pick up the stray packets, "and if it's a shitheap and people like us sit around and make fun of it and say it's a shitheap, then I'll still win because, no matter what, I'll have more sugars." Together, we organize the packets by color and place them back in the caddy. "So do what you want to do, Dennis." concludes Ross. "Because ultimately no one gives a damn."

I pick up the original Equal, the one that represents all the naysayers of the world, and stuff it back into its home. "What's wrong with my shirt?" I say.

Three days later, Ross is the first to arrive at our Screening Party, celebrating not only the toe-tapping wonder of *Flashdance* but my induction into the DVD fraternity. My excitement is soon dampened, however, when Ross dumps a beat-up VHS copy of *Flashdance* on the coffee table and informs me that taking your passion and making it happen is not something that can be done on DVD, at least not at the present time.

"What the fuck?" I gripe. "Is Cynthia Rhodes holding out for money?"

"But I got good news too," he says before holding up a UCLA catalog. "I signed up for the class yesterday. I'm making a movie."

"Congratulations," I say, patting him on the shoulder. "If there's anything I can do to help, let me know."

"You wouldn't happen to have $20,000 lying around?" he asks.

"No, but you can borrow *Coyote Ugly* if you want. You know, to learn from."

One by one, we give big coyote welcomes to the rest of the crew, who, as they enter, express enthusiasm about my new electronics purchase. Their bubbles are soon burst, however, when I break the news that we're still VHS-ing it today as *Flashdance* isn't available on DVD.

"What the fuck?" gripes Tony. "Is Cynthia Rhodes holding out for more money?"

"You two are so redundant," says Ross.

"Be that as it may," I say, reclaiming the floor, "I'd still like to show off my purchase, so here, without further ado, is my favorite DVD discovery to date: Tyra Banks ruminating on the intricacies of her craft on the commentary track of *Coyote Ugly.* Hit it, Ross."

Ross unpauses the movie and we join the action in a scene where bartendresses Tyra Banks, Bridget Moynahan, and Izabella Miko count their tips after work over heaping plates of junk food in a Manhattan diner. "This is my big scene," announces Tyra on the commentary track. "I was a little skinny, though. Like I wasn't eating carbs back then and I was about 10 pounds lighter. I think I look a little too modelish, so I decided to put my pounds back on for my acting."

"God bless DVD," says Marcus, raising his hands to heaven.

Just then, the doorbell rings. Odd, considering we're all here already and we haven't ordered any take-out yet.

"It's Tyra," figures Tony. "She's come to apologize for all those times she was modelish."

"Oh, I totally forgot," says Lauren. "It's probably Shawn."

"Shawn who?" asks Dr. Beaverman, a certain edge creeping into her voice. Though she's never said so, I have a hunch Dr. Beaverman doesn't cotton much to interlopers.

"Shawn from hip-hop class," says Lauren.

"Shawn from hip-hop class?" I practically shriek.

"I thought it would be good to have a real professional dancer here for *Flashdance,*" explains Lauren.

"If only the filmmakers had been so thorough," says Tony.

"Is somebody going to get the door?" says Marcus after the bell rings for the third time.

I check my appearance in the entryway mirror and psyche myself to greet the mocha-skinned, dreadlocked, dimple-cheeked, young-looking-but-who-knows-how-old-he-is dancer boy who gets his considerable groove on in the front row of the street dance class Lauren and I take Wednesday nights. Though I've been a member of the Shawn fan club for months, I've probably only ever said two words to him in my life, which is two more words than he's said to me, though he has nodded at me four times and smiled at least twice.

I rest my hand on the doorknob, then turn to my guests and say, as quickly and quietly as possible, "I think Shawn is totally hot, but Lauren and I have no idea what blows his skirt up, so be on the lookout for clues and call me into the kitchen and slap me if I start to act like an asshole. Tony and Marc, if Shawn flirts with you, you both have drug habits and jealous boyfriends who are totally racist, just like you." With that, I open the door.

"Hey," says Shawn. "For a second, I thought I was in the wrong place."

"No, this is it," I say, ushering him inside.

This is the first time I've seen Shawn when he wasn't dressed to move. I'm not surprised at all to see he cleans up well, in low-slung jeans, beat-up sandals, and a clingy sleeveless T-shirt that reads "Jesus Kinda Likes Me." Get in line, Lord.

While I fetch Shawn a Coke in the kitchen, Lauren introduces the rest of the group and tries to explain to Shawn what it is we do here. When she finishes, Shawn eyes the rolling cassette recorder on the coffee table and says, "I sort of have a *Flashdance* story, but it's kind of embarrassing. You want it?"

"I want it," I say, handing him his Coke. Oh, God, was that as loaded as it felt?

"Remember that moment where Jennifer Beals slides her foot up into the guy's crotch?" he asks. "Well, I had this one summer where I was obsessed with crotches and I would watch that scene over and over again."

"Guess that answers the skirt question," says Ross.

"What question?" says Shawn.

"It's not important," I stammer. "I'll tell you later."

Suddenly, Marcus, in what's clearly an attempt to dispel the current awkwardness, hoists a leg onto the sofa arm and stretches over it, claiming he needs to be warmed up if he's going to watch this movie and avoid injury.

Shawn laughs and says, "This is actually the movie that made me start dancing."

"What, you were scrambling to get out of the theater and you figured a jazz run was just as effective as normal running?" says Tony.

Shawn laughs at this, much to my relief. "Nah," he says. "I remember thinking, *I want to turn like she does. I want to jump like she does.* It was interesting, because my really macho brother, who I used to be in a gang with, took me to the movie because he was into break dancing. After that, I quit the gang and started taking dance classes behind his back. God, I sound like someone from *A Chorus Line.*"

Uh-huh, and the tune that comes to mind is "I Hope I Get It."

"How many times did you see it?" asks Lauren.

"Three or four in the theater," says Shawn.

"I've got you beat," boasts Marcus. "When I was in college, I saw it 10 times."

"Of course you did," says Ross. "It was probably a great place to pick up guys."

"This was before I knew I was gay," says Marcus.

"Wait a second. Stop the presses," says Lauren. "You saw *Flashdance* 10 times and you didn't know you were gay?"

Marcus shakes his head no, and before I have a chance to prepare Shawn, the train for St. Olaf has left the station. "I saw it when it first came out in like April," Marcus remembers. "After that, I'd tell people about it and everybody else wanted to see it but they'd be like, 'No one will go with me,' so I was like, 'I'll go with you.' It got to the point where people would tell their friends, 'You want to see *Flashdance*? Call Marcus. He'll go with you.' "

"You were like the official *Flashdance* ambassador," I say.

"Not a lot of competition for that job," says Dr. Beaverman.

"People would come up to me and say, 'Hi. I don't know you but my friend said you would go see *Flashdance* with me because you already saw it eight times,'" recalls Marcus.

"You went with *strangers*?" I ask.

"A couple of times," he replies. "Once with my roommate's co–teaching assistant for Human Sexuality, and I forget who the other person was. Then, during the summer, my friend Matt, who's gay now too, we'd have nothing to do so we'd be like, 'Let's go see *Flashdance*.' "

"Let me get this straight," says Lauren. "The two of you think, *There's nothing to do, let's go see* Flashdance *for the 10th time,* and you didn't know you were gay?"

Marcus just shrugs.

"You should have called me," says Lauren. "I would have told you."

"Can I just say that I'm gay and I've never had that little to do?" remarks Tony.

"I didn't know I was gay either when I saw it," I report. "I remember seeing the commercial for it and thinking Jennifer Beals was so beautiful that I had to see her. I was like, 'I *love* her.'"

"You know you're gay when you're going, 'I *love* her,'" argues Lauren. "That's not like 'Oh, I would love to have sex with her.' It's like, 'Oh, my God, I *love* her.' Very gay."

"Also, I was taking a jazz dance class when it came out," I say, "and I wrote a paper on *Flashdance*."

"Another clue," says Lauren.

"I wasn't kind, though," I recall. "I wrote that it was kind of hacky. I thought she was beautiful, but I didn't think it was a good movie."

"So you thought that because you were being catty, that wasn't gay?" asks Lauren, growing more incredulous with each reply.

"Take it from me," says Ross. "Straight men could give a shit about this movie. They were thinking, *What do you mean, I don't get to see her tits? I thought she was a hooker.*"

"Oh, I almost forgot," Marcus says, digging in his jeans pocket. He pulls out a rumpled slip of paper and reads from it. "174631503." We just look at him. "That's Jennifer Beals's character's Social Security number," he says proudly. "They mention it in the movie and I wrote it in my journal the fourth time I saw it, or maybe it was the fifth. You know what? It was the fifth because I borrowed the pen from my roommate's T.A. friend. I also wrote down her address: Alexandra Owens, 7 Wood St., Pittsburgh, PA 15222."

"This is going to be one long fucking party," says Ross.

I take that as my cue and start the movie already. Seconds later, the word *Flashdance* scrolls across the screen in giant blood-red letters. "This looks like a horror movie," says Tony. "It's like Clive Barker's *Flashdance.*"

"It *is* a horror movie," says Dr. Beaverman.

Soon, Irene Cara's Oscar-winning song "Flashdance (What a Feeling)" kicks in on the soundtrack over various establishing shots of rainy-day Pittsburgh. "I went to college there. Carnegie Mellon," says Lauren. "And every time my friends and I drove over that bridge, we all sang this."

"The lyrics refer to 'a world made of steel, made of stone,'" remarks Dr. Beaverman. "The metaphors in this movie are about as subtle as Bruce Jenner's face work. This is a cold, hard, impenetrable world, but this girl, this rainbow child, Jennifer Beals, is made of music. She's going to take her passion and she's going to make an *indentation* in that world of steel, by God, if it takes 16 dance doubles to do it."

"Did you guys know that one of her dance doubles was a guy?" asks Shawn.

"No, but I remember reading in *People* that the dance double from *Footloose* was married to the dance double from *Flashdance,*" boasts Marcus.

"They actually held their whole ceremony in silhouette," says Tony, nodding. "And the wedding video is all quick cuts and backlighting."

"The dance double from *Footloose* was my dance *idol,*" I gush. "His name was Peter Tramm and he worked all the time, like he was the blond guy in the ZZ Top video 'Sharp Dressed Man.' I think he died of AIDS. I have this 'Cher at Caesar's' concert video from the '80s where he humps her in a giant stiletto."

"Are they sure it was AIDS?" says Dr. Beaverman. "Maybe it was embarrassment."

"The shoe thing was kind of cheesy," I admit. "But I would have done it in a heartbeat. I would have been like, 'Move that ankle strap, Cher. I'm coming in.'"

As the opening credits unfurl, we see the names of the folks behind *Flashdance*—executive producers Peter Guber and Jon Peters, producers Don Simpson and Jerry Bruckheimer, director Adrian Lyne, coscreenwriter Joe Eszterhas—all of whom have, in the years since, become some of Hollywood's biggest power brokers. "Before the movie came out, they all thought it was a big abortion and they were afraid to release it," says Tony of the big names behind *Flashdance,* who, it's rumored, have about one soul between them. "Then it came out and made like $170 million and everyone involved, even like Michael Eisner and Dawn Steel, who were somehow in on it too, were rushing to take credit. It's like, all of a sudden Guber and Peters were *geniuses.*"

"I was just about to say that," says Ross.

"Losing your touch, film geek?" teases Tony.

"You watch one *Behind the Music* and you think you can horn in on my act," taunts Ross.

"For your information," says Tony. "It was an *E! True Hollywood Story.*"

"Why don't you two just make out and get it over with?" says Lauren.

Back on the screen, we get our first good look at our steel town heroine—Alex, according to the name on her welding helmet—when she removes her headgear to wipe the sweat from her brow. "Alex is a woman in a man's world," says Dr. Beaverman. "She's got a man's name, a man's job, and a blowtorch as a penis."

"And she's mustache-y," adds Tony.

"You think every girl's mustache-y," carps Lauren. "We could be watching *Curly Sue* and you'd think the little girl was mustache-y."

"I just call 'em as I see 'em," says Tony. "Don't you see it, Dennis?"

"I've made a deal with this movie from the first frame that I'm going to love her *the way she is,*" I assert.

Across the room, I see Shawn's eyes fill with affection as the film takes us to Mawbry's Bar and our first big dance sequence, set to "He's a Dream" by Shandi. Grab a towel, folks, because this is the number where Alex lies back on a chair, yanks a chain, and gets drenched with water from above.

"I'm loving watching this scene," I confess. And I'm not just saying that so Shawn will think I'm a champion of the dance.

"None of the customers in that bar are loving it, though," says Ross. "They're like, 'Show us your bush!' "

Soon, we're introduced to the other dancers who shake their moneymakers at Mawbry's. They include Cynthia Rhodes of *Dirty Dancing* and *Staying Alive* fame, a banana-eating black chick named Heels, and, finally, Margo, a long-in-the-tooth redhead who is so world-weary I keep waiting for her to break into "Private Dancer." Or keel over dead, one of the two.

"Dennis, remember I told you my Cynthia Rhodes story the day we met?" says Dr. Beaverman.

"And several times since," I say.

"And I've yet to see it in print, so here it goes again," says Dr. Beaverman. "Cynthia Rhodes and her husband, Richard Marx, the rocker—and no, I never slept with him—used to eat breakfast at Jinky's in Sherman Oaks one table over from me every Saturday. And let me tell you, she'd have to do *Staying Alive* and *Dirty Dancing* back to back to burn off the calories she'd inhale in one breakfast."

Shawn finds this hysterical; I'm not sure why. But I'm happy about it.

"I believe her preferred poison was the banana nut pancakes," continues Dr. Beaverman. "But she'd also order eggs, bacon, juice, and then she'd Hoover up something from Richard's plate. I'd always try to eavesdrop on their conversation and one time I think she was telling Richard that she didn't think the Beatles were that great. That's my Cynthia Rhodes story."

"I can die now," says Ross, with a melodramatic sigh.

"I suppose you can do better," says Dr. Beaverman.

"Actually, I can," Ross replies. "I have a Jennifer Beals story and it involves boob poking."

"Pause the tape," says Tony.

"I saw her at my dry cleaner's a while back," says Ross. "She brings in this lacy black bra and she says to the seamster guy, 'There's a wire poking out. Could you cover it with some material, because it's jabbing me right here?' And she starts poking her boob in the dry cleaner's. That's it."

"I can die now," says Shawn, much to our collective delight.

We return to the movie to discover Alex back at the steelyard, flipping though a copy of *French Vogue* with the late Gia Carangi on the cover. "I know women who walk around in boots like that and they are not reading *French Vogue,*" grumbles Lauren. "They're reading *Cat Fancy* and *On Our Backs.*"

Soon, Alex's swarthy boss, Nick Hurley, played by Michael Nouri, swaggers up and says, "I saw you dance. What's a dancer doing working as a welder?"

"I want her to be like, 'I don't fucking know, dude. This is my first movie. It's in the script,'" I say.

"Cream relaxer was available was in 1982, wasn't it?" Tony asks. "Couldn't those two have gotten a twofer at a salon somewhere?"

"I know women who walk around in boots like that and they are not reading *French Vogue,*" grumbles Lauren. "They're reading *Cat Fancy* and *On Our Backs.*"

Alex makes a date with her boss, then returns to her warehouse home to drink from a Diet Pepsi can with a style of lettering that hasn't been seen since Hands Across America. Then she dances around the warehouse to Michael Sembello's "Maniac," blowing off her loyal mutt, Grunt, who clearly needs to visit a fire hydrant, stat.

"If she were a real ballet dancer she'd be taping her toes, not the balls of her feet," Shawn informs us.

"The lyrics of this song talk about telling the dancer from the dance," says Dr. Beaverman, "which is a phrase from one of my favorite poems, 'Among School Children' by William Butler Yeats." Dr. Beaverman gestures to Tony to pause the VCR and recites from memory:

Labour is blossoming or dancing where
The body is not bruised to pleasure soul,
Nor beauty born out of its own despair,
Nor blear-eyed wisdom out of midnight oil.
O chestnut-tree, great-rooted blossomer,
Are you the leaf, the blossom or the bole?
O body swayed to music, O brightening glance,
How can we know the dancer from the dance?

We all feel oddly enriched by her recitation and applaud accordingly. Shawn smiles at me as he claps. It seems I may have just scored a few points. And here I thought snagging a guy in L.A. was all about cutting out carbs and other such modelish pursuits.

"Yeats's point is that when it comes to great art, you cannot separate the *artist* from the *artwork,*" Dr. B. explains. "Except in the case of this movie, which is clearly not great art, because the dancer and the dance were separated not once but many times, by both men and women, at least one of whom was French, and if you question that separation, I suggest you check with payroll."

Pleased with herself, Dr. Beaverman gives Tony a nod. He restarts the movie in time for us to get a heady dose of Jennifer's trademark superfast running-in-place. "That ass does not jiggle one ounce," Lauren groans. "Is it tasty treat time yet?"

"Not yet," says Marcus. "I'll tell you when."

"I'm fascinated with the ass-cam," says Tony. "Operating that was a someone's full-time job for months. I bet their chiropractor bills were enormous."

Soon, Mr. Ass-Cam gets a short time-out so we can see what the full-bladdered Grunt thinks of the Maniacal goings-on. "Maybe it's because I'm not really a dog person," I say, "but I hate in movies where they're like, 'Let's get the dog's reaction. That'll be cute.'"

"If Eszterhas had his way, the dog would have been licking his balls through this whole scene," says Ross, as Alex finishes her dance and we cut back to Grunt to witness his delight in how visibly pooped his mistress's workout has left him.

"This is right down the street from where I went to school," says Lauren during the next scene, in which Alex stops by the prestigious dance academy where she dreams of studying to pick up an application. "This building is not as dark as that anymore because they sandblasted it."

"The same can be said for a few members of the cast," says Tony.

Back on the screen, Alex is feeling despondent over her inability to fill out a simple application, so she pedals across town to visit her elderly gal pal Hanna, a former ballerina with one foot in the grave.

"How does she know Hanna?" I ask.

"We never find out," says Marcus.

"Hannah's just there to die," says Ross. "She's the Obi-Wan Kenobi of *Flashdance.*"

Then it's off to confession, where Alex prattles on about her fear of auditioning. Her priest seems rather uninterested in Alex's plight, which is not surprising considering the man probably signed on to hear about same-sex fantasies and hit on altar boys. Counseling wanna-be Fly Girls was not part of his plan, or the Lord's, for that matter.

"I want her to be like, 'I can't stop flashdancing, father,'" says Ross. "'I've flashdanced 25 times since my last confession. I've got to stop! *I've got to stop flashdancing!*'"

"This is supposed to show us her spiritual side," says Dr. Beaverman. "And yet her whole world is so about *her.* She gripes to the priest that she doesn't think she's going to make it in the dancing world. It's all about her, folks. She's not asking to be a better person. She doesn't say, 'Forgive me for causing my dog to explode with piss because I had to do a routine to "Maniac."' It's all about her and her leotard dreams. It's official. I hate her."

Then it's back to Mawbry's, where Richie the untalented comic–fry cook exhorts the crowd to give it up for Cynthia Rhodes as Tina Tech. With that, our favorite Jinky's carbo-loader kicks into her big number, "Manhunt," in which the Animotion refugee flips backward off a faux brick wall, then crawls toward the camera like Wendy O. Williams looking for a lost contact lens.

"I wonder if Richard Marx has ever said, 'I knew from the moment she did that first cooter-slam, we were meant to be,'" I say.

"I bet she's still finding glitter in the strangest places," says Tony.

"Oh oh oh oh oh," pants Marcus, jumping up excitedly and pulling another piece of paper from his pocket. "This was in *The Hollywood Reporter* yesterday," he says, then reads aloud: "20th Century Fox will partner with Columbia Pictures to finance the Mariah Carey starrer *All That Glitters,* which Fox will distribute domestically and Columbia will handle internationally. Written by Kate Lanier, *Glitters* is set against the background of the New York club scene and centers on a singer who overcomes a troubled childhood to rise to the top of her profession."

Marcus tosses me the clipping and I rest it on my face like it's some kind of newfangled aromatherapy stationary. "At last, a reason to go on living," I say, sighing.

"No shit," says Marcus. "I'm considering it part of my drug cocktail."

I run into the kitchen and magnet the clipping to the refrigerator next to our burgeoning list of Filthy Sanchez definitions. When I return, Cynthia's still cooter-slamming to beat the band, while Alex, Heels, and Margo, perched around a table in full costume, cheer her on. "How slutty must the girls across the street at Zanzibar be if these girls are the classy ones?" I wonder. "I mean, they look like Vanity 6."

The next scene finds Alex cheering on another friend: her figure skating pal Jeanie, who's competing in a big ice meet, Salchow-ing her ass off to the strains of Laura Branigan's "Gloria."

"Is she really skating?" asks Shawn.

"Uh-huh," says Marcus.

"You've gotta give her props," I offer. "In a movie full of phonies, she's the real deal."

"According to E! this girl is dead," reports Tony. "She had an aneurysm when she was like 30."

Alas, Jeanie, my so-called "real deal," soon bites the ice. And when she can't find the wherewithal to get back up, Alex rushes to her side and comforts her friend dutifully.

The night's not a total bummer for Alex, though. Later, back at her home sweet Home Depot, she enjoys a romantic interlude with her boss, Nick.

"I want Michael Nouri to look around and go, 'Maybe if you got a one bedroom apartment like a normal person, you wouldn't have to work two jobs,'" says Lauren.

"While driving her to the bedroom on a forklift," I add.

It's in this scene that we finally get our iconic Jennifer Beals: the wide-eyed dreamer from the poster who loves nothing more than to lounge around the warehouse in an old gray sweatshirt with the neck cut out. "This movie led me to ruin my entire wardrobe for the summer of '83," grumbles Lauren. "Actually, I had cut my shirts up *before* that, but then the movie came out and made it supertrendy. You couldn't wear them after like September without embarrassing yourself."

"This movie has planned obsolescence built into it," says Dr. Beaverman. "It was created to be a *Flashdance* in the pan."

It's clear none of us know what she's talking about but aren't sure we should ask for clarification. "Planned what?" wonders Shawn, who doesn't know better.

"Planned obsolescence," repeats Dr. Beaverman, while casually hitting pause on the remote. "It was a marketing ploy back in the '50s. Designers would deliberately overstylize products so they would only have a brief time in the sun. Take, like, a pink-and-charcoal two-tone sedan from the '50s with the big fins. The designers knew it could only be considered au courant for one season. After that, it was just laughable, and they knew people would *have* to buy another car right away or risk being ridiculed. Employing planned obsolescence was a way to keep people coming back for more."

"So what did we all buy into after *Flashdance*?" wonders Tony.

"Homosexuality, apparently," says Lauren.

We rejoin the movie to find our plucky protagonist spouting her "close your eyes and see the music" spiel to Nick while casually digging around in her sweatshirt and removing her bra. "I wonder if that bra was jabbing her in the boobs too," muses Ross. "Maybe her boobs are the problem, not the bras."

"I tried to take off my bra like that once," recalls Lauren. "It's not as easy as you'd think."

"Please, it's totally easy," argues Tony. "I did it last Halloween."

"I've got five bucks on the gay guy," says Ross, tossing a fiver on the coffee table.

"He's all talk," scoffs Dr. Beaverman. "My money's on Lauren."

We pause long enough for Tony and Lauren to agree to a postmovie showdown and for the rest of us to place our bets. Marcus and Ross go with Tony while Shawn joins Dr. Beaverman in backing Lauren. Though I daresay the smart money is on Tony, I opt to join Dr. B. and Shawn because suddenly I want to do everything with Shawn.

When we resume the movie, Alex is back at work looking all moony after an evening of lovemaking with her boss. "This is where Gloria Allred should show up and serve Michael Nouri with a summons for sexual harassment in the workplace," says Marcus.

Instead, we get the "Lady, Lady, Lady" montage where Michael and Jennifer pitch all manner of woo in such grimy urban settings as a junkyard and an abandoned building. "For our two-week anniversary, let's go to a crack house, whaddaya say?" says Tony.

"She has just gone to bed with her boss," Dr. Beaverman reminds us. "And all she can talk about is *herself* and how *she* feels when *she's* dancing. She's not saying, 'You were incredible: tender, yet strong.' She's saying, 'When I'm dancing, I can pretend I'm someone else!' And he's sitting there putting up with it. Most guys would've walked right out of that junkyard. It's all 'me, me, me' with her, and I'm sick of it. They should have called that song 'Egomaniac.'"

Though her love life is in full bloom, Alex still prefers to play pissed-off-at-the-world when she's dancing. In her next Mawbry's showstopper, set to Laura Branigan's "Imagination," Alex, in whiteface, has a full-on mental breakdown while a symphony of strobe lights beat down on her. "Time for my 'What a Feeling' brownies!" announces Marcus, before running into the kitchen to retrieve them. "They're both non-fat and sugar-free," he says, returning with the treats. "And we're eating them now because this scene is Jennifer at her most artificial."

"Beals probably wasn't even in the country when this was shot," I say, reaching for a brownie. "She was at a friend's wedding in Barbados."

"Or at my dry cleaner's poking her boobs," says Ross.

"Those weren't actually very large shoulder pads for that period," says Lauren, pointing to Alex's red suit jacket. "They were wearing larger shoulder pads on *Designing Women*."

"She's Julia Sugarbaker in Kabuki makeup," decides Tony.

"If she welds during the day and dances at night," says Shawn, as Alex seizures her way into a checkerboard-patterned corner, "when does she build all those sets?"

"Well, her pantry is a lumberyard," I say. "That helps."

"Beals probably wasn't even in the country when this was shot. She was at a friend's wedding in Barbados."
—Dennis

The next night, while attending the ballet with Hanna-Wan Kenobi, Alex spots her boyfriend-boss with an icy blond on his arm. Furious at this betrayal, she stops by his house on her way home and hurls a rock throw his window. "My opinion of her just changed," declares Dr. Beaverman. "That's the best thing she's done this whole movie. Finally, the sparks are flying. Good for you, Yalie."

Still distraught over Nick, Alex arrives home to more bad news. There's a puddle in her warehouse and she doesn't know if it came from the dog or the radiator. "I want her to be like, 'Hmm, it doesn't *taste* like dog piss,'" says Tony.

The next day at work, Alex admits to Nick that she was the one who busted his window. Nick claims that the blond is his ex and that they have to appear at the ballet together for philanthropic reasons. And Alex actually buys it. To celebrate their renewed faith in one another, they go to dinner at a fancy restaurant. It's here that Alex proves she can be as slutty offstage as on by orally molesting her defenseless lobster entrée and then sliding her stockinged foot up into Nick's pin-striped crotch.

Remembering that this is the scene that got Shawn through puberty, we all can't help but glance over at him. "OK, now I'm embarrassed," he says, burying his face in his hands.

"Funny, that's exactly what she said," I say.

A few scenes later, Nick ducks into a local diner to place a phone call to the dance academy on Alex's behalf. We all dissolve into a giggle fit of disbelief when 10-time *Flashdance* viewer Marcus utters aloud a line that Michael Nouri, on screen, mouths silently: "Coffee."

"You can't stop yourself, can you?" says Tony.

Marcus just shrugs.

"You loop better than anyone in the movie," says Ross.

"Did you yell that line out in movie theaters like the eighth and ninth time you saw it?" I ask.

"No," says Marcus. "I wanted to let people experience the silent coffee moment on their own."

A few days later, Alex takes a break from welding to open a letter from the dance academy. She could have easily done it at home on the crapper in front of Grunt, but Alex prefers to read her mail where there's dry ice and backlighting. What girl doesn't?

That night, she goes out to dinner with Nick to celebrate the fact that the dance school wants her to audition. On the car ride home, she revels in the fact that her man's considerable clout afforded them special treatment at the restaurant. Then, when Nick lets it slip that that same clout helped get her the audition, she pitches a five-alarm Shit Fit, shrieking at him to "Stop the goddamn car!" in the middle of a busy tunnel.

"Ever since this movie," I remark as Alex stomps away, "whenever I ride through a tunnel with someone, I have to stop myself from yelling 'Stop the goddamn car!' and walking home."

"She is such a hypocrite," bellows Dr. Beaverman. "She was just waxing all romantic about how wonderful it was to whiz to the front of the line at the restaurant and yet she doesn't want his connections to get her the audition. Her morality is so incongruous it's laughable."

Making matters worse for Alex is the fact that her friend Jeanie, the ice skating failure, has started coochie dancing at Zanzibar. Ms. Beals, who I maintain is more compelling in her scenes with her friends than her scenes with Michael Nouri, marches in like the cavalry and rescues her. Later, she returns home to find Grunt feeling just as lost and disillusioned as she is. "I really hate dumb dog moments in movies," I reiterate.

"Like when Jeanie fell on the ice, you mean?" asks Tony.

Then Nick shows up for a huge screaming match. Unable to convince Alex to forgive him, Nick storms out in a huff, but not before laying out the message of the movie: "If you give up your dream, you die," a pearl of wisdom I suspect Nouri may have plagiarized from a needlepoint wall hanging in his plastic surgeon's office.

Then Hanna croaks, making our heroine even more bummed out than before, if that's possible.

Alone with her broken dreams, Alex mopes around the warehouse and smokes for the first time in the movie. It's one more out-of-nowhere character wrinkle than I can handle. "As much as I love Ms. Beals," I start, "Alexandra Owens doesn't add up to a real person. It's like all those Hollywood heavies who made this movie each wrote down three character traits on a Post-it and the writer had to work them in somehow. She reads *French Vogue,* she goes to confession, she smokes, she thinks it's funny to pretend to direct traffic. I keep waiting for her to show us her Pez collection."

"The push for eccentricity is just too much," agrees Dr. Beaverman. "OK, so she's wacky. She rides a bike everywhere and she's got a little bit of Katharine Hepburn in her. We get it, already."

Then Alex quits her job at Mawbry's, confesses that she gave head to a lobster, and finally we've made it to the Big Audition Scene, which, according to the recently E!-ducated Tony, had to be reshot because Michael Eisner thought the first version was duller than an Osmond bachelor party.

Trembling with nervousness, our aspiring ballerina puts "Flashdance (What a Feeling)" on the turntable. Then, as the school's doddering panel of experts looks on dubiously, she pulls a Jeanie and falls flat on her ass, just seconds into her routine.

"Another dumb dog moment," says Ross.

But Alex isn't down for long. Once that beat kicks in, she gets her groove back and soon the uptight panelists are tapping their toes, unable to resist our girl's streetwise exuberance.

"Wouldn't it be awesome if they started stuffing dollar bills into her unitard?" says Lauren. "The fat guy could ask her if she has change for a five."

As Ms. Beals or whoever executes the famous move where she sashays along the table, pointing her fingers at individual committee members, Tony bursts into a number from *Dreamgirls,* "And *you*...and *you*...and *you,* you're going to love me-e-e." After belting the hell out of that final note, he simmers down and reports that according to E! Jennifer Beals had four, count 'em four, dance doubles for this scene: Marine Jahan, an acrobat, a UCLA tumbler, and, as Shawn informed us earlier, a male break dancer.

"The guy had a mustache too, if I remember right," adds Shawn, "and he refused to shave it off."

"He probably wanted to make sure he matched Jennifer," says Lauren.

"I knew you'd come around," grins Tony, before grabbing the remote and freeze-framing on the aforementioned male break dancer, curled up in a ball, mid floor-spin.

"Look at those muscles rippling," says Dr. Beaverman.

"Jennifer Beals is a bottom," says Marcus. "Good to know."

We never see how Alex's big audition number actually ends, which, as an aficionado of ending poses, I've always thought was a cop out. Instead, we cut to Alex dashing triumphantly out of the building where her boyfriend–boss–string-puller, Michael Nouri, waits with an armful of roses.

"He would have gotten a ticket for parking there," Lauren informs us. "It's actually a sidewalk."

"As long as there's a citation being given," says Tony, "would anyone object if I checked the box marked 'split ends'?"

"She gives him one flower back," I notice. "What does that symbolize?"

"Thank God you were useful," mutters Lauren as the credits begin rolling.

"Exactly, Lauren," says Dr. Beaverman, getting up to stretch her legs. "This is supposed to be the female *Rocky,* but Rocky didn't have any connections. And Jennifer Beals did."

While Dr. Beaverman rants, Shawn and I simultaneously reach for the last "What a Feeling" brownie, then opt to split it.

"Of all the people in this movie chasing after their dreams, Alex was the one who made it," Dr. Beaverman continues. "Not Jeanie the skating stripper or Richie the hack comic. Of course, in both of those cases, you could blame it on other things: Jeannie had that loathsome 'Gloria' song and Richie had that loathsome hat, but the real truth is, they didn't pull any strings—or any other appendages, for that matter—and Jennifer Beals did. So, in other words, it's perfectly acceptable for a woman to *get a leg up,* so to speak, by using a man. In fact, it's encouraged. The message is, for a girl to be Rocky, she needs a man. And I do not approve. Dr. Beaverman does *not* approve."

Suddenly, as if to prevent Dr. Beaverman from continuing, Ross jumps up, runs behind the love seat, and starts massaging Tony's shoulders Burgess Meredith–style. "You ready to make daddy some money?" he asks.

"I was born ready," says Tony, glowering across the room at Lauren.

"Bring it," says Lauren, glowering right back.

"Is this going to take long?" asks Dr. Beaverman.

We all jump into action at once. Lauren begins a series of stretches while Tony runs out to the garage to retrieve his Bag of Shame—an Army-issued duffel overflowing with costumes and accessories he's pilfered from past stage extravaganzas. Ross collects five bucks from each of us and places the bills in the *Flashdance* video box for safekeeping. I dash back to my bedroom and return with two sweatshirts, one plain gray and one black with the *Les Miz* logo that I swear I didn't buy and have never worn and I don't even know how I ended up with it. Marcus rewinds the movie to the "Maniac" scene so we'll have some energetic accompaniment for our competition. Dr. Beaverman crouches down in front of Lauren and gives her a woman to woman pep talk that includes references to both Billie Jean King and "the eye of the tiger." Shawn just takes it all in.

After arguing over who gets saddled with the *Les Miz* shirt—Tony's argument is that since he's crossing gender lines to don a bra, the least Lauren can do is look like a musical theater geek for five minutes—the adversaries disappear into the bathroom and return a few minutes later ready to rumble.

"Both bras are securely fastened?" inquires Ross, assuming the role of referee.

"Yeah, we checked each other's," reports Tony.

"His is actually much cuter than mine," says Lauren. "Big surprise."

"Competitors, sit on the floor and assume the Jennifer Beals position," says Ross, holding up the video box to illustrate. "When I say go, you will reach into your shirts and start the removal process. The first flashdancer to remove his or her bra and pull both hands free is the winner."

"You want a piece of me, bitch?" Lauren barks.

"I was just about to ask you the same question," Tony retorts.

We gather around our respective contestants. The tension is almost unbearable. OK, it's not. It's actually quite bearable, though I'm a little thrown by how badly I want Lauren to win. You may theorize that I'm carrying some smidgen of internalized homophobia—if Tony loses, then I can believe that us gays aren't really *that* gay—but if that were true, would I be running into the kitchen for a dish towel so that I can kick off the competition with the Cha Cha DiGregorio drag race layout from *Grease*? I don't think so. I want Lauren to win because I think if she does, Shawn, in his excitement, will touch me.

"Oh your marks," bellows Ross, "get set, and...go!"

I do my best Cha Cha, Marcus cranks the music, and Tony and Lauren go to it, utilizing wildly different strategies.

Tony's poking around inside his top like, well, a maniac who has misplaced his pet ferret. Lauren, meanwhile, is more calm and methodical. It's as though she were appearing here today to promote her new book, *Zen and the Art of Flashdance Bra Removal.*

As the pair wrangle, Shawn squeezes my shoulder, leans in, and whispers, "This tension is too much." No shit, I think.

And then, suddenly, Lauren, cool as a cucumber in a crisper, pushes her arms out through her sleeves, as though she's yawning. An unadorned but durable B-cup wonder dangles from her right hand. Overcome with the adrenaline of victory, Shawn hugs the fuck out of me for about 10 seconds. Dr. Beaverman gives Lauren what I'm willing to bet is her first high five ever and predicts the Wheaties people will be calling any minute now.

Tony, meanwhile, is contorted in a heap on the floor, spitting and growling like Russell Crowe at a press junket. After a few more seconds of this, he simmers down and calmly pushes his arms trough the sleeves, revealing, for the first time, his lacy pink Wonderbra.

"You were right, Lauren," says Dr. Beaverman. "His is cuter."

Forty-five minutes later, I walk back into the living room after escorting Shawn to his car and talking his ear off. Everyone's gone but Tony.

"Just so you know," Tony says, "I kinda let her have it. I thought it would bring you and Twinkletoes closer together. Was I right? He seemed pretty into you."

"We're having dinner tomorrow," I say, unable to keep from smiling.

"Stick your foot in his crotch under the table," advises Tony. "Something tells me he goes for that kind of thing."

WHITNEY, BABY, ONE MORE TIME

"If you really concentrate," advises Marcus, as he, Lauren, and I make our entrance into the Mayan, a giant, multilevel, Aztec-style nightclub in downtown Los Angeles, "you can totally feel the Ghost of Whitney Past in this place."

"That must be why I'm sweating already," mutters Lauren.

The Mayan, Marcus informed us as we drove here, was where director Mick Jackson shot part of *The Bodyguard,* specifically the sequence where Whitney Houston, in her film debut as stalked superstar Rachel Marron, does a surprise club performance of her song "Queen of the Night" and gets stage-rushed by overzealous fans. She's then rescued, of course, by the film's surly title character, played by Kevin Costner, who sprays the crowd with a fire extinguisher and then carries his client to safety.

"I've never seen *The Bodyguard,* believe it or not," says Lauren as we sidle up to the bar.

"OK, now we *have* to do it," I decide. The moment Marcus mentioned the film outside, I knew it was a grade A primo Screening Party candidate. And now that Lauren's outed herself as a *Bodyguard* virgin, it's simply a must-do. "This Sunday, then."

"Plus it'll start getting us in the mood for Mariah's movie," says Marcus, who is literally counting the days until the former Mrs. Tommy Motolla makes her film debut later this year. "Did I tell you they've changed the name from *All That Glitters* to *Glitter*?"

"That'll make engraving those Oscar statues easier," says Lauren.

The reason the three of us are here tonight, apart from looking for little plaques that say "Whitney Passed Out Here" and killing time until *Glitter,* is to watch Shawn shake what his momma gave him in "Sunset Strips," a burlesque-style AIDS benefit starring L.A.'s sexiest professional dancers in heavily choreographed, lightly costumed production numbers. My guess is that it's going to be similar to Tony's *Man-O-Man* show except the cast members tonight, in addition to including women, are not as likely to be drunk, high, straight, or untalented. Furthermore, I doubt we'll see any lotion-shooting bananas. But I left my leather jacket in the truck just in case.

My *Man-O-Man* refugee roomie had hoped to join us tonight, but he ended up working late. Yes, that was the word *working* you saw back in that last sentence. It gives me great pleasure to report that two weeks ago, Tony started toiling as a personal assistant for a blond, 30-something TV actress who's dramatic on her series but funny on talk shows. I can't tell you who it is, but if I did, the odds are good that you would have the following response: "Oh, I love her. Is that show still on?"

Tony was referred to the actress by the star's previous assistant, whom he knows from the gym. After one quick interview, in which Tony shrewdly complimented the actress on how real she was in her early indie films even though he's never seen any of them, the position was his. Since then, he estimates, the ratio of mundane tasks to cool tasks is about 15 to 1. For every end-of-season wrap party at Moomba, which is where he is tonight, there are 15 trips to the dry cleaner's. He also spends a lot of time playing Switzerland to her warring lawyer and publicist, who have always despised each other. All in all, he's happy with it and says his boss is nice and no crazier than anyone in her position would be. She did, however, have her new puppy's larynx removed because she couldn't deal with the barking.

"He's the best one up there," declares Lauren when Shawn makes his first half-naked appearance in a crazy-sexy-cool, all-male version of "Big Spender" from *Sweet Charity.* When Marcus seconds the motion and directs a few innuendo-laced comments my way about Shawn's considerable flexibility and "ballet booty," I just smile and nod, as if to imply, "You have *no* idea."

The truth is, I don't have that much of an idea myself. OK, I have *some* idea. Though Shawn has stayed over a number of times in the three weeks since the *Flashdance* party, our time together seems more about affection than desire. And that's not just because I wouldn't know a slutty phase if it came up and fucked me in the ass.

There's a definite chemistry between us, but there's some kind of disconnect in the way it's expressed. To use a bit of dance terminology, it's like our counts are off.

It became obvious to me after like date 2 that this wasn't forever. For starters, Shawn's a good deal younger than I thought he was, though I can't tell you how much younger exactly. He refuses to tell anyone his age because he thinks people will make assumptions about him based on it. Apparently, he'd much prefer to have people think of him as that paranoid guy who won't say how old he is.

He also seems to think wristwatches are just something cute to wear to set off an outfit. Our first few dates all began the same way, with me standing in front of a venue, like a restaurant or theater, looking at my watch and exhaling into my nonexistent bangs, and then him wandering up whenever he damn well pleased, usually 20 to 30 minutes after the designated time. If I were really into him, this perpetual tardiness would drive me crazy, but I'm not, so it's just sort of moderately annoying.

Being late isn't the only tap dance Shawn likes to do on the space-time continuum. On the plus side, he has this Endora-like way of popping up when and where you don't expect him. Like last week I was watching *Divas Live* over at Lauren's, and in he wanders, halfway through Shania, saying he happened to be driving by and saw my truck.

Then he put his adorable head in my lap through the finale, made out with me on the sidewalk for a while afterward, and then went away. It was perfect.

Shawn's propensity for now-you-see-him, now-you-don't entrances and exits, coupled with the fact that I can take or leave this so-called relationship at any given moment, has earned him a nickname: the Accidental Boyfriend. And, to be honest, after the heartbreak and histrionics of my last foray into Loveland, I kind of don't mind the flukiness. I don't know if this is good or bad, but I've come to the conclusion recently that I don't want to be the best thing that ever happened to someone. Not right away, anyway.

So, in other words, while Shawn may have excellent legs, my relationship *with* Shawn probably doesn't.

"Does anyone have any singles?" I ask my companions as "Sunset Strips" nears its sweat-soaked conclusion.

Lauren shakes her head no.

"I just have 20s," says Marcus.

"He's worth a 10 then," I say, pulling a bill from my wallet.

The dancers have just taken their final bows, and now they've all returned to the stage to try and raise a few more bucks for the cause by go-go dancing in a rotating line around the foot of the stage. When Shawn grooves his way to our area, I run up, tuck my 10-spot in his white boxer briefs, then hand him the flowers I brought for him. He hands me one back, *Flashdance*-style, then grabs the back of my head and plants one on me, all without losing the beat.

"I hope you're happy," scolds Lauren when I return from my mission. "Now everyone who tips him is going to expect a kiss like that."

"I think Shawn can take care of himself," I say.

"If the crowd starts rushing him like Whitney," Marcus asks, "would you risk your life to run out on the stage with a fire extinguisher and carry him to safety?"

"Probably not," I say.

•

Shawn is the first to arrive to our *Bodyguard* Screening Party a few days later. Oh, wait, no, he's not. In fact, I don't even know if he's coming. I left him a message inviting him, but I haven't heard back. I don't call him the Accidental Boyfriend for nothing.

Everyone else is in attendance, though, or will be soon. Tony just called on his cell. He's about 10 minutes away on his way back from a boutique in Beverly Hills, returning his boss's designer gown from last night's People's Choice Awards. At least the designer, whom we'll call Designer Von Queen, was told it was for the People's Choice Awards. In truth, it was for the private party Tony's boss went to instead. She just told the designer it was for the media-covered People's Choice Awards so she should get it for free.

Tony arrives home just in time to hear Marcus start into St. Olaf story, version 10.0.

"It was my first relationship with a guy," Marcus recalls, "one of those one-month, desperately-in-love kind of things that meant everything at the time. The guy was named Bruce and he was an aerobics instructor."

"Of course he was," says Ross.

"High or low-impact?" wonders Lauren. It's her business, after all.

"It started out high-impact and then turned into no-impact, seemingly overnight," laments Marcus. "I first saw him on the sidewalk outside the gym—this was when I was still living back East—and I started going to his aerobics class three times a week at 6 o'clock in the morning just to see him. He had the most perfect little ass in the entire world, and, of course, back then everyone was in spandex."

"Is that the *Bodyguard* connection?" asks Dr. Beaverman, wanting to cut to the chase. "Spandex?"

Marcus shakes his head no and continues. "So we only went out like three or four times, but it was enough for me to learn what I'd be missing when it was taken away. Then he just started not returning my phone calls, and the after-class chitchatting got less and less, and finally I just stayed home and got fat because I felt foolish going."

"That's the *Bodyguard* connection!" says Dr. Beaverman, triumphantly. "Foolishness."

"No, no," says Marcus. "So, for like the next month, when I was showering for work, I would play that song from *The Bodyguard* that goes, 'I have nothing, nothing, nothing if I don't have you,' and scream my guts out."

"That's the *Bodyguard* connection," says Dr. Beaverman. "Screaming your guts out."

"That's the *Bodyguard* connection," confirms Marcus, before picking up the DVD of the movie and gazing fondly at the image on the cover of Kevin holding Whitney like a ventriloquist dummy. "It was my big daily cathartic ritual for weeks. The voice of Whitney Houston got me through my first broken heart."

Ross, taking a surprising interest in the mating habits of the urban homosexual male, has a question. "Did you change the words to 'I have nothing, nothing, nothing if I don't have *Bruce*'?" he wants to know.

"No," says Marcus, laughing. "But only because in my mind I was singing it *to* him." Marcus returns the DVD to the coffee table and says, "Anyway, I never saw him again after I quit going to class, but I think of him every time I hear that song."

"It's weird," says Ross, removing the *Bodyguard* disc from its case and loading it into the player. "I know all the songs from this movie by heart but I've never owned the CD. I think if you were alive in the world in 1992, you just sort of *came down* with them."

"Like cooties," says Dr. Beaverman.

I'm about to press play when Tony's hand shoots up. "Before we start, Dennis, I have a question," he says, in an unnecessarily businesslike tone. Since he's been working for the TV star, he's made a conscious effort to be as 'detail-oriented' as his padded résumé claims he is. "Do you want to issue a cap on wig jokes up front?" he wants to know.

I ponder the query for a moment, then hand down my ruling. "No," I say firmly.

"Better to have too many and have to whittle it down than to miss a gem because we've already hit our quota."

"It's like me at the Souplantation," says Lauren, referring to one of our favorite all-you-can-eateries. "I take as much as I want in the salad area because you never know what kind of muffins they're going to have at the end until you get there."

Once we start the film, it takes Dr. Beaverman about a millisecond to psychologically peg Kevin Costner's character, tortured ex–Secret Service agent Frank Farmer. "The surface syndrome is, of course, commitment phobia," the good doctor discerns after Kevin proclaims that he's no good in a permanent position. "Notice that the song on the radio as Kevin's being coerced to take the job guarding Whitney is 'Walk Away Renee.' The subtext is 'Don't come too close, honey.' Unfortunately, there's a not a song called 'Walk Away Rachel Marron,' but given the percentage of the budget that went toward wigs, they were lucky they had any money left over for licensing."

"He got totally ragged on for this haircut at the time," I say, referring Costner's Caesar do. "But I think he looks hot."

Lauren shoots me a look that seems to say, "Are you high?"

"I have to say that," I admit, "because my hair's been doing the same thing for the last 10 years."

"Dennis's hair knows the words to one song," says Tony, delivering my time-honored, all-purpose, self-deprecating hair quip so I don't have to.

"The hair is an homage to Steve McQueen," says Ross, serving up the first Fowler Fun Fact of the day. "Lawrence Kasdan originally wrote this script for Steve McQueen back in the '70s."

Our affection toward Kevin and his hair begins to ebb when it becomes obvious that he's selected jet-laggedness as his character's defining personality trait. "I bet the gag reel's full of shots of him actually falling asleep," figures Tony.

When Kevin pulls up to Whitney's palatial L.A. mansion, Ross informs us that the same swanky pad was used for the harrowing horse-head scene in *The Godfather.* Like the poor chap in that film, Whitney's also had a terrifying bedroom intruder. Hers apparently mistook her pink bedspread for a blue dress from the Gap and let fly with some serious man seed. Given that all of us except Lauren have seen the film before and know that the ultimate perpetrator is female, it seems that whoever sowed the seeds of love on Whitney's bedspread would have to have been *hired* to do so. "What if you were the guy paid to stain the bed," I suggest, "and you got in there and you couldn't finish?"

"Maybe you could improvise," says Marcus, "like, with a stick of gum."

"Not very menacing," says Dr. Beaverman.

"I'd bring it from home," says Tony, "in some Tupperware. You really want to lock in that freshness."

Kevin makes his way inside to find a horde of dancers, crew people, and hangers-on slaving away on Whitney's latest music video, which, in terms of its art direction, has obviously been inspired by Fritz Lang's classic *Metropolis.* "German impressionism is one of Whitney's favorite film genres," figures Ross.

"Whitney's the only actress working in film today whose hair has a chin strap," says Tony, when we get our first good look at the superstar.

"Who shoots a music video at their *house*?" wonders Lauren as Kevin and Whitney shake hands and size each other up. "I mean, she's got all these dancers and grips running around and she's surprised there's come on her bedspread?"

For his part, Whitney's slimy publicist, played by Spandau Ballet founder Gary Kemp, reckons the jizz bandit is probably the same perv who's been sending the diva threatening cut-and-paste letters. "You know, that note could double as a song order for Rachel's next gig," says Tony as the camera zooms in on the menacing missive. "OK, Knuckles, I'm opening with 'Marron Bitch,' then going right into 'I Have Nothing,' then finishing big with 'Whore Queen of Darkness.'"

"Who shoots a music video at their house? I mean, she's got all these dancers and grips running around and she's surprised there's come on her bedspread?" —Lauren

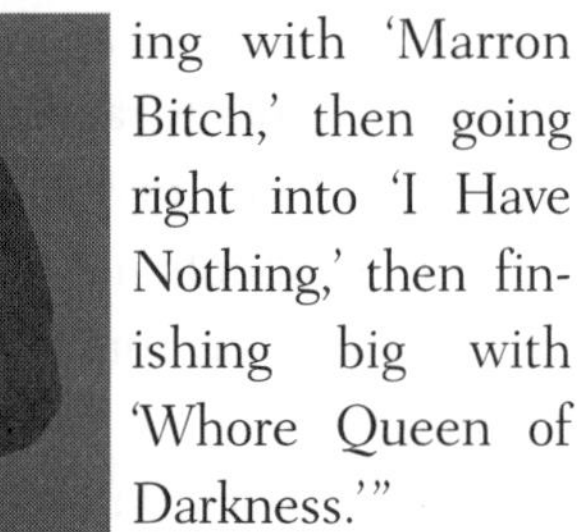

"Notice that the word *whore* is one piece, one font," Dr. Beaverman points out. "Which can only mean one thing: It was cut from the Christina Aguilera newsletter."

When "I Have Nothing" starts playing over a scene of Whitney's unseen stalker pasting together another note, Marcus, the song's number 1 shower warbler, pretends to dab away a tear, then disappears into the kitchen. He emerges a few seconds later with a Styrofoam plate covered in tinfoil. "What smells so good?" says Lauren, perking up like Scooby-Doo at snack time.

"Pineapple upside-down cake," Marcus announces.

"What does that have to do with *The Bodyguard*?" asks Lauren.

"There's crack in it," says Tony.

"No, there's not," snaps Marcus. "I refuse to buy into the tabloid rumors with my dessert. We should be supporting Whitney right now, especially after all the dance mixes she's given us." With that, our budget gourmet removes the foil and unveils his creation. "Pineapple upside-down Cake," he says, showing it around the room like a kindergarten teacher during story hour, "like this movie, is interesting in concept, but when you really think about it, it makes no sense at all."

"Boy, you're reaching with that one," says Lauren.

"Don't eat it, then," says Marcus.

"That shut her up," observes Dr. Beaverman.

Back on the screen, Kevin has reluctantly accepted the job guarding Whitney and now he's dissecting her every move and wig flip. Though I'm sure Whitney must be paying him well, my fantasy is that he's hanging around for one reason and one reason only: He's hot for Whitney's supersexy driver, Henry, played by Christopher Birt, whom Kevin tellingly refers to as the "cocky black chauffeur."

"Break me off a piece of that Kit Kat bar," I say in my best Kim Cattrall purr, during a scene in which Kevin lets Cocky handle his gun. "Something's shifted in me in since the last time I saw this, because I don't remember being hot for the cocky black chauffeur. Why isn't that guy on *Law & Order* or something?"

"I am detecting a bit of sexual tension between to two men," confirms Dr. Beaverman, as Kevin gives Henry a private lesson in defensive Town Car driving. "And I'm not just saying that so you'll get up and get Dr. Beaverman another gin and tonic to wash down this cake with."

"The cocky chauffeur/cocky bodyguard interplay also ties into my cake," boasts Marcus, "because there is definite fruitiness involved, but it's buried underneath."

Given that Kevin is used to calling the shots, it's no surprise that he visibly bristles when he has to take orders from Whitney. A prime example of this dynamic is the pained look he shoots Whitney's also-ran sister, Nicki, when his superstar charge stops outside a restaurant to pose for a photo with a young fan.

"Wow, Whitney's being nice to the little people," marvels Lauren.

"That's how you know it's fiction," figures Ross.

"My celebrity poses for pictures all the time," boasts Tony. "She loves her fans. The only time she doesn't want to be photographed is when someone lower than her comes up to her on the red carpet. She tries to only be photographed with stars that are her level or higher. In fact, at the *Saving Silverman* premiere the other night, I was totally on Sally Kirkland Watch."

Slightly more believable than Whitney's fan photo moment is a later scene in which our sassy songstress sits blissfully by the pool, listening to herself on a Walkman. Her self-centered reverie is interrupted, however, by the construction going on nearby so she charges inside and bitches Kevin out about all the changes he's instigating. "We're seeing the beginning of their sexual power struggle here," says Dr. Beaverman, as Whitney rants on while whipping herself up a foamy white smoothie snack. "Costner has a problem with nonsubmissive women who pull the superiority act on him. That's why he's looking at the contents of that blender very enviously. She has the scrotum here, folks, and he's shriveling in his pants."

The sexually charged sparring continues in the next scene when the pair go shopping. "You probably won't believe this," says Whitney, disappearing into a fitting room, "but I have a reputation for being a bitch."

"I'm sorry, are we rolling?" says Tony, voicing what he assumes to be the diva's next words.

Whitney goes on to blame the tabloids for her disagreeable temperament, explaining that so many bogus stories have run over the years that painted her as a cranky pain in the ass, she figured she might as well *be* a cranky pain in the ass. "Oh, so it's other people's fault?" Lauren scoffs.

"Of course, Lauren," says Tony. "That's, like, Celebrity 101."

"Costner's hating this shopping business," I observe, as Kevin's eyes grow more and more lifeless by the second.

"Of course he is," says Dr. Beaverman. "Remember, his name is Frank Farmer. He acts defiant to pretend he's above her, but in actuality he's just a farmer among moneyed people and it pisses him off."

Despite their outward friction, deep down the twosome are beginning to warm to each other. In one key moment, Kevin stares raptly at Whitney's video in the guest house. Meanwhile, Whitney is upstairs entertaining lusty thoughts of Kevin while a hairdresser tends to her locks. "I love the idea that she actually has her hair done while it's on her head," remarks Tony. "It's more like, 'Let me crimp your hair, Miss Marron.' 'Here, take it, I'm going for a swim.'"

"What I love is that he literally *becomes* her stalker," says Lauren. "I think if you had a bodyguard, it would really creep you out to look in the guest house and see him pleasuring himself to tapes of you."

Just then, Tony's cell phone rings. "It's my boss," he says, getting up to go into the kitchen. I pause the movie, not only because I don't want Tony to miss the big Mayan scene but also because listening to Tony talk to his actress can be really entertaining.

"What do you mean, they you sent a bill?" he says, suddenly distressed. "How did they find out? $1,500 for that stupid thing? No, I didn't mean stupid like that; you looked gorgeous. Of course I didn't say anything about the party. A stain? Where? Well, it wasn't me; I didn't even take it out of the garment bag. So should I go pick it up if they're making you pay for it anyway? No, of course not, you shouldn't have to. OK, call me back and let me know what they say. It's going to be fine. Don't worry. Bye."

When we rejoin our saga, Whitney, posse in tow, is striding purposefully out of her mansion wearing a mysterious black-hooded cape. "She's got an appointment to play chess with Max von Sydow," figures Ross.

"Oh, shit," says Tony, returning to the front room.

"Was that what it sounded like?" I ask.

"Uh-huh," he says nervously. "It'll be fine. She's having her agent call. That should take care of the problem."

Tony gestures to me to start the movie. When we rejoin our saga, Whitney, posse in tow, is striding purposefully out of her mansion wearing a mysterious black-hooded cape.

She's got an appointment to play chess with Max von Sydow," figures Ross.

"I have no idea why I think that's so funny," I say, laughing.

"It's a reference to this Ingmar Bergman movie, *The Seventh Seal,* where Max von Sydow plays chess with Death," explains Ross. "Plus the word *Sydow* is always funny."

"I want Kevin to say, 'I have a suit just like that at home, only mine's white and has little holes for the eyes,'" says Lauren.

Instead, Kevin gives Whitney a small pager/crucifix that she's to squeeze if she gets in trouble. "Ho-jack," I name it.

Trouble comes soon enough, when Whitney takes the stage of the hey-we-were-just-there Mayan nightclub to lip-synch "Queen of the Night." When the track kicks in, our diva doffs her hood to reveal a metallic *Metropolis* getup and starts rocking the house. Unfortunately, before she can even take it to the bridge, some nervy crowd members jump onstage and start rocking the house with her. The next thing you know, she's body surfing on an ocean of extras and screaming her crimped head off. "I wonder if when celebrities watched this movie, they related to Whitney," I muse. "Like Brett Butler was sitting in the theater thinking, 'I gotta get me one of them Ho-jacks.'"

"Does your celebrity have a Ho-jack?" Lauren asks Tony.

"No, but she has a Jack Russell terrier named Jack," replies Tony, "who's probably sitting in his $500 doggie bed right now thinking of fun places in the house to poo."

Thinking fast, Kevin grabs a nearby fire extinguisher, squirts it into the crowd, and, after physically assaulting several innocent fans—personal injury lawsuits were apparently not a consideration—he carries Whitney away like a rag doll. "We have a poster!" says Lauren, holding up the DVD cover for effect.

"Notice how you don't see her face," says Ross. "She was a major superstar at the time and yet I think the studio thought it would be bad for box office to have a black woman in an embrace with a white man so her face is hidden. They also hemmed and hawed about how much to show of them making out."

"Speaking of love among the races," says Lauren, "where's the Accidental Boyfriend?"

"I have no idea," I say.

Back on the screen, Cocky drives Whitney and Kevin to safety, while Dr. Beaverman breaks down the sexual symbolism we saw in the previous scene. "That extinguisher was the first hard object that's been in front of Costner's pants since the Reagan years," she asserts.

"And did you see that stream?" adds Marcus.

"Exactly," confirms Dr. Beaverman. "The only time that he can effectively get it up for her is when she's a helpless piece of limp macaroni. When she's frightened to death, he's got a rocket in his pocket, i.e. the fire extinguisher. Again, it's a whole power thing, and now he's back on top."

At this point, Lauren brushes the cake crumbs off her hands and pulls from her bag several sheets of address labels, a roll of stamps, and a stack of postcards with her head shot on it. "I'm sending out fliers for my gig next week," she explains while dealing each of us a card. "I want to pack the place because I have a manager coming to see me. So save the date."

We all agree that we'll do our best to be there. Then Ross, looking on as Lauren labels her first card, says, "I wish I'd thought to bring a project."

"Start stamping, sweetheart," says Lauren, handing him half her stack of cards.

Though Kevin saved the day at the Mayan, not everyone's taking to his macho heroics. Tony, Whitney's Danny Aiello–esque security guy, is feeling particularly obsolete and expresses his frustration by attacking our hero while he's in the kitchen cutting into a peach. Though I like to imagine the two men are fighting over the affections of Cocky, Dr. Beaverman has more likely theory. "Kevin clearly has a castration fixation," she declares. "That's why he's always throwing knives around. He has to feel superior to others because of his own deeply buried feeling of inferiority. Having no chin has certainly not helped."

Kevin's alpha male ego takes another blow the next morning when Whitney, looking all dewy in sweats and a scrunchie, asks *him* out on a date. "Isn't that sexual harassment?" asks Lauren.

"Technically, yes," says Marcus, our resident law expert. "But it's OK because she's sort of cute and earnest here."

"As much as I like to make fun of her," I say, "Whitney's pretty good in this movie, like she's holding up her end of the deal. What's sad to think about is, *Could she do it now*?"

Lauren, in the middle of a stamp lick, groans agreeably. "This is like watching an old Katharine Hepburn movie, like from the '30s when she was all gorgeous and fabulous," she says, "except it's not 70 years ago that *The Bodyguard* was made."

"Notice Kevin's face when she asks him out," interrupts Dr. Beaverman. "He's freezing in his boots."

"How can you tell?" wonders Ross. "That's the same expression he's had the whole movie."

Though clearly threatened, Kevin accepts Whitney's proposition and takes her out to an old samurai film in Koreatown. "She's like, 'As long as we're here, Kev, why don't we visit the ancestors of my hair,'" says Tony.

After the movie, the couple grab a drink at a nearby country bar and slow-dance to a low-key version of "I Will Always Love You" sung by John Doe from the band X. It must be all Whitney can do to not look into the camera and whisper, "I'm going to sing the shit out of this song in about 20 minutes, people, just be patient."

When the song ends, Whitney tells Kevin she'll protect him and he's so emasculated by it, he almost has a facial expression. Hoping to tip the balance of power back his way, he takes Whitney back to his place, but, once there, she upsets the gender cart again by fiddling around with Kevin's cherished samurai sword. "I'm surprised she doesn't strap it on," says Dr. Beaverman, when Whitney points the blade into Kevin's chest. He responds to the pseudopenetration by snatching Whitney's sheer blue scarf from around her neck and tossing it heavenward. Together, they watch it drift down onto the sword and get sliced in two.

"I want her to be like, 'That's coming out of your paycheck, asshole,'" says Tony. "'You could have just said, 'It's sharp.' "

"If I were still single, I would find this scene so depressing," says Lauren, "because I've been on that same date a million times, where you go to some creepy guy's basement apartment and look at his sword and he cuts up your scarf. Trust me, it's *not* charming."

"The scarf symbolizes her long-lost hymen," declares Dr. Beaverman. "He *had* to chop it off with the love sword. Only then can he kiss her and subsequently bed her."

Which he then does, though the filmmakers hardly show any of it. "We would have had more on-screen nooky if they were the same race, right?" I ask.

"Totally," confirms Ross, "or if the film were set in New Orleans."

The next day, Whitney starts in with the morning after moony talk and, not surprisingly, her issue-encumbered manservant can't deal. "Have I done something wrong?" Whitney asks him.

"Whitney's wig in this scene is like a tricornered hat. I keep waiting for her to cross the Delaware."
—Dr. Beaverman

"Oh honey, rewind," says Tony.

"He's totally playing head games with her," observes Lauren, "but I'll give him this; he knows how not to fuck up a lady's wig. Notice how perfect it looks. She must not have blown him."

Whitney and Kevin's mutual frosting-out continues at a party thrown in Whitney's honor, in a swanky penthouse in Miami. We know the soiree's for her because of the exploding "Rachel!" fireworks on the balcony. "Whenever your celebrity is being stalked and you go to another city," explains Tony, "you want to have fireworks that say their name so that the murderers will know exactly where to look. A big neon arrow is also a nice touch."

"Whitney's wig in this scene is like a tricornered hat," says Dr. Beaverman. "I keep waiting for her to cross the Delaware."

In an attempt to get a rise out of Kevin, Whitney sneaks away from the party with a mysterious stranger, who turns out to be an old Secret Service colleague of Kevin's. Her ploy seems to do the trick. "Wait a second," I say. "Did Kevin just have a facial expression?"

"Nope," says Lauren. "False alarm."

"There was something on the lens," says Ross.

When a party bimbo with enormous earrings approaches the stone-faced Kevin and coos, "I've been watching you from across the room," Kevin responds with a terse, "Why don't you go back there and keep watching?" Though the comeback is funny in a *Mad Magazine's Snappy Answers to Stupid Questions* sort of way, I can't help but feel sorry for the well-meaning lady. "She's probably thinking, *I'm going to go home and cry now,*" I say.

"I'd be like, 'Fuck you, man,'" barks Ross. " 'I hope you direct yourself in a shitty movie about a postapocalyptic mail carrier and it tanks, asshole.'"

When the stalker crank calls Whitney in Miami, the tension becomes too much. So Kevin hauls the ice queen and a portion of her posse off to the comparatively safe frozen tundra to hang out with his dad, played by Ralph Waite, a.k.a. Pa Walton. "Kevin told her there would be snow, so she agreed," figures Ross.

"Wouldn't it be great if every time they cut to Ralph Waite, he was just finishing a dirty story about *The Waltons*?" I say.

"I'll do my best," says Tony.

My joke jukebox of a roommate cranks out his first selection when Kevin and Ralph sit down for a game of intergenerational chess. *"So one day we're on a coffee break and that fucking commie, Will Geer, just whips it out,"* says Tony, in a homespun live-from-Walton's Mountain drawl. *"I mean, what the fuck?"*

Once night falls, Whitney's loser sister, Nicki, musters up her nerve up and puts the moves on Kevin. None of us are surprised when he clenches up. "He doesn't know what to do with a women whose hair is attached," figures Lauren.

"Il Postino can't deliver," agrees Dr. Beaverman.

The next morning finds Kevin roaming the grounds with Ralph Waite. *"And it turns out they weren't even freckles!"* exclaims Tony, reprising his role as Pa Walton. *"Ellen Corby and I laughed till we cried."*

Soon Kevin happens upon some mysterious tracks in the snow. "Elk?" he wonders.

"Gaffer," says Ross.

Meanwhile, Nicki has come out on the porch to commune with nature and sing "Jesus Loves Me." Her reverie is dashed, however, when Whitney saunters out and starts riffing circles around her. "I want Nicki to turn to Whitney and be like, 'Jesus also loves *straight* tones, as it turns out,'"says Tony.

"Why doesn't Whitney just go all the way and change the words to 'Jesus Loves Me Better'?" I wonder.

"I keep waiting for Ed McMahon to come out and go, 'Nicki Marron, 1¾ stars! Rachel Marron, 4 stars!' " says Lauren. "We have a new *Star Search* champion!"

Unfortunately, before Ed can charter a plane, boats are blowing up and Nicki cracks, confessing to Kevin that she, in fact, is the one who wants Whitney dead and that she commissioned a hit man to make it happen. "He doesn't even know who hired him," she sobs. "I went to a bar in East L.A...."

"His name was Rico, he wore a diamond..." adds Marcus.

No sooner does Nicki come clean about the hit man business than she's accidentally shot and killed by the very lowlife she hired to rub out Whitney. Jeez, is it hard to find good help these days or what?

"Music executive Nicki Marron was gunned down last week in a lakeside retreat..." says a news announcer over shots of her rainy-day funeral.

"Her superstar sister, Rachel, will be singing at the funeral," I add, in my best announcer voice. "Call Ticketmaster for dates and showtimes."

"In a surprise turn, Nicki Marron's funeral has been extended for two more weeks!" Tony adds.

"The rock 'n' mourn Glass Casket Tour will be coming to an arena near you!" I continue.

"Hello, Cleveland! Goodbye, sis!" shouts Ross.

"Thank you! Rest in peace! Good night!" proclaims Dr. Beaverman.

I'm working on a Sisterpalooza quip to add to the heap when Tony's cell phone rings again. He answers it with an anxious, "Hi," then runs into the kitchen. I put the movie on pause because, as delicious as *The Bodyguard* is, it can't hold a candle to the real-life melodrama unfolding on the other end of that cell phone. "What did they say?" asks Tony. "Oh, my God. Did you tell them everybody else does it?" After a long pause, Tony asks, "How do you know it was Debra Messing? Anybody at the party could have talked." Which is followed by, "Oh, that makes sense. She totally is." Tony's portion of the conversation ends with, "It's OK, don't cry. No, I'm not doing anything. OK, I'll be right over. There's a new box of those ice cream sandwiches you like in the freezer. Don't do anything crazy. Bye."

Tony hangs up and walks back into the front room. "I have to go," he says, grabbing his organizer.

"Before you go," says Lauren, "let me see if I got it right."

"I can't talk about it," says Tony, digging his car keys out of his pocket.

"Then just nod or something," suggests Ross.

"OK," says Lauren, breathlessly, "Your boss got a designer to lend her an expensive dress for an awards show and he said yes thinking it would be photographed like crazy, but she wore it at a private party instead and now he found out and he's making her buy it."

"And there's a stain," interjects Marcus.

"And your boss thinks Debra Messing was the bitch who sang," I add.

Tony gives us a little nod, shrugs as if to say, "I can't believe this shit," then dashes off.

Though it's sure to pale in comparison to the Saga of the Duplicitious Starlet, we restart the movie to watch the big, climactic Oscar sequence, where Whitney competes for Best Actress, Robert Wuhl handles the emcee duties, and Kevin wanders around backstage like he owns the place. "The day that Arli$$ hosts the Academy Awards…" says Ross.

"Is the day that Whitney Houston wins one," says Dr. Beaverman.

Sure enough, the Oscar goes to Whitney. She glides to the stage and is about to claim her trophy when shots ring out. "The hit man chose the Oscars to make his move because it's easy to get in and out of and there are no witnesses," says Ross.

"Why is someone still shooting at her if Nicki's dead?" I wonder.

"Because Nicki said the guy she hired would never stop," recalls Lauren, "not until the job was done."

"You're following this movie better than I am and you've never seen it before," I marvel. "*And* you brought a project."

Kevin, of course, rushes in and saves the day, but not before taking a shot in the arm, which, I maintain, is exactly what he's needed all along. As he lies bleeding on the stage, Ross voices what he imagines Kevin's final utterance would be if he were, in fact, dying. "Bi-i-itch."

Just then, there's a knock at the door. I open it to discover Shawn, dressed in red sweatpants and a white wife beater that's soaked through to the skin. It works on him. "It's almost over," I say hastily. "Come in."

The rest of the gang wave hello, then turn back to the screen where Whitney and Kevin kiss and say goodbye on a tarmac after which we cut to Whitney belting out "I Will Always Love You" and sweating buckets—a proclivity that has continued unabated to this day.

"Sorry I'm late," whispers Shawn. "I was at a callback."

"For what?" I ask.

Shawn smiles and points toward the ceiling, Travolta-style.

"*Saturday Night Fever*?" I guess.

"National tour," he replies.

"How'd it go?" I ask.

"I got it," he says.

"Oh, my God," I say, then give him a big congratulatory hug. Lauren catches my eye over Shawn's shoulder gives me a look that says she'll feel bad for me if he goes away. I try to give her one back that says don't sweat it.

"It makes zero sense that they wouldn't continue their relationship," carps Marcus, when the film cuts from Whitney singing to Kevin hard at work on his new assignment, guarding some famous priest at a Rotary meeting in the First Presbyterian Church of Iowa Rapids. "Big stars always have boyfriends in other states."

"Yes, but this way everyone winds up where they should wind up," concludes Dr. Beaverman. "Whitney's off on the Ashes to Ashes Tour and Costner's guarding some of his own people for once, the Presbyterians and the Rotarians, and take it from me, a more frozen, expressionless people you're never going to find."

Unfortunately the last shot of the movie is not Kevin and Cocky running off together to Ibiza, but Kevin standing behind his new cleric client, who clutches the Ho-jack cross as he prays. "Kevin Costner looks like he's going to fall asleep," observes Shawn before helping himself to the last piece of pineapple upside-down cake.

"Please," says Dr. Beaverman. "I've been making that same face for last hour and 45 minutes."

"Done," chirps Lauren, holding up a stack of stamped and labeled postcards.

"How many years after this do you suppose Whitney and Kevin exchanged Christmas cards?" I wonder as the credits roll. "I say two."

"I say one," counters Ross, "like the Christmas this movie came out, and by the following year, it was over."

•

"*The Bodyguard* is exactly the experience I would want to have if I had a bodyguard," says Lauren, reading from her trusty joke notebook a week and a half later, "which is a hot guy who's going to protect me a little and fuck me a lot."

"I like it," I say, laughing, "but I like some of your other stuff better, like that bit about the Gap billboard."

The two of us are nursing Diet Cokes at the back bar of the Ha Ha Café and Comedy Club in North Hollywood, where Lauren's scheduled to take the stage in less than an hour. I'm the first of our group to arrive, so she's trying out a few new gags on me. "Before I forget," I tell her, "Tony wants you to know he's coming, but he'll probably be late."

"Are they going to do it?" she asks excitedly.

"As far as I know, it's still on," I say.

"Oh, my God," she gasps.

As of an hour or so ago, Tony's plans for tonight centered around getting his actress ready for this evening's SAG Awards, where she's going to debut a head-turning new creation by Designer Von Queen. The catch is that since the day of *The Bodyguard* party, she and Designer Von Queen have been at war, serious war. It's like Bosnia with publicists. So tonight, when Ms. Thing saunters down the red carpet, telling Joan and Melissa and whoever else will listen that her gown is Designer Von Queen couture, she's actually going to be wearing something Tony got off the rack from a Ross Dress for Less and spent the last 48 hours tackying up as much as possible. He did this by enlisting another operative, one with sewing skills and a penchant for mischief. Together, they combined elements from every bad red-carpet dress of the last 20 years. www.GeenaDavis.com was a particularly handy resource.

I know what you're thinking: *The woman is crazy*, and all I can say to that is, well, yes. According to Tony, what started out as a drunken revenge fantasy has somehow turned real. He tried to play devil's advocate, by pointing out that the pictures would haunt her for years, but she wouldn't budge. Apparently, she's convinced herself that what she's doing is political, that she's not just making an ass of herself, she's making a statement, about Hollywood excess and the shallowness of celebrity culture. When Tony suggested that she could make the same statement by donating tonight's goody-filled gift bag to charity, she looked at him like he was crazy.

"I wish I could just tell that story tonight," says Lauren. "It's so much funnier than any of my material."

"No, it's not," I tell her.

"*There's* our little superstar," says a voice from behind us.

We turn around and discover two women and one guy, who happens to be very cute. Lauren introduces them as Theresa, Stacy, and B.J., all coworkers from the gym, then goes backstage to prepare for her set.

Before you know it, Theresa and Stacy are all over each other like Anne and Ellen at the White House—nothing like a pair of fit lesbians in the first blush of love, I always say—leaving me to chat up B.J. With the Accidental Boyfriend off to New York to rehearse for *Fever,* I'm on the market again. And then some. It's like Shawn was the appetizer, we've cleared the crumbs, and now I'm ready for the main course.

When B.J. tells me he's just moved here from Boston, I'm not at all surprised. There's a lack of self-consciousness about him, a measure of goofiness, that guys who look that good and live in L.A. seldom have, because they've worked so hard and sacrificed so much to become desirable, they won't dare risk looking foolish, even for a second. B.J. clearly doesn't have this problem, because when the godforsaken "Macarena" comes on the jukebox, he hops off his stool and insists I learn the steps.

Though B.J.'s super amiable and actually asks questions in addition to answering them, I'm not getting a flirtatious vibe from him. One good thing about having an Accidental Boyfriend–type experience, as inconsequential as it all was, is that it reminds you of what someone's face looks like when they're into you. If you go a while without seeing it, you start imagining sparks where none exist. I don't think there's a spark with B.J., but I'd love to be proved wrong.

He's in the middle of describing his new '70s disco sculpt class when Lauren's boyfriend, Barry, arrives with flowers, followed soon after by Ross and Dr. Beaverman. I introduce my friends to B.J. and the lesbians, then we all caravan to a long table near the stage. Once there, I save two seats, one for Tony, who I knew would be late, and one for Marcus, who should have been here already.

They're both still MIA when Lauren takes the mike a short time later. After a dodgy start—she made a really peculiar face when she came onstage, then took 10 or 15 seconds to utter her first word—she starts to rally. The riff she was able to concoct from her unreasonable rivalry with a Gap billboard goes over well, especially the ending where she claims Barry once called her Rachael Leigh Cook during sex. "He didn't just say Rachael, either," she rants. "He got all three names out. After he got me off, I was like, 'We have to move.'"

Suddenly, Marcus, harried and out of breath, sits down next to me. "There was a situation at work," he explains. "How much did I miss?"

"Like 10 minutes," I tell him.

For her next act of hilarity, Lauren launches into the ever-popular I-Got-My-Period-at-*The Vagina Monologues* monologue. I turn to Marcus, expecting to share a conspiratory smile, but he looks totally stunned. "What?" I whisper.

He takes a pen from his pocket and writes, "That's Bruce, my aerobics guy," on a napkin, then draws an arrow pointing to the end of the table where B.J. sits, laughing his supercute head off.

"I Have Nothing?" I write back, garnishing the title of Marcus's heartbreak anthem with a sprightly pair of music notes.

As he nods, I watch what's left of the color drain from his face.

The remainder of the set goes well for Lauren, and though I do my share of chortling, I'm a bit preoccupied with the B.J. revelation. At one point I start to daydream a scenario where B.J. and I fall madly in love and have Marcus over for dinner, during which the three of us laugh ourselves silly about the whole kooky situation over a really good bottle of wine. I don't even drink wine.

God, I hope he remembers Marcus's name. I hate it in movies when there's that exchange—designed to illuminate one character's complete insignificance to another character—that goes like this:

OK, pretend Ben and Jack have screwed and are running into each other some time later, or that Jack toils as a peon under Ben in a high-pressure work environment.

Ben: Oh, my God. It's so good to see you, John.
Jack: It's Jack.
Ben: Right, Jack.

I know it happens in real life, but I think the frequency with which it happens in movies is grossly disproportionate to the frequency with which it happens in real life, and it always takes me out of the story.

"Oh, my God, Matthew?" says B.J. after the show.

"It's Marcus," says Marcus.

"Right, Marcus," says B.J.

OK, I'm an asshole. We're in the back bar area now, and I have just brought Marcus over to B.J. to get reacquainted. "I started going by B.J. when I moved to L.A.," he explains when we ask about the name change. "Bruce just has all these sort of gay connotations."

"And B.J. doesn't?" I say.

"I know," says B.J., laughing, "but that's a *good* gay connotation."

While Marcus and B.J. catch up, I go to the other end of the bar and join Barry, Ross, and Dr. Beaverman in congratulating Lauren.

"Did you see me almost barf at the beginning?" Lauren asks us.

"Is that what that was?" asks Ross. "You just looked sort of constipated."

"The microphone smelled so bad, you guys, like it had been stuck up somebody's ass," Lauren groans, "but other than that, isn't this place cute?"

Before we can answer, the talent manager woman Lauren had invited swoops in and takes her off to a corner to talk business. Then Tony wanders in.

"Oh, my God, what happened?" I have to know.

"I talked her out of it," he says, with a strange mixture of pride and disappointment.

"Yesterday, I secretly called another designer and arranged for a nice dress as a back up in case she changed her mind at the last second, and she did. She decided she didn't want to be political tonight. She wanted to be pretty."

"What girl doesn't?" mutters Dr. Beaverman.

"But you should see that other dress," says Tony. "It's like Kim Basinger collided with Chloë Sevigny and now they're going to do the Charleston to a song by Cher." Tony takes a swig of his hard-earned margarita, then adds, "Oh, wait, you'll see it. I have pictures."

"Of course you do," says Ross.

The next day, I'm returning some CDs I borrowed from Tony's bathroom—yes, I was craving *The Bodyguard*, I admit it—when I see a familiar face looking up at me from Tony's trash can. It's a photo of B.J. on a business card. Handwritten under the printed name and phone number are the words, "Call me, cutie."

Why do I suddenly feel like Nicki Marron, sitting on that cabin porch, trying to get through a goddamn verse of "Jesus Loves Me" without have to harmonize with Whitney?

"He stuck it in my back pocket when we were leaving the club last night," Tony explains, when I bring it up later.

"Did you even talk to him?" I say, trying to sound as matter-of-fact and un-Nicki-like as possible.

"A little," he says. "He was nice."

"Did you mean to throw it away?" I ask, holding it out to him.

"Yeah," he says.

"OK," I say.

With that, I toss the card back in the trash, then wonder if I would have done the same thing had it ended up in my pocket. Ultimately, maybe, but I would have explored the loophole situation first.

"I can't go out with that guy, Dennis," Tony says. "It would just be awkward, and people's feelings would get hurt. My friends are more important."

And he totally means it. He's always been that way, as loyal as the day is long. And if you don't believe me, you can ask his actress.

THANKS FOR SHARON

Let us begin this installment with two totally unrelated pieces of advice:

1. If you're going to invite people over to your house to watch Paul Verhoeven's 1992 thriller *Basic Instinct,* be prepared to hear the following words and phrases on your answering machine: coochie, cooze, honey pie, honey pit, honey bunches of snatch, flat-ass, and shitheap.

2. If you're ever going to have one of your friends pretend to work for a messenger service that they don't actually work for, pick someone ugly. And if they're not ugly, ugly them up as much as possible. And if they have nice arms, for God's sake, don't let them wear a tank top. I learned this lesson the hard way and now, I fear, we may all end up paying.

It started so innocently. A few days after Lauren's show at the Ha Ha, I got a phone call from a woman named Marlene Meyer, vice president in charge of development at Seraphim Filmworks, a production company I'd never heard of until that moment. It seems Ms. Meyer's gay ob-gyn had just finished reading my novel, *Misadventures in the (213),* and told her he thought it would make a good TV show. She claimed he offered her this tip while she was in the stirrups, but maybe she was just trying to be colorful. "So I want to read it ASAP," she gushed. "You gays always know what's funny first." (I didn't feel the need to tell her that the book's been out since '98.) "I'm transferring you to my trusty assistant, Tad, who's going to give you our address," she chirped. "Messenger a copy of the book right over."

Of course, I agreed to do just that. Now, I've never used a messenger service before, nor do I really have the cash to blow on one, so I enlisted my newly unemployed roommate to do the deed. Yes, folks, after six frenetic but fabulous weeks as a personal assistant to a TV drama queen, Tony's back on the job market. His glam gig came to an abrupt and disheartening end last week when the actress's series got the ax after four seasons of well-paying mediocrity. Three days after the word came down, she checked herself into rehab, telling Tony before she departed that she was going to have to trim the fat from her entourage. "She literally said 'trim the fat' to my face," carped Tony when he returned home that day. So now my roommate inexplicably thinks he's carrying around 30 extra pounds that none of the rest of us can see. "She's not even that much of a drunk," he continued. "I think she just wants to meet guys."

At this point, you're probably wondering why I didn't just deliver the silly book myself. I would have—I'm certainly not above it—but I have my mystique as an artist to consider. I wanted Ms. Meyer to think I was too busy being a creative genius to run the kind of bullshit errand that only non–creative geniuses should have to bother with. In fact, I'd prefer that she think I have some freak neurosis keeping me away—like I can't drive westbound down Sunset Boulevard on days that start with T without experiencing stigmata—than that I'm waiting by the phone, ready to do whatever she says for however much money she offers.

Call me jaded, but in matters of love and show business, I think crazy trumps available every time.

So I waited in the truck while Tony—experienced operative that he is—dashed into the office and made the drop. When he emerged triumphant a few minutes later, I treated him to fajitas at Marix.

Now, however, I kind of want to make him puke them up, and here's why: Though I never explicitly stated it, it was *not* part of the plan for Tony to give Tad, Ms. Meyer's trusty assistant, his phone number, let alone fondle him in our condo complex hot tub, which Tony implies that he did on their third date.

Yes, kids, Tony and Tad are an item. They've practically been joined at the hip-huggers since the moment Tony—clipboard in hand, pen behind ear, pager at the ready—sauntered into the Seraphim office to deliver my book. In other words, my aura of artistic mystery lasted roughly 15 seconds. Apparently, Tony and Tad had a good laugh with Marlene over the whole silly ruse via speakerphone a few days after the drop-off when Tony showed up at Tad's office with a lovingly prepared picnic lunch. That's what he tells me, anyway; I wasn't there.

I've not heard one peep from Marlene Meyer since our initial phone conversation. Tad claims she's still interested in my book, but that she's been too busy giving birth to triplets to read it. Yeah, I've heard that one before.

I know what you're thinking: I'm being petty and stupid and I need to chalk it the fuck up and move on, and you're totally right. But the truth is, I have a funky feeling about Tad, and *that's* what this is all about. There's something about him that's *not quite right.* Or not quite right for Tony, anyway. He's always perfectly pleasant, but think it speaks volumes that Tony hasn't told him the Rutherford Shelton story and doesn't plan to. I mean, Tony has told that story to strangers on the street. There are baristas at our neighborhood Starbucks who know the Rutherford Shelton story. They give us free frappucinos every time Tony retells it.

That said, I'll soon have a chance to further define my Tad aversion, or perhaps transcend it, as Tony's invited him to our *Basic Instinct* Screening Party.

"It's not just because I can't stand to be away from him," Tony said defensively, when I wondered aloud how the presence of a newcomer would affect the group's chemistry. "It's one of Tad's favorite movies ever. He's seen it a zillion times, and so he has lots of inside poop. I thought you'd appreciate it. Besides, *you* invited Shawn over."

I wanted to remind him that *Lauren* invited Shawn, but I stopped short when I realized, again, that I was being petty and stupid and needed to chalk it up and move on. So instead I said, "I'm being weird. I'm sorry. I'm sure it'll be fine."

•

"Can we be mean in front of him?" asks Marcus, who's come over early to bake vagina cupcakes in our oven.

"Totally," says Tony. "But you're never mean."

"I wasn't talking about me," says Marcus.

"Oh," says Tony, taking a moment to reflect on his own quotient of mean. "Please," he says finally, "Tad's got a great set of humor."

"You just said *set* of humor," I point out.

"You know what I mean," mutters Tony, before disappearing into the bathroom to light his Screening Party potty candles, a ritual he's taken to with ever-increasing gusto as the parties go by. Dr. Beaverman told me just last week that her favorite moment of *The Bodyguard,* bar none, was draining her bladder and breathing in the scintillating aromas of jasmine and vanilla while Whitney wailed "I Will Always Love You" 20 feet away.

While Tony's in the bathroom, Marcus takes a break from beating his cake batter, leans over to me, and whispers, "So, is this Tad guy nice?"

"He's nice," I concede. "But they sort of have to be nice to me."

"What's he look like?" he asks. "Blond, Tony said."

"Yeah, and kind of fat," I reply.

"Really?" says Marcus.

"No," I say.

Both Marcus and I find this exchange inexplicably hysterical. We're still giggling about it a few minutes later when Ross and Dr. Beaverman wander in.

Tad arrives next, carrying flowers and wearing khakis that fit him really well and a pec-hugging black sweater. OK, I admit it. It's possible I haven't taken to Tad because he's crazy great-looking and the first time I met him he made the following declaration while eating McDonald's french fries on my couch, shirtless: "Oh, I can eat whatever I want. I know it's going to catch up with me someday, but it hasn't yet, knock wood." So maybe I hate him because he's beautiful. I'm totally willing to entertain that possibility.

After introductions all around, Ross makes a big show of removing the *Basic Instinct* DVD from its Video Master bag and propping it up on top of our entertainment center. "Oh, my God!" I say excitedly. "Our first *real* DVD party!"

Though we watched *The Bodyguard* on DVD, I'm not counting that as an official DVD party because that disc had no special features at all, not even a "Making the Weaves" featurette. The *Basic Instinct* disc, however, looks to be jam-packed and fun-filled.

I'm perusing the list of extras when the phone rings. Marcus answers it in the kitchen. "It's Lauren," he calls out. "She's coming from Pasadena and doesn't know how to get here from there." Lauren is two weeks into a four-weekend comedy writing workshop held at some community college in Pasadena. "Does she want the 5 or the 134?" Marcus asks.

Tony takes the phone from Marcus, gives Lauren the directions, then listens for a moment. "The usual chips and stuff," I hear him tell her. "We may order pizza. And Marcus is making cupcakes with labia on them. No, shaved, I think. They smelled delicious, but we're not allowed to eat them until the interrogation scene. Cool, see you soon." Tony hangs up, returns to the front room, and says, "She said she'll be here in 20 and to start without her if we want."

To buy Lauren some time, I turn the floor over to Marcus, our resident tangent master, for this month's St. Olaf story. "All I remember is that, after seeing this movie, I went out and bought an ice pick and then I couldn't really find any use for it," he says.

"Well, it makes a mess," complains Tony, curling up on the floor next to Tad. "The ice goes everywhere and you step on it later."

"That's your whole story, Marcus?" Ross asks. "You didn't go out and kill anybody or move to San Francisco or sign up for gynecology school or something?

Marcus just shrugs.

"I saw this movie at the AMC Century City," recalls Dr. Beaverman, "and I will never forget how the audience roared with laughter when Michael Douglas walks to the bathroom and shows his ass. I'm telling you, people were beside themselves."

"Most people think this movie's all about punani," Ross notes, "but it's also about ass: crazy, misguided, Michael Douglas man ass."

As Tony and Tad get cozy of the floor, all limbs and tangles, I suddenly remember I have pretzels from Ralph's that I've forgotten to put out. "I went to see *Basic Instinct* with this guy from dance class named Walter," I recall, on my way into the kitchen, "and I wasn't sure if it was a date or not."

"God, you've changed so much since then," teases Tony.

I flip Tony a quick bird, then rip open the pretzel bag and set it on the coffee table. "I also remember nicknaming it *Basically, It Stinks* because I didn't think it was very good. But since then I've become obsessed with *Showgirls* and *Starship Troopers,*" I say, referring to Paul Verhoeven's deliriously fucked-up follow-ups to *Basic Instinct,* "so I'm excited to give this another look."

"Verhoeven's sick as fuck," confirms Ross, "and I love every single moment of his movies. He'll go places other mainstream filmmakers would never go." For emphasis, Ross gestures to Marcus's cupcakes, fresh from the oven and grouped together on a green plate like a bouquet of snapdragons.

"But this is so superior to his more recent movies," remarks Tad.

There's a hint of...what?...pretension, maybe, to Tad's tone that makes the hair on the back of my neck stand up. Again, I admit, I may just be biased because he can grow bangs.

"It's pure Hitchcock: icy blond femme fatale, San Francisco, sexual perversity, flawed cop," Tad spouts, as though he were a pitching copy ideas for the film's poster. "I wrote a 20-page paper on the Hitchcockian overtones in *Basic Instinct* when I was at Cal Arts."

"I'm sorry," says Dr. Beaverman.

I can tell by the suddenly constricted look on her face that she didn't mean to say that out loud.

"I'm not," Tad snaps back. "I got an A on it."

"Remember how gay groups were protesting this movie by telling people in advance who the murderer was?" I recall, trying to change the subject. "Well, I remember coming out of the theater and *wishing* someone had told me who did it because I was clueless. I needed, like, Melissa Etheridge with finger puppets to break it down for me."

"She wasn't even out yet," remarks Marcus. "Isn't that weird to think about? When this movie came out, we had no Melissa, no Ellen, no Elton, no *Will & Grace*."

"No Sam Harris," I offer.

"Wait a goddamned minute!" barks Tony. "Sam Harris is *gay*? Sam Harris from *Star Search*? Is *gay*?"

"I know," I say, nodding gravely. "It took me a while to get used to it too."

"So maybe the gays were right to raise hell about this movie," says Marcus, continuing with his thought. "Maybe that's how change happens."

"My boss, Perry, protested this movie," says Ross.

"Perry, who took our pictures?" says Marcus eagerly. "Sexy, bald Perry?'

Ross nods.

"He doesn't seem like the protesting type," I say.

"Call him at the store," suggests Ross.

I get Perry on the line at Video Master, confirm that he indeed has a *Basic Instinct* story, then put him on speakerphone so that everyone can hear. "Is the caller there?" I say.

"Yeah," says Perry. "So *Basic Instinct* totally changed my outlook. I was in my mid 20s, living in New York, and I was protesting with a bunch of other gay people in front of this theater on Fifth Avenue. We were leafleting and yelling things like, 'Catherine did it!' and 'This movie demeans lesbians!' And a very nice woman who was in line came up to me and said, 'Have you even seen this movie?' and I ranted back to her, 'I don't have to see this movie. I'm not giving them my money.' And she said, in a very nice way, 'You should see it.' And so about six months later, I secretly rented it, and I was appalled at myself because I *loved* the film. I thought that if it had been directed by a woman, it would have been the opening night film at the gay film festival and the lesbians would have been on their feet cheering female power. So I decided right then not to ever protest something that I hadn't seen with my own two eyes. Look, I got a customer. I gotta go. Have fun."

"Thanks, Perry," I shout. "We'll save you a vagina cake!"

With Lauren still en route, I click on the making-of documentary, playfully entitled *Blonde Poison,* to see if we can discover anything more about the protests.

It turns out there's a whole section about it, during which we learn several interesting things. We learn that the on set protests took place in San Francisco and that some 150 homosexual hell-raisers showed up on the first night of shooting and remained a presence for 18 nights—chanting, flashing lights into the camera, and even holding signs up to passing drivers that said "Honk if you love the 49ers." According to producer Alan Marshall, some 26 people were arrested that first night. He knows, because as the person whose name was on the 300-foot restraining order, he had to do the arresting. Police would bring protesters before him like he was some kind of pharaoh and he'd say, "Yes, arrest them." For his part, Verhoeven—who always maintained his film's treatment of sexuality as a "nonissue" was good for the gays—got a perverse kick out of the whole to-do, which is kind of why I love him. As for the actors, according to cinematographer Jan De Bont, the controversy took its toll on them, making them feel as though they were doing something dirty, which, thank God, they were.

We also learn that there was a big powwow between the filmmakers and the activists where the gays reportedly showed up with a list of proposed script changes. God, I would have loved to have seen the look on Verhoeven's face when the protesters suggested why don't they just make Michael Douglas the killer and Sharon Stone the detective. That'd be a quick, easy fix.

And last but not least, we learn that Queer Nation cofounder Jonathan Katz, one of the gay talking heads featured, is quite attractive and has nice floppy gay hair. Even nicer than Tad's.

Having gotten our fix of the furor, I click back over to the main menu, which features, among its several alternating images, a shot of Sharon dragging on a cigarette. "Oh, wait, I have a story," remembers Ross. "One of my customers at the store was a P.A. on some Sharon Stone movie a few years ago and he said she colors like a maniac."

"Colors what, her hair?" asks Dr. Beaverman.

"No, like with crayons," says Ross. "He said that she was always sending him out for coloring books. Of course, this guy could be totally full of shit. He returns his movies stoned most of the time."

It takes us a moment to digest this peculiar tidbit of gossip, much longer than if Ross had reported that Sharon had, say, taken a part in a fourgy with two grips and a gaffer in the catering truck. The innocence of Sharon's alleged predilection seems to have stymied us a bit. Finally, Tony speaks. "I bet she'd eat the crayons too," he says.

"Oh," says Tad, wearily, "this is going to be gossipy?"

Everyone except Tad takes a sip of beverage. It's as if someone had proposed a toast.

"I wish Lauren would get here," says Marcus.

In a last ditch effort to give her another minute, I click through the various chapter headings and read them aloud, a pastime, I discovered with *Coyote Ugly,* that can be quite entertaining. "The first chapter is 'Johnny Boz and the Ice Pick,'" I announce.

"Don't they sing 'Runaround Sue'?" asks Dr. Beaverman.

"'Love Hurts,'" I continue. "'Interrogation, Catherine at Play...'"

"'In the Fields of the Lord,'" adds Ross.

"That's odd," I say, when I get to chapter 16. "There's actually a heading called 'Basic Instinct.' I wonder if when you watch that section, it's like watching the whole movie in 10 minutes."

"Worth a try," says Dr. Beaverman.

"'No Luck With Women,'" I read on, "'Gus Gets It,' and 'Minks and Rugrats.'"

"That last one's actually a coloring book," says Tony.

With that, Tad lets out an audible sigh and suddenly we're knee-deep in a river of social discomfort. Something has to fill the silence, so I decide it might as well be the reason we're all here. I click on "play movie" and soon the room is bathed in the hauntingly atmospheric strains of Jerry Goldsmith's Oscar-nominated score. Though full of tension in its design, the music seems to work on us like a miracle salve, smoothing out the rough edges that existed before its arrival.

The credits end, and our story begins with a shot of a naked and nubile blond—it's either Sharon or someone super Sharonesque—grinding atop a man we'll learn later is a '60s rock star and club owner named Johnny Boz. "Is that Sharon's ass," I ask, as our sex kitten binds Johnny's hands with a white Hermes scarf, "or a stunt ass?"

"It was all her," Tad informs us. "None of the actors used doubles. Verhoeven told them up front, 'If you're going to be in my movie, you have to do everything I want,' and they all went for it. You have to respect that kind of bravery."

Tad's point is perfectly valid, and yet I sort of want to hurl. It's not *what* he says so much as the I-read-*Variety*-and-do-script-coverage-for-a-living manner in which he says it.

When the blond, who possesses what Ross effusively describes as a "pretty awe-inspiring natural rack," whips out an ice pick and makes a Boz-kabob out of poor Johnny, the gore-averse Dr. Beaverman covers her face with her hands until the coked-up has-been is good and dead. She emerges just as Michael Douglas arrives on the scene, playing Nick Curran, a seen-it-all San Francisco detective with a weakness for just about everything. "There's come stains all over the sheets," a low-ranking member of Nick's cop posse informs him.

"Wouldn't it be awesome if that was the line that got that actor his SAG card?" says Tony. "If I ever get a SAG card, I hope it's because I delivered some kind of come update."

Michael's too good a cop to just take the guy's word for it, so he checks out the stains himself, using a special pair of high-tech porn goggles. "Who was just there, the Oakland A's?" marvels Ross, when we get a load of the load.

"Does semen really glow in the dark like that?" I wonder.

"Mine does," brags Ross. "I drink a lot of Mountain Dew."

With that, a brief, but unmistakable grimace passes over Tad's face, the subtext of which is, "I don't wish to imagine that guy even *having* a load." Thankfully, Tony misses it, as he's looking at the screen. Double thankfully, just then Lauren comes ambling in, *finally.* "I got a little lost," she says, catching her breath. "I thought Tony said take the first *right* after Victory and it was the first *light.* It's the Asian in me flipping the consonants." She plops down on her regular sofa cushion and says, "OK, what have I missed?"

"Some guy with a big load got ice-picked to death and Sharon Stone likes to color in coloring books in her trailer," I say.

"OK," says Lauren.

Tony introduces Lauren to Tad while I fetch her a Coke from the fridge. Meanwhile, on screen, Michael and his transplanted country boy partner, Gus (George Dzundza) arrive at the mansion belonging to Sharon Stone's character, ice queen novelist Catherine Tramell, who they've been told was Boz's girlfriend at the time of his death. Sharon's not home, so our public dicks chat up Roxy (Leilani Sarelle), Catherine's tough-talking friend, instead. "Half boots," says Lauren with a sigh. "A lesbian dead giveaway."

Roxy tells the cops they'll likely find Sharon at her beach house. When they arrive, sure enough, there's Ms. Stone, sitting in an Adirondack deck chair, alone with her fucked-up thoughts, proving that just because a girl's a diabolical, murderous wonderfuck doesn't mean she can't curl up in a cozy J. Crew sweater set and appreciate a pretty view of the Pacific.

"Her last name is Tramell," Dr. Beaverman says, pointedly, "which is just an accent mark away from being the verb 'trammel' as in 'to enmesh.' She's going to have no trouble trammeling up Michael's life because he, it seems, never learns to keep it in his pants, no matter how many movies just like this he turns up in."

After exchanging pleasantries and a few furtive glances, Michael begins peppering Sharon with questions about her dead ex, like "How long had you been dating him?"

"I wasn't dating him," Sharon replies, her voice both husky and bloodless. "I was fucking him."

"With my vagina," clarifies Ross.

"Speaking of which," says Lauren, grabbing herself a cupcake. "I haven't had lunch."

"Not yet," says Marcus, giving her hand a playful smack. "Soon, though."

Lauren scowls at him but returns the treat to its plate.

"Did you go home with him?" Michael asks Sharon.

"Please, you saw the bedspread," says Tony.

Placated for now, Michael leaves Sharon and heads off to visit to Jeanne Tripplehorn, as Beth Garner, a police psychologist who's dead serious about her work, but who also occasionally enjoys being sodomized. Apparently, Michael goofed up a little on a recent case and accidentally shot some tourists, so, as part of his penance, he has to periodically check in with the company shrink. "Oh, boy," groans Tony. "I'm really sorry I trotted out my mustache material on Jennifer Beals. I didn't think I'd need it again so soon."

"Tripplehorn?" I ask.

"Oh my *God,*" he replies. "Beals was like Def Con 2, 2½ maybe. Tripplehorn is a solid 4. She looks like she's in one of those 'Captain Morgan was here' rum ads."

During a scene featuring a bunch of cops around a conference table, we learn that Sharon's last novel, *Love Hurts,* in addition to sharing its name with a Nazareth song that was later covered by Cher, just happened to be about a retired rock and roller who gets ice-picked by his girlfriend.

The cops figure that's reason enough to haul Sharon's ass in for questioning, so Michael and Gus return to the beach house to fetch her. After learning she's a suspect, Sharon, cool as Vanilla Ice, disappears into her bedroom, flashes her ass to Michael, and emerges a few moments later in her favorite interrogation dress, her hair pulled up in a tight Grace Kelly twist. "There must have been 16 gay stylists positioned in that bedroom," I figure. "It's like working pit crew at the Indy 500."

"Only not as tranquil," says Dr. Beaverman.

During a claustrophobic coastline ride to the police station that Tad points out is reminiscent of Hitchcock's *Vertigo* as well as *To Catch a Thief* and *Suspicion,* Michael and Sharon discuss her writing career. "Sharon's pen name is Catherine Woolf," remarks Dr. Beaverman, "another man-eating reference, and not a very clever one either. How much did Joe Eszterhas get paid to write this? A million?"

"Three, actually," says Tad.

"Then I should get a fiver for sitting through it," figures Tony.

At this point, Tad extracts himself from Tony's lap, pretends to stretch, then leans with his back against the couch. It's the first time I've ever seen Tad and Tony sit in the same room together as separate entities.

"Ms. Tramell has waived the right to attorneys," Michael explains to the crew of horny detectives at the outset of Sharon's illustrious interrogation scene.

"But she did send her lighting people in," says Tony.

"No shit," says Ross. "It's like she's giving her testimony on the Starship Enterprise."

"Are you a Trekker, Ross?" I have to ask.

"I have Trekker leanings," he confesses, "but I wouldn't describe myself as a full-on Trekker."

"Because it would be OK if you were," I say.

As the cops question Sharon, and fret about how they're going to walk to sixth period with raging hard-ons, we inch closer to what I maintain is the most unsettling shot in the whole film. I refer, of course, to the "Newman Zoom," that moment when the camera and Sharon's prime inquisitor—played by bespectacled, round-faced actor Wayne Knight, a.k.a. *Seinfeld*'s Newman—move toward each other in one quick dizzying swoop. Even thinking about it makes me light-headed.

Then the Newman Zoom happens and, praise God, we all survive it unscathed.

"Grab your cupcakes, everybody!" Marcus announces.

"Oh, thank God," says Lauren, before snatching a cake and taking a giant bite.

"Wait, not till she flashes it!" scolds Marcus.

I can't tell exactly what Lauren says back to him, as her mouth's full, but I'm pretty sure it's either "Fuck off" or "Fuck you," one of the two.

Wanting to give proper credit to the chef, I pause the DVD briefly and ask Marcus to explain today's culinary creation. "The cake is devil's food, duh, because she *is* the devil," he says animatedly, as though he's an actor introducing a movie clip on *The Tonight Show*. "The icing is white because she always wears white, and the toothpicks, of course, represent the ice pick."

"What does the diamond-shaped red icing design on each cupcake represent?" I ask. Of course, I know the answer already. I just want to see what word he'll use.

"Her pussy," he says. "Bon appetit."

"In my memory, it seemed like a much more explicit shot," I complain.

"What did you think?" says Tad haughtily. "That Sharon was going to open it up with her long fingernails like in *Hustler* and you'd hear it go 'Cli-i-ick?' "

"Wouldn't that have been something?" says Ross dreamily.

With that, I unpause the DVD and we watch, rapt, as Sharon asks Michael if he's ever fucked on cocaine, a question that, in Verhoevenland, is such a no-brainer that I'm surprised Michael doesn't snap back, "Does a bear shit in the woods?" Then Sharon methodically uncrosses her left leg and replaces it with her right. "It's coming up, right?" I pant, like a 5-year old waiting for Christmas.

"That was it," says Marcus.

"That was *it*?" I ask.

"Yeah, that's it," says Ross. "Go back and pause on it, Dennis."

Though I'm a relative tenderfoot with the DVD remote, I nail the shot on the first try. There it is, folks, the moment Sharon later claimed she was hoodwinked into serving up. The moment a hairy-pitted Florence Henderson would later make fun of in a parody for the MTV Movie Awards. The moment that inspired weeks of international water cooler discussion and at least a dozen cupcakes. "You hardly see anything," carps Tony, "just a few blond pubes."

"Which I left out of the recipe," says Marcus. "Hope that's OK."

"In my memory, it seemed like a much more explicit shot," I complain.

"What did you think?" says Tad, haughtily. "That Sharon was going to open it up with her long fingernails like in *Hustler* and you'd hear it go 'Cli-i-ick?' "

"Wouldn't that have been something?" says Ross dreamily.

Sensing his *Hustler* comment may have rubbed me the wrong way, Tad tries to win back a few points with another film history lesson. "Verhoeven got the idea for that moment because when he was in college there was this older woman he'd see at parties who would flash her crotch like that," he explains. "Finally, one of his buddies went up to her and said, 'Do you know everyone can see your vagina?' and she said, 'Of course I know. That's why I do it.'"

"I'm sure Sharon found that story very comforting," says Lauren.

"Thank God it's not Demi Moore, or there'd be hair hanging off the end of that chair," says Tony.

Finally, Tony catches one of the cavalcade of persnickety faces Tad's pulled today. Of course, it would be impossible for him to miss this one, as it's aimed right at him and features what appear to be daggers, though they could very well be ice picks.

When I switch to the commentary track to get a little insight on the famous shot, the first thing we hear is cinematographer Jan De Bont saying, "That specific shot almost made her a star."

"You said it, Jan," I say. "We didn't."

Ross suggests we listen on to see if the horny foreigners Verhoeven and De Bont say anything about how Sharon later claimed she'd been duped and didn't realize what was happening. Our curiosity is rewarded soon enough. "If you put a camera between someone's legs and you have a little light there, it's most likely that you will see something," says De Bont.

"Is that really true, though?" says Tony, playing devil's advocate. "I want to try something. Lauren, spread your legs." In one quick medley of movement, Tony puts a cupcake in her hand, grabs her wrist and positions it in her crotch with the cake facing out. Then he takes my Canon instamatic from the bookshelf, positions it between Lauren's knees, and aims it at the cake. "Do you notice that?" he asks her. "Be honest. Tell us exactly how you feel."

Lauren takes a moment to consider the question. "Yes," she says, deliberately. "I have a camera between my legs and I definitely notice it."

"Another mystery solved," says Tony.

Tony returns his props to the table but not before snapping a shot of Lauren's cupcake crotch that I'm sure will end up on our refrigerator. "You're going to have fun explaining that to the guy at the photo lab," chides Tad.

"That'll be nothing after the turd pictures," muses Ross.

"What turd pictures?" asks Tad.

"He had one of his stripper buddies pinch a loaf in a fish and chips tray," explains Ross, completely oblivious to Tony's pained "shut the fuck up" expression. "And then he put it in this guy's mailbox in England who thought we were being too mean."

Tad makes a face like he's just spent the last two hours watching the Newman Zoom on a continuous loop. "That is so vile," he says finally.

"It's not as vile as it sounds," Tony says defensively. "I'll tell you all about it later. You'll probably think it's funny. Everyone else does."

Meanwhile, back on the screen, Michael has just dropped Sharon off at her mansion. Given that the last thing they discussed before she darted inside was the blond banshee's no-panties policy, it's not surprising that Michael leaves feeling hornier than the cast of *American Pie.* And, since he can't remember the address of Blow Buddies, he has no choice but to get liquored up and head to Jeanne's place for some knock-down, drag-out intercourse. "I love what Verhoeven gets people to do," I marvel as Michael rips Jeanne's silk blouse open and slams her against the wall. "This was her first movie after studying drama at Julliard. Could you imagine? One day you're doing the campus production of *A Doll's House* and the next you've got your tits out and Michael Douglas is banging the holy hell out of you."

"He's only able to bang her with gusto because he's thinking of Sharon Stone," Dr. Beaverman says. "Let's face it, he can go there with Tripplehorn only if he completely fantasizes that she's someone else, someone who doesn't have the fashion sense of Columbo."

As Michael shoves Jeanne over the sofa and mounts her doggy-style, we take a straw poll in the room as to which orifice he's invading. When it comes up 4–3 in favor of the back door, I switch over to the commentary track in hopes of settling the matter. "You're not even sure if he's in her vagina or if it's anal sex," says Verhoeven.

"This was Jeanne Tripplehorn's first movie after studying drama at Julliard. Could you imagine? One day you're doing the campus production of *A Doll's House* and the next you've got your tits out and Michael Douglas is banging the holy hell out of you." —Dennis

"Well, that clears that up," says Marcus.

"She's an insult to the psychiatric profession," fumes Dr. Beaverman. "She's the needy woman who will stand by and take crumbs. You can tell she didn't send away for her degree from a diploma mill like I did."

"Speaking of which, I haven't heard much about Ivy-by-the-Pacific on ESPN lately," says Ross, turning to Dr. Beaverman. "Will we see the Fighting Ivys in a bowl game this season?"

"Doesn't look like it," says Dr. Beaverman. "But there's talk of getting a second phone line."

As Jeanne and Michael continue to rut like pissed-off bunnies—this is what O.J. Simpson must have had in mind when he coined the term "wrasslin"—Tad informs us that the gay protesters also took issue with this scene, even though it doesn't have any gay content.

"Maybe they were thrown by Jeanne's 5 o'clock shadow," speculates Tony.

"Actually," says Tad, curtly, "they said it was a date rape."

"But what's a Paul Verhoeven movie without some forcible sex?" asks Ross. "It's like a Gene Kelly movie without dancing."

Soon Michael finds himself back at Sharon's beach house, getting a lesson in introductory ice picking. "I like rough edges," Sharon says as an explanation for why she doesn't just pick up a few ice trays from her Tupperware lady and save the strain on her wrist.

"I have a question," I declare, taking the floor. "Is Sharon Stone *good*?" I ask. "Does she have it?"

"Absolutely, she does," gushes Tad. "She's a total star."

"Because I came into this party ready to gun for her," I continue. "But the fact is, when she's not on-screen, it's a big drag."

"Huge drag," agrees Tony. "All we get is Michael Douglas and a bunch of guys who look like the Commish."

"And Jeanne Tripplehorn," adds Marcus.

"I was including her in that grouping," clarifies Tony.

By this point, I'm tired of trying to artfully describe the various disapproving faces Tad keeps pulling. If I wasn't, I'd stick another one in here and it would be a doozy.

"I liked Sharon so much better when she was the mysterious femme fatale," muses Dr. Beaverman, "as opposed to the celebrity we know today. She could never play this role now because she's given us far too much information. She's blown her cover and now she's the Zsa Zsa Gabor of the 21st century. And that's with deep apologies to Zsa Zsa."

"She got an Oscar nomination for *Casino,* don't forget," Tad reminds us, because neither Rutherford Shelton nor Sharon herself is here to.

Before long, Michael gets his undisciplined ass taken off the case. By now, however, he's so ensnared in Sharon's web of sexual intrigue that he can't just forget about her and take in a Sex Addicts Anonymous meeting. No, not our Michael. Instead, he stalks Sharon to a gigantic cathedral-slash-rave club, which is what the DVD package must mean when it says Michael "descends into San Francisco's forbidden underground."

"Sharon looks like a million bucks here," I say as Ms. Stone, in a gold minidress, does the Lesbian Lambada with Roxy while making eyes at Michael.

"Yeah, but she only got paid $200,000 to do the film," says Tad. "By way of comparison, I just read in the *Reporter* that Leelee Sobieski got a million to do *The Glass House.*"

"Who?" asks Lauren.

"Helen Hunt Jr.," I say.

"Oh, her," says Lauren.

"My point exactly," says Tad, with a smug smile.

By now, Michael's so hot for teacher, he'll do anything Sharon wants. This includes accompanying her home and allowing her to tie him to the bedpost Johnny Boz–style. "He's so *stupid*!" shouts Lauren.

"Straight men come off worse than anyone in this movie," opines Tad, in a manner that strikes me as oddly disembodied. It's like he heard Camille Paglia say it on *Nightline,* and then adopted the sound bite as his own.

"Most straight guys would do the same thing," asserts Ross as Michael makes a meal out of Sharon's honey pie, a moment that, courtesy of the MPAA, Americans had to wait for the unrated Director's Cut to enjoy. "Deputy Cock is calling the shots."

"Has anyone considered that maybe she ties Michael Douglas up because he's lousy with his hands?" suggests Dr. Beaverman. "I say he's a frat boy in bed and *that's* why she has to do all the work."

Remarkably, Michael lives to see the other side of his orgasm, then takes his post-coital saunter to the bathroom, nude. And we *see* him do it. *From the back.* Suddenly, my living room erupts with a wake-the-neighbors combination of screams, gasps, flying sofa cushions, and exclamations of "Oh, my God." It's like we're watching *America's Funniest Home Videos* and a cat has just fallen from a six-story building and landed on a sun-bathing obese woman, who then vomits.

"I never go to the gym and my ass is better than that," claims Ross, the first of us who's actually able to form words.

"He may be in San Francisco, but that ass is in San Luis Obispo," says Tony.

"And this was almost a decade ago!" Dr. Beaverman points out. "C.Z. Jones is probably building a sand castle out of that thing as we speak."

As someone with a few problem body parts of my own, I have to stand up for Michael here. "Judging by his pecs, it looks like he worked pretty hard to get in shape for this movie," I remark. "He probably just figured, 'Screw it, my ass is never going to get any better than this, so here it is.'"

Tony zooms back and pauses, then crawls to the screen and points to the empty space between Michael's thighs, just below his Oscar-winning butt crack. "He is taped to high heaven," Tony asserts. "It's like an original Hershey Bar: no nuts."

"This is making my teeth hurt," says Marcus.

"Lauren, you're in fitness," I say. "You've got two months until shooting starts and an hour a day with Michael Douglas. What do you do?"

"I would have probably done whatever they did," she says, shrugging. "You can't change genetics. Steroids would have given him a Butterfly Ass."

"Isn't that a Mariah Carey album?" asks Dr. Beaverman.

"I like it just the way it is," I conclude. "Concave."

Michael makes it to the bathroom, where he comes upon the jealous, biker-jacketed Roxy, and tells her that her gal pal, Sharon, is the "Fuck of the century." He doesn't specify which century. "Roxy's wearing lip liner only," groans Lauren. "That's a negative portrayal of lesbians right there."

Then Michael and his concave ass go back to bed to find Sharon curled up like a sleeping baby, a blissful smile on her face. Though she may well be visualizing her next act of just-for-the-fuck-of-it homicide, I like to imagine she's dreaming about her life after the movie comes out—a life of *Esquire* "Women We Love" covers, standing-room-only AmFAR auctions, and the occasional Oscar appearance where she'll steal the show with a perfectly timed bon mot. "This movie is the most fun to watch when you think of it as Sharon Stone's damn-the-torpedoes attempt to become a movie star," I remark.

"Totally," agrees Tony. "Right here, she's thinking, 'Move over, Demi. There's a new sheriff in town.'"

"Sharon had been working for years in B movies like *Police Academy* when this script came along," Tad informs us. "No one who was hot at the time, like Kelly Lynch or Jamie Lee Curtis, wanted to do the nudity, so Sharon was like, 'I don't want to do another fucking Allan Quartermain movie. Give me the damn thing.' Then she realized, 'I could tear this role up, and I could be *huge*!' And it worked!"

"And we've been enjoying her movies ever since," says Marcus.

A few scenes later, Michael meets up with portly Gus at a western-themed dance bar because, according to Ross, fat people love country music.

"Gus becomes more and more of a good ol' boy as the movie goes along," I observe, as Gus lets Michael try on his Stetson hat. "By the end, I predict he's going to suggest they open up a can of whoop-ass on Sharon."

"While banjo music plays in the background," adds Ross.

Michael leaves Gus and heads unwittingly into a parking garage where a black Lotus comes out of nowhere and attempts to run him down. Thinking fast, he jumps into his own car and chases after his attacker. Suddenly, it's as though he's back on *The Streets of San Francisco,* flying over hills and spinning out around corners. Though the sequence is energetically shot and scored, something's missing in it for me. And that something is a certain baby-adopting, Gap T-shirt–espousing, coloring book aficionado named Stone. "You know that whoever Sharon was banging at the time of the premiere leaned over to her here and said, 'When you're not on-screen, it's not as good,'" I say.

"I think it was Faye Dunaway," says Lauren. "I remember reading that when they applauded at the premiere, Sharon got weak-kneed and fell back and Faye Dunaway caught her and said, 'Now you can do anything you want.'"

"And the very next day," says Tony, "she started giving her private lessons in how to be crazy."

The car chase ends with the Lotus driver careening off an embankment and dying. It turns out to be Roxy. "See how Verhoeven keeps his women beautiful?" says Tad as Michael rolls over Roxy's dead gay body to reveal her perfectly made-up face. "She's the first female killed in the movie and she doesn't have a scratch on her."

In a subsequent scene, Michael does a little research and learns that Roxy razored her brothers to death several years earlier. "That's another reason why the gays were upset," says Tad, with visible testiness, "because the movie asserts that Roxy slashed her brothers because they didn't understand her. Well, I *want* people to think I might take a knife out because I have questions about my sexuality."

Where the hell is *this* coming from?

Tad rants on. "It means, don't fuck with me about it because you know what, I *do* have a problem, and it's *you*!"

Stunned into silence by Tad's psycho outburst, we watch without so much as a titter until the scene where Sharon visits a mysterious elderly friend named Hazel Dopkins, played by Dorothy Malone, the ruby-lipped, gray-tressed veteran actress who won an Oscar for playing a nympho in 1956's *Written on the Wind.* "Dorothy Malone looks like the picture in Goldie Hawn's attic," decides Tony.

Everyone thinks this is hilarious except for you-know-who. Great set of humor, my ass.

The plot, such as I'm following it, thickens considerably when Michael discovers that Jeanne and Sharon were pussy partners back in college. When he goes to Jeanne's and confronts her about it, she barks, "What am I supposed to say? Hey guys, I'm not gay, but I did fuck your suspect?" When Michael continues to press her, Tripplehorn shrieks, "You think I could *kill* somebody?"

It's more than Tony can take. "I don't even have the balls to kill this lip hair at the root!" he hollers, speaking for Jeanne.

Which is the straw that breaks the camel's back.

Tad, the veins on his forehead on the verge of bursting, stands up and says, "You know what? I have to go. I just remembered I have something to do." He's out the door before I can even offer him a snatch for the road.

I try not to look at Tony, but I can't help it.

"I know," Tony says, then leaves to chase after Tad.

"Those two are either going to break up or have the best sex ever," figures Lauren.

By the time I'm able to quell my feelings of anxiety and guilt and turn my attention back to the movie, I've lost whatever grasp I had on the plot. Marcus tries to get me up to speed, but it just doesn't take. "I know, it makes no sense," he admits, when I express my bewilderment. "When Sharon was in college in '83, she would have had to be thinking about her future career in homicide and how she was going to set up Jeanne Tripplehorn, who would coincidentally be around."

Then Jeanne shows up and reaches into her trench coat pocket for her Bart Simpson key ring, only to get shot by Michael, who realized while he was waiting in the car that Gus was in danger. Though it's all quite twisted and climactic, all I can think is, "God, *The Simpsons* has been around *forever*."

Then Michael returns to the beach house, where he sneaks a peek at Sharon's new novel and reads that the amiable partner of the central cop character gets murdered. Luckily, Gus is unharmed when Michael hooks up with him later in the city, where they ride together to an office building to follow up on a lead Gus got earlier. Gus insists Michael stay in the car because he's on leave, then says, "I'll be in Suite 405."

"Strumming a banjo," I add, speaking for Gus.

"Singing Fee-Fi-Fiddley-Eye-Oh," says Ross.

Before he can even find a piece of straw to stick in his mouth, Gus gets his George Strait–loving ass ice-picked to death in the elevator. Then Jeanne shows up and reaches into her trench coat pocket for her Bart Simpson key ring, only to get shot by Michael, who realized while he was waiting in the car that Gus was in danger. Though it's all quite twisted and climactic, all I can think is, "God, *The Simpsons* has been around *forever*."

"I want that guy from the beginning to show up and go, 'Lieutenant, there's come all over these elevator buttons,'" says Ross, as the cops show up and try to make sense of it all.

In the wake of Jeanne's death, the cops go to her apartment and discover all sorts of incriminating photos, including a picture of Jeanne and Sharon at their college graduation that was clearly taken the first week of production. "Sharon planted them," Marcus informs me.

"Got it," I say, though I'm clearly as clueless as I was when I saw this movie at the theater in '92.

"What this movie subliminally says is that all women are crazy," declares Lauren.

"It's not saying it subliminally," counters Dr. Beaverman. "It's in labia-pink neon. It's a very mistrustful film toward women. The lesbian part is just to emphasize that point. It's a gender thing. Women can be the biggest weakness; not booze, not cigarettes, those can be conquered. But if you give in to your basic instinct for sex, all the rest of your willpower and your discipline will just go right out the window. Women will be the death of you."

Unfortunately, the movie isn't over. We still have to go back to Michael's apartment for the film's final scene, which finds our shrewd seductress grinding away on top of Michael in a position we've seen her in several times already. "She's supposedly the fuck of the century," I comment, "but it's exactly the same every time."

"She's a one-trick pony," says Ross. "But it's a hell of a trick."

As they stew in the afterglow, Sharon's hand inches its way under the bed. Is she reaching for a condom? Some komodo dragon chow? Her brand new *Rescuers Down Under* coloring book and 64-pack of Crayolas with the built-in sharpener? Of course not; it's another damn ice pick. She must buy those fuckers in bulk.

Though the odds are good that she's going to put an end to Michael's sorry existence here and now, we'll never know for sure if she does, because just as it looks like she's going to do the deed, the music climaxes and the screen goes black. "I don't think she would have killed him then," muses Lauren. "She would have killed him when he was really getting on her nerves, like when he didn't throw his dirty socks in the hamper or when he was saying something to her like, 'Jesus, Catherine, how long does it take you to get ready?'"

As the credits roll, Marcus bemoans the fact that we don't have a Diane Warren–penned love theme to take us out. "Like 'Pick Me' by Richard Marx," he suggests.

"Or 'Love on Ice' by Expose," says Lauren.

"How 'bout 'Pick Me (Love on Ice)' by Richard Marx *with* Expose," suggests Ross on his way to the bathroom.

"Have ever told you guys about how I used to have breakfast next to Richard Marx?" asks Dr. Beaverman.

"Yes," replies everyone within earshot.

As I retrieve the empty glasses from the front room and head into the kitchen, Dr. Beaverman picks up my cassette recorder and speaks directly into it. "I think the moral of this story, especially for men, is that you must control your basic instincts. If you let the woman on top, she'll kill you. That phallus that Sharon's packing is always erect, always lethal, always potent, and can penetrate right into the heart if you allow it. In other words, *watch your ass,* Michael Douglas, so we don't have to."

"Jesus, it's like Wicks and Sticks in there," says Ross, returning from the can. "I feel so pretty now."

•

A half hour later, everyone has gone home but Marcus. He's in the kitchen collecting his cupcake fixings and listening to me feel guilty about the Tad-Tony debacle. "It's like I did some kind of roommate voodoo curse on Tad or something," I fret. "I should have given him more of a chance."

"Were you ever less than cordial to him?" asks Marcus.

"No," I say.

"Then I wouldn't worry about it," says Marcus. "They're probably blowing each other in Tad's SUV as we speak."

Just then, Tony walks back in, his face tear-streaked and ruddy. He's about to head straight to his room and slam the door, but first he has an update to deliver. It's not really a come update, but in a way, it sort of is. "It's over," he says.

I wish I could give him his SAG card.

'ROID RAGE

"Talk about a disaster," says Ross as I stand sweating in front of the TV pushing every button on my DVD remote and some simultaneously. "This column's going to write itself."

"The movie ain't on here, you guys," I announce. "This is just the extra stuff. We're screwed."

"Or spared," says Dr. Beaverman. "Depends on how you look at it."

"I actually like this movie," says Tony, with utter sincerity. "I saw it at the Burbank AMC by myself in the afternoon and I walked out of the theater totally pumped up and proud to be an American."

We all just look at him.

"Seriously, you guys," he adds.

"Well, I feel like I just dodged a bullet," says Dr. Beaverman.

Our trouble began earlier today when I plunked down the slightly scandalous sum of $50 for the DVD "Criterion Version" of *Armageddon.* (I don't know what criterion means. Does it mean there are critters in the movie?) Most mental health professionals, present company included, would call such a purchase a cry for help, but to me, it's just a healthy collision of impulse buying and conscientious journalism.

See, Matt in London is putting together a special issue of *British Premiere* all about disaster movies. Our mission, should we choose to accept it, is to examine one of the most commercially successful disaster films of all time, director Michael Bay's 1998 asteroid epic *Armageddon.*

Why don't we do a *real* disaster movie, like *The Poseidon Adventure* or *The Towering Inferno,* you may wonder? God knows, I did. Well, Matt seems to have those movies covered by another writer who's dedicated a good chunk of his career to the genre. So it looks like that guy gets Pamela Sue Martin treading water on an inverted ocean liner to the music of Maureen McGovern and we get Liv Tyler blossoming into womanhood on an oil rig to Aerosmith. Life isn't fair.

So, in the hopes of compensating for that chasm of fun, I brought home the special two-disc DVD with Bay's lovingly compiled bells and whistles only to discover, with a living room full of guests, that all I *got* was bells and whistles. The disc with the actual movie is MIA.

"That's what you get for not letting me bring the movie," says Ross, scoldingly.

"You told me yesterday that someone had checked out the DVD a month ago and never returned it," I remind him.

"Well, we have three copies of the tape," he says.

"But you yourself keep insisting DVD is far superior," I argue.

"It is," he says, "but tape is better than nothing, which is what we have now, nothing."

"Just be quiet for a second!" I holler. "And let me figure out what to do."

Inspired by the sudden tension in the room, Lauren brings her hands to her face and, in her best disaster movie babe wail, shrieks, "We're all going to die!" The word "die" goes on for like 10 seconds.

"Pull yourself together, woman," Marcus barks, and then fake slaps her across the face. "The only way we're going to make it through this is if we stick together."

"I just need a second to think!" I insist. "How about this for a plan?" I say after massaging my temples for a few seconds. "I'll go to Twisted Video just down the street...get the movie on VHS...we'll watch that...and I'll return the DVD to Virgin and get my money back tomorrow."

"That sounds crazy," says Marcus. "But it just might work!"

"You're not leaving me here," vows Lauren. "If you're going, I'm going with you."

"Yeah, me too," says Marcus, putting his hand out in front of him.

Lauren and I place our hands on top of his.

"I'm in," says Ross, topping the stack. "I'm afraid it's our only hope."

The four of us turn to Tony and Dr. Beaverman, who are perched together on the sofa thumbing through the latest *In Style*. "Are you guys in?" I ask.

"Actually, we're going to stay here and color her hair," says Tony, while running his fingers through various strands of Dr. Beaverman's war-torn coif.

"Do what you want," I spit. "But I won't be responsible for what happens."

On the way out, Marcus falls to his knees in front of Dr. Beaverman. "If I don't make it back, I want you to do something for me," he says, before pulling a chain from around his neck and placing it over Dr. B's head. "This is my trusty St. Anthony medal."

"I thought you were Jewish," says Dr. Beaverman.

"It's a long story," says Marcus. "Anyway, if I don't make it back, give this to that guy I met at the Abbey the other night who still hasn't called and probably never will."

"What's his name?" asks Dr. Beaverman.

"His name," says Marcus, "is Diesel Jeans Cute Ass."

"He's part Indian," I say.

As we ride to Twisted Video, I recall for my friends my tragic history with the disaster movie genre, or, more specifically, how *The Poseidon Adventure* ruined my childhood. In short, it scared the bejesus out of me. I'd wake up in the middle of the night convinced that a giant wall of water was heading for my bed. It was only when I managed to flip on the light that I remembered that I lived in Arizona, which is not exactly tidal wave country. "I refused to watch disaster movies for years after that," I say. "I remember going to see some Disney movie and they showed the trailer for *Airport 1975* and I literally ran to the snack bar like I was running for my sanity. I was very vigilant about keeping images of panicked stewardesses and trapped character actors in leisure suits out of my consciousness."

"When I watched those movies I never really thought that I would be the one to die," boasts Lauren. "I thought I would be the one still treading water when everyone else was dead. I'd practice in the pool, just in case."

This, it turns out, is just the beginning of Lauren O'Donovan's Disaster Movie Scenario Preparedness Regimen.

"You know what else I do?" she says. "Whenever I sit in an outdoor café, I always wonder how quickly I'd be able to get out of the way if there was a bus careening toward me."

"Listen to this, you guys," says Ross, from the backseat. "'Despite what you may have heard, *Armageddon* is a work of art,'" he says, reading from the liner notes that came with my bum DVD. "I love it when the packaging starts out with an apology."

"That's so weird," I say. "You'd think they would have realized that if a person blew 50 bucks on the thing, they were already hooked."

"'Those who claim,'" Ross reads on, "'that it was hard to tell where characters were in relation to each other in space should take another look...'"

"But if we don't see it the first time, then it's sort of failed, right?" suggests Marcus. "That's like saying, 'I'm going to be confusing and unclear and call that my style and think less of you if you don't get it.'"

We arrive at the store, and, once inside, hang together for dear life so that if an earthquake hits and tears a gash through the center of the building, we'll all get sucked in together.

"Oh, great, it's pan-and-scan," grumbles Ross after plucking the *Armageddon* box off the shelf. "That means we won't see, like, 30% of what was filmed."

"You say that like it's a bad thing," says Lauren.

"To the counter, then!" I command, doing my damnedest to keep morale up through this trying time.

On our way, Ross deviates from our Irwin Allen improv to comment on the store's categorization system, which he describes as both "arbitrary" and "piss-poor."

"What do you expect for 99 cents, even on weekends?" I say. "Besides, people don't usually come here for mainstream movies. There's a huge porn section in the back."

I hand the clerk, a mustachioed Latino named Raul who's always sort of done it for me, the empty video box. While he's retrieving the tape proper, Lauren decides to change the subject. "What's with your roommate, Dennis?" she asks. "He doesn't seem like himself." At last, someone's commenting on the rainbow-colored elephant that's smelling up my living room. I was wondering how long it would take. "I mean, he hasn't said one smart-ass thing all afternoon."

"And he was all gung ho about *Armageddon*," adds Ross. "*Armageddon*!"

"It's spooky, you guys," I say, relieved to actually be talking about it. "He doesn't even make fun of *Entertainment Tonight* anymore. That used to be our favorite pastime. Last night, he said he thought Jann Carl was insightful. Insightful! It's like he's been replaced by a pod person."

"A Stepford fag," says Lauren.

While I dig out my driver's license for Raul, Marcus gets Ross and Lauren up to speed on what he knows of Tony's mysterious transformation. "Remember that guy Tad he was dating?" he says. They both roll their eyes and nod. "Well, as they were having their big breakup fight after *Basic Instinct,* Tad said something to him like, 'Maybe your life wouldn't be such a mess if you weren't such a snide bitch.' Like maybe he'd have better luck with jobs and relationships and just, like, life if he weren't so negative."

"Who made that guy Karma Kop?" asks Ross. "By the way, Dennis, if you write what I just said, I want 'cop' to be spelled with a K."

"Done," I say.

"So Tad didn't stick," Lauren clarifies, "but Tad's Guide to Life did?"

"So it seems," I say. "Tony's been writing in a journal too and taping all the Dr. Phil episodes of *Oprah.* It's total Invasion of the Roommate Snatchers."

My disaster movie costars and I look at each other for a moment and then share a collective shrug.

"You still have *Centerstage, Spray It Forward,* and *Jizz Junkies 4* checked out," Raul informs me without taking his eyes off the screen. "You gonna return them all together?"

"Yeah," I say as coolly as possible, though I'm cringing inside.

"Dude, you gotta watch out for this fucker," Ross tells Raul, while patting me on the shoulder. "He *never* rewinds."

"I totally rewind and you know it," I say to Ross. "I totally rewind," I say to Raul before following my charges out.

The second we're back on the road, Ross has a question for me. "So, Dennis, how's *Jizz Junkies 4*?"

"Not as good as *1,*" I say, trying to camouflage my embarrassment with shtick, "but better than 2 and 3." Then, before Ross can ask me anymore questions about *Junkies* and their *Spray,* I change the subject. "My favorite *Armageddon* story actually comes from Matt, my editor," I say. "A few months before the movie came out, the studio showed like 50 minutes of footage to journalists at Cannes. Well, Matt was there, and he said that half the audience was roaring with laughter by the end. Then, Bruce Willis gets on the microphone afterward and says, 'I'm glad you all found the end of the world so funny.'"

We're still laughing about Bruce when we get back to the condo and find Tony and Dr. Beaverman holed up in Tony's bathroom like mad scientists. "We'll be ready in two minutes," Tony hollers over the sound of running water. "Just have to rinse, dry, and unveil."

A few minutes later, Dr. Beaverman emerges from Makeoverland with a towel on her head.

"So, let's see it," says Lauren.

"Not yet," says Dr. Beaverman. "I'm going to pick a moment in the movie where we really need the distraction." She takes her usual place on the sofa and says, "You've seen this movie before, right, Dennis?"

"They were showing it on a plane I was on," I say, "but I didn't rent the headset. I just remember looking up from time to time and thinking that Bruce Willis was really orange."

"Well, I've never seen it," says Marcus.

"Then there's no St. Olaf story," says Ross, reaching for the remote.

"Not so fast," Marcus says. "I didn't tell you the *reason* I didn't see it."

"Should I build a fire?" I ask.

"Ever since I was a wee lad," Marcus begins, "I loved learning about mythology. As a result, I've always known a lot of really great words that a lot of my friends didn't know."

"Like 'supercilious,'" says Lauren.

"Kiss my ass," I mutter.

"Well, one of my favorite words is 'Armageddon,' which means 'the end of all that is,'" Marcus continues. "I've known that word since I was like eight years old and now all of a sudden it's the name of a big dumb movie and I can never use it again without people thinking I got it from a big dumb movie. I've lost one of my favorite words forever."

"You can have supercilious if you want," I offer. "I've hardly touched it."

"Zephyr was another one I loved," Marcus continues. "It means 'a gentle west wind,' and the same year I lost 'Armageddon,' Madonna put 'zephyr' in 'Ray of Light' and cheapened that."

"As she does so many things," says Dr. Beaverman.

"So what words do you have left?" wonders Tony.

"Seraphim," says Marcus, "which is an angel of the highest order."

"Good luck holding on to that one," says Ross, just back from the can. "That's a Sarah McLachlan song waiting to happen."

"Seraphim is that company Tad works for," says Tony.

"Damn it!" whines Marcus. "Well, I also have Priapus, the son of Aphrodite and Dionysus. Priapus personifies male procreative power."

"I thought that was Mick Jagger's job," says Dr. Beaverman.

"So to be priapic," Marcus continues, "is to be overly concerned with masculinity."

"So one might say, 'This movie is positively priapic,'" I propose, while sticking the tape into the VCR.

"One might," says Marcus, smiling, happy to have passed on a little of his hard-earned knowledge.

"You guys, pay special attention to Ben Affleck's teeth," advises Ross as I start the movie. "In his earlier movies he was more snaggletoothed. Jerry Bruckheimer, the producer of this movie, spent something like 20 grand to have them fixed."

"There's more porcelain in that mouth than in the men's room at Grand Central Station," adds Dr. Beaverman. "I know because I've used it."

"Ben Affleck's mouth, or the men's room at Grand Central?" I ask.

"I've always thought that Ben Affleck was a very handsome guy," remarks Tony.

We wait for some kind of caveat or a punch line but none comes. Ben Affleck's handsome, that's it. Unfortunately, before we can bask in Ben's handsomeness, we have to endure a voice-over from Charlton Heston telling us that the last time an asteroid like this hit was way back "when dinosaurs ruled the earth."

"To put that in perspective," says Lauren, "this was about the time Cher was graduating from high school."

"Dennis, when you write this up for the magazine, could you change that to the year that Cher contemplated signing up for GED classes, but skipped," requests Dr. Beaverman. "I want it made clear that she's no high school graduate."

The miseducation of Cher properly logged, we're soon treated to one of the few action sequences in the film that doesn't scream out for subtitles: A meteor shower takes Manhattan, toppling buildings, killing innocent extras, and wreaking all manner of fiery havoc.

"Well, that's one way to get Bernadette Peters off Broadway," figures Dr. Beaverman.

Soon the asteroid is given a name: Dottie, after the wife of the stargazer geezer who first spotted it. The old guy figures it's a perfect moniker as his beloved wife is a "life-sucking bitch from which there is no escape," not unlike the asteroid.

"Well, that pretty much sums up what men think about women in this movie," mutters Lauren. "If you're not Liv Tyler, you're a life-sucking bitch."

"There isn't an individual shot that lasts more than five seconds," I observe, referring to the frenetic directing style of Michael Bay, veteran of *The Rock* and a bunch of soft drink commercials. "When the rocket finally blasts off, the countdown's going to go, 'Ten, five, one!'"

Soon, NASA, represented by a leg-braced Billy Bob Thornton, reports to the president that the situation is indeed dire. "It's what we call a global killer," says Billy Bob. "Nothing will survive, not even bacteria."

"Not even Cher," says Marcus. "Well, OK, maybe Cher."

"No more Cher jokes," I advise the room. "We're already over quota. Try substituting Liza."

Billy Bob decides that civilization's only hope is to drill a hole in the asteroid and impregnate it, if you will, with a nuclear bomb. To do this, NASA must enlist the world's preeminent maker of holes. Enter Bruce Willis as Harry Stamper and his ragtag team of roughneck oil-drillers, featuring Oscar-winning screenwriter Ben Affleck as A.J. Frost.

"Ben Affleck is not a roughneck no matter how many times Bruce Willis says he is," insists Lauren, during a scene set on an oil tanker in the South China Sea in which Bruce busts in on Ben while he's knocking boots with Bruce's porcelain-skinned daughter, Grace, played with doe-eyed earnestness by Liv Tyler. "Any man who exfoliates more than once a week is *not* a roughneck."

"Is Bruce being genuinely protective here, or is he just jealous?" wonders Marcus as Bruce fires off bullets and smart-alecky dialogue while chasing Ben around the tanker.

"Good observation, Marcus," says Dr. Beaverman. "There is a very sick little triangle going on here in the South China Sea. Bruce is hot for Liv, which is not terribly surprising, because he is, in essence, a man-child, a Peter Pan who refuses to grow up. I mean, he's balding and he's still trying to do bangs."

Tony gets this strained, disconcerting look on his face, like "I was just about to point that out," but says nothing.

Bruce and Ben's oil rig showdown climaxes when Ben tells Bruce he needs to hear five words from him. Unfortunately, I can't tell you what they are because we're too preoccupied coming up with our own versions to listen to Ben's.

"That's a nice toupee, Bruce," suggests Ross, counting the words on his fingers.

"Is it just my ethnic bias, or does Liv look like a hostess at P.F. Chang's? I keep waiting for her to hand Billy Bob a menu." —Lauren

"Matt Damon's a big bottom," says Marcus.

"Who names a kid Tallulah?" I offer.

We look to Tony for his contribution, but he just smiles blankly while opening a bag of Doritos. This is worse than I thought.

Before you know it, Bruce and Liv are being whisked off to NASA, where Billy Bob explains that the country needs Bruce to save the world. "This is a man who can't even save Planet Hollywood," says Dr. Beaverman. "And somehow they expect him to save Planet Earth."

"See, you guys, Bruce is orange," I assert.

"Is it just my ethnic bias, or does Liv look like a hostess at P.F. Chang's?" says Lauren, referring to the ingenue's Pan-Asian dress and hairstyle. "I keep waiting for her to hand Billy Bob a menu."

After much haggling, Bruce accepts Billy Bob's challenge, with one condition: "I want to take my own men," he says.

"And I want the film to cut away from me after every three words so I don't have to learn any lines," I add.

"It's a deal!" says Ross.

The next sequence, in which we meet the members of Bruce's drill team one by one, is like something out of *The Bad News Bears in Breaking Training*. Fortunately, for those of us trying to keep track in the peanut gallery, the film's army of screenwriters have given each driller one defining character trait, sort of like the seven dwarfs. There's Steve Buscemi as a strip-club aficionado (Horny), Owen Wilson as a yee-ha–hollerin' Texan (Hicky), Will Patton as the guy who ran out on his wife and kid (Deadbeat Daddy), the fat guy who's really into doughnuts (Fatty), the big black guy who likes to raise hell on his Harley (Bad-Ass), and, last but not least, our two leads, Ben Affleck (Hottie) and Bruce Willis (Orangey).

After an extended training sequence, we learn that blastoff is imminent when Billy Bob tells the gang, "Both shuttles will take off Tuesday at 6:30 P.M."

"There'll be a layover in Cedar Rapids," adds Ross.

"And a 15-year-old stewardess for you to harass," says Dr. Beaverman.

"The in-flight movie is *Bounce.* Sorry, A.J.," I say.

"Who do I talk to about ordering a kosher meal?" wonders Marcus.

We look to Tony, who would normally provide the wisecrack de résistance, but his mouth is full of one of Marcus's M&M and Pop Rock cookies. "These are delicious," is all he says.

Before takeoff, Bruce convinces NASA to give the gang a few hours to eat doughnuts, titty bar–hop, and, in the case of Ben and Liv, toy with career suicide in one of the most inane romantic exchanges in film history. I'm referring, of course, to the *Armageddon* animal-crackers-in-my-poop-shoot canoodling scene. "The best we can hope for," says Dr. Beaverman, as Ben trots out a faux crocodile hunter accent and flirtatiously dances an edible gazelle across Liv's supple belly, "is that no animal crackers were harmed in the making of this film."

"They should have used McDonaldland cookies," I say.

"Oh, my God!" gasps Marcus. "We lost the Grimace in the Batcave. I'm sending Mayor McCheese in after him!"

Then, as if the scene isn't unsettling enough, it hits me that it's Liv's real-life dad, Steven Tyler of Aerosmith, singing on the soundtrack, thereby turning our sick little triangle into a sick little rectangle, or octagon if you count the whole band.

"I don't care how much you love these two stars," says Ross, on his way to the kitchen for another beer, "this scene is unwatchable. Armagettin' out of here."

"Then let's unveil your hair," suggests Tony, turning to Dr. Beaverman.

Dr. Beaverman gets an anxious look on her face.

"It's that or the animal cracker scene," says Lauren.

"Well, since you put it that way…" says Dr. Beaverman, sitting up straight on the couch.

As Liv and Ben kiss and coo on screen, I tap a drumroll on the coffee table with my index fingers. Then Tony grabs the corners of Dr. B's towel and, with a quick flick of his wrists, whisks it away to reveal a home color job that is, I'm happy to report, an unqualified success. Even damp and unstyled, Dr. Beaverman's newly honey-colored hair looks better than I've ever seen it. She steps slowly to the mirror, shakes it out, takes it in, then turns to Tony with a look of excitement and gratitude. Tony smiles proudly. How can someone who's so good at so many things have such a hard time finding their place in the world?

It's a testament to Ben Affleck's star power and those million-dollar choppers that the actor survived the animal cracker scene, but why, oh why, does he have to push his luck by croaking out the John Denver-penned "Leavin' on a Jet Plane" on his way to the shuttle? "This is the one scene where you could literally see the dollar signs in their eyes," says Ross as the rest of the drillers, one by one, join in the sing-along.

"What girl would make out with her boyfriend in front of her father like that?" wonders Lauren as Liv straddles Ben and sucks his face. "She literally mounted him in a sundress in front of her daddy."

"We have liftoff," confirms Ross.

"Isn't there some kind of rule that says you have to wear panties at NASA?" I wonder.

"And notice the resentful looks Bruce keeps shooting Ben," says Lauren.

"That's because he's thinking, *Why did you have A.J. sing some dead guy's song when you could have had my band for cheap?*" says Dr. Beaverman.

Then, before lasting off into the great unknown, Ben gives Liv a final goodbye kiss. "See you at the premiere," chirps Marcus.

Once the goodbyes are uttered, we get to the famous *Right Stuff* rip-off shot of the whole posse, outfitted in orange jumpsuits and striding slo-mo style down the tarmac. "Bruce is like, 'OK guys, even though we're all in these suits, I'm still Orangey,'" I say.

"In the movie theater, this blast off sequence was really powerful," asserts some guy on the love seat who goes by the name of Tony, as our heroes rocket into space in two separate shuttles: *Freedom* and *Independence*. "You forget what a big deal it is every time a space shuttle goes up. We just take it for granted."

Up until now, the on-screen goings-on have, I'll grant you, been a bit on the cheesy side, but at least they were comprehensible. The stuff that happens in outer space is so visually confounding that I may just refer to it in future paragraphs as "space stuff" and "more space stuff." I apologize for that in advance.

"When I saw this in the theater, it was easy to follow," argues Tony when I express my bewilderment. "You could really feel everyone in the audience getting into it. I mean, the seats would literally shake because of all the bass."

Though none of us—save my animatronic roomie—can tell you what's actually happening, the film's Freudian implications are crystal clear, at least to Dr. Beaverman. "This film is about a little boy, Bruce Willis, who can't grow up and his fight against the father who is trying to pull him into the masculine world," the good doctor explains. "The man-child, of course, does not want to go into Daddy's world, which implies commitment, responsibility, and putting in time with women who can no longer fit into sundresses. So he has to kill off the bad father, who is represented in this case by a giant fiery testicle. Yes, kids, the asteroid is Daddy."

We all take a moment to digest this nugget of symbolism.

"Then who's Mommy?" wonders Tony. "Liv Tyler?"

"Mommy can be read as the hag astronaut wives, who actually expect some help raising their children," Dr. B. replies, "or it can be read as Mother Earth, because these cosmic Teletubbies still miss Mommy. That umbilical cord, believe it or not, stretches all the way into outer space."

"I'm guessing that Billy Bob's leg brace is also symbolic," I offer.

Dr. Beaverman nods. "His phallus is wounded," she says dryly. "He's got a crimp in the ol' member, which is why he can't go into space with the more virile men and why Bruce trusts him to stay on earth with his daughter."

Now that our heroes are Dottie-bound, one would think the thrills and chills would kick in, but, alas, the space shenanigans are so busy and loud—like Elton John "Crocodile Rock" loud—that I, for one, would rather be wandering the halls of NASA with Liv Tyler.

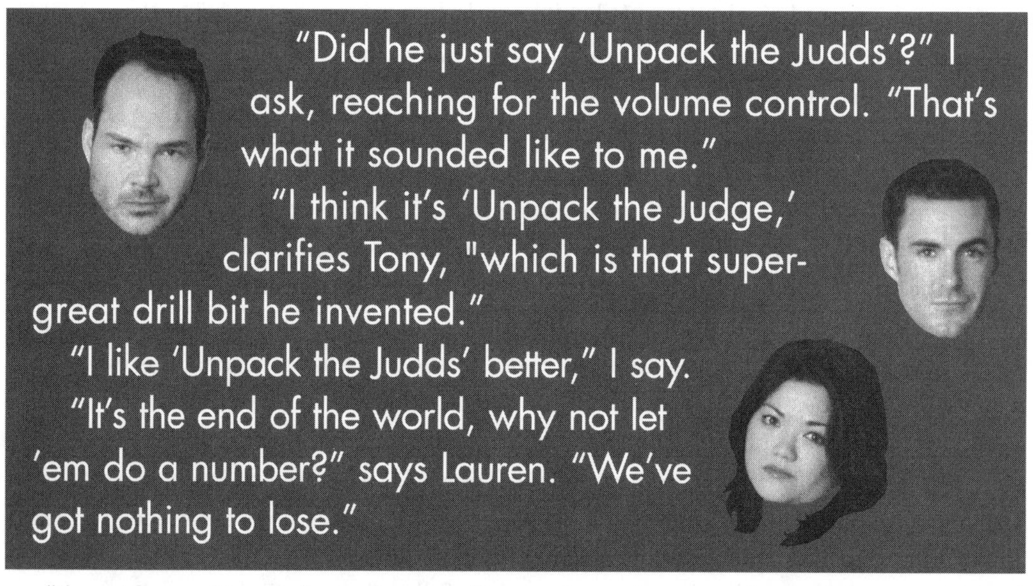

"I'm with you, Dennis," says Lauren. "I want her to log on to BetseyJohnson.com and run up Bruce's credit card so she'll have something cute to wear if the world doesn't end."

"And then go into the bathroom and see what it would look like if she cut her hair," says Marcus.

"And then find her G spot with a beaker," offers Ross.

"And change her nail color," I suggest. "I want there to be a shot of her wagging and blowing on her wet nails and saying, 'How's my daddy doin'?'"

We look to Tony again, but all he says is, "God, Liv's beautiful standing in front of the flag like that. I totally get why she's a movie star."

We try to take his observation seriously, but when Ross says, "Liv Tyler *is* Patton," we can't help but dissolve into giggles.

Back in outer space, the two shuttles become separated when Ben Affleck's craft crash-lands 26 miles off course. Meanwhile, more space stuff is unfolding in Bruce's little corner of the asteroid. I'm pretty sure it involves Bruce preparing his massive tool for penetration, then having one drill bit after another break on him. Finally, his frustration builds to the point where there's only one option. "Did he just say 'Unpack the Judds'?" I ask, reaching for the volume control. "That's what it sounded like to me."

"I think it's 'Unpack the Judge,' clarifies Tony, "which is that supergreat drill bit he invented."

"I like 'Unpack the Judds' better," I say.

"It's the end of the world, why not let 'em do a number?" says Lauren. "We've got nothing to lose."

"Maybe Bruce wants to give the asteroid one good reason to never to come to earth," suggests Dr. Beaverman.

Bruce gets the Judge sufficiently unpacked only to discover that he's lost communication with earth. By the time it's restored, our orange-hued hero has only one thing on his mind.

"Houston, I promised my little girl that I'd be coming home," he says, earnestly.

"She's sitting her cleaning out her purse," drawls Marcus as Billy Bob.

"What's she wearing?" I ask, assuming the role of Bruce.

"The P.F. Chang's dress," says Marcus.

"Oh, that little black number with the flowers?" says Ross, sharing Bruce duty with me. "She's so hot in that. Are her legs crossed or uncrossed?"

"Crossed," says Marcus.

"Hair up or down?" I ask.

"It was up," says Marcus. "But then she got bored and brought it down. Oh, wait, she's putting it up again."

Meanwhile, in a gravity-defying image straight out of *Shitty Shitty Bang Bang,* Ben maneuvers his armadillo to Bruce's area of the asteroid. No, *armadillo* is not a euphemism for penis. It's actually a big crazy space tractor vehicle thing. Now the gang's all together again except for a few people on Ben's team who died, and I'm not sure who they are because it was all so fast and blurry. I'm thinking, though, that if you're a Hicky fan, you might want to start shopping for a black dress.

We zoom back a bit and agree that yes, it was Owen Wilson as Hicky who went to the great press junket in the sky.

"If your hot buddy died in space, would you look to see how he was hung?" I wonder.

"Totally," says Lauren. "It's like, 'Wow, Hicky had a Prince Albert. Who knew?'"

"They say you get bigger in space," remarks Marcus, "because you don't have gravity weighing you down."

"Who's with Affleck, the Russian space station guy?" I ask as Ben navigates his armadillo through the cavernous 'roid.

"Yes," says Ross, "and the pants-less corpse of Owen Wilson."

"I'd like to see him explain that to Bruce," says Dr. Beaverman.

"What happened to Hicky's spacesuit, Ben?" I ask as Bruce.

"Umm, it disintegrated in reentry," stammers Marcus as Ben.

"Why's his ass bleeding?" I implore.

"Because…he, um, fell on a stalagmite?" says Marcus.

"I think you mean 'tite,'" I say.

"He sure as hell was," says Marcus.

"And scene!" we proclaim, simultaneously bringing our hands over our faces like the final curtain of a play.

Meanwhile, back on earth Billy Bob tells Liv the good news about Ben by saying, "Your boyfriend's back."

"He's not my boyfriend," Ross replies breathlessly. "He's my fath…oops!"

"I want Liv Tyler to be on the floor doing Abs of Steel," I decide. "You just see two feet in heels poking up over a console and Liv huffing, 'Any word from Harry? I don't want to miss a thing!'"

Then, more space stuff happens in space and this space stuff involves one of the non-oil drilling real astronauts getting pissed and pulling a gun on Bruce. "What's that guy doing with a gun in space?" wonders Lauren.

"Guns sell more toys," replies Ross. "On the DVD you stupidly bought, which I've seen before, Michael Bay literally admits that's why there's a gun in the movie."

"In other words, it would have been just as true to the reality of the situation for the guy to hurl an Easy-Bake Oven at him," says Dr. Beaverman.

The pressure to save the world and outgross *Deep Impact* at the box office soon begins to take a toll on our heroes. Steve Buscemi's character, Horny, begins the first movement of a Hissy Fit, most of which he does with his mouth agape. "Steve's got, like, an extra tooth in his front palate behind his other teeth," observes Marcus squeamishly.

"Affleck's hand-me-downs," deadpans Ross.

In the blink of an eye, Horny spirals from Hissy through Conniption to full-on Shit Fit, leaving his cronies no choice but to tie him up and gag him. This, I'm not that surprised to learn, brings back memories for Lauren. "I used to have my sisters tie me up in a chair," she recalls, "to see how long it would take me to get out in case I ever got kidnapped."

"And they say the American family is dead," says Dr. Beaverman.

Bruce soon makes the painful discovery that the trigger to detonate the nuke has been irreparably damaged during the journey, which means that someone must stay behind and sacrifice himself to save the world. The gang decides to draw straws to see who the lucky martyr will be. "I love that it's so badly directed that you can't tell who actually picked the short straw until Ben Affleck says his line and you realize it's him," remarks Ross.

"I think they all have short straws," says Dr. Beaverman, "if you know what I mean."

"I miss Owen Wilson," says Tony out of nowhere.

"So do I," I echo.

"Me too," says Marcus.

All this Hicky-missing starts my mind wandering and, before long I hit on what I think would have been the perfect tag line for the poster. OK, maybe not, but it would have gotten *my* ass in a theater seat, anyway. "You guys wanna hear my new tag line?" I ask. No one protests, so I clear my throat, move my open hand up across my face like I'm reading a billboard and say: "In space, no one can hear your balls slap against your dead buddy's ass."

Even the Stepford fag chuckles at this.

"I'm glad you think the end of the world is so funny," spits Ross.

"Meanwhile, back at NASA," says Lauren, "Liv's taken all the bobby pins out of her hair and lined them up on the radar screen and then put them back in."

"While watching *Titanic* on Starz," says Ross.

"And now she's trying to interest Billy Bob in a Cosmo quiz," adds Dr. Beaverman.

"And I'd rather be there!" I whine.

Short straw or no, Bruce isn't about to let Ben hog all the glory, so he insists on being the one to go down with the spaceship. Noble, sure, but I'm guessing he just wants to steer clear of any misbegotten sequels the movie might spawn. "Before he signed on to the movie, Bruce made them promise that his character would die," Ross confirms.

"Denzel Washington did the same thing in *Malcolm X,* if I'm not mistaken," says Lauren.

"The fact that Bruce Willis would rather die than come back to earth and face normal sex serves as a paradigm for the state of male sexuality as we know it today," fumes Dr. Beaverman. "There is no mature sexuality in American myth. The men in modern pop culture don't want to take out the garbage for no woman. They want to penetrate, they want to invade, and they want to be bad little boys."

"I know I promised you I was coming home," Bruce says to Liv during their final goodbye scene, which, with its umpteen TV screens, appears to have been shot at Circuit City.

"Everything good I have inside me I have from you," Liv blubbers to Bruce.

"Including a two-headed fetus and a couple of Keebler gazelles," says Dr. Beaverman.

Then, quite spectacularly, Ben and his surviving cohorts leave Bruce behind and hightail it off the asteroid, vowing never to discuss what they did to Owen Wilson's dead body.

Left alone, Bruce reaches for the detonator, which, surprisingly, is so crude looking it appears to have been made by Fisher-Price. "Baby's First Nuke," says Ross.

With that, Bruce blows the bitch up, saving the world and becoming so orange in his final moments, I'm surprised they didn't name him Julius.

"Very typical of a commitmentphobic man-child," says Dr. Beaverman. "Drill deep, explode, then never be heard from again."

Our triumphant roughnecks return to earth to receive a hero's welcome from their freshly scrubbed womenfolk. Liv, hair up again, appears to be wearing NASA-issued lipstick and I'm guessing the shade is Challenger Red. Even Deadbeat Daddy's wife and child have shown up. "He's like, 'Security, get that woman and child away from me,' " orders Ross. " 'I've got a date with Carmen Electra.' "

"These astro-pigs can come right off that plane," carps Dr. Beaverman, "having dumped in their moonsuits for weeks, with curiously strong dog breath, and still get major lip locks from these women, who've had to bathe and Listerine and douche within the last five minutes. It's really an unfair world. Bruce just saved a totally unfair world."

As the credits roll, we're treated to home movies of Ben and Liv's wedding, in which the happy couple are flanked by head shots of Bruce and the other fatalities of the mission, because, as Ross puts it, "No wedding is complete without visual references to the dead."

We sit motionless for a moment, as drained and catatonic as the survivors of your average *Airport* movie. Then Marcus grabs his empty Tupperware cookie tray and says to Dr. Beaverman, "Can I have my medal back?"

Dr. Beaverman reaches to her neck but finds nothing. "Oh, no," she gasps.

Panicked, she plumbs the sofa cushions around her but only finds remnants of snack foods from the last millennium. She dashes, like she's been sped up in postproduction, to the bathroom and when we catch up with her she's down on her hands and knees tossing discarded towels around frantically.

Marcus, for his part, seems calm, though there is a visible lump in his throat.

"I think I see it," says Tony peering down the drain. "Something's catching the light."

We all turn to Ross at the same moment.

"Oh, so because I'm straight, I'm suddenly Schneider from *One Day at a Time*?" he asks.

"Look, I just did her hair," argues Tony. "I lived up to my stereotype, you could at least try to live up to yours."

Using the few tools we have in the house, Ross crawls under the sink and begins to tinker. "There's a scene just like this in *Spray It Forward,*" he remarks. "Isn't there Dennis?"

"Uh-huh," I say, "only it's better because the plumber doesn't have any lines."

"This has to be the most people ever crammed into one bathroom in L.A. without drugs being the motivating factor," says Lauren.

I'm sure Dr. Beaverman could respond to Lauren's comment with a slew of juicy anecdotes, but she doesn't seem to be in the mood. Instead, she puts her hand on Marcus's shoulder and says, "I am so sorry about this."

"It's totally OK," Marcus assures her, though it's obviously not OK, not totally anyway.

"But you said before there's a story behind it," says Tony.

"There is," says Marcus, "but it's kind of long."

"That's never stopped you before," says Lauren, before closing the toilet lid and taking a seat.

"It's going to take me a while to unscrew this," adds Ross.

"OK, here goes," says Marcus. "After I found out I was HIV-positive, I quit my job as an attorney and went to work at the AIDS Ride. My thinking was, it would be less stressful. Right. So one day I went to the doctor for my checkup and he told me that my viral load had gone from 2,000 to 12,000. In three months!"

"Dennis, this wrench totally blows," gripes Ross from under the sink.

"It's all we have," I say.

"Would it help if we unpacked the Judds?" asks Lauren.

Marcus is the only one who laughs.

"Go on with your story," Dr. Beaverman tells him.

"So my doctor strongly suggested that I switch medicines," Marcus continues, "and that was flipping me out too, that the medicines I had were failing me. So I called work and said I wasn't coming in that day because I needed some time to figure out why things were getting worse for me instead of better. Roger, my new boss at the AIDS Ride office, called me back and lashed out at me for taking the day off. And then he told me I was 'perfectly fine.' He's like, 'There's nothing wrong with you.' "

"How would he know?" asks Lauren.

"Exactly," says Marcus. "Anyone who's not infected can't say 'There's nothing wrong with you' to someone who is. Then, he said something about how I was filled with self-pity and always need to be coddled."

"Maybe he thought you were me," offers Tony. It's the first remotely sarcastic comment he's made in weeks. It's like a tiny window into the padded room where the new Tony keeps the old one.

Marcus smiles at Tony and continues. "If someone had said that to me now, I'd beat the shit out of them," he asserts, the fury audible in his voice. "But back then I just kind of took it. So I hung up and I just literally curled up in a ball on the floor and started crying and crying. Finally, I called my friend Marty, who's also positive, and he said, 'Come over now.' I went to his house and told him the story and totally lost it in front of him, which was the first time I'd cried in front of someone since I'd found out 2½ years earlier."

Dr. Beaverman brings her hands to her face but says nothing.

"Then Marty took the medal from around his neck," says Marcus, getting softer as he nears his conclusion, "and put it around mine and said, 'This is St. Anthony, the patron saint of lost souls or those who are on a journey. It will keep you safe.' It was one of the kindest things anyone ever did for me."

"If we don't find it," says Dr. Beaverman, her voice a touch raspier than usual, "I'm taking you to the store and buying you a new one."

Marcus nods. "It's not like I wear it all the time," he says. "I just put it on every once in a while to sort of put myself back on the right track."

Having run out of story, Marcus looks down at Ross. The rest of us do the same, even though our fix-it man is starting to sweat through his old Tom Petty T-shirt. It seems better than looking at anyone's face. A minute or so passes before anyone speaks.

"What have we here?" says Ross, melodiously.

Ross's fist emerges from underneath the cupboard. He opens it to reveal something small and shiny: a quarter. And under it, Marcus's trusty St. Anthony medal, tangled in its grimy silver chain.

"Oh, thank God," says Dr. Beaverman before snatching the medal away. She pads it gingerly with a hand towel and then she puts it around Marcus's neck and pats his chest maternally.

"Take the quarter too," Ross says.

For some reason that has to do with lightening the mood, I decide now might be a good time to sing the theme from *The Poseidon Adventure.* "There's got to be a morning after…"

Lauren and Tony join in for the second line. "If we can hold on through the night…"

Unfortunately, none of us knows the third line, so we kind of hum for a second, then give up and head to the kitchen to eat stuff.

•

Later that night, I return *Armageddon* to Twisted Video along with the other titles I have checked out. Before giving me my change, Raul reveals to me that he cried during *Armageddon* when Liv Tyler was saying goodbye to Bruce Willis for the last time. I don't think he's at all ridiculous.

WOMAN 'N' THE MOON

"We're going to do rock and roll today! And we're going to be in a movie! In *our* movie, we're real! We fight, we scream, we talk dirty, we smoke grass! So, in the lingo of the movie, I say, all of you motherfuckers, have a great time!"

I read that quote with as much mid-'70s, me-generation gusto as possible to Marcus, Lauren, and Dr. Beaverman, the first three guests to arrive at our Screening Party for director Frank Pierson's 1976 rock-and-roll melodrama *A Star Is Born.* I then inform my guests that those strange and powerful words were uttered by the dirty-talkin', grass-smokin' queen of all motherfuckers, Barbra Streisand. The setting was Sun Devil Stadium, a 50,000-seat outdoor arena at my alma mater, Arizona State University, where rock promoter Bill Graham, at the behest of Barbra's then-boyfriend, hairdresser-turned-film producer Jon Peters, staged a daytime megaconcert that would be shot for the film. To ensure a big and enthusiastic crowd, Graham had brought in ringers like Peter Frampton and Santana to perform alongside Streisand's costar Kris Kristofferson, but long delays and the ingestion of various substances had the crowd growing restless. It was during one of the many breaks in the action that Barbra took the mike and delivered what I've taken to calling her "Let's Do Some Rock, Motherfuckers" speech.

"It's a shame that just isn't a little bit longer," says Lauren. "I could use it as an audition monologue the next time I have to play crazy."

"She also came out and sang 'People' at one point," I report, "to sort of keep the crowd happy. I don't know if she called them motherfuckers first or not." At that point, Dr. Beaverman shows us what it would be like to see Barbra go from "Let's Do Some Rock, Motherfuckers" to "People who need people" in 0.5 seconds.

"I like some of her records," says Marcus, chiming in from the kitchen, "but she doesn't really *send* me, you know. Like I got the Bette Midler gene and the Cher gene but not the Barbra Streisand gene."

"Me neither," I admit.

"I used to baby-sit this boy named Taylor who definitely has the Barbra Streisand gene," remarks Lauren while strategically placing the candles from Tony's bathroom around the front room. "I mean, he knew all the words to "Don't Rain on My Parade" by the time he was 3. One day he asked me to put red nail polish on him, and I said, 'No, but we can put green on one finger.' When it dried, he came back in with a tutu and he said, 'Can I put it on?' and I said, 'Of course you can.' He said, 'Would you put it on me?' I said, 'Of course not.' So he stripped down naked in the kitchen and put on the tutu himself. Playing in the background, I believe, was Barbra Streisand's *Broadway Album,* which I had been subjecting him to since he was born."

"I think track 3 on that is 'It Feels Good (In Your Butt)'," I say, "if I'm not mistaken."

"So his mother came home," Lauren continues, "and saw him in the tutu, and I told her he did it himself and she goes, 'Oh, is *that* the way we're going?' Then he came skipping in and asked her if he had to take it off, and she goes, 'No, I think we're going to leave it on for daddy.' Now, her husband's like this really butch, Italian Catholic construction worker. So I baby-sat Taylor again a week later, and all he could talk about is how he was going to be a working man when he grew up and drive a truck and have a family. He repeated it about eight times while we were coloring."

"How did he feel about *The Mirror Has Two Faces*?" wonders Dr. Beaverman. "Did that snap him out of it?"

"I don't know," says Lauren, laughing, "but something inside me really died that night. I literally had to get up and leave the room. Now when I see him, he's playing soccer and baseball, which is great, but there are moments when he gets so frustrated he bursts into tears for no reason, and I wonder if it's because he'd rather be, you know, wearing a tutu and listening to *Yentl*."

"Maybe he really likes soccer and baseball," offers Marcus. "I did when I was a kid."

"Really?" I ask.

"No," says Marcus.

"Maybe he'll grow up to be a total straight jock," says Lauren, "but the last time I sat for him, he was taking a bath, and he scooped all the bubbles into like a one-strap gown and went, 'Look Lauren, it's a dress.'"

"All right, you win," concedes Marcus.

With that, Marcus walks in from the kitchen carrying a white cake topped with a recent photograph of Barbra in a hot pink star-shaped frame that has the word *Hollywood* stenciled in one corner. It isn't until I touch it that I realize that in addition to being blindingly fluorescent and dangerously pointy, the frame is furry.

"It's yours to keep," Marcus says of the photo. "I'm not taking it with me."

"Is there anything about the cake itself that's Streisand-centric?" asks Dr. Beaverman before pinching a taste of frosting.

"Not really," says Marcus, "though I did end up making the icing four times. It's not that I was being difficult or bitchy. I just wanted to get it right."

Suddenly we're interrupted by the fax machine, which rings twice, then stops. "That's the signal!" I gasp. "They're on their way home."

"Hide the cake!" says Dr. Beaverman.

"I'll light the candles," says Lauren.

"Oh, my God," says Marcus, dashing back into the kitchen. "Why am I so nervous suddenly?"

"Leave it to me, kids," says Dr. Beaverman. "This is my field of expertise."

A few minutes later, the four of us are sitting casually in our usual spots in the candlelit living room when Tony and Ross arrive.

"Any luck?" I ask Ross.

"Some great stuff for the adults," he replies. "Some OK stuff for the kids."

"We found some perfect Cub Scout uniforms," Tony says.

Ross and Tony spent this morning shopping for costumes for Ross's film, *Renaissance Boy,* which after several months of rewriting and preproduction, is scheduled to shoot later this month. Ross told Tony that his "eye for style" would be a great help when it came to planning the costumes, hair, and makeup. Though this is essentially true, the real story is that we just needed someone to get Tony out of the house so we could conspire against him in peace.

"I bought some Kleenex at 7-Eleven," says Tony, tossing a box of tissue onto the coffee table. "This movie makes me bawl my eyes out."

I look from Lauren to Ross to Marcus to Dr. Beaverman. Dr. Beaverman gives me a small nod.

"Tony, we're not doing *Forrest Gump* today," I say, then switch off the lamp, so only candles light the room. "There's been a change of plans."

"What are we doing then?" he asks. "What's with the candles?"

Ross pulls the video for *A Star Is Born* from behind his back, places it on the coffee table then spins it like top. When it finally stops revolving, Barbra and Kris, naked and embracing, are facing right side up directly front of Tony.

"What the *fuck*?" says Tony. "Is this some kind of voodoo thing? What are you guys trying to do to me?"

"Save you," I say.

"From yourself," says Dr. Beaverman.

"We're only doing this because we care about you," stresses Lauren. "Please know that."

"Is this some kind of…" Tony struggles for the word for a moment, and then it comes to him. "Intervention?"

"Yes, it is," I say. "The only difference is, there's booze in the kitchen if you want any."

"I'm fine, thanks," he says, defiantly.

Dr. Beaverman scoots closer to Tony on the sofa and takes both his hands in hers. "Tony, for the last two months or so, you have tried valiantly to be what you think is a good person," says Dr. Beaverman, using air quotes to emphasis the words "good" and "person." "And we all commend you for that. The recycling, the compliments, the random acts of kindness, the volunteering—these changes are undoubtedly for the better, and we all admire you a great deal for instigating them. However, there are parts of the old Tony that we miss desperately, and more importantly, we think you miss them too."

"Sometimes," I say, jumping in, "I can see a thought pop into your head, but instead of saying it out loud, you, like, squelch it. Last night, when Kelly Preston let bugs crawl all over her on *Celebrity Fear Factor* and then John Travolta showed up and they did the Walk of Shame together, I thought your head was going to explode. That kind of repression can't be healthy, right?" I look to Dr. Beaverman as if to say, "Back me up here."

"It's *not* healthy," confirms Dr. Beaverman, "though it does raise some interesting questions: What *is* healthy? What is *right*? What is the more true way to live? To be what one thinks is a 'good person'?" Again with the air quotes. "Or to be oneself?"

"Oneself, oneself," pants Ross.

Tony sits silent for a moment, then says, "You sort of know why I'm trying to change my attitude, right? Like you *get it,* right? Because I need things to go better in my life, my so-called life. It's a serious thing and I'm serious about it."

"We know that," insists Marcus, while the rest of us bob our heads like those dolls you see on dashboards.

"Are you happier lately?" says Lauren. "Honestly?"

Tony gives an "I don't know" shrug.

"We're not asking you to be mean to people in the real world," Lauren says.

"But you can be mean to people on *The Real World,*" I add. "And *Road Rules* for that matter."

"We're asking you to say what's on your mind," concludes Lauren.

"Might I suggest a little experiment?" says Dr. Beaverman. "Think of this room, this holy room, with this wonderful box we call a television, as your haven, your free zone, a safe place where you can say and do and feel anything you want, without judgment or recrimination." Dr. Beaverman's pin-striped DKNY slacks may not be down around her ankles, but make no mistake, she's totally pulling this out of her ass. We all are. "That way," she continues, "you can go forth into the world purged, oozing love, joy, and positivity from every pore, because you got all the bad stuff out watching *A Star Is Born.*"

"And *Queer as Folk,*" I add hastily. Suddenly I'm a slimy senator on a pork-barreling spree. "Can we include that in there too?" I ask. Dr. Beaverman gives me a resigned nod. "I can't get through it without you, Tony," I plead. "If you're not going to comment on it with me, we might as well get rid of Showtime."

"OK, who thinks Tony should go back to being himself?" says Ross, cutting to the chase.

One by one, our hands go up. Marcus's hand is last, and once he's in, he says, "That's five."

"Six if you count Matt in London," I add, putting my hand on Tony's shoulder. "Matt's extremely concerned. He thinks that without you being you, we'll totally lose our edge."

"You can inch into it slowly," Dr. Beaverman assures him. "Maybe just start with some cheap shots about her hair and nose. Then, as you start getting your sea legs, throw in something about Jason Gould or the nails. Whatever you choose to express, just know we'll be right here with you."

Tony just shakes his head and stares dazedly at one of the candles.

"Dennis, read him the 'Let's Do Some Rock, Motherfuckers' thing," urges Lauren.

I do just that. I even attempt a Barbra imitation, but Tony remains catatonic. Hoping a little visual stimulation will snap him out of it, Marcus rushes into the kitchen and returns with the Barbra cake.

"Christ on a bike!" Tony exclaims, diverting his eyes from the sweet-smelling confection as though it were a ball of fire.

"I think you mean, 'Christ, soft as an easy chair,'" corrects Ross.

"And Marcus isn't taking the Barbra picture with him," I say. "We have to keep it."

Tony turns slowly back and stares the Barbra cake down like a boxer waiting in his corner for the bell to ring.

"And if you don't think she's got it coming," I say, grabbing a stack of white paper from under the coffee table, "I suggest you read this. It's an article Ross found called "My Battles with Barbra and Jon." It's written by Frank Pierson, the director of *A Star Is Born* and an Oscar-winner for the screenplay of *Dog Day Afternoon,"* I explain as I pass out the copies. "It ran in *New York* magazine in November 1976, just before the movie came out. It's the kind of tell-all story you wish someone from every nightmare movie had the nerve to write afterward, just really well-written and superdishy, and it goes on for pages and pages and pages."

" *'I want it,' Barbra shrieks in a baby's desperate wail,"* says Dr. Beaverman, reading aloud one of the article's juicier pull quotes. *"It has the power of primitive will, deep and full of loneliness..."*

"If 10% of what's in here is true," Ross tells Tony, "she deserves whatever you can dish out."

"And if we ever think you're being a bad person, like in the real world, we'll tell you," promises Lauren.

"If I start," Tony says deliberately, "I'm afraid I won't be able to stop."

"That's why we're here," says Dr. Beaverman, "to ease you back into it. With *love.* Now," she says, clapping her hands expediently, "on with the show. Do you have a story for this movie, Marcus?"

"This movie, no," Marcus stammers, "but when I saw *The Main Event...*"

"Good," says Dr. Beaverman, cutting him off, "because I do. This may come as a surprise to you all, but in all my years, I've only been kicked out of a movie theater once, though I've walked out of many a movie."

"I walked out of *The Gun in Betty Lou's Handbag,"* says Marcus boastfully.

"I think the real question is, why did you walk in?" says Ross.

"Anyway, back to me," says Dr. Beaverman. "It was this very movie I was evicted from.

It was 1976, San Francisco, and I was watching *A Star Is Born,* probably in some sort of bicentennial-themed jeans and tube top, and we got to the scene near the end where Barbra Streisand's crying and holding this unraveling cassette in front of her face. Well, there was this reverential hush over the theater and I said, 'Look, she's crying tapes,' and the usher came up and said, 'I'm sorry, you have to go.'"

"I don't get it," says Marcus. "Crying tapes?"

"You'll get it when the scene comes along," snaps Dr. Beaverman.

"In 50 *years,*" groans Ross, wagging the remote about impatiently.

"OK, we're starting," I say. With that, Ross hits play, and soon the six of us are rocking out to "Watch Closely Now" as performed by Kris Kristofferson's coke-addled rocker character, John Norman Howard.

"Are we meant to find him sexy?" wonders Lauren as Kris peels off his shirt, revealing a boyishly hairless torso. "I mean, there are four and 20 blackbirds baked in that beard."

"He never really had a dewy period, did he?" says Tony. It's not the typical, biting, below-the-belt quip Tony's known for, but it's a start.

"We're supposed to think of Kris as a great rock star who's on a downslide," explains Ross. "According the article Dennis just passed out, Kris prepared for his drunk scenes by getting drunk."

"And I just might have to do the same," says Dr. Beaverman, raising her martini glass.

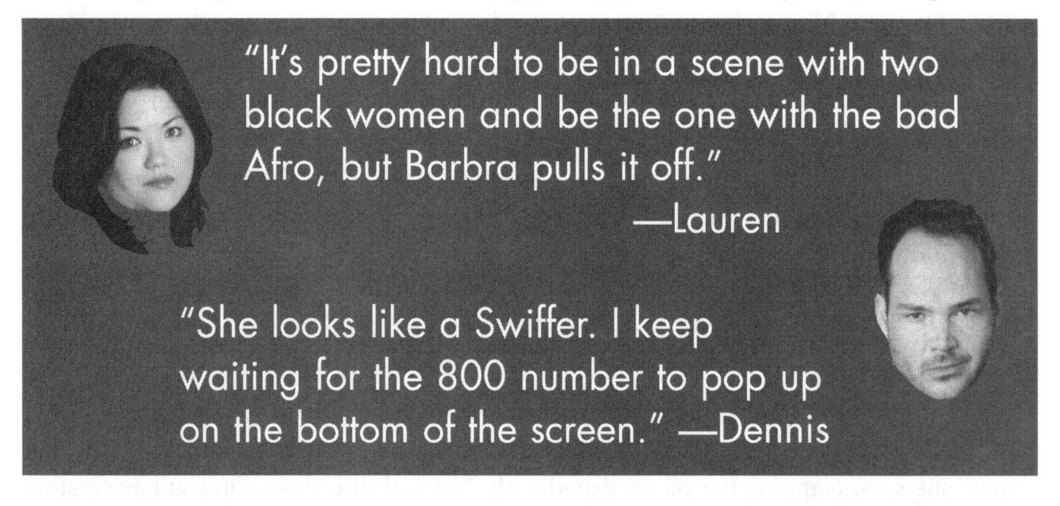

During a postconcert limo scene in which a depressed Kris nearly spills vodka all over his face ("Any kind of antiseptic is a good step," figures Dr. B.), Kris gets a talking-to from his beleaguered road manager, played by Gary Busey. "I love that Busey is presented as a figure of responsibility in a story about substance abuse," I remark when Gary urges Kris to get a good night's sleep before the big show tomorrow. "I mean, imagine the sculpture you could make from the mangled motorcycles of those two."

Kris ignores Busey's advice and instead hauls his wasted ass to a dive bar. It's here we get our first gander at Barbra Streisand as Esther Hoffman, the huge-haired lead singer of the lounge trio the Oreos. "It's pretty hard to be in a scene with two black women and be the one with the bad Afro," Lauren says, as the ladies perform the spunkily choreographed "Queen Bee," "but Barbra pulls it off."

"She looks like a Swiffer," I say. "I keep waiting for the 800 number to pop up on the bottom of the screen."

"Her backup singers must be thinking, *We marched in Atlanta for* this?" says Dr. Beaverman.

"Do you suppose they're rejects from some '70s group like Sister Sledge or A Taste of Honey?" wonders Marcus.

"No," snaps Tony, raising his voice for the first time in weeks. "I think they're Groundlings, because this is a goddamn *comedy.*"

Oh, my God, is that vitriol I smell? Could the old Tony be returning to us at last? Across the room, I see Dr. Beaverman look heavenward and mouth the words, "Thank you, God." I then return my attention to the screen just in time to see Barbra turn upstage in her skintight polyester slacks and introduce us all to the *real* star of *A Star Is Born.*

"We have ass!" I announce.

"Let's count the gratuitous ass shots," suggests Marcus.

"Hope you have an abacus," says Lauren.

"Abacus, hell," scoffs Dr. Beaverman. "We're going to need the accounting firm of Price Waterhouse."

"There's number 3!" says Marcus.

(In the interest of space and reader patience, future Ass Shot Updates will be indicated by a simple number in parentheses.)

All this talk of Babs and her ass prompts Ross to say something that not only flabbergasts me but makes me question whether I really know him at all. "Have you guys ever seen that footage of Barbra giving a blow job to a guy and then getting it up the ass?" he asks.

"*What?*" I gasp. I couldn't have heard that right.

"There's this porno flick she must have done when she was like 16," he continues. We all just stare at him dumbfounded. He may as well have said, "Oh, have I told you guys? I'm a cannibal."

"Let's count the gratuitous ass shots." —Marcus
"Hope you have an abacus." —Lauren
"Abacus, hell. We're going to need the accounting firm of Price Waterhouse." —Dr. Beaverman

Frustrated with our unanimous incredulity, Ross grabs the remote and presses pause. "No one's seen it?" he asks. "No one's even *heard* of it?"

We all just shake our heads. Ross must just be stressed from prepping his movie, I decide. I gesture for him to unpause, but he ignores me. "Her fan club claims it's not her," he insists, "and supposedly they bought up all the copies."

"It's a total urban legend, like Richard Gere and the gerbil," asserts Lauren. Ross just shakes his head.

"What does she do in this video?" I ask Ross, with the same inflection I'd use if I were saying, "So the aliens hooked you up to the sensors, and *then* what happened?"

"I told you," says Ross emphatically. "She sucks a guy off and then she takes it up the ass."

"It's called *Up the Sandbox,*" says Dr. Beaverman.

"Have you seen it with your own two eyes?" I ask.

"Yes," he insists, "when I was in high school. If it's not her, then it's someone who looks like her. I may have been stoned, but I'd know that nose anywhere. I think James Garner's in it too."

"Oh, *that* one," says Tony. "They show that all the time on E!"

"That's the *Before They Were Rock Stars* I want to see," I say, laughing. "Could you imagine the announcer? 'Recognize any of these famous assholes? One of them belongs to a Funny Lady who went on to make beautiful music with Don Johnson and Bryan Adams. The answer when we return.'"

"I can't believe none of you has ever even heard of it," fumes Ross.

"Who's screwing her in it, Bob Crane?" asks Dr. Beaverman.

"Screw you all," barks Ross. "Someday I'm going to track down that movie and make you all eat your words."

When we restart the movie, Barbra finishes "Queen Bee," then ditches the other Oreos to sing the ballad "Everything."

"This song makes me think of the first guy I was ever really, really obsessed with," I confess. "I was a junior in college. His name was Adam, and we were dancers together in the campus production of *Oklahoma!* and I was so hot for him. We were also in this class called Review Ensemble together, and this was one of the songs he sang for that."

"Did anything ever happen?" asks Marcus.

"No," I say. "He was straight." I didn't realize that was my big laugh line, but apparently, it is. "There was one night where I spent the night at his dorm and I think something *could* have happened," I continue. "I remember him saying something sort of provocative, but before I could even process it, he sort of laughed it off and my window of opportunity closed. Looking back, I don't know if I wish I had made a move, because he ended up sort of dumping me as a friend anyway. If we had fooled around, I would have been a mess for two semesters."

"And you've applied that same cautious strategy to your crushes ever since," teases Tony.

"OK, now you're being mean in the real world," I say.

As Barbra croons on about all the things she wants, *Nightmare on Elm Street* actor Robert Englund turns up as the irritating companion of one of Kris's biggest lady fans. "Oh, my God, it's Freddy Krueger!" says Marcus, as the couple plops down uninvited at Kris's table.

"No, it's not," says Tony. "Barbra's just being backlit."

"Speaking of which," says Ross, laughing, "the subject of backlighting comes up over and over in this article by Pierson. Apparently, Barbra was obsessed with it."

Back on screen, Kris is getting more and more fed up with his loudmouthed tablemate. Finally, he punches him in the face. An all-out bar brawl erupts, but before Kris can finish what he started, he's led to the back door by the perpetually halo-headed Barbra. Once outside, the couple hops into Kris's waiting limo.

"God, you've got incredible eyes," Kris tells Barbra as the rain beats down on the car.

"Would you mind uncrossing them for me?" says Tony, before erupting into the kind of convulsing giggle fit one might see in a detox center. He's back, folks.

As they ride, Kris continues to give Barbra compliments on her angelic voice and beautiful mouth. When the couple arrive at her place, 211 Orchid St. in Hollywood (Marcus makes a note of it), Kris follows her up the stairs and lets fly with a line I'm willing to bet Barbra penciled into the script herself.

"You've got a great ass," he says. (4) "You live alone?"

Though Kris is itching to come in and get a piece of that great ass, Barbra resists his advances and instead invites him to come back a few hours later for breakfast. He honors the request, though none of us can figure out why.

"This guy would not even be interested in her, OK?" groans Lauren, as Barbra ushers Kris into her cozy apartment, which, according to Pierson, the actress decorated herself with carloads of tchotckes she brought from home.

"What does he see in her, Dr. Beaverman?" I ask.

"She's disciplined, nurturing, keeps a nice house," says Dr. Beaverman as Barbra serves up the pizza Kris brought as well as Ass Shots 5–7. "She's the perfect Jewish mommy."

"Eat your breakfast," Barbra nags.

"See what I mean?" says Dr. Beaverman.

By now, Kris is so inexplicably smitten with the bed-headed songstress that he invites her to come with him to his big outdoor concert that afternoon. This, of course, is the Sun Devil Stadium sequence where Barbra gave the "Let's Do Some Rock, Motherfuckers" speech. As the pair flies over the arena in a chopper, I must admit it's pretty spectacular to see a crowd that large and effusive that isn't computer-generated. Her potty-mouthed cheerleading worked.

When Kris takes the stage, Barbra looks on from the sidelines and does her best wide-eyed babe-in-the-woods ingenue routine. "At least with the Judy Garland *Star Is Born*, you bought her as a nobody," remarks Ross, "but I ain't buying it from Babs."

"I'm so sick of her ugly duckling shtick," groans Lauren. "She *knows* she's going to get screwed. She *knows* it."

"I like the way she looks at him," I say, "like she's already making a list of his flaws in her mind. She can't even give in to one moment of pure romanticism without being judgmental."

"She thinks she can fix him," says Dr. Beaverman.

Barbra's this close to jotting down a list of vocal coaches for Kris, I'm sure of it, when the coked-up rocker dashes off the stage, borrows a motorcycle from a fan, and starts daredeviling about like he's Gary Busey on Red Bull or something. "Pierson tells this crazy story about how Jon Peters wanted to hire Evel Knievel to be Kris's stunt double for this scene," says Ross, as Kris careens off the stage and drags several speakers with him. "He wanted Knievel to, like, fly onto the stage from the audience and crash into the instruments and while Pierson and Peters were arguing about it, all Barbra could talk about was how there weren't enough close-ups in the movie and how when she worked with Willy Wyler, there were close-ups in every scene."

With Kris off to the hospital, the sequence ends with a long shot of Barbra standing alone in a deserted parking lot. She doesn't lay eyes on Kris again until weeks later, when they coincidentally meet up at a radio station. "Everywhere you go, fighting breaks out and things get broken," Barbra rants at him. Nothing gets Kris sexed up like a good scolding from Mommy, and so it's no surprise they end up going back to his L.A. mansion together.

Though Kris seems happy to just hang out in the billiard room and tell Barbra how "cute" she is, I'd much prefer if he gave her the grand tour of the place. "This waterbed is where I knocked up Rita Coolidge," I say as Kris, "the first time."

"Excuse that IUD," says Ross, taking over as Kris. "Suzi Quatro was here over the weekend and left half her shit behind."

"This is the room where I got really blitzed and had a three-way with Loggins and Messina," says Tony, "and now I can't find the seven-ball."

Soon, Kris tries to get another rise out of Mommy by letting loose with a can of spray paint on his own wall. "He's writing 'Help!'" figures Tony, before we realize that Kris has actually spelled out "Esther" backward, or ass-backward as the case may be. (12)

"Aren't you going to cross my *t*?" Barbra asks him.

"Yes, Mommy," says Marcus.

"He's going to be so pissed when he sobers up and realizes he tagged his own house," Lauren says.

"Wait till he realizes he banged her," adds Tony.

The banging proper doesn't actually go down until after a scene Pierson claims he cribbed from a real-life jam session he witnessed between Streisand and songwriter Leon Russell, where Kris and Barbra sit at the piano and write a song together.

"It's 'Songs in the Key of Ass,'" says Tony as Barbra noodles away on "Lost Inside of You" while Kris croaks out lyrics.

"You're so *good,*" Barbra coos to Kris between bouts of schoolgirl giggling.

"Everything's always a big fucking joke right before you screw for the first time," remarks Dr. Beaverman. "After they sleep together, they will never sit at the piano again."

"She'll be like, 'Quit that racket!'" I say.

"She's so close to that beard, I'm sick," grumbles Lauren.

"That's because they're shooting her through it," figures Tony.

After they make love, Barbra does the most sensible thing she's done in the whole movie: She gets Kris Kristofferson into a bathtub, albeit a bathtub lined with empty beer containers.

"Look at that can of Schlitz," says Ross, nostalgically. "Or should I say, 'Look at that can *and* the Schlitz.' "

In the next scene, a guitar-strumming Barbra wants to take a break from practicing, but Kris pushes her to keep going. "See, now he's criticizing her," points out Dr. Beaverman. "Before the sex, it was just gales of laughter."

"I want him to go, 'You know that guitar really hasn't sounded the same since I shoved it up Buffy Sainte-Marie's ass,' " says Ross.

Instead, Kris begins grooming his songstress squeeze for her own shot at stardom. Before long, they're in the studio together working on demos. "Both Barbra and Kris recorded most, if not all, of their vocals live, while they were filming the scenes," Ross informs us. "You got to give 'em credit for that."

And I do. As Barbra holds Kris's hand and sings the Oscar-winning "Evergreen," I find myself surprisingly moved, enriched even. "*Barbra sings to make you forget every other thing she has ever done or said,*" says Ross, reading aloud Pierson's description of the day they filmed the first musical number. "*You feel excited and wonderful. She throws it away as though it were a gift not worth having.*"

Pierson's observation, I think, really nails the reason I've never jumped on the Barbra bandwagon. It is my belief that if God or the Universe or Whoever's on High gave you the ability to do something well, be it sing or write or paint blue dogs, you should trot it out occasionally, especially if it's something that could bring pleasure and inspiration to others. And ideally, you should trot it out joyfully and beat your chest like Celine if the spirit moves you. Barbra acts as though every time she opens her mouth to sing one note, you've just asked her for a ride to the airport. "There's this subtext under a lot of her performances that says, 'I'd rather be doing something else,'" I remark. "But I can't figure out what that something else is."

"Shopping for Tiffany lamps," figures Marcus.

"Is that it?" I say. "That's when she's genuinely not cranky, when she's rifling through fabric swatches at the Malibu compound?"

Out of nowhere, Lauren lets out a loud yawn, then gets up from the couch and takes a new position sprawled on the floor. "I was up so late last night waiting to go on at the Comedy Store," she explains, closing her eyes. "Wake me when the star gets born."

"It's about to get born," I promise. "In this next scene, I think."

"I know something that'll wake you up," says Marcus, before heading into the kitchen for a cake-cutting knife.

We're all enjoying our first mouthfuls of cake when Kris gives Barbra her big break by dragging her out onstage at a benefit concert he's doing and insisting she sing for the people. "This is like buying a ticket to Limp Bizkit and having Charlotte Church come out and doing a few songs," says Ross as Barbra starts into the schmaltzy "Woman in the Moon." (13)

"Kris can't even organize his own bowel movements," gripes Tony, "and yet he's managed to get Barbra's backup singers there, give them corsages, and make sure his band knows her songs."

Slowly but surely the crowd starts to warm to her. "Maybe they think she's Peter Frampton," I suggest.

"Except she doesn't come alive," says Marcus.

"She doesn't come at all, I'm afraid," says Dr. Beaverman.

Though Kris doesn't go to the trouble of sending out announcements or passing out cigars, I believe this is the scene where the star officially gets born, because when Barbra finishes her song, the crowd goes apeshit.

"I want her to become an instant pain-in-the-ass diva after one song," says Lauren, "just pulling out a list of demands for the dressing room and being like, 'Where's my tea set? I need my tea set!' "

The audience insists on an encore, so as Babs launches into the lounge favorite "I Believe In Love," I launch into another story from my college days. "I've performed on that very stage," I boast. "It's Grady Gammage Auditorium at ASU, where I starred as a Teen Dancer opposite Russ Tamblyn in *The Music Man.* It was the first time I ever got paid to perform, and I was so proud of myself that I Xeroxed a copy of my $75 paycheck because it said "actor" on it, and sent it home to my mother as a little souvenir. Well, she didn't get that I was just being show-offy, and she deposited it in my account and it went through."

"*That's* how I should raise money for my movie," says Ross as though he could have had a V8, "just deposit every check twice."

Barbra leaves the stage only to be immediately accosted by a mob of reporters and photographers. When Kris rescues her from the throng, she rewards his chivalry by proposing, and soon the two are tying the knot in a corny wedding scene in which Barbra sports baby's breath in her hair.

"That baby had the croup," says Tony.

Then it's off to the Arizona desert, where the newlyweds bulldoze away on their pueblo-style dream house. (16)

"If you build it, she will come," I say.

"This is like *Little Jew on the Prairie,*" says Marcus, as Barbra and Kris pretend to do manual labor.

"Why couldn't this be *Tremors*?" laments Ross. "I'd love to seem them get attacked by a big giant worm right about now."

With Barbra's stardom in full ascent and Kris's fizzling in a puddle of booze, things start to get a little tense around the pueblo. At one point, Kris tears off on his motorcycle for yet another dangerous spin that ends with him wiping out. Barbra, ever the devoted little wife, just throws up her hands like a befuddled substitute teacher then joins Kris in the mud for some down-in-the-dirt lip-locking. (19)

"We've got a Dirty Ass Shot!" proclaims Marcus.

"Please, they've all been dirty ass shots," says Dr. Beaverman. (20)

By this point, Esther's career is skyrocketing so spectacularly that only a montage with lots of camera clicks can do it justice. On the flip side, Kris soon learns from his bandana buddy, Gary Busey, that his band will be touring without him.

"Now did Kris quit or did they dump him?" I wonder.

"It doesn't matter, Dennis," insists Tony. "This movie is about her ass. What movie are you watching?"

The emasculation of John Norman Howard continues back at the L.A. mansion, where Kris has to take not only Barbra's constant smothering but her calls as well. It's too much for his fragile ego to take, so he decides not to show up for Barbra's big night at the Grammys. Given that she's both codependent and dateless, it's no surprise that Barbra seems a little down in the dumps at the ceremony. Still, that doesn't begin to excuse the look of complete and utter disgust and disdain that Babs pulls when presenters Tony Orlando and Rita Coolidge announce that she's won. If you were to judge only by her facial expression, you'd swear that Rita, Tony, Telma Hopkins, Joyce Vincent Wilson, and hell, let's throw the country group Alabama in there as well, had all taken a dump on her new Donna Karan poncho and then tossed it at her. But no, she's just winning a Grammy.

Sensing an opportunity to get interactive and keep Lauren awake, I grab the remote. "I want to try something," I say, then rewind to the moment just before Rita announces the winner. "Hey, Barbra!" I say, in the friendliest inflection I can muster. "If you're free on Saturday, I was wondering if you could help me move."

With that, I press play and Barbra gives me and my simple request the most soul-shattering fuck-off-and-die look this side of a *Charmed* table read. We all, I'm not too modest to say, find this quite funny. "Tony, you want a piece of this action?" I ask.

My just-back-from-the-brink-of-decency roommate nods eagerly as I zoom back to Rita's announcement. "Hey, Barbra!" he says. "I'm from the Make-a-Wish Foundation, and this is little Timmy. He's going to die this afternoon, and he was hoping you'd sign his poster of *Nuts*." I press "play," and with just a glance, Barbra tells Tony and Timmy and the entire Make-a-Wish Foundation and their families and pets to fuck off and die, in that order.

"I've got one, I've got one," says the now wide-awake Lauren. "Hey, Barbra!" she starts. (If this game catches on as a national pastime, I think it should be called "Hey, Barbra!") "My husband and I are having trouble conceiving and I was wondering if you wouldn't mind letting our doctors scrape inside your uterus and remove some of your remaining eggs."

Barbra gives Lauren the look. More laughter all around.

Ross's turn. "Hey, Barbra!" he shouts aggressively, as though he were one of a gaggle of unruly reporters. "Why don't you tell us about that underground movie where you get fucked up the ass by James Garner?"

More laughter, the kind you think you may die from.

Marcus's "Hey, Barbra!" offering is the short but sweet, "Mom, I'm gay." Dr. Beaverman, meanwhile, is too busy hugging the arm of the sofa and gasping for breath to contribute. "I think I can bring it home," offers Tony, raising his hand. "Hey, Barbra!" he hollers. "I don't know how to tell you this, but I just came back from the future, and it turns out you're going to marry James Brolin."

I let the tape play on after Barbra gives the look, but we're all too busy catching our breath in the wake of "Hey, Barbra!" to pay much attention to what's happening on-screen. It appears as though Kris has shown up drunk and wandered onstage during Barbra's acceptance speech.

"What is it, is it me?" pleads Barbra to Kris after she drags him to a nearby bathroom. "Am I doing something wrong?"

"Do you want it alphabetically or in order of scene?" poses Tony.

In the following scene, set during a rehearsal for her TV special, Barbra scores her highest points on the believability scale when she rationalizes her diva behavior to her manager by saying, "I'm not trying to be difficult or anything. I'm just trying to get it right."

Things go from bad to worse for Babs when she returns to the mansion and finds Kris in bed with a waif-like interviewer, who tactfully tells Babs to lighten up because Kris couldn't get it up anyway. "You can trash your life, but you're not going to trash mine!" Barbra shrieks before flying out of the bedroom in a fury and then trashing the house.

Kris follows her downstairs, and after Barbra yells at him to fight for her, he pins her to the floor. "A lot of this fighting stuff," says Ross after Barbra spits in Kris's face, "like the screaming and the spitting, is based on Barbra's real-life relationship with Peters. They wanted to show people how passionate their love was."

Soon, the couple goes from spitting and screaming to sighing and crying, prompting Ross to read us another juicy passage from Pierson's article. *"Kris cries readily; she needs menthol blown in her eyes to make them tear. Kris apologizes. "Jesus, Barbra, I'm sorry. I wish I could do something to help you. I'm not giving you what you need." Barbra takes me aside. "Did you hear what he said? The ego! He thinks what he does controls what I do!"*

Despite her rage at Kris's infidelity, Codependent Barbie ends the scene by sucking face with the same hygienically challenged has-been she called a "son of a bitch" only minutes ago. (26) "It's the classic 'I hate you, fuck me' syndrome," says Dr. Beaverman with a sigh.

In the next scene the lovers return to the desert for more quality time together. It's then that a burning question pops into my mind. "Who feeds the horses when they're not at the pueblo?" I wonder.

"Craft Services," figures Marcus.

"Oh," I say.

In a rare moment of tenderness, Kris stares at and then touches Barbra's nose while she sleeps.

"He's thinking, *Her dick must be huge,*" says Ross.

"It *is* huge," says Lauren.

"I think he just wanted to see if it's real," Tony figures. "He thought it came off with the glasses."

"Look at her," Dr. Beaverman says when Babs opens her eyes and gazes needily into Kris's eyes. "Even in repose, she's smothering."

With a distant, get-me-the-fuck-out-of-here look in his eyes, Kris tells the ol' ball and chain he's going to go for a drive. Then he hops into his 'Vette, pulls the tab on a Schlitz, and pops Barbra's "Lost Inside of You" in the 8-track. It's all so deliciously '70s, I half expect Jackie Gleason to pull out from behind a clump of cactus in a cop car and chase after him.

We soon find ourselves back at the L.A. mansion, in the company of a grieving Barbra, who almost loses it completely when a workman accidentally puts her dead husband's music on the boom box. "How do you turn this thing off?" the befuddled hired hand asks Barbra.
"That's what I've been wondering for the last hour," mutters Lauren.

"I'm going to go out on a limb here," I announce, "and say that I like Kris Kristofferson in this movie. He may have been drunk half the time, but there's something touching and real about him."

"He did the best he could under the circumstances," concurs Ross.

Then, just as I've gone public with my affection for Kris, the Movie Gods go and take him away from me. We cut to a shot of Kris's little red Corvette, totaled and resting on its side in the Arizona boondocks. "She's still smothering him," Dr. Beaverman says after Barbra rushes up to Kris's dead body at the accident scene.

"It's the only time he didn't pull away," Marcus points out.

"It's as stiff as he's ever been too," says Lauren.

"She's really underplaying her grief here," I notice. "You'd think she'd really go to town with the hysteria."

"She's saving her energy to argue with the insurance adjuster," figures Ross.

We soon find ourselves back at the L.A. mansion, in the company of a grieving Barbra, who almost loses it completely when a workman accidentally puts her dead husband's music on the boom box. "How do you turn this thing off?" the befuddled hired hand asks Barbra.

"That's what I've been wondering for the last hour," mutters Lauren.

"This is the part where I got kicked out," recalls Dr. Beaverman wistfully as Barbra nags at dead Kris, then holds his unraveling demo to her face and, yes, cries tapes like one of those puppets in *The Lion King*.

"Oh, now I get it," says Marcus. "She's crying tapes. That's kind of stupid."

"I can just imagine the grip going home to his wife and saying, 'Barbra kicked ass tonight,'" says Ross. "'There was not a dry eye on that set, man.'"

The film ends, not with an ass-shot recap montage alas, but with one endless close-up of Barbra in concert singing about what she would do for "one more look" at her dead lover.

"Then get a shovel, you lazy bitch," barks Tony.

As the widow sings her heart out, Tony imagines what it would be like if Barbra turned up on *Crossing Over* and contacted Kris on the other side. "I need to acknowledge a broom," says Tony as psychic John Edward, "but it's not used to cleaning… It's a flying broom… Does that mean anything to you?"

"I don't know," I say, laughing. "I think I'd rather see them work out their issues on *Tattletales*. I want Barbra to wear the headphones upside down so she doesn't wreck her 'fro and Kris to show up drunk and take a leak all over the Banana Section."

Barbra seamlessly segues from her mournful ballad to a rockin' reprise of "Watch Closely Now," during which she does what I like to call the Chicken Dance, a series of insane hand and neck movements I'm sure we'd all find endlessly hilarious if we weren't so damn drained.

Finally, the screen goes black.

As the credits roll, we learn not only that Barbra was responsible for the "musical concepts" but that her character's wardrobe was "from Ms. Streisand's closet."

"That's like admitting you farted in an elevator," I remark before stopping the tape for the final time.

"Speaking of credits," says Ross, "Pierson claims that at one point Streisand tried to get him to share directing credit with her. She was totally serious."

We all just shake our heads in disbelief.

"She was just trying to get it right," concludes Marcus.

•

Two weeks later, Marcus and I are driving down Franklin Avenue in Hollywood when a certain street sign catches my eye. "That's Orchid," I shout, "the street Barbra's apartment was on in *A Star Is Born*."

"I know, but there's no 211," says Marcus disappointedly. "I looked it up on

MapQuest the day after we watched the movie. She supposedly lives at 211, but the street numbers start at like 1000."

"Oh, well," I say. "They got everything else right."

The two of us are on our way to Togo's to pick up sandwiches for the cast and crew of *Renaissance Boy* who are working at a nearby elementary school. Marcus has volunteered to be in charge of catering for the shoot. Tony, believe it or not, is helping wrangle the child actors. Lauren is assisting with makeup and playing a two-line role as a toy store clerk. And I'm doing whatever Ross needs me to do at any given time. As for Dr. Beaverman, she couldn't get off from work or simply had the foresight to claim she couldn't. She's with us in spirit, though.

We're four days into the five-day shoot, and so far Ross has had three Shit Fits, six Conniption Fits, and one Hissy. The Hissy was by far my favorite because it was super gay and it happened in front of the kids. Fits aside, I think Ross is doing a bang-up job. He would totally belong in the director's chair if we actually *had* a director's chair. It just wasn't in the budget.

Marcus and I are trying to find a place to park when my cell phone rings. It's Ross, clearly in the throes of another yet-to-be-defined fit. "I'm having a problem with one of the actors," he grumbles. "Marjorie, who's playing the school principal."

"She's so nice," I say. "What's the problem?"

"She's *so nice*," Ross echoes. "She's been palling around with the kids so much that now she's like their friend and the scene's not working. I need them to be fucking *terrified* of her."

"What can I do?" I ask.

"Give me Beaverman's phone number," he says.

Start shopping for cigars. Another star's about to be born.

FEVER ALL THROUGH THE NIGHT

"Where do you go when the record is over?"

That's the tag line on the movie poster for *Saturday Night Fever,* the 1977 John Badham–directed, Norman Wexler–scripted disco classic that gave us John Travolta in a body-hugging white suit as dance-floor god Tony Manero as well as a slew of toe-tappingly delicious tunes from the hirsute and harmonious Brothers Gibb. As a hormonally confused preteen with an unnatural jones for cocky guys in polyester shirts and painted-on Angels Flight slacks, I interpreted that tag line literally: When the record was over, you went straight to the back seat of your nerdy friend's jalopy and banged TV's Angie.

It isn't until right this second, as I hold in my hands a weather-beaten copy of the soundtrack (on vinyl, no less), that the line's existential overtones (i.e. "What are you doing with your life, Tony Manero?") register with me at all. Until today I just thought that when the record was over, you got laid. Someone got laid, anyway.

Maybe it was my age at the time. Maybe it was the way those unnatural fabrics caressed every curve and crevice. Maybe it was the moment when Donna Pescow walks up to Travolta with a handful of rubbers and literally begs him to stick it in. Whatever the reason, *Saturday Night Fever,* more than any other movie, represents sex for me. It proved that a guy could dance around his bedroom in his underwear, as often was my wont, and still be thought of as masculine and desirable. Not only were sex and dancing not mutually exclusive—which seemed to be the conventional wisdom in my small-town universe—they were connected. Tony Manero wasn't sexy *in spite* of his dancing. He was sexy *because* of it. This was a new concept to me.

I wasn't alone, as it turns out. Three time zones away, another young man with a penchant for the boogie was getting just as sexed-up by *Fever* as I was. "Remember that scene in the back bar of the disco where there was the stripper chick?" Marcus asks me, as the two of us inspect the photos of Travolta and Company inside the album cover. "Well, guess what happened to me in that scene the first time I saw the movie?"

"Hard-on?" I say.

"First one ever, although I prefer the term *boner,*" Marcus says, smiling at the memory. "*Saturday Night Fever* was the first R-rated movie I ever saw. I was 14 and my friend Danny was 15, and he told the girl behind the counter that he was 18 and I was 17, and she bought it. I walked out of there thinking R ratings equaled boners."

The *Night Fever* soundtrack is one of several milk-crates-full of Dr. Beaverman's old LPs we're trying to unload today in front of Ross's place in Studio City. His 24-unit apartment building is having its annual yard sale–gossip fair–wienie roast. With Ross still a good 10 grand away from finishing postproduction on *Renaissance Boy*, the rest of us—save Dr. Beaverman, who avoids the sun like a vampire—have brought over carloads of our unwantables in hopes of helping the cause. My goal for today, apart from convincing Ross to hit on his foxy new neighbor, Renee, is not to leave with more junk than I came with. So far I've shown remarkable restraint; I've only purchased one item, a just-like-new copy of *Staying Fit!*—John Travolta's 1984 workout book in which the dimple-chinned actor, still pumped up and waxed from *Staying Alive,* demonstrates his favorite exercises with a little help from *Taxi* redhead Marilu Henner and a wide array of headbands. My plan is to present the tome, which set me back a whopping $1.75, to Shawn as a break-a-leg gift. Yes, the Accidental Boyfriend is back in town—though we've yet to meet up—performing for the next month in the touring company of *Saturday Night Fever: The Musical.*

Though the "merchandise" we're trying to sell today isn't exactly flying off the grass, it's a beautiful day to be outside and we're having a nice time. Ross is in particularly good spirits. His sister phoned as we were setting up this morning to tell him his mother's doctors think they got it all. They even went as far as to use the term "cancer-free." He says it was the best "Edelweiss" call he's ever gotten.

What's more, my film-freak friend survived his first shoot as a movie director and feels good about what transpired, Shit Fits and all. Dr. Beaverman, as Ross put it, "kicked major acting ass" in her two-minute scene as Mrs. Peevner, a persnickety junior high school principal, and was such a hero to the production that Ross almost had her wear a cape. The child actors' visible uneasiness while in her formidable presence was exactly what the director ordered and then some. When I asked Dr. Beaverman later what she did to prepare for the scene, she said, "I just tried to imagine they were children."

Since the shoot, Dr. Beaverman's favorite thing to do is prattle on like a self-serious starlet at a press junket. The other day I asked her if she had been in our condo complex's Jacuzzi since they retiled it, and she said, "No, but I would if it were integral to the role and really moved the story along." Did you watch *Survivor* last night? "Yes, and it just underlines my point: There are no good roles for women." Are you going to pop by Ross's yard sale this weekend? "Doubt it. I just can't deal with the paparazzi."

While Dr. Beaverman will have to wait to start fielding follow-up offers until people actually see the film, Tony's gratification was instant. The mother of the kid who played the Renaissance Boy's best friend was so impressed with the amiable way he corralled the movie's youngsters that she offered him a management position at Gym Dandy, a fitness and recreation center for kids she owns in Sherman Oaks. That's right, folks, my former male strip-show performer roommate who once ordered a shit hit on an innocent British mailbox and enjoys talking about anal sex in an Angela Lansbury brogue is now working with children. And liking it fine.

"I've been there one week," says Tony, between bites of chili dog on Ross's apartment complex lawn, "and I can already tell you everything you'd ever want to know about boogers."

"Why are they called boogers?" asks Marcus.

"Because they taste like boogers," replies Tony. "What else would you possibly call them?"

"Travolta actually thanks the company who donated his tanning bed," marvels Lauren while giggling her way through *Staying Fit!* "I can't believe you're going to give this to the Accidental Boyfriend. How can you part with it?"

"I know," I say. "I'm going to be like that teenage girl who gets knocked up and at the last minute decides she wants to keep the baby. I'll be sitting on my front porch with a rifle going, 'You can have my copy of John Travolta's *Staying Fit!* when you pry it from my cold, dead fingers.'"

Just then my cell phone rings. It's Shawn, of all people. Proving that just because he's been doing eight shows a week in various corners of the country doesn't mean he's lost his flair for spookily well-timed entrances and exits.

"Have you gotten your tickets yet?" he asks.

"No," I tell him, then start into some half-assed excuse about trying to get everyone's schedules coordinated.

"You have to come on the 18th," he says, cutting me off. "I'm going on as Double J." Normally, Shawn plays the ensemble role of Disco Patron/Puerto Rican Drug Dealer, though he understudies several juicier parts, including Tony Manero's jive-talkin' right-hand man, Double J. "The guy who usually plays him has a wedding to go to," Shawn explains. "This is probably my only chance to do it."

I lower the phone, then ask my fellow yard salespeople if they're free on the 18th. Everyone nods affirmatively. "The 18th looks good," I tell Shawn. "We can check with Beaverman tomorrow night. You're still coming, right?"

"Totally," he says.

"Don't be late, then," I say, turning briefly into supernag Esther Hoffman Howard from *A Star Is Born*. "You're like the guest of honor," I say, softening a bit.

"Cool," says Shawn.

"Where the fuck is he, magician school?" I rant the next night when Shawn fails to show up on time for our *Saturday Night Fever* Screening Party. I even scheduled it for a Monday, the one night he doesn't have a show, but our expert witness is nowhere to be found.

"Screw him," says Lauren.

"He already has," quips Ross.

No, he hasn't, I think, *technically,* but Ross doesn't need to know that.

"Let's just go," groans Tony, 25 minutes after our designated start time. "I've got a Mommy, Me, 'n' the Mat class to teach at the crack of ass. I need my sleep if I'm going to keep those pain-in-the-ass brats entertained."

"I don't know how you cope with those kids," says Dr. Beaverman. "I'd open a vein."

"I was actually talking about the mothers," says Tony.

"Was Travolta a big star yet when this came out?" wonders Lauren, while reading the back of the *Fever* video box. That's right, I said video box. Once again, Paramount, the studio that let us down with *Flashdance,* has failed to deliver a DVD version of one of its most popular movies ever.

"He was already huge because of *Welcome Back, Kotter,"* says Ross, serving up his first Fowler Fun Fact of the day. "In fact, the movie had a lot of trouble shooting on location in New York because Travolta's fans would turn up and start screaming and carrying on. It got so bad they started issuing fake call sheets to confuse people as to where they were going to be."

"Maybe Shawn got a hold of one of those," says Marcus, chiming in from the kitchen, where he's taping a homemade "Countdown to *Glitter*" calendar with a giant shot of a windblown Mariah on my refrigerator. "We have a month to go, people. After that, nothing is ever going to be the same."

Having delivered his *Glitter* update, Marcus returns to the front room as I slide the *Fever* tape into the VCR. "This movie is very nostalgic for me," says Dr. Beaverman. "I remember walking into the theater in Berkeley and the girls were screaming like they were at a concert or something. This was a matinee too. It was the most exciting movie I'd ever seen in my life." Dr. B. shakes off the memory, then takes a swig of her cosmo. "Of course, I've become so jaded now," she sighs. "Even if I were rummaging under Robert Downey Jr.'s sofa cushions, I couldn't summon up a feeling as pure and genuine as that again."

I press "play" and the film opens, with a shot of a bell-bottomed Travolta strutting down the sidewalk in his working-class Brooklyn neighborhood to the strains of the Bee Gees' "Stayin' Alive." As he happens by a shop that sells men's platform shoes, he holds his own Boogie Shoe up to the window and gives us a little bounce.

"That's not his foot, it's a double's," purports Ross. "Travolta claims he'd never jiggle that way."

"That's not what I read in the *Star,"* says Tony.

Just then the doorbell rings. I pause the movie and open the door to discover Shawn, sporting huge '70s hair, a clingy disco shirt that employs most if not all of the colors in the brown family, painted-on bell-bottom jeans with square-shaped stitching all over them, and a single thick gold chain with one of those squiggly horn things hanging from it. It's the first time I've laid eyes on him since he left L.A. for New York a few months ago, and the sight almost takes my breath away.

Before I can tell him how foxy he looks, he pulls a long-sleeved T-shirt with the *Fever* logo on it from behind his back and tosses it into my chest. All is forgiven.

"Sorry I'm late, everyone," he says, coming inside. "I was doing the bump with a black Mormon girl."

"Of course you were," says Dr. Beaverman.

After insisting that Shawn give us a twirl and fetching him a Coke, I restart the movie. "This is where I start to sing but I'm not onstage," says Shawn as the Bee Gees head into the chorus of "Stayin' Alive." "I'm off in the wings with my little Janet Jackson mike."

When Travolta stops at a pizza joint for a couple of slices, the girl behind the counter, played by Travolta's real-life sister, Ann, greets him by name. "That moment is in the musical," reports Shawn. "Half a day rehearsal just so this idiot girl, Jillian, could say, 'Hey, Tony, two or three?' in an eight count. I wanted to strangle her. She's the girl with the cards I was telling you about, Dennis."

"What cards?" asks Marcus.

"She has this deck of Inner Peace Cards," Shawn explains, "and before every show she goes around to everyone and makes you take one."

"Is she the black Mormon girl?" asks Dr. Beaverman.

"No, the black Mormon girl's cool," says Shawn, "but this other girl's totally annoying, with her flowery cards that say, like, 'I love myself' and 'My body's a temple' and shit. I can tell she's tired of doing it, but she thinks if she stops, something horrible will happen, like she'll fall into the orchestra pit or something."

The credits wind down, and we discover that all that strutting was leading Travolta to his dead-end job at the local paint store, where one of his customers is played by Travolta's real mother, Helen. "In his job he's surrounded by all the colors of paint and yet he's really in the nuts and bolts of the working world," remarks Dr. Beaverman. "All the colors he really sees are in a paint can so he has to color his own world with the disco at night."

Dr Beaverman knocks back the last of her cosmo, then continues. "I remember reading an interview with Travolta in *Time* magazine when this movie came out where he quoted Diana Hyland," she says, referring to the actor's *Eight Is Enough* actress lover, who died of cancer in Travolta's arms during the shoot. "He said, 'Diana told me this script had all the colors.' I always thought that was a very evocative quote. Of course, it was the '70s, so she was probably on LSD at the time. Or maybe I was."

After work, Travolta heads to the house he shares with his parents, younger sister, and grandmother. He's barely in the door before his movie mom harangues him for arriving so late. "Where you been?" she bellows.

"I was doing a scene with my *real* mother," I say.

"And she's is the shittiest actress, Fake Ma," adds Tony. "It took her 14 takes to buy the paint. She's worse than my sister with the fucking pizza. You can't believe the day I had."

Then Travolta heads upstairs and begins his getting-ready ritual. This involves much striking of poses, drying of hair, clasping of necklaces, and, sigh, adjusting of basket. "That moment where he zips up his pants over his crotch kills me," I confess. "I literally lose my mind."

Shawn smiles at me, then stretches his denim-clad legs out in front of him on the floor and leans back on his elbows.

"The only time you see a man in dusty rose double-knit Sansabelt pants anymore is in Leisure World or West Palm Beach," laments Dr. Beaverman, "and it's a damn shame."

When the family's unemployed patriarch wanders into John's bedroom to say that dinner's on the table, our hero just keeps on grooving, right in his Dad's face. "I danced around my room like that all the time, but I would never have done it in front of my father," I reveal. "It would have been like underlining the fact that I wasn't exactly the kind of son he had in mind. Dancing was like a dirty little secret, right up there with masturbation and watching *For Ladies Only.*"

Before hitting the town, Travolta must endure a family dinner during which his impossible-to-please parents bombard him with criticisms like, "You should have been a priest like your brother."

"Ma, I'm gay," says Tony, "but I'm not *that* gay."

"A lot of the father's anger is jealousy over his son having a life," says Dr. Beaverman as Papa Manero continues to berate his son, "but it's also because Tony is a convenient scapegoat for the father's own frustration at being such a prime loser. Because of his joblessness, the rigidly defined boundaries of the traditional nuclear family are slipping in the Manero household. Normally the father is expected to earn the money and the woman is expected to cook and spread her legs. When those roles are upset, the woman can become dominant, as she is here, and the son takes over the father's role. It's all very Oedipal and confusing. I need another drink."

As Tony fetches Dr. B. a refill, and the Maneros continue to shovel food into their gaping mouths, I ask Shawn if they use real pasta in the musical, and if so, who cooks it. "We get it from a local restaurant," he replies. "It comes on a Tuesday and it has to last through the following Sunday. They keep reheating it. I always try to grab a little on Tuesday or Wednesday, but by the weekend it's so gross that the people onstage don't even eat it. They just push it around their plates."

"Boy, he's a great openmouthed chewer, John Travolta," muses Marcus.

"One of the best we have," concurs Ross.

When Papa Manero hauls off and smacks his son, Travolta barks back, "Watch the hair. You know I work on my hair a lot, and he hits it. He hits my hair."

"That line was actually an ad-lib," Ross informs us.

"One of the ways Tony Manero holds his crazy world together is by being a little obsessive-compulsive," observes Dr. Beaverman. "Everything has to be just so because the only control he has is over his clothes, his dancing, his hair, and the number of untalented family members he can weasel into the cast."

In the next scene, Tony meets up with his gang, the Faces, which is made up of the drug-taking, poufy-haired Joey (Joseph Cali), the hot-headed, poufy-haired Double J (Paul Pape), the soon-to-be-hospitalized, poufy-haired Gus (Bruce Ornstein), and the car-owning, eager-to-please, poufy-haired Bobby C. (Barry Miller).

"There's a famous essay by S.I. Hayakawa that compares men's choice of cars with their penises," says Dr. Beaverman as Travolta hops into Bobby C.'s beat-up Chevy. "This four-wheeled hunk of junk that takes these boys to their fantasy world shows us that their masculinity is very, very tenuous. All of their external trappings—the clothes, the car, their machismo—are just smoke and mirrors. They're Bob Dole, if we go by the car."

"The creators of our show couldn't get a car on the stage," says Shawn, "so they reinterpreted this scene to be a tap number to "Boogie Shoes."

"That I gotta see," says Lauren.

As the Faces drive down the boulevard, Travolta complains to his buddies about their drug taking and tired music selections. "Very early on, Tony distinguishes himself from the other lowlifes in the car," points out Dr. Beaverman. "He's bothered by their tapes and their drugs. He's already targeted for the future. He's sensitive. He's contemplative. He may not look it, but there's potential there."

"Do you guys take drugs in the show, Shawn?" asks Lauren, as Joey pops a couple of feel-good pills on the screen.

"Tic Tacs," says Shawn, "and we always get reprimanded, like, 'Don't eat the Tic Tacs offstage,' because the orange ones tend to disappear."

"I bet it's the chick with the Inner Peace Cards," figures Ross. "She seems shifty to me."

Soon our fab five putter up to their favorite nightspot, the 2001 Oddyssey. "This reminds me of the epic poem *The Odyssey*, which describes the long, wandering journey of Odysseus, a Greek hero of the Trojan War," says Dr. Beaverman. "One might argue that Tony Manero is like a contemporary Odysseus, except instead of the Trojan War, he's a hero of Trojan Condoms. Oh God, I'm good."

On their way inside, the Faces discuss such scintillating topics as spics, niggers, the pope's ass, and how horny they all are. I can't imagine that kind of un-PC chitchat made it into the sanitized, family-friendly stage version. "We have the 'I'm horny' conversation but not the rest," says Shawn, "and then we start flap-ball-changing...right about *here*."

Travolta and his boys don't tap, however. Instead they strut into the disco like they own the place, past all manner of poly-clad extras, as Walter Murphy's "A Fifth of Beethoven" blares on the soundtrack. Lauren can't help sighing. "Oh, the Qiana, oh, the humanity," she cries out.

"Here's my problem with this period in time," announces Tony. "Everyone looks so *drowsy.* All the women look like they got in a convertible with their hair wet, put on a backwards baseball cap, and just drove."

As the extras boogie-oogie-oogie on the club's light-up dance floor, Marcus sneaks into the kitchen and returns with today's taste sensation: cupcakes topped with either red, blue, or yellow frosting, positioned in his Tupperware cupcake-taker so as to evoke the colorful floor pattern of the 2001. Before allowing us to eat, he pulls out a pair of flashlights, points them at his creation, then rotates them in time with the music. It's all so genius I almost hate to ruin the effect by taking a cake, so I wait for Lauren to dig in first. She doesn't disappoint.

I take my first bite as Donna Pescow makes her entrance as Tony's codependent disco moll, Annette. When Travolta tactlessly informs her that she's not his dream girl, Pescow snaps back, "You want a dream girl, then go to sleep and have a nightmare!"

"Or take a train to Broadway and see *Dreamgirls*, you fag!" barks Tony.

The two finish their verbal sparring, then take the floor together. As they get their tightly choreographed groove on, the club's Ron Jeremy–looking DJ, Monty, gets on the mike and crows, "It's so beautiful, man. I like your new haircuts. I like that polyester look, man."

Thank God, I think. I thought I was the only one.

"The guy who plays Monty, the DJ, in our show is, like, my best friend on the tour," reports Shawn. "His name's Carl and he's totally obsessed with the '70s. He always wears '70s T-shirts and stuff, and I think his hair would be bushy like that even if he weren't in the show."

"I used to have a T-shirt that said DISCO KID," remarks Marcus, prompting our group to rehash all the lamentable slogans we sported back in the day in the name of fashion.

"My mom gave me a shirt she got free from Del Monte for buying corn or something," recalls Lauren, "and it said I'M A HUMAN BEAN. I wore it for my school photo two years in a row. I want to believe that was accidental."

"My mom used to wear this shirt that said FOXY LADY, and she had these really big jugs too," recalls Ross, "and I'd be like, 'Hey, Foxy Lady, gimme some lunch!' "

"My classic '70s shirt was both shocking and subversive," I boast. "It had a cartoon of a bunch of donkeys in the back of a truck, and it said HAULIN' ASS. I had to be careful where I wore it because it was so naughty."

"Carl always wears this yellow shirt with a frowny face on it that says POW'S NEVER HAVE A NICE DAY," says Shawn. "He's also got this super decked-out '70s van that he bought when we were in San Diego last month. It's got, like, shag carpet, an eight-track player, a fold-down bed, a little mini roller skate for a key ring, the whole bit."

"Does it say DREAM MAKER on the side?" I ask. "I say that because when I was in high school, there was a guy named Lorenzo Olmos who had DREAM MAKER on the back of his Trans Am. He was a senior when I was a sophomore. I sat near him in shop class. I remember one day he was talking to this guy, Victor, about how if you were going to wear disco pants, you had to wear bikini briefs under them, no other kind of underwear. Like he was giving him pointers on how to be a disco stud. Then he noticed that I was listening to them, and he told me to stop or he was going to break my scrawny neck. Last I heard, he was like 5 foot 3 and 300 pounds."

"Carl's van says DREAM WEAVER," Shawn tells us.

"See, I was close," I say, delightedly. "It's always 'Dream' something."

Back on screen, Travolta, having finished his dance with Donna, scans the dance floor and spots the woman who will change his life forever, *All My Children* alum Karen Lynn Gorney as the shimmy-happy and sophisticated Stephanie Mangano.

"She can dance, you know that," Travolta tells his buddy Joey over the din of the Trammps' "Disco Inferno."

"*That's* the reason Travolta was nominated for an Academy Award for this," says Ross, "because he successfully delivered that line without cracking up."

"I'm surprised Joey didn't turn to him and go, 'Wait, are we looking at the same girl?'" says Tony.

After a scene in the club's back bar, during which Annette asks Tony to be her partner for the upcoming dance contest and Marcus fends off a flashback boner watching the topless stripper, we head outside to Bobby C.'s car. There we discover Tony's buddy Double J getting busy with an unnamed disco doll in the backseat, while Joey and his date stand outside and wait their turn.

"It's happening? It's happening?" Double J groans, determined to give his partner the big O.

"Remember the '70s, when you would just come in front of your friends?" says Tony.

"At this time in the 20th century, there was no stigma to one-night stands," says Dr. Beaverman, punctuating her thought with a loaded clearing of the throat. "It was perfectly OK for respectable people to have them. The car thing is a bit much, but by and large, it was not a big deal. Not just the lowlifes of Brooklyn did it."

We head back inside, where another disco groupie grabs Travolta, plants one on him, then squeals, "I just kissed Al Pacino!"

"You're thinking of *Cruising*, lady," mutters Ross.

"Which we'll get to," I assure my guests.

Then, in a sequence that inspired suburbanites the world over to sign up for disco classes at their local Y, Travolta leads the rest of the club's surefooted patrons in a rousing line dance to the Bee Gees' "Night Fever." Even Double J, who is surely spent from all that backseat banging, joins in the fun.

"I wonder if Double J rushed through the foreplay so he could get back inside in time for the number," I say.

"Notice how Travolta saved him a spot next to him," remarks Marcus as the crowd moves as one on a smoke-machine cloud. "Maybe he jiggles that way after all."

The next morning finds our hero back in reality, sprawled out on his bed in his black bikini briefs. "That, my friends," says Dr. Beaverman, as Travolta gives his package a good-morning adjustment, "is the best-looking goody trail Dr. Beaverman has ever seen on film."

"And yet nobody talks about the eyeliner," marvels Tony.

"This was when the dimple in his chin was still sexy," remarks Lauren as Travolta gazes at himself the mirror.

"Now he uses it for dipping sauces," says Ross.

In the afternoon, Travolta reunites with his flunky pals to shoot a few hoops. When some unsuspecting gay men sashay by carrying dance bags and wearing jeans tucked into their boots, the Faces, save the more empathetic Tony, harass them with jeers and shoves.

"Shawn, do the Faces bash the gays in your show?" I ask.

"No, the gays *are* the Faces in my show," he says. "I mean, during tech rehearsal, the straight crew members had to take us outside and show us how to throw a punch and dribble a basketball. You'll see. I do as little dribbling as possible, but I'll tell you, I'm Michael Jordan compared to the guy who plays Joey. You guys are going to die when you see him."

After getting a raise at the paint store, then having his pop piss on it, Tony heads to the dance studio to rehearse with Annette. When she hits on him for the millionth time, he suggests that she figure out which she's going to be, a nice girl or a cunt. He's still waiting for an answer when he spots his dream girl, Karen Lynn Gorney, in a neighboring studio, wearing a less-than-flattering off-white leotard and tights.

"They couldn't have given her a black leotard?" wonders Lauren, as Karen gracelessly swings her leg hither and yon at the ballet barre. "It's like, 'Here Karen, here's your sack of potatoes.'"

"And just go ahead and wear the bra and panties underneath," adds Tony. "They won't make you look lumpy."

After putting Annette through her paces, Tony sends her on her way so he can hit on Stephanie. "You're a very good dancer, you know that?" he gushes, though she's glaringly not. Still, Ms. Gorney does her part to keep the 'good dancer' illusion alive. When we leave her, she's even got one leg propped up on the barre. "It took a dozen teamsters half an hour to get her ankle up there," I say.

"And then, as a joke, everyone left the set," says Marcus.

"*That's* why we haven't seen her since," says Lauren. "She's still there!"

When Travolta returns home that night, he learns that his brother, Father Frank, played by Martin Shakar, has left the priesthood and devastated his parents in the process. "The situation with Father Frank is supposed to show us that the ritual of the church is no longer relevant in 1977," says Dr. Beaverman. "New rituals have taken over: the ritual of dancing, the ritual of getting ready for Saturday night."

The next time Travolta returns to the dance studio, he tells Stephanie he wants her to be his partner in the big dance contest, then asks her out for coffee. Across a diner table, she talks her suitor's ear off about how much she's changing and growing as a person now that she's started working as a secretary at a Manhattan entertainment company. When he fails to ooh and aah over her story about meeting Laurence Olivier, Stephanie calls her love-struck Lothario a cliché and says, "You're nowhere on the way to no place."

"Well, this date's going well," says Marcus.

"I am probably the only person in the universe who loves the character of Stephanie," remarks Dr. Beaverman. "On paper, that is. Embodied by Karen Lynn Gorney, well, it just blows." I ask Dr. B. to expound. "This girl is so desperate to get out of her hideous rut of a working-class background," she says. "She's passionate. She's rude. She's disdainful. But behind all that is absolute fear and desperation. You have to have a chip on your shoulder if you're going to do a bold, risky thing like move to Manhattan and you're young. I have never seen anything wrong with that, probably because I had a little bit of that in me too, and I was just as rude and disdainful."

"The thing that killed me about this movie when I saw it is that I knew I was Annette, but I wanted to be Stephanie. That struggle has stayed with me my whole life. I thought, *I'm always gonna be Donna Pescow, looking to get in Karen Lynn Gorney's Danskin wrap-around dress."* —Lauren

Speaking of rude and disdainful, Travolta is both and then some to Donna Pescow when he tells her outside the dance studio that he's going to dance with Karen Lynn Gorney in the big contest instead of her.

"Jeez, that's gotta hurt," mutters Lauren.

"Why do you hate me so much?" Annette pleads to Tony in one of my favorite moments in the flick. "All I ever did to you was like you."

"It's a real tribute to Travolta's charisma that he could be such an asshole and still have everyone like him," says Ross.

"The thing that killed me about this movie when I saw it is that I knew I was Annette, but I wanted to be Stephanie," reveals Lauren. "That struggle has stayed with me my whole life. I thought, *I'm always gonna be Donna Pescow, looking to get in Karen Lynn Gorney's Danskin wraparound dress.*"

Lauren's not the only one trying to get into that dress. Travolta's more smitten than ever when Stephanie shows up at their first practice session in a blue belted leotard that's a considerable improvement over her first rehearsal getup. "That's going to be her character arc, covering her ass more and more with each practice," figures Tony. "She's like, 'I'm late, but I'm French-cut.'"

As the couple compare and contrast various hustle styles together, it becomes obvious that Travolta is going to hold on to the illusion that Gorney can dance until the bitter end. "How come we never talk about how we feel when we're dancing?" he asks as they walk home from practice.

"Because I'm trying to remember the goddamn steps," says Lauren.

Tony invites Stephanie to meet him at the 2001 that Saturday, but she doesn't show, which leaves our working-class hero in the remarkably youthful hands of Fran Drescher. The future *Nanny* plays a a disco groupie named Connie who pops up at Tony's table and purrs, "Are you as good in bed as you are on that dance floor?"

That line of dialogue, more than any other in the film, has always resonated with me, and not just because Fran's inimitable voice has a way of blowtorching itself into your memory bank. No, that line haunts me because it implies that if one has confidence in the former area, one should have confidence in the latter. Apparently I didn't get the memo.

"The girl who plays the Fran Drescher part in our show already knows the answer to that question," reveals Shawn. "She's slept with half the cast, including the guy who plays Tony, and a couple of girls."

"Fran's hand on his ass in those pants makes me crazy," I feel the need to announce, as John and Fran strut out onto the floor.

"I wonder if being in this movie affected how much she was able to lie about her age when she did *The Nanny*?" says Lauren, as Tony and Connie fumble through a few twirls together.

"I was actually 12 when I did *Saturday Night Fever,*" says Tony, delivering a spot-on Fran imitation. "*I got my tits at 10. Ha ha ha ha ha ha.*"

Soon, Tony tires of Fran and her two-year-old tits and ditches her to do a spectacular floor-clearing solo dance to the Bee Gees' "You Should Be Dancin'."

"Wasn't this song a few years old when this movie came out?" I ask.

"Yes, but Travolta liked rehearsing with it, so they put it in the movie," explains Ross. "He worked on this scene with Deney Terrio for seven months before they shot, and he almost cried when he saw the first cut of the film because the director and editor had used all these close-ups and Travolta felt like all his dancing was lost. So he called the producer, Robert Stigwood, who let him go into the editing room and put it together himself. It took him all of five minutes because it's pretty much just the master shot with, like, one close-up where John goes like this." With that, Ross stands, plants his Doc Martens, and demonstrates the move where John points in a half circle around the room. We applaud vigorously.

"You as good in bed as you are on the dance floor?" Marcus asks.

"Better, actually," says Ross.

Rub it in, I think.

"We call that step the Shampoo," says Shawn, pointing to the screen, as Travolta rapidly waves his clasped-hands over and behind his head. "That one there's the Chicken," Shawn continues, as Travolta dances on. "There's the Poke, the Genie."

"I thought Travolta would be a better dancer," says Tony

"I think he's fucking awesome," I argue.

"It's like he's making the music go," agrees Ross. "Like the music is happening *because* of him. *That's* how good he is."

When Travolta starts into an impressive series of rotating splits, Marcus takes us on a short jaunt to St. Olaf country. "I was at Janet and Debbie Dialto's Sweet 16 Party—they were twins—and this guy, Jeff Block, made everyone step back so he could do that step," Marcus recalls. "I was standing next to my friend Matt and I said to him, 'Jeff's not only a bad dancer but a total asshole too.' And just then, Jeff slipped and broke his wrist and I was *euphoric*. It was almost as if I had *caused* it."

Like Jennifer Beals in the *Flashdance* finale, John doesn't give us a big ending pose. Instead he just chugs off the floor and suddenly it's "All Skate" again. Meanwhile, back at the Faces' table, Bobby C. seeks guidance from Father Frank about his pregnant girlfriend who refuses to have an abortion. "This scene shows that when you've given up the old religious rituals, as Frank has, you're left with the new rituals, which are empty and shallow and meaningless," says Dr. Beaverman. "They cannot help you in moral issues, like the one that Bobby is wrestling with, which his why Frank has no choice but to take his pullover sweater and extremely wide-knot tie and haul his ass out of the disco."

Travolta, meanwhile, having been stood up by Stephanie, figures he'll settle for Annette, so he takes the needy fireplug to Bobby C.'s backseat. When the pair discover they're shit-out-of-condoms, Tony wisely opts to avoid the pickle that Bobby C.'s gotten himself into and says, "Just give me a blow job."

"Is that line in the stage version?" I ask Shawn.

"Only the matinees," says Shawn.

Soon daylight comes and brings with it a scene in which Tony borrows Bobby C.'s car in order to help Stephanie move to Manhattan. Though his dweeby friend can't stop talking about how "paralyzed" he is over his girlfriend dilemma, Tony's so horny for Gorney that he completely blows him off. "Here's where Bobby C. breaks into song and sings 'Tragedy' in our show," explains Shawn, as Bobby dissolves into tears.

"Those *shoes* are a tragedy," groans Tony, in regards to Bobby C.'s comically skyscraperesque brown-and-white platforms.

"Guess who I had a crush on when I first saw this movie?" asks Lauren. "Now, remember, I was a total teenage codependent."

"Not Bobby C.," I say.

"Of course, Bobby C.," says Lauren. "I remember thinking, *I'll totally pay attention to you, Bobby. I'll get an abortion in a heartbeat if that's what you want. Let's call the clinic.*"

As Tony and Stephanie cross the bridge into Manhattan, to what sounds like the karaoke version of the film's love theme, "How Deep Is Your Love," I recall for my guests how a girl named Charlene Raingarten sang along to that record in my junior high talent show. "She was very quiet," I remember, "so it was like watching her stand there with a mike while listening to the Bee Gees."

"This song makes me think of the Great Skate in Phoenix, Ariz.," says Tony. "It was always a ladies' choice."

"I remember the Solid Gold Dancers doing a couple dance to it," says Lauren. "Darcel was being spun around on the floor and I remember thinking, *That gay guy's going to step on her hair.*"

"My association with this song is happy because it comes at the end of the show," chirps Shawn. "When it starts, I'm usually pulling the dance belt out of the crack of my ass, putting my real underwear on, and getting change for the Coke machine."

"What's a dance belt?" asks Ross.

"It's like a jock strap for dancers," I explain, grateful that my five years as a cruise ship entertainer have finally come in handy. "The strap goes right up the back like a thong and pulls everything up in front. Not very comfortable."

"I've actually figured out a way to pull mine out of my crack in front of 2,000 people," boasts Shawn. "When we all do the Travolta pose, with our right hand pointing in the air, I just sneak my left hand behind and do a quick yank."

"The classic misdirect," says Tony.

"I'll have to watch for that," I say.

" 'How Deep Is Your Love' makes me think of this jerk I used to, uh, *see*," reveals Dr. Beaverman. "We moved to L.A. together from Berkeley. Then one day he just took off and became a roadie for Bob Seger."

"I'm sorry," I tell her.

"So was I," fumes Dr. Beaverman, "because he left the apartment half-painted. I had to pay an illegal alien $250 to finish it."

"So how does the song figure in?" wonders Marcus.

"Oh," she says, getting her train of thought back on track. "Because before we moved, I made him give his last pair of brown Angels Flight slacks to Goodwill. He was cleaning out his closet and I said, 'If I'm giving away my Candie's mules, then those pants are going.' So he put on the *Saturday Night Fever* soundtrack, slipped into the pants, and took one last look at himself in the mirror before reluctantly parting with them. And I'll tell you, he reminded me until the last time I saw him, which was years later, of that sad day when I made him give up those cherished, Sansabelt Angels Flight pants that reminded him of his glory days." Dr. Beaverman picks up her cocktail from the table but doesn't drink from it. "And I can't tell you how happy that made me, to have caused him pain." Then she drinks.

It isn't until we're well into the next scene—where Tony and Stephanie carry boxes into her new apartment—that I realize Ross and Marcus haven't regaled us with their "How Deep Is Your Love" stories.

"I fold," says Ross, as though this were a game of anecdote poker.

"Marcus?" I ask.

"My memory is Shawn pulling the dance belt out of the crack of his ass," he replies. "It's only a few minutes old, but it's a goody. Every time I hear that song, I go right back."

While checking out Stephanie's new digs, Tony has an awkward encounter with his unrequited love's sugar daddy, a snobby record producer Stephanie met at work who treats her as badly as she treats Tony. When Tony confronts her about the relationship later in the car, she breaks down and reveals that her snooty, sophisticated act is just that, an act. "Part of Tony's journey is to learn how to be a man rather than just *act* like a man with these exaggerated macho aspects," remarks Dr. Beaverman. "This is the one time when he is an absolute man, when Stephanie starts to cry and he takes over and tells her not to worry."

Tony's mature phase, however, proves to be short-lived. Soon he's stirring up more mayhem with the Faces by attacking the Barracudas, a rival gang they believe put their friend Gus in the hospital. "That guy would be me," says Shawn, pointing out a bandana'd Puerto Rican homeboy who gets punched out by Double J.

"Do you have Barracuda girls fighting like they do in the movie?" I ask.

"No," says Shawn. "It just seems that way."

Because of the injuries Tony sustains during the rumble, our disco stud has to compete in the big dance contest with a bandage on his cheek. Luckily, it's white and looks polyester, so it goes with his signature three-piece suit.

"The late Gene Siskel, of Siskel and Ebert, bought that white suit at an auction," reports Ross. "*Saturday Night Fever* was, like, his favorite movie ever."

"I wonder what he did in it," ponders Tony. "You know he was locking the bedroom door and finding out how deep his love really was."

"My fantasy is that he would wear it to the *Chicago Tribune* Christmas party every year," I say, "then get really hammered and dance around like a crazy person and make everyone uncomfortable."

Before watching Tony and Stephanie trip the light fantastic, we meet one of the other couples in the competition, Shirley and Chester, an African-American duo who get down with the genie to "Open Sesame" by Kool and the Gang. "I understudy Chester too," says Shawn. "That's why I was doing the bump with a black Mormon girl earlier."

When Chester and Shirley finish, Tony and Stephanie take the floor. "He's so underdancing to be with her," I remark, as Travolta dips and twirls his dazzlingly mediocre partner to the song "More Than a Woman." "He's moving like he's under water compared to that dance he did earlier by himself."

"Where's Cha Cha DiGregorio when you need her?" wonders Tony, referring to the leggy Latina who snatched Travolta away from Olivia Newton-John during the dance contest in *Grease*. "I'm surprised Monty the DJ didn't announce them as 'Tony Manero and Guest'!"

Hector and Maria, a seemingly double-jointed Puerto Rican couple, are next up and scorch the floor. Even Tony thinks they deserve to take the trophy, but they don't. First place goes to our home-turf favorites, Tony and Stephanie. Disillusioned with his hollow victory, Travolta stomps across the room and gives the trophy to the more deserving couple, Maria and Hector. Then he drags Stephanie outside to Bobby C.'s backseat—where else—and tries to get busy with her, but she's having none of it. "I'm just dumping my bullshit all over you," she barks at Travolta after he calls her a cock tease. "Selling my act on you, using you."

"I remember watching this scene and thinking, *I've really got to get the snotty, hard-to-get thing down and put guys down more,*" recalls Lauren. "She's been ripping him a new one for the whole movie and yet he's totally obsessed with her."

"If Travolta's parents didn't treat him like a pile of dog turds, he probably wouldn't put up with her cruelty," asserts Dr. Beaverman. "The impossible approval he seeks from her is just a transfer from his childhood."

When Tony refuses to take "no means no" for an answer, Stephanie kicks him in the nuts and flees, leaving the backseat free for Donna Pescow to take on both Joey and Double J in pre-*Angie* tag-team rape. "Maybe I saw the PG version, because I don't remember this part," says Lauren disgustedly as a drugged-up Donna sobs and wails through the gang bang. "This is really awful."

"You proud of yourself, Annette?" Travolta asks Donna afterward. "Now you're a cunt."

"There's a woman named Annette on my floor at work," says Marcus. "I pass her in the hall every day and I so want to say, 'You proud of yourself, Annette? Now you're a cunt,' but I don't think she would like it."

"There's a woman named Annette on my floor at work. I pass her in the hall every day and I so want to say, 'You proud of yourself, Annette? Now you're a cunt,' but I don't think she would like it."
—Marcus

"Never know until you try," urges Ross.

"Is the 'cunt' moment in the musical?" I ask Shawn.

"We say 'slut,'" replies Shawn. "Our show is so cleaned-up compared to the movie—like, the worst word we use is 'bitch.'"

"Who gets to say it?" asks Tony. "I bet it's the guy who can't dribble. He's like, 'Throw me the ball, bitch.'"

The Pescow rape is soon eclipsed by a tragedy so tragic that it's foreshadowed in the musical by a song called "Tragedy." I'm referring, of course, to the moment Bobby C., unable to cope with his girlfriend problem and fair-weather friends, says screw it and takes the Nestea Plunge off the Brooklyn Bridge.

"Bobby ended up where he did because he was confused about what being masculine is all about," theorizes Dr. Beaverman. "He tries to be a nice guy. He's generous with his car. He tells Tony he thinks Stephanie is nice even though she insults him. He tries so hard to be accommodating, and yet he fails in the masculine sexuality department because he knocks up a girl. He gets *caught* and subsequently kills himself." Dr. B. puts her hands over her ears as Donna Pescow wails hysterically. "Although perhaps he didn't mean to," she reconsiders. "Maybe he was just going for a swim and those big white Pee-wee platforms weighed him down. It's like, 'Look out, Jimmy Hoffa, here comes Bobby C.!' "

Overcome with feelings of alienation and regret, Travolta spends the night aimlessly riding the subway in Gene Siskel's white suit while the Bee Gees' version of "How Deep Is Your Love" plays on the soundtrack.

"Kids, this is not a very good movie," decides Tony.

"I think it is," says Ross.

"I love it," I insist. "It's my favorite movie we've done."

"Because it's entertaining?" asks Tony.

"Because it seems real to me," I say. "I think the desperation in the movie is very real. I love that it was a pop-culture phenomenon and yet it didn't pander to the audience by telling us what we wanted to hear. It was brutally honest about its characters."

"It feels like someone's vision to me," remarks Ross, "even though John Badham, the director, was brought on 2½ weeks before they started shooting. Originally, John Avildsen from *Rocky* was supposed to direct, but he got fired because he wanted to make a lighter movie than Travolta and the producers wanted to make."

"I also have a soft spot for Tony Manero," I admit, "because his motivations come from this place inside him that have nothing to do with his fucked-up family or his crazy environment. He has this yearning in his heart for something better and he tries to follow it."

In the film's final scene, our shattered hero follows his heart to Stephanie's place, where he apologizes to her for his backseat impropriety. "It won't happen again, I promise you," he vows.

"No more raping," affirms Lauren.

"Look at that panty line on her," groans Tony.

"She's had it the whole movie," says Marcus.

"I know, but in a bathrobe?" Tony replies.

The movie comes to a tender, understated finish when Tony and Stephanie vow to be friends and help each other. The camera freezes on the couple embracing in Stephanie's windowsill. "I just love where they freeze it," says Dr. Beaverman, her voice a tad raspier than usual. "You will never see a movie like that anymore with such a sweet, hopeful, non-ironic ending. Today's culture doesn't embrace movies that play it straight. It's a lost moment in time."

Normally, Dr. B. would punctuate a thought like that with some kind of twisted reversal or punch line, but I'm not expecting one today. "I'm sorry I wasn't exactly a barrel of laughs this time out," she says, getting up to leave. "It's just that Dr. Beaverman is the roughly the same age as John Travolta, albeit better preserved, and so this movie represents a time when were both at our fighting weight, so to speak. I'll be my old disapproving self by next time, I promise."

"You can disapprove of my musical," offers Shawn, with a sweet, guileless smile.
"Thank you," says Dr. Beaverman. "I'm sure I will."

The following Sunday, I meet Marcus, Lauren, and Ross in front of the Shubert Theater in Century City, where, in a few minutes, Shawn's going to make his first-ever appearance as Double J, Tony Manero's loose-cannon pal whose hobbies include uppers, raping and tap dancing, in *Saturday Night Fever: The Musical.* Tony and Dr. Beaverman, who should be here any minute, are riding together because they both had classes to teach this afternoon. His is called Tumbling for Tots; hers, Penis Envy, My Ass: Articulating and Wielding the Phallus Within. If those two aren't a remake of *Freaky Friday* waiting to happen, I don't know what is.

Though reviews of *SNF: The Musical* have been less than stellar, we'll be fine if the show is half as diverting as the conversation Lauren and I strike up in the will call line with Cheryl and Shirley, two middle-aged sisters from Long Island who now live in Encino.

"I haven't been to this theater since I saw *Cats* here in the '80s," Shirley remarks, after we tell the ladies to watch for our friend, Shawn.

"I never did see *The Cats,*" says Cheryl. "Is it good?"

"Fabulous," says Shirley.

"What's it about?" wonders Cheryl.

Lauren and I share a look that says, "This should be good."

"Well, there's all these cats running around," explains Shirley, employing the kind of accent you'd hear at a Great Neck city council meeting. "One cat, in particular, is very old...and very tired...so all the other cats...put her on a giant tire...and *blow* her through the ceiling."

Maybe you have to be here to appreciate it, but Lauren and I think Shirley's capsule review of *Cats* is about the funniest thing we've ever heard. Truth is, though, she's right. That's exactly what happens in that fucking show.

"What's so funny?" Ross asks, when we return to him and Marcus with the tickets. While I do my best to re-create Shirley's spiel, Lauren writes it all down in her little notebook so she can work it into the act later.

"What's so funny?" asks Tony, rushing up with Dr. Beaverman, just as I finish my Shirley imitation. I let Lauren do the honors this time, and she does them hilariously. We're all still tittering when we take our seats inside the theater, just seconds before the lights go down.

On the drive here, I made a mental list of things to watch for based on the backstage anecdotes Shawn told us about the cast. The first thing I notice is that Jillian, the Inner Peace pizza girl, seems pissed off and not that talented.

As for the basketball boys, Shawn warned us we might die laughing, and we nearly do. Not because of Shawn, however. His three dribbles, as Double J, are perfectly convincing. Watching his buddy, Joey, bless his heart, is like seeing Liberace turn up on *The Battle of the Network Stars.*

It pains me to report that the company slut, who you'll recall plays the Fran Drescher role, is out sick tonight, so we're seeing an understudy. I like to imagine that the original Fran screwed her way right into a coma.

The big moment I've been waiting for, Shawn's end-of-act-one dance belt yank, is, as promised, scarcely visible to the naked eye, even with binoculars. What's more, he's really, truly good in the show. I knew he was a great dancer, but his talent for acting has taken me by surprise. As for the production as a whole, it doesn't live up to its gritty source material, but it makes me want to dance, and that should count for something.

A few minutes after the final curtain, we meet Shawn, in an outfit only slightly less '70s than his show duds, at the stage door and smother him with comments and compliments. After making sure I present him with the *Staying Fit!* book—Lauren was certain I wouldn't be able to part with it—everyone heads home, except me.

"Wanna see the stage?" Shawn asks.

"Totally," I say.

As we pass through the dressing room, I spot the Inner Peace pizza girl in front of her mirror rifling frantically through her dance bag. "This isn't funny, you guys," she says, clearly on the verge of tears. "OK, if I don't have my Inner Peace cards back by Phoenix, I'm going to be so mad and hurt, I won't be responsible for what happens. Seriously, you guys."

Shawn ignores her and leads me upstairs, where his buddy Carl, a.k.a. Monty the DJ, snaps a few pictures of us goofing around on the set. Look, we're on the bridge! Look, we're in the DJ booth! Look, we're at the Maneros' dinner table, but we're not eating the pasta because it's been here all week! Can you dig it? I knew that you could.

When we go back downstairs, nearly everyone is gone. Shawn starts to stuff *Staying Fit!* into his bag but can't resist giving it a quick thumb-through. While he does, I peruse the long rack of costumes, trying to decide which disco shirt is my favorite. It's a really tough call.

"Put one on," Shawn says. "I know you're dying to."

Don't think the idea hadn't occurred to me.

"I don't want to get you in trouble," I say.

"You won't," he assures me. "The costumes get dry-cleaned tomorrow, anyway. Try some pants too." Is he for real? "My shoes are 9. Will they fit you?"

"They should," I say.

I settle on an ensemble, then disappear behind the rack to try and fit into it. The second I put on my-my-my-my-my boogie shoes, the Chorus Boy I Could Have Been assumes control of my body and insists that Shawn show me a few eight-counts of disco-ography.

"You pick up fast," he says, smiling at me in the mirror, somewhere between the Shampoo and the Chicken.

"I have a good teacher," I say.

I'm about to dazzle him with a Genie-Poke-Shampoo combination when Shawn says something to me that totally shatters my concentration. "Are you as good in bed as you are on the dance floor?" he asks.

"Probably not," I say, before I have a chance to think about it. I shouldn't have said that, I think.

I try to laugh it off, but Shawn doesn't laugh. Instead he pulls a set of keys on a mini roller skate key ring from his bag and dangles them in front of his open polyester shirt. "How are you in a van?" he asks.

YOU CAN BALL ME, AL

This is not intended as an indictment of the homosexual world, but is set in one small segment of that world, which is not meant to be representative of the whole.

That's the disclaimer that appears on the screen at the outset of *Cruising*, director William Friedkin's Manhattan murder mystery set in the world of gay leather sex that ruffled all sorts of feathers when it was shot in 1979 and released in 1980. Activists, at the time, raised holy hell over the movie, arguing that it would perpetuate negative stereotypes of gay people and result in more violence directed toward them. Though I'm confident that what will transpire in my living room today won't do either of those, I'm opening with the disclaimer, because who the hell can be sure about such things?

We're off to a provocative start, that's for sure. Marcus has just showed up on my doorstep wearing a leather harness, no shirt, and threadbare 501s, carrying his cupcake-taker in one hand and what appear to be penis-shaped Rice Krispie treats dipped in fudge in the other.

"They're penis-shaped Rice Krispie treats dipped in fudge," he confirms, handing me the plate. "Get this," he says, while I pull him inside before we spook the neighbors, "my mother called when I was making them. I had butter all over my hands and I was shaping the ball sacs and I was like, 'I'm cooking, Ma, I'll talk to you tomorrow.'"

"Oh, my God, is that a harness?" says Tony, arriving a minute or so later.

"Oh, my God, is that face paint?" replies Marcus.

"I was hosting a birthday party for a bunch of 4-year-olds," Tony explains, "one of whom did a number in his pants. That number was two. Happy Birthday."

"Where'd you get the harness?" I ask Marcus, while admiring the way the leather straps lift and separate his perky pectorals.

"Wait," says Tony, before Marcus can answer. "I've got to wash this paint off my face and then I want to hear all about the harness."

By the time Tony gets cleaned up and lights his Screening Party potty candles, Lauren and Ross have arrived, along with Ross's friend from work, Perry, who it turns out is a bonafide *Cruising* aficionado. Ross figured it might be wise to invite someone over to represent what's sure to be the unpopular opinion, like having a Republican on *Politically Incorrect*.

"So my harness," Marcus starts, "I bought it at the Leather Shoppe in San Francisco..." I decide instantly that I'm going to spell "Shoppe" with two p's and an e regardless of whether that's accurate or not. "I tried on four or five, maybe," Marcus continues, giving us a little twirl, "but this was my favorite. I got it for $65, down from $100, because I flirted with the clerk and let him fit it on me in the dressing room."

"Were you naked while he did it?" Tony wonders.

"Of course not," scoffs Marcus. "I had my pants on."

"Well, you don't have to say it in that *voice,* like 'What a stupid question,'" Tony snaps back, "like it's so farfetched that I would think you were naked. You were getting a discount on a harness at fucking Marshall's Leather Dress for Less, but *I* made it dirty. Forgive the fuck out of me."

Marcus laughs off Tony's scolding, then pulls a yellow piece of paper from his back pocket. "This came free with purchase," he says, handing it to me. It's a two-sided card with the headline "The Hankie Code" that lists over 50 different colors of handkerchiefs (as well as other nonhankie items like a chamois, a HandiWipe, mosquito netting, and a Ziploc bag) and the sexual messages they send when dangling from the back right pocket or the back left. "Heaven forbid people should actually have to have a conversation to discover that they both like shrimping—whatever that is," I say, looking over the card. "Did you guys know there's a difference between a red hankie and a *dark* red hankie?"

"Red's fisting, isn't it?" says Perry. I nod affirmatively.

"You answered that really quick," Ross says to Perry. Perry just shrugs.

"What's dark red?" Lauren wants to know.

"Dark red is two-handed," I reply.

"E-e-ew!" says Lauren, burying her face in a sofa cushion. "I had to ask."

"So basically, dark red hankie stands for C-section," Tony clarifies, before taking the card from me.

"We have this video at the store where a guy makes it with a fire extinguisher," says Ross. "A fire extinguisher! I always wondered what would happen if there was a fire and they actually needed it."

"Mustard worn on the left means eight inches or more," says Tony, reading from the card. "Orange means anything, anytime, anywhere."

"How can you tell in a dark club if it's mustard or regular yellow?" Lauren wonders.

"Or an unlit park, say?" I add.

"You got me," says Tony. "I'm just glad they don't get into the J. Crew colors. It's like, 'Is that ecru or bone?' 'Look, just stick your leg up my ass, that's the bottom line.'"

Just then, Dr. Beaverman bursts in, in the throes of a kind of Conniption no hankie could begin to describe. "Can I complain about something before we get into this?" she says, fuming. "How *desperate* and/or poor or greedy is Anne Murray? How many infomercials must she *have* to hawk her wares? Is she trying to pay off a lawsuit from some gym teacher who's threatening to go public or what? Because every time I turn on the television—winter, spring, summer, or fall—she's got a new collection of cover songs. And everything is in the key of Bea Arthur. She can't even hit the high notes in 'Snowbird' anymore. It's *terrible,* Dennis. *I am sick of her ass!*" Tony hands Dr. Beaverman a manhattan, in honor of the city that never stops *Cruising,* then leads her to her usual spot on the couch. She takes her first swig, then lets out a long guttural sigh. "Thank you," she says. "I feel much better now."

"OK, who's seen this movie?" I ask. Marcus, Perry, and Dr. Beaverman raise their hands. Actually, Dr. Beaverman raises her glass. "So we're not going to have any Fun Facts from you today?" I ask Ross.

"Perry's my Fun Fact for today," Ross says, patting his tank-topped colleague on the shoulder. "Show 'em your thing, Perry."

"That was quick," says Dr. Beaverman. "I don't even have a buzz on yet."

"I brought something from my personal collection," says Perry, digging in the pocket of his leather jacket. What could Perry's thing be, I wonder? Handcuffs? Poppers? A Ronco Hanky Be-dazzler for that extra special touch? No, it looks like some kind of printed matter. "There's a whole section in here called 'The Men of Cruising,'" Perry says, handing me an old copy of the gay jack-off rag *Mandate.* "The editor of *Mandate* went undercover as an extra and he interviewed other gay extras and wrote all about what it was like on the set and how they felt about being there."

I open Perry's cherished magazine, then read aloud, the first quote that catches my eye, from Clif Coleman, a 21-year-old artist and *Cruising* extra: *"I have never experienced such hatred in the air,"* he says of the hostility between the protesters who wanted to shut down the movie and the gays who thought Friedkin should be allowed to make it. *"It's so tense you could cut it with a knife. My lover wants us to move to Iowa."*

"Speaking of knives," says Lauren. "Can we cut the penises now, Marcus?" She doesn't even wait for an answer before disappearing into the kitchen for a knife. While she slices and serves, I read more quotes from the leather-clad, bushy-mustached *Men of Cruising*. *"There's so much hypocrisy,"* carped Gene Ford, 30, another extra who worked as a pastry chef by day. *"I saw one gay restaurant owner protesting* Cruising, *yet he served orange juice in this restaurant all through the Anita Bryant controversy."*

For John Edward Burke, an actor-director, it was a First Amendment issue first. *"I know the movie can be interpreted as exploitative, but once you censor one word in a book or movie, you're in trouble,"* he asserted. *"I'm appalled that the gays in this city don't understand the larger implications. After* Looking for Mr. Goodbar, *straight psychopaths did not start killing the Diane Keatons of this world in singles bars.* Cruising *is an effect, not a cause."*

"The whole gay movement is about freedom of expression," echoed Steven Dasaro, 31, a painter. *"Isn't the image of gays this movie depicts better than suggesting that all homosexuals are nelly faggots? When I protested on Gay Liberation Day back in June, the TV cameras were always on the queens. On the set of* Cruising, *there were* men."

In his thoughtful first-person article, John Devere, the undercover *Mandate* editor, reiterated that the extras *"were not empty-headed partygoers unaware of the issues. One recurrent observation was that the men who frequent the world being depicted were* in *the movie and did* not *object to their world being depicted. Middle-of-the-road gays, they thought, were the ones who didn't want the leather fringe seen by middle America, even though the world certainly exists. Many felt that the protests were as much a protest against the leather world itself as they are against Friedkin's film."* He went on to report that the background actors provided their own clothes and accessories and that *"Friedkin repeatedly urged the background actors not to wear, say, or do anything they would not ordinarily do in a bar situation."*

That included knocking back a few real drinks, sniffing real poppers and doing other things for real as well. *"Some people were having real sex, but Friedkin didn't ask anybody to,"* said Kurt Bieber, a *Cruising* extra professional actor and who also worked on *Can't Stop the Music* and *Dressed to Kill,* lucky bastard. *"No way would I suck cock in front of a camera. But I think I am in the film kissing a guy."*

"OK, *now* I'm dying to watch this movie," I declare, closing the magazine.

"I saw *Cruising* when it came out," says Dr. Beaverman, "but I don't remember anything about the story. All I remember is like a quarter of the audience walked out and it was all men who left. You would hear these straight guys going 'Ugh!' and then see them storm out. I remember thinking, 'How easy is it for a straight man to watch an incredibly graphic scene of a woman being raped?' Nobody walks out of *The Accused.* But these guys see another guy simulating a blow job with a jacket covering his face and they can't stay in the theater. They thought they would turn gay if they just sat there for one more second."

"They just might have, if my experience is any indication," says Marcus. "I was in high school, senior year, and there were six of us, all guys, who were going to the movies."

"This one always has a story," Ross says to Perry.

Cue the St. Olaf theme music.

"Three of the guys refused to see *Cruising,"* Marcus starts, directing his story to Perry, the one with the fresh attention span and endless eyelashes, "and they saw some John Ritter movie where he played a superhero."

"Hero at Large," says Ross.

"Me and the two other guys went to see *Cruising,"* says Marcus, taking three Tootsie Rolls from the dish on the table and placing them on top of the *Cruising* video box. "And eventually all three of us came out of the closet. David came out first, then left the group because he thought we wouldn't understand him," Marcus continues, while taking one of the Tootsie Rolls and placing it at the corner of the coffee table, all alone, "and given how immature we were, he was probably right. Matt came out a few years later, struggled with it, then looked up David in the New York phone book." Marcus moves another Tootsie Roll from the video box to the corner. "Then David invited Matt to group therapy, where Matt met his boyfriend, Ed," he says, adding a happy new

Tootsie Roll to the pair in the corner. "And now they've been together 10 years. Then, once I saw Ed and Matt together," he says, picking up the Tootsie Roll from the video box that represents himself and reuniting it with the others, "I saw how normal it was to be gay and then I came out."

"And then I bought a harness," concludes Ross.

"And then I bought a harness," says Marcus, placing the original trio of Tootsie Rolls as well as the new boyfriend Tootsie Roll on top of Perry's *Mandate*. "So *Cruising* made all three of us gay," he concludes, doing a little dance with two of the rolls. "At the time, though, it scared the shit out of me. I didn't sleep for three nights thinking, *If I do that stuff, I'm going to get hacked to bits. If Al Pacino can go down the stony end, I can go down the stony end.*"

"Do you mind if I eat one of your friends?" says Lauren, reaching for a Tootsie Roll.

"Eat Matt," says Marcus. "He owes me a phone call. Besides, David died of AIDS in 1993." With that, I take the David Tootsie Roll and place it in the buff arms of the Joey Lawrence doll that looks down over the room from the top shelf of the entertainment center. It's the closest my condo comes to having a heaven.

"I participated in a protest against *Cruising,*" reveals Perry, "in Cincinnati, no less. I was in high school, and I was obsessed with this guy who went to the University of Cincinnati, who was very political. We had previously protested some movie with Talia Shire where there were lesbians or rape scenes or something."

"*Windows,* I bet," interjects Ross, as though he's trying to win Ben Stein's money.

"That sounds right," says Perry. "I never knew anything about what we were protesting. I just went along because I was in lo-o-ove."

"What did you do," I ask, "yell at all the suburban people?"

"Suburban people didn't go to *Cruising,*" scoffs Perry. "It was just the other three fags in Ohio. We didn't yell, though. Mainly, we were just having a presence there and I think we had fliers that said, like, 'If you don't want your cock cut off, stop *Cruising*.'"

"Well, since you put it that way," says Ross.

"Listen to this, you guys," says Tony, holding up the *Cruising* box. "The very first line of the synopsis is, 'A cop goes undercover to *ferret out* a killer.' Am I the only one that raises an eyebrow at that? Dennis, you're a writer, how often do you use the expression *ferret out*?"

"Only when I'm writing about *Cruising,*" I admit.

"Thank you," says Tony, grabbing the remote and pressing play. "That's all I'm saying."

Before we get to the see any hankie panky, the disclaimer I mentioned earlier appears on the screen.

"Does anyone know who John Rechy is?" asks Perry asks us.

"He's a gay writer, right?" I say.

"Yes," says Perry. "His earlier novels are set in the same sort of world as this movie. From what I understand, Friedkin showed Rechy a cut of the movie a few days before it opened and Rechy was the one who suggested the disclaimer."

Finally, the film opens, *Blue Velvet*–style, with an unsuspecting civilian happening upon an errant body part. In this case it's some man in a boat discovering a dead gay arm off the port bow. "They know it's gay because it's floating in the water with a limp wrist," says Tony, before demonstrating.

After a scene in which two asshole cops harass two leather drag queen hookers who look like they're on their way to a Sexy-Sandy-at-the-end-of-*Grease* look-alike contest, we make our first visit to a gay leather bar. It's the Cockpit, located, appropriately enough, in Manhattan's meatpacking district. We're led into the "private club" by a mysterious long-haired fellow wearing a biker jacket and aviator glasses.

"There's more jockstraps in this movie than in *Rudy,*" marvels Ross, as director Friedkin (who also adapted the screenplay from the 1970 novel by Gerald Walker) serves up several long tracking shots of the Cockpit's colorful clientele, most of whom are either having sex, dancing, or having sex while dancing. Though I'm tempted to just watch the horndog extras, I figure I should try to follow the plot, which seems to involve a conversation between a supersexy, muscle-bound, jumpsuit-clad bar goer and the man in glasses we followed inside who we've come to realize is the killer. We know this because he speaks in an oddly disembodied and creepy baritone that was clearly provided in a looping studio. "He's very, 'Do you like scary movies, Sydney?'" says Tony in his best *Scream* voice.

The two men head to the low-rent St. James Hotel together where Supersexy Guy, now wearing just a jockstrap, saunters over to *Scream* Voice Guy and kisses him. He then rubs his hands down his trick's leather jacket and unzips his fly. "I bet the Foley artists on this movie went *insane,*" I say. "Banging a rutabaga against a leather jacket for weeks on end can really take it out of you."

The pair fall into bed together, and it looks like it's just going to be another night of hot sweaty man-ramming. That is, until *Scream* Voice Guy whips out a knife and holds it up to Supersexy Guy's throat as though he were trying to get himself kicked out of the *Big Brother* house.

"Um, did we choose a safeword yet?" stammers Marcus.

"It's William Friedkin, so this is probably going to be really graphic," cautions Ross, referring to the man behind such hard-hitting films as *The Exorcist, The French Connection,* and *The Boys in the Band.*

Ross's words of warning come a bit too late, as *Scream* Voice Guy has already set about doing his business, hacking away at Supersexy Guy like the host of a Ginsu infomercial.

"There are frames of actual gay porn edited into this sequence," Perry informs us. "Go back, Dennis, and do a frame-by-frame."

Though this is not the kind of scene I particularly want to linger on, I follow Perry's instructions. Sure enough, there's clearly a shot of man ass being penetrated.

"Oh, my God!" gasps half the room.

"I cannot believe that," says the none-too-easily shocked Tony. "This calls for another slice of chocolate-covered cock."

"Friedkin allegedly put subliminal frames in *The Exorcist* too," says Perry.

"Oh, wait, I do have a Fun Fact," says Ross excitedly, "William Friedkin is the youngest person to ever win an Oscar for directing. He won for *The French Connection* when he was 32."

"Yes, but could he host a face-painting birthday party?" says Tony, his mouth full of Rice Krispie treat. "I think not."

The next scene takes us to the morgue, where a coroner tells Paul Sorvino as Detective Edelson, over the din of a distant bone saw, that the killer's semen had no sperm in it. This new wrinkle in the case causes both Lauren and Marcus to simultaneously suggest that a certain male box office star with no known biological offspring might be our killer, but I refuse to include the actor's name here out of fear of lawsuits.

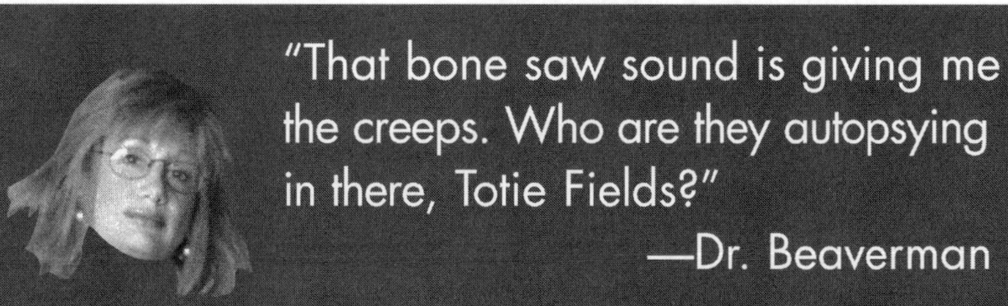

"That bone saw sound is giving me the creeps," Dr. Beaverman gripes as the saw grinds on and on and on. "Who are they autopsying in there, Totie Fields?"

After a scene at a Manhattan police station in which one of the transvestite hookers from earlier gripes to Sorvino about the abusive cops, we're finally introduced to our protagonist, newbie New York cop Steve Burns, played with body-waved ambiguity by Michael Corleone himself, Al Pacino.

"Does anyone here think Pacino is hot?" Tony wants to know.

"Not me," says Lauren. "He looks like Peter Brady with that perm."

"I was going to say Lily Tomlin," says Dr. Beaverman. "For me, the height of Pacino's hotness was *Bobby Deerfield*."

I turn to Perry, who gives me the so-so hand signal while Marcus and Ross shake simultaneously no, as if their heads are connected by a strand of fishing wire. That leaves me. "I kind of think he *is* hot," I admit. When everyone erupts in gross-out noises, I backpedal a bit. "But I'm going to hold out for the tank top before I give my final answer."

Back on the screen, Al is about to have his dull but manageable heterosexual world rocked when Sorvino calls him in for a private conference. "Did you ever have your cock sucked by a man?" Sorvino asks him. "Ever been porked or have a man smoke your pole?"

"Just that one time by Jimmy Caan on *The Godfather*," says Marcus, "but we were in love."

Sorvino then asks Al if he'd like to "disappear" into the leather gay netherworld and ferret out the guy who's killing all the homos. "Nobody can know what you're doing," Sorvino emphasizes. "Whaddaya say?"

Al pretends to think about it a bit before saying yes yes yes. Actually what he says is even more telling than yes yes yes. "I love it," says Al.

"It is Dr. Beaverman's opinion that there's no way in hell that a straight policeman is going to take this assignment in a million years for a million dollars unless he has some kind of tendency toward homosexuality already," asserts Dr. Beaverman.

"Al's character was actually based on a real guy," says Perry, "His name is Randy Jurgensen, and he was a consultant for Friedkin on *The French Connection*, and he plays a detective in this movie. There was a rash of killings similar to the ones in this movie that took place in New York City the '60s and '70s, and Jurgensen went undercover to ferret out the killers. I don't think he ever caught them, though."

"I just think Al's got to be a little bit willing to have his 'pole smoked,' as Paul Sorvino so delicately phrased it," says Dr. Beaverman, continuing with her thought. "I mean, he doesn't even go home and sleep on it."

He does, however, go home and sleep on Karen Allen, who plays his dishwater-dull girlfriend, Nancy. "Al must be thinking, *Please send me out with a decent bang, you dried-up hag,*" I say, as Al and Karen cuddle in bed together the night before Al's descent into the land of man milk and honey.

"Please," scoffs Ross. "He's probably already taping pictures of Shaun Cassidy to her back."

Though Karen peppers Al with questions about his top secret assignment, all he can tell her is that if it goes well, he'll be promoted to detective.

"*I can't say anything else about it,*" says Tony as Al, "*but can you shave the crack of my ass? I'm going to bend over and you do what you need to do. I swear, it's work-related.*"

The next day Al embarks on his trip to Gayberry RFD. He's not going it alone, however; he's brought along a few carefully chosen props, like worn jeans and a leather jacket, which he unpacks from a black suitcase. "I want to get a suitcase like that and start all over," I confess. "I've been doing the gay thing *all wrong*."

"One night of nooky in a '70s van and suddenly you're a man-whore," chides Tony.

"There should be a scene where, like, Q gives him his special gay gadgets," suggests Marcus.

"*This is the* Funny Girl *original cast album,*" says Ross in his plummiest British accent. "*Please return it intact, 007. And I expect those anal beads to be returned sterilized and still on the string.*"

While organizing his closet, Pacino discovers that his new apartment is so gay that he'll have to rid it of all-male porn rags straight away if he ever wants to get some decent shut-eye. "It kills me that he's throwing away that perfectly good '70s porn," I lament as Al hauls his stack of *Honcho*s and *Mandate*s out to the trash can in the stairwell.

"I'm with you, Dennis," says Perry. "How 'bout we split 'em?"

While in the hallway, Al meets his affable neighbor Ted Bailey (Don Scardino), an aspiring playwright whose dancer boyfriend is out of town doing a new musical.

"I like the way Al's leaning against the wall," muses Lauren, as the two men chat each other up. "It's like he's already trying out moves."

"It's a very saucy lean," agrees Ross.

The neighbors hit it off instantly and are soon dashing out together for a bite to eat. "Look at the way they come out of the front door like, 'We're new friends now!'" observes Tony. "It's so shmiel-shmazel."

Over breakfast, Al lies and tells Ted he's a recent art-school dropout looking for work. "That's not what I would have said," says Tony. "I would have been like, 'Yeah, I'm a Frankie Valli impersonator. Uh-huh, out of work.'"

"Boys, you would know better than I, but aren't there a lot of carbohydrates on that table for supposedly gay people?" Dr. Beaverman says as Ted and Al dig into their greasy diner food. "Where were the lo-cal scrambled, egg-whites-only, broiled-chicken, no-cheese omelets? I'm thinking there was no gay consultant on this film."

"Speaking of food," says Lauren. "I noticed somebody's little cupcake-taker in the kitchen. Are we getting another treat?"

"Oh, I nearly forgot," Marcus says, jumping up and running into the kitchen. When he returns, he sets his trusty cupcake-taker on the coffee table, then pauses the movie. "I give you…my *Cruising* Cream-Filled Butt Cakes!" he proclaims, before unveiling a collection of circular yellow cakes with white cream oozing from their centers. "You bake them like normal cupcakes," he explains, gesturing like Vanna, "then a minute before they're ready, you split the tops and shoot the holes full of vanilla frosting."

"Hoo-*hah*!" bellows Tony as though he's channeling Al Pacino's cranky, blind Army colonel from *Scent of a Woman*.

Tony's hoo-*hah* gets the biggest laugh of the party so far. So it's no surprise when, a moment later my roommate announces a plan to issue more hoo-*hahs* throughout the afternoon as the spirit moves him. "But they won't all be happy hoo-*hahs* like that one," he advises us. "Some might be sad hoo-*hahs* or frightened hoo-*hahs*."

Guess I'd better unpack my adjectives.

When we restart the movie, Ted's in between burger bites and confessing to his new friend Al that he's "scared to death of cruising." It's at this point that I admit to my guests that I'm a little foggy on the actual definition of cruising. "The movie acts like it's something you're either doing or not doing, like flashing or streaking," I say, "like you have to shift into this strange, hyperhorny state of consciousness."

"In my neighborhood, cruising is just walking," says Marcus. "At any moment it could happen."

"Suddenly you are *cruised*," says Perry ominously.

Soon Ted brings up the recent rash of gay killings, and I'm surprised Al's ears don't literally perk up like a dog's. "This is so *I Know Who You Butt-Fucked Last Summer,*" carps Tony. "Oh, you're new in town? Let me tell you the legend of the *gay killer.*"

When night comes, Al takes his act to the streets, skulking past a crowded row of Village hotspots. "Notice the names of these bars," instructs Dr. Beaverman. "The Ramrod, the Iron Horse. It's all about that erection with men, whether they're gay or straight."

Al's introduction to the world of rough trade continues when he pops into a leather shoppe where the proprietor, played by Powers Boothe, gives him a crash course in Hankie Appreciation. "A light blue hankie in your left back pocket means you want a blow job," explains Powers. "Right pocket means you give one…"

"One over your face means you rob banks in the Old West," says Marcus.

"One on your head means you're Isaac Mizrahi," says Lauren.

"The handkerchief semiotics have Dr. Beaverman quite baffled," gripes Dr. Beaverman. "Who knew such a coding existed? I feel like I need a paint chart here."

"Where's my little card?" asks Marcus.

"I think it's under the Butt Cakes," I say.

Lauren lifts up the cakes, retrieves the Hankie Code card, and passes it to Dr. Beaverman. "This is astounding," says Dr. Beaverman while looking over the card. "I mean, what if you're a Gene Anthony Ray and you just need a do rag for dance rehearsal? You can't just choose any old do rag. You put the wrong color on your head and suddenly Debbie Allen's peeing on you."

"The handkerchief semiotics have Dr. Beaverman quite baffled. Who knew such a coding existed? I feel like I need a paint chart here." —Dr. Beaverman

Now that Powers has broken the code for him, Al's ready to go where the boys are. And where better to do that than the Wolf's Den, another West Village watering hole and sex parlor. "Dr. Beaverman, unbelievably, has never been in a gay bar," reveals Dr. Beaverman, as Al makes his way through the roomful of libidinous leathermen. "Are these guys supposed to be in shape?"

"Seriously, you've never been?" says Tony.

"I know," Dr. Beaverman says with a shrug. "It doesn't track."

"We'll have to rectify that," vows Marcus.

"My point is, there's a lot of jiggling cellulite going on, more than I thought there'd be," says Dr. Beaverman, "and I'm feeling much better about myself as a result."

"I'm so surprised at how graphic this is," I admit. "This is back when R really meant something."

"Actually, there was a big controversy with the ratings board on this movie," says Perry. "Friedkin submitted the film six or seven times, and each time the board gave it an X rating. The last time, they gave Friedkin a list of three changes to make that would allow them to give it an R. Friedkin agreed to make the cuts, but when the film was released, some members of the board claimed that Friedkin never made the cuts he said he would."

"So this is like an X-rated episode of *Columbo,* basically?" clarifies Ross.

"Yes," says Perry, "though I can't imagine Peter Falk doing poppers in a pair of chaps. Angela Lansbury, maybe."

"Next week on *Murder, She Felched,*" says Tony.

Al takes a position against a back wall and tries to be blasé, even though just about everyone around him seems to be involved in some act of sodomy. "There's a tiny part of me," I hedge, "that watching this thinks, *I want to visit that land of big crazy mustaches but just not get murdered.*"

"E-e-ew," moans Tony.

"Tony, I have a dark side," I whine.

"I'm with you, Dennis," says Perry charitably. "I could do without the homicide part, but everything else is worth a look-see."

"This movie is totally wrong," I reiterate as one creepy guy after another gives Al the evil eye, "but you have to admit it's got nerve. It would never get made today."

"That's what I love about it," says Perry. "I'd take it over *The Broken Hearts Club* any day."

When a sex pig in a light-up belt spots Al's yellow hankie, he saunters over, assuming it's just a matter of minutes before he's peeing all over our hero, but Al tells him he just likes to watch. This goes over about as well as live singing at a Paula Abdul concert. "If you like to watch," the guy barks, "take that hankie out of your pocket, asshole!"

"Al looks like he's going to cry," observes Ross.

"Hoo-hah," Tony says sadly.

When the next scene finds Al screaming out "Yes! Yes!" while pumping iron in his apartment, none of us are the least bit surprised. "This is right on the money," I assert. "He's gotta work out now because he's not enough the way he is."

"One night at the Wolf's Den and he's already body dysmorphic," adds Tony, nodding.

After doing a little more half-assed cruising, Al rendezvous with Paul Sorvino in a pool hall. As our hero, dressed in a baggy and unflattering brown shirt and matching pants, updates Paul on the investigation, I can't help suspect that Al secretly misses his gay clothes.

"He's looking at Paul Sorvino like, 'Wow, straight people really are boring and less attractive,'" Lauren says.

"I want Paul to be like, 'Hey, one of the balls is missing!'" says Ross.

"Hoo-hah!" groans Tony as if he has a pool ball wedged in his ass.

Before hitting the Hershey highway, Al has one more thing to tell his boss: "You dropped your chalk."

"Oh, that old saw," groans Dr. Beaverman.

From the pool hall, we cut to a scene featuring a huge gaggle of men glaring at each other and drooling. But we're not back at the Ramrod or the Cockpit or the Wolf's Den, we're in the Rambles section of that most revered of tourist attractions, Central Park.

"Park cruisers don't gather in huge packs like that, do they?" I wonder, as the massive throng scope each other out. "It looks like the sidewalk in front of a Poppers Anonymous meeting."

"There should be one of those dispensers at the corner where you can take a number," says Marcus. "Now servicing 78."

"I just think this world is overpopulated," I continue. "There's just so many people everywhere."

"There were," says Perry.

"They all died," says Marcus.

It's here in the park that our deep-voiced killer picks up his next victim, a wavy-haired stud with a sexy Roman nose who, like the killer himself, also has an oddly disembodied voice. As they walk together into the park, I half expect one of them to turn into the Thriller. "This was where the Foley artists were really starting to go, 'Oh, Christ,'" I mutter, as the sounds of boot steps, crickets, and jangling leather jackets compete for space on the soundtrack.

"Maybe the Foley people really got into it," counters Tony, "like, 'Mr. Friedkin, I put a few squirrel sounds in with that rim job. Hope you don't mind. I was feeling artsy.'"

After taunting his trick with some nursery-rhyme-sounding chant, our killer stabs Roman Nose Guy in the back before they even have time to blow each other. Meanwhile, in another corner of Gotham, Al vigorously gives it to Karen Allen while sporting his new studded leather bracelet. "Pacino only enjoys sex with Karen Allen when he's got this other thing going on," grumbles Dr. Beaverman. "It's just like a man. Men can never just have straightforward sex. They have to have a little touch of perversity." When Perry raises a quizzical eyebrow, Dr. Beaverman clarifies her remark. "By that I mean perversity in terms of the straight world," she emphasizes. "I'm not saying there's anything perverse about gay sex."

"You've obviously never had any," says Marcus.

The next morning, over coffee, Karen tries to engage Al in conversation. Unfortunately, I can't tell you what they talk about because I'm preoccupied with what I imagine must be going through Al's head right now. "I want him to look around the room and go, 'I hate our drapes,'" I say.

"I want her to catch him in the shower rubbing steel wool on the crotch of his jeans," says Marcus.

"I read somewhere that the script was so top secret that Friedkin only gave Karen Allen the scenes she was in," remarks Perry. "Could you imagine what she must have thought when she saw the finished movie?"

"She was like, *I thought Al was going undercover at the circus, but I couldn't figure out how the Crisco fit in,*" I suggest. "*This leather netherworld makes so much more sense.*"

After more shmiel-shmazel luncheonette bonding with neighbor Ted, Al returns to the Cockpit just in time for Precinct Night, a theme evening where all the patrons dress like extras from *S.W.A.T.* Needless to say, our undercover brother is the only one who didn't get the memo. "You've got the wrong attitude," the bare-chested bouncer tells Al. "I'm afraid I'm going to have to ask you to leave."

"*Hoo*-hah," Tony says indignantly.

As Al makes his way to the exit, I have a point to reiterate. "I think the extras are over the top in terms of their horniness. Wouldn't some of them be enjoying a beer between partners? This is like all-skate, all the time."

"And this is before Viagra," Marcus reminds us.

Dejected, Al climbs the stairs to the exit. He's followed outside by an adorable pouty-lipped young Latin cutie who reminds me of Jesse from the *Fame* TV series. "If that bulge in your pants ain't a knife," the cutie says to Al, "why don't we take a walk?"

"Say yes, Al," I plead.

"Say yes, Al," everyone else echoes.

"*Dear Diary,*" says Lauren breathlessly. "*He walked right up to me on the sidewalk. He was so cute and then, Diary, he asked me! He asked me to take a walk with him. Oh, Diary, I almost fainted!*"

When Al refuses Pouty's proposition with a curt, "Not tonight," Tony has no choice but to let out a self-loathing "Hoo-hah!"

Later, Al wrestles with his desires and inhibitions while Karen services him. Meanwhile, our killer continues his murderous ways across town. His next victim is a bearded boutique owner he hooks up with in an adult bookstore. "What is it with the hard rock music everywhere?" wonders Lauren, as the killer and boutique owner disappear into a booth together. "Is that what the gays were listening to?"

"They wanted to attract the frat audience," figures Ross.

Soon the knife comes out and blood is flying everywhere. Some drops even splatter the unsuspecting porn stars on the screen. As the killer inserts another coin into the peep-show slot and takes off, the talk in my living room turns to the virtues of old-school '70s porn versus today's shit, and soon Marcus is begging Tony to do his time-honored Falcon Videopac announcer impression. "At the end of this one brand of gay porn videos, they have trailers for other movies," I explain, trying to get the heterosexuals in the room up to speed. "Well, the voice-over guy tries to sound ultra-ultra-butch, but his s's give him away. Tony has him down pat."

"Do it, do it, do it," says Lauren, clapping her hands eagerly.

Thrilled to be performing something besides "Itsy Bitsy Spider" to toddlers in party hats, Tony hits the pause button, clears his throat, and starts in. "*Falcon Videopac 23,*" he hisses. "*DenniS and Tony have Some friendS over to watch a movie. Pretty Soon, the clotheS come off and the room explodeS in a torrent of heavy-duty fuck and Suck action. Then muScle Stud MarcuS jackS off in his hand and offerS it to Dr. Beverly Beaverman as a Symbol of his love in* A Gift I Made Myself."

"Seriously, there's a movie called *A Gift I Made Myself*?" wonders Lauren between guffaws.

Tony nods. "Can I just say that my birthday's coming up next month," stresses Ross, "and I'd prefer it if you got me something from a store or nothing at all. Thank you."

When we stop tittering and unpause the movie, Al's making another Cockpit stop, this time in a body-conscious black tank top. "He's in the tank top and I'm still in," I admit. "I still think he's sort of hot."

"You're on your own, Dennis," says Perry.

"Wait, is that a sling in the background?" asks Tony, sitting up straight.

"Oh, yes," says Perry.

"Rewind," says Dr. Beaverman. "Dr. Beaverman doesn't see the sling."

I rewind to a long shot, and there, clear as the nose on Al's face, is a wooden frame with chains hanging from it. A handful of men are gathered around it as a leather-chapped man reclines in the sling and awaits his fate. When Dr. Beaverman claims she's still a bit lost, Marcus crawls to the television and points to the screen like a weatherman in a harness. "This black leather part is one leg," he explains, before moving his finger across the screen, "and this is the other leg." Not content to let it go at that, he adds, "and we've got a cold front moving down from Minneapolis to the crack of his ass, but the weekend should be sunny."

"That guy looks like Bruno Kirby," says Lauren when we finally get a good look at the fister.

"In a role that will surprise you," adds Ross.

"I have to say," I start, "that most of the time when straight people make movies with same-sex contact, you get the feeling that they got exactly the footage they needed and no more. Like that big kiss between Tom Selleck and Kevin Kline in *In & Out,* I bet they did it once and then broke for the day so that everyone could take a bath. This movie, on the other hand, is *going to town.*"

"Yeah, but the big movie star's not taking part," says Dr. Beaverman. "That's an important distinction."

"And they're going to town with the wiggiest ass stuff they can find," grumbles Ross. "The way Friedkin shot that fisting scene makes it look like those guys are torturing him."

"Rent *Falcon Videopac 37,*" says Marcus. "Same basic vibe."

"They're not showing kissing or anything romantic or sensual," continues Ross. "Everyone's just standing there grimly."

"They can't film a fisting scene and have everyone be all 'Woo-hoo' about it," argues Lauren. "Even *I* know that."

"My point is," I say, "if you were going to shoot this script—not that that's a good idea necessarily—Friedkin really shot the hell out of it."

"But the guys don't even talk to each other," says Ross. "I haven't seen anybody smile. Everybody's just glowering at each other."

"Just another night at Rage," says Marcus.

"Remember, kids, it's a netherworld," says Dr. Beaverman, "a leather netherworld, at that. Romance is anathema."

Getting one's groove on, however, is not, and that's really good news for fans of Bad Movie Star Dancing like me. I can hardly contain my euphoria when a swarthy, sweat-covered superstud approaches Pacino and says, "Hey baby, what's happening? Wanna dance?"

"Say yes, Al," we all say.

And then he does.

"Wait, I just had a VH1 Flashback," Ross announces, as Al nervously follows his paramour out onto the floor and starts boogying. "I was in a club once and they were projecting a loop on the wall of like three seconds of Al Pacino dancing. It would just play over and over. And it liberated me, in a way. I felt like nothing I could ever do on the dance floor would be as insane as Al. It was like the nuttiest thing I'd ever seen."

And it still is.

"Oh, my God!" shrieks Lauren as though she were watching Kate Winslet eat her own placenta.

"He's going to blow his cover," frets Marcus as Al alternates between Streisand's chicken dance, some hankie sniffing, and few moves obviously inspired by the novelty single "Kung Fu Fighting." "Everyone's going to be like 'Cop!' "

"Even the guy getting fisted is like, 'Damn, that guy can't dance,' " I say.

"Of course, he's only able to say that because the guy standing up goes like this," says

It's here that *Cruising* goes to Bad Movie Valhalla, when one of the detectives, unable to get a confession from Pouty, opens the interrogation room door Mystery Date–style to reveal a Shaq-sized black man wearing only a cowboy hat and a brown jockstrap.

Tony, holding up his hand as if he's a ventriloquist operating a dummy. "Bruno's like, *'Say hello, to the nice people.' 'Hello, nice people.'* "

"Now say good night, Fisty," says Ross, getting into the act.

"Good night, Fisty," we all say.

After a scene in which Sorvino and Al talk murder weapons, Al finally goes home with his prime suspect, the pouty-lipped young Latin pup who wanted to go for a walk with him earlier.

"Hoo-*hah,*" says Tony breathlessly.

Weird Al and Pouty Lips go to sleazy hotel room where a wired-for-sound Al gets Pouty to tie him up. Before they can get seriously busy, however, Al's plainclothes cop cronies bust in and spoil the fun. "This is based on something that really happened to

Randy Jurgensen," says Perry. "He was wearing a bug like that, and they lost transmission so the cops broke in and found him half naked with a guy who ended up not being the murderer."

The cops take Al and Pouty down to the police station for questioning. It's here that *Cruising* goes to Bad Movie Valhalla, when one of the detectives, unable to get a confession from Pouty, opens the interrogation room door Mystery Date–style to reveal a Shaq-size black man wearing only a cowboy hat and a brown jockstrap. Without saying a word, the man marches in, slaps Al right off his chair and leaves. "What was that?" Al shouts. "What did he hit me for?"

Good fucking question.

"What the *fuck*?" says Ross, speaking for everyone.

"This must come under the orange hankie," figures Lauren. "Anything, anytime, anywhere."

"*Excuse me, Jennifer,*" says Tony as if he were speaking into an intercom. "*Can you send out the giant black man in the cowboy hat and jockstrap, please? And hold my calls.*"

"That was completely, completely surreal," says Dr. Beaverman.

"And worth another look," I say, before grabbing the remote and rewinding.

"This scene actually got laughs in movie theaters," says Perry, as we watch the scene again.

"Knock me over with a feather," says Dr. Beaverman.

"So did the scene where Al dances," Perry adds, "and the moment at the end where he says, 'Hips or lips.'"

"Hips or lips?" I echo, my curiosity clearly piqued.

"You'll see," promises Perry.

"Maybe this is meant to be like Friedkin's version of a gay porn movie," offers Tony, when the giant black man returns to slap the shit out of Pouty. "In gay porn, when you go to the police station, you get laid."

"Did I ever tell you guys about when I saw that Jeff Stryker prison play *Hard Time*?" says Marcus, who never met a tangent he couldn't go off on. "Well, at one point Jeff comes out in the audience and slaps his dick around in your face. I had to get my whole outfit dry-cleaned because he was all oiled up. I was so livid I almost sent him a bill."

"I got that beat," says Tony. "It was at an APLA benefit in 1990. I was the volunteer in charge of getting the stars to the green room and I was assigned Jeff Stryker. So we were going to the stage, and I said, 'I have to pee,' and he said, 'Me too,' which is like every non–porn star's nightmare, that someday you're going to have to pee standing next to Jeff Stryker."

"Oh, I get it," says Dr. Beaverman. "This Mr. Stryker is well-endowed."

"Totally," says Tony. "So we're both peeing and we finish and I zip up, and I swear to God, he goes, 'You wanna see it?' His subtext was so like, *As long as it's out, I might as well give the kid a thrill.*"

"What did you say?" asks Lauren.

"I was like, 'Uh, no,'" says Tony.

"No?!" Marcus, Perry, and I shout simultaneously.

"I was caught unawares," says Tony, defensively. "I was like 20 and totally freaked out. Besides, we were running late."

"How long does it take to look at a penis?" asks Lauren.

"You'd be surprised," says Marcus.

We turn our attention back to the screen in time to learn, from one of the detectives, that Pouty Lips can't be the killer because his semen has swimmers. "I think that's Randy Jurgensen, the guy this was based on," says Perry, pointing to the most bushily mustached of the group of investigators. "I remember reading this article about him in which he said he was walking down Christopher Street one night in full leather, with a star painted over one eye, arm in arm with a couple of gay guys, and his girlfriend's brother drove by and recognized him."

"What happened?" I ask.

"Well, he couldn't blow his cover, so they ended up breaking up," says Perry.

"Boy, you really have good Fun Facts," says Lauren. "No offense, Ross."

The news about Pouty's grade A sperm means Al's back to square one. To make matters worse, when he turns to Karen Allen for comfort, she calls him on the fact that there hasn't been any hoo-*hah* in their relationship in ages. "Is it me?" she asks him. "Are you turned off to me?"

"No, you're just boyish enough to keep my interest," says Ross.

"Like she's the litmus test now?" carps Lauren.

"I want Al to be like, *Honey, do you think it looks dumb when I dance with my arms up, because Pouty says it does but I don't think it does,"* I say.

"What I'm doing is affecting me," Al says instead, before agreeing to Karen's suggestion that they cut each other loose for a while.

"This just goes to show that if you hang with them faggots long enough," asserts Perry, "you will turn into a filthy queer just like them."

"What's taking you so damn long, Ross?" asks Tony.

Freaked out by his buried desires, Al meets up with Paul Sorvino, rags on him for his barbaric treatment of Pouty, then tells him he wants off the case. "I can't do the job," he pleads. "Things are happening to me!" Before Al can throw in the hankie, however, Paul gives him something new to go on, yearbook photos of all the students who took a class from the dead gay Columbia professor.

Al looks them over when he gets home and soon comes up with a new prime suspect, Stuart Richards, a bratty Columbia coed who, quite surprisingly, is writing a thesis on the roots of the American musical theater. Next thing you know, Al's alternately stalking and cruising the guy.

"Why is the alleged killer jogging in jeans?" wonders Lauren as Al watches Stuart return to his apartment from a run.

"They're not jeans," replies Marcus. "They're sweats that look like jeans. I used to have a pair."

Al follows Stuart around for a few days, waiting for an opportunity to break into his apartment. When he finally does, he discovers a closet full of leather gear and nothing else. "Stuart doesn't have any other clothes, just leather?" I ask.

"And sweats that look like jeans," Lauren reminds me.

"He lives a simple life," says Tony.

"I have to say, I miss the Cockpit scenes," I say wistfully. "The smell of the Crisco, the roar of the crowd."

"Do you think any gay man who's studying musical theater is going to have an apartment decorated like that shithole?" scoffs Dr. B. "I mean, there's not one palm frond in the whole place, nothing retro, no tacky chic, no framed *Chorus Line* posters. Again, where was the consultant?"

"I think Friedkin claimed later that the killer wasn't gay," says Perry.

"*What*?" says Marcus. "There was semen in the victim's butt."

"I know," says Perry. "It doesn't add up."

Al finally hits pay dirt when he comes upon a box full of letters Stuart wrote to his father but never sent.

"Hoo-*hah*!" Tony exclaims.

After a scene in a park between Stuart and his father that I'm not sure is meant to be real or a figment of Stuart's imagination, it becomes clear that this sweatpanted Sondheim buff is, in fact, our killer and that the badly looped voice we hear every time he kills is Stuart channeling his disapproving pop.

"Don't tell me this is all going to come down to father-son issues?" carps Dr. Beaverman. "Of course, it sort of makes sense, as this was the beginning of the Reagan years, Reagan being everybody's daddy. He wasn't my daddy, though. I didn't claim him."

Though it seems Al has enough evidence to have Stuart arrested, he decides instead to go *mano a mano* with the serial killer. So, decked out in his cutest cruising duds, he follows Stuart to a bench in a dark section of Riverside Park. "This is kind of hot," says Lauren as Al and Stuart size each other up and wander off together. "Straight people never do it this way, and I wish they would, just, like, stare at each other for an hour and then go do it. Think of how much you'd save on your cell phone bill."

Al wants to take Studly Stu back to his pad in the West Village, but Stu would rather get it on here in the park. This spooks Al a bit. "I'm not too crazy about public places," he says.

"Don't worry, Dorothy," Stu chides, "there's nobody around."

"I'm so glad he called Pacino on his uptight bullshit," says Tony. "It's like, *This movie's called* Cruising, *all right? Don't get all prissy on me now. It's the third reel, for crying out loud.*"

Al gives in and lets his paramour lead the way to a clearing near a tunnel. Then Stuart asks Al how big he his, to which our undercover cop replies, "Party size." Although I'm sure this is meant to imply that Al's packing, I can't help being reminded of the two-inch mini Snickers I gave out last Halloween.

Once they settle on a sex spot, Stuart informs Al that he "doesn't do anything." Our hero assures him that's cool then says the three little words that set every gay man's heart aflutter, "Hips or lips?"

Though the room cheers, I have to admit I'm a bit befuddled. "I don't fully understand the question," I reveal as Al shucks his pants, "especially since the other guy already said he doesn't do anything."

"The killer's a major top looking for trade," huffs Ross, spewing forth terminology I had no idea he was up on. "When Stuart says 'I don't do anything,' that means, 'I don't suck, I don't get fucked, so you're going to take my penis somewhere in you. Hips or lips?'"

"Very impressive, Ross" says Tony. "You butch it up a little and you could do gay porn voice-overs."

It looks like Al's going with option B, because when I turn my attention back to the screen, he's dropping to his knees. "Notice how he put his jacket on the ground so he wouldn't get his knees dirty," observes Lauren. "He's so gay now."

"And he did the Gap trifold," adds Tony. "Always a dead giveaway."

Then Al tells Stuart that he wants "to see the world," which I think is just a fancy way of saying, "Can I press my eyes up against your goody trail?" Alas, before Al can do either, Stuart's reaching for his knife. Luckily, Al gets to his first, and the next thing you know, the guy who "doesn't do anything" is getting penetrated big time.

The next time we see Stuart, he's laid up in a hospital bed being told by Paul Sorvino that his prints are on the peep show coin, so he's pretty much fingered, and not the good kind of fingered either. Paul then welcomes Al to the detective division, and gives him the rest of the week off to deal with his possible gayness.

A few days later, Al's sweet gay neighbor, Ted, is found stabbed to death in his apartment. "That position that Ted is sprawled in was actually inspired by a David Bowie album cover," Perry informs us.

"Jesus, you *do* have good Fun Facts," Ross concedes.

Which brings us to the film's final scene, with Karen and Al back together in their apartment. "I want to tell you everything," Al says, calling out to Karen while he shaves in the bathroom mirror. In the front room, Karen slips into Al's leather jacket and cap as if she just might Go West herself, then walks ominously toward the bathroom. As Al gazes into the mirror, haunted and confused, sort of like all of us, he hears her jangly, leather-jacketed approach.

"So Pacino is now the new self-loathing homosexual on the block?" I ask.

"Code name: Shmazel," mutters Tony.

"We never really know if he is," says Perry, as the credits roll. "It could have been Al who killed Ted, or it could have been Ted's jealous boyfriend."

"I'm so confused," admits Lauren.

"It says right here on the box that *Cruising* doesn't answer all the questions it raises," Tony points out.

"You can say that again," says Ross.

"Well, psychologically speaking, we've got several things going on in this movie," says Dr. Beaverman. "First, there's the matter of Stuart's repressed rage at his father. 'Oh, what havoc one can wreak with a coercive parent,' the movie seems to say. It could turn you into a murderer, basically. First a homosexual, then a murderer. However, we also have the environment versus heredity argument to consider. Some might say this movie shows that if you put someone in a homosexual world, they'll turn right into Boy George, but I find that difficult to believe. I think heredity plays a part that is ignored here, and I resent the implication that clothes a man make, in this case bad clothes and even worse accessories."

"Speaking of which, Dennis," Ross calls from the kitchen where he's wrapping the leftover penis treats in tinfoil, "do you want to try on my harness before I go?"

I'm powerless to say no, so we head to my room, dig out my best-fitting ratty jeans and clunkiest boots, then embark on my rough trade makeover. I'd like to say I take to the look like Liza to a painkiller, but the truth is, it takes us a pathetically long time to get the tangled up contraption on me and when we do, the results are less than spectacular. Maybe stubble would help.

"So?" asks Perry, after I put my shirt back on and return to the front room. Though the question's meant for me, Perry's looking at Marcus when he asks it. And smiling expectantly. Interesting.

"Are you going to start running with the shadows of the night, Dennis?" asks Lauren.

"No, but I'm going to stop eating bread," I say.

"I have to say this does not get my thumbs-up," asserts Dr. Beaverman, depositing her three-times-empty highball into the sink, "not my thumbs, not my fist, not my billy club, nothing. Everything's down. It's all droopy and down." She walks back into the front room and grabs a Butt Cake for the road. "In fact, I have to say I prefer the Huey Lewis and Gwyneth Paltrow version of Smokey Robinson's "Cruising" over this Al Pacino version of *Cruising,* and that's saying a mouthful, so to speak."

"Hey," I offer, opening the door for her, "at least there was no Anne Murray."

•

Though I can't decide whether I think it's bad or brave, sexy or stomach-turning, irredeemable or landmark, *Cruising* stays with me, and a few days later I go to the library to ferret out all the info about it I can. The last time a movie sent me to the library for personal rather than work-related reasons was in 1983. The film was *Body Heat,* Lawrence Kasdan's 1981 film noir throwback starring Kathleen Turner as the femme fatale who manipulates William Hurt into killing her husband. A female college friend and I happened upon it one night on cable, and as the film twisted and throbbed to its surprise denouement, my world was irrevocably rocked. I was soon obsessed and watched the movie every time it aired, decorated my room with the poster and lobby cards, signed up for a fan club some *Body Heat* boosters back East had started, and yes, went to the library to learn more.

Not surprisingly, there was considerably more ink spilled about *Cruising* than there was about *Body Heat,* most likely because the latter didn't make people want to strangle each other. *Cruising,* it seems, did, and it's going to take me hours to get through this sizable school of microfiche.

One of the first things I learn is that, according to Richard Goldstein of *The Village Voice,* the battle over *Cruising* was the first time in history a citizens' protest had been waged against a film before it was in the can. Spearheading the early protests, it seems, was that paper's own Arthur Bell, a fiercely opinionated columnist who regularly wrote about New York City's gay issues, including the real-life murders that inspired the film. After getting his hands on an early draft of the much-guarded script, Bell wrote that *Cruising* "promises to be the most oppressive, ugly, bigoted look at homosexuality ever presented on the screen.... It will negate years of positive movement work and may well send gays running back into the closet and precipitate heavy violence against homosexuals. I implore readers...to give Friedkin and his production crew a terrible time if you spot them in your neighborhood."

Anti-*Cruising* momentum built from there, and soon a string of riots erupted in the Village, with both gay protesters and policemen sustaining injuries. As filming continued, Bell went on an ABC morning show and urged viewers to do violence against the production. The incensed writer, who proudly compared his original column denouncing *Cruising* to the Declaration of Independence in terms of the gay community, later admitted in *The New York Times* that yes, he had urged violence during his TV appearance, but added, "It was last-minute advice, and I'd had only two or three hours' sleep the night before. If my head had been clearer, I would have said, 'Aim your violence against the cameras, because their violence will be aimed at us.'"

Friedkin didn't take Bell's attacks lying down. "To say that a film that has not been made yet is going to cause people to kill gays is, in my opinion, wishful thinking on the part of the people who've made that accusation," Friedkin told the *Times.* "I believe that Bell and all the others who have said this film will cause gay men to be murdered *want* that to happen so they can come out in print and say, 'We told you so,' and get more publicity for themselves."

As for my opinion, I was pretty much in his corner until I read the remarks he made at a press conference following a media screening of the film. Now I'm not so sure, though you have to give him credit for facing the press at all. When asked if Al Pacino's character committed the final murder after realizing he was gay, Friedkin replied, "I myself was not sure whether there was one killer or more than one." He went on to stress that the violence the film depicted was all perpetrated by a heterosexual. Why then, someone asked—as Marcus did during our Screening Party—was semen found up the first victim's butt? "That's a difficult question," Friedkin replied. "I'll have to think that over." Those are pretty vague, mealy-mouthed answers for a filmmaker who clearly gets off on pushing audiences' buttons. Of course, Friedkin might have just been freaked out at the time, because at that same press conference, his nemesis, Arthur Bell, jumped from his chair, walked down the theater aisle, and spat, "I condemn you. You are the worm of worms!"

If I were the age I am now and living in Greenwich Village at the time it all happened, I don't know where I would have come down on the *Cruising* debate. I've never felt it was the job of artists to make me feel good about myself. I just want them to tell me the truth, some truth, anyway, even if it's ugly. Of course, it's easy for me to say those things today, 22 years later, when there are all manner of gay and lesbian images in our culture, images we might not have gotten to yet had people not raised holy hell over *Cruising*. I do know, however, that if Randy Jurgensen, the cop whose story inspired the film, sat down next to me at a dinner party, I'd want to know every fabulous, fucked-up, fascinating detail of his foray into the leather netherworld, and I'd want to see pictures if he had them. Why shouldn't someone be allowed to make a movie about that?

A week and a half later I report my findings to the rest of the gang, save a curiously late Lauren, as we stand in line to get into '70s Disco Saturdays at Oil Can Harry's, a been-around-forever dance club in Studio City. We've gathered here tonight to pop Dr. Beaverman's gay-bar cherry.

"So do you think the people who made the movie were homophobic?" Ross asks me, after I finish telling them about Arthur Bell's "worm of worms" tirade.

"No, I don't," I say. "I think they just thought it was a exotic backdrop for a thriller, like sending Melanie Griffith into the Hasidim in that other shitheap."

"*A Shiksa Among Us,*" says Marcus.

"Maybe it was originally supposed to be a serial killer in outer space," suggests Tony, "and then they were like 'We don't have the budget. Let's just make him gay.'"

"I can't believe how long this line is," says Marcus, looking up and down the queue. "It's not usually like this," he says to Dr. Beaverman.

"It's Bear Night," explains a tall, bearded guy standing in front of us. "They Bear Night once a month."

"What does Bear Night mean?" asks Dr. Beaverman.

"It means that I'm going to be the belle of the fucking ball," mutters Ross.

"No word from Lauren?" says Tony.

I shrug, then pull out my cell phone to check my machine at home. There's one message, from Lauren, left about two hours ago, when I was out to dinner with Marcus. "Hey, it's me," she says. "I'm going to be late tonight because I'm doing a last-minute set at the Laugh Factory as an audition for this young comedians TV special. My manager's been trying to get me in front of these people for ages, and it's kind of a big deal. I'll meet up with you guys later. Wish me luck."

I relay Lauren's exciting news to the rest of the gang, then laugh my head off as Marcus, Tony, and Ross take turns doing the Al Pacino dance to "You Should Be Dancing," which we can hear playing inside the club. "I hate when they play all my favorite songs while I'm standing in line," I lament. "Watch, once we get inside, they'll play a bunch of songs I've never heard of."

"As long as it's not Anne Murray, I should be fine," says Dr. Beaverman.

When I look back to see how long the line has gotten behind us, I see Lauren stomping up the sidewalk. If the look on her face is any indication, her "big deal" set must not have gone well.

"Why didn't you tell me the magazine went under?" she says to me, angrily.

"What magazine?" I say.

"Fucking *British Premiere,*" she says.

"It went under?" says Marcus.

The guy behind Lauren is enjoying a cigarette, so it's hard to tell how much of the smoke in the air is his and how much is literally coming from Lauren's ears. As I stare at her, speechless, my heart pounds in time with the distant music. Scratch that, it's faster.

"Before I do my set," Lauren starts, "my manager takes me to the bar and introduces me to the talent booker of this big show, Roger something, and I'm being charming and witty and all that, and then he says, 'This is my girlfriend, Sarah.' Sarah, it turns out is from England, so I go, 'Oh, my friend writes this column for *British Premiere* called Screening Party, and her eyes get all big and she goes, 'Oh, I *love* Screening Party. It's so fab.' So I go, 'I'm in that. I'm the girl aerobics teacher–comic who puked during *Jaws,*' and she goes, 'Oh, you're all so funny. I read the *Pretty Woman* one to my girlfriends over the phone and blah blah blah.' So suddenly this Roger guy can't get enough of me and I'm thinking, *I'm in. I'm going to be on TV.* Then suddenly Sarah goes, 'Too bad about the magazine, though, isn't it?' and I'm like, 'What are you talking about?' She goes, 'It went belly up months ago.' I was like, 'Really?' and of course, I can't let it go and just do my set. I have to fucking challenge her about it, like, 'Well, that's impossible, because we're still doing parties,' and she goes, 'No, my sister Fiona used to work at *British Premiere.* They're no more.' Like two minutes later, I was onstage. So what the fuck, Dennis?"

"It folded," I say.

"When?" says Marcus. It's one word, but it feels loaded with sadness.

"A few months ago," I say. "*Armageddon* was the last one Matt assigned me, but it never ran. The last one that was published was *The Bodyguard.*"

"That was back during the *spring,*" says Ross incredulously.

"Why didn't you just tell us?" asks Tony.

"I don't know," I stammer. "I was trying to find another home for it, but I haven't been able to. I didn't want to kill the momentum, so I didn't say anything." Though Lauren is the only one visibly miffed, and with good reason, everyone else just looks sort of bummed out and befuddled. "Never Can Say Goodbye" starts playing inside, another of my favorites, but suddenly I don't feel like dancing. "Things like this," I say, "tend to run their course, you know. It's like the college play that's really fun and when it's over, everyone swears they're going to hang out all the time and then they never do. Well, I wasn't ready for this to be over. I'm so sorry about tonight, Lauren."

There's an uncomfortable silence as we realize that the people around us have picked up on the tension. Finally, Ross fills it. "Dude, I don't know if I speak for everyone," he says, "but I don't give a shit that there's no magazine. I'd still show up. Where else am I gonna get to use all the useless stuff I know about movies and laugh my ass off and eat tasty treats? Hell, I haven't *read* any of the articles in months."

"You haven't read them?" I say.

"Not since you started E-mailing them," he tells me. "I fucking hate E-mail."

The rest of the gang pretty much echoes Ross's sentiments, save Lauren, who remains silent. It looks like the world might not end after all. "So," says Dr. Beaverman, putting her arm around Lauren's shoulder, "how did your set go?"

"How do you *think* it went?" Lauren says, trying to laugh so she doesn't do the opposite.

"Did the microphone stink?" asks Tony, trying to lighten the mood a bit.

"No, but *I* did," Lauren snaps back. "I was so off my game it wasn't even funny. I think my manager might dump me now." Her eyes start to well, but before any tears can fall, she looks at me and says, "I have to go," then turns and walks down the sidewalk.

"I'm going to go talk to her," says Marcus.

Two songs later they're still not back and the line has hardly moved at all. "Dr. Beaverman is suddenly feeling very tired," says Dr. Beaverman. "Can we feed the bears another night?"

Tony volunteers to drive her home. When Ross suggests he and I get some pie at Dupar's down the street, I say sure. Pie seems like a better plan than anything else I can think of.

Years ago, when I was working as an entertainer on cruise ships, part of my job was to choreograph passengers for a big lip-synch show. Each cruise, I would turn a group of fun-loving ladies into "Aretha Franklin and the Franklinettes," and they'd wow their fellow guests with a rousing, tightly choreographed rendition of "Respect." One cruise in particular, I had these four supernice women from England who were really into it. We rehearsed for hours, and by the day of the show they were so excited they could hardly speak. As goofy as it all was, for those few days it really meant something to them. They were going to be stars.

Well, show time arrived and I took a seat in the balcony of the theater fidgeting like Fosse at the opening of *Sweet Charity.* But when their music started, the curtain hadn't been opened yet. When my girls finally appeared, they were 12 counts behind the music in terms of their steps, and they proceeded to remain 12 counts behind for the entire number. It was officially a train wreck and I could see the sad, panicked looks on their faces, like *This wasn't supposed to happen. This was supposed to be fun, not heartbreaking.* I thought about jumping up and saying, "Stop the tape! Let them start over!" but I stayed in my seat. My insides ached. It was like the Queen of Soul herself had left Detroit and taken up residence in my small intestine.

I felt miserable about my free-falling Franklinettes for weeks after that, in a way that was completely unwarranted, I'll grant you. It was a cruise ship lip-synch show, for crying out loud, not *Showtime at the Apollo*. Still, I remember thinking that it was the worst thing that had happened to me all year.

That feeling I had after that show, let's call it the Aretha Ache, is not unlike the one I have right now as I slide into a booth at Dupar's. When it comes to failure, it seems, I'm OK with my own. My dreams get dashed against the rocks, I can chalk it up, say I did my best, and not lose a lot of sleep over it. But the idea that I somehow blew it for someone else, that's another matter.

"It was shitty timing, Dennis, that's all," says Ross, between bites of apple pie. "She'll get over it."

"Hey," I say, hoping to change the subject. "There's something I've been wanting to ask you, but I keep forgetting." I push my half-eaten piece of cheesecake across the table to Ross as a peace offering and say, "What's number 1 on your all-time top 10?"

"You've been wanting to ask me that, huh?" Ross says with a laugh, clearly aware that since the day we met I've gotten a sort of perverse kick out of *not* asking about it.

"I really want to know," I say.

"*Body Heat,*" he says, then flags the waitress over for more decaf.

Ross and I have the same favorite movie. I want to tell him that, and go on and on and on about it, but I think if I do it now, tonight, he'll *really* think I'm patronizing him. "I love that movie too" is all I say.

We pay the check and walk out to the parking lot. "So, we still doing *Top Gun* next week?" he asks me. "I want to start looking stuff up. That fucker Perry really raised the bar on Fun Facts."

"I don't know," I say. "I have to smooth things over with Lauren."

"She'll be in," figures Ross. "She's the one who's always talking about how she's convinced Tom Cruise is animatronic."

Ross gives me a hug. "Thanks," I say.

"You're welcome," he replies. "Now say good night, Fisty."

"Good night, Fisty."

CAREY ME HOME

We don't end up watching *Top Gun* as planned, but it's not because Lauren is unforgiving or Tom Cruise got wind of our cruel intentions and sicced Pat Kingsley on us. No, it's because, at the last minute, Ross was able to charm his way into a few more hours of free editing time during which he put the closing credits on his film. *Renaissance Boy* is now finished, though no one, except Ross, his instructors, and his editor, has seen a frame of it. He and a few of his classmates are unveiling their opuses next week at a screening and reception at UCLA. We've all marked our calendars. Marcus plans to bake Medieval Muffins, whatever they are, and Dr. Beaverman has hired a publicist. I'm kidding, she hasn't. She is, however, having Tony touch up her roots.

Yesterday, when the invitations to the screening arrived in our mailboxes, I asked Dr. Beaverman if she thought it was going to be weird to watch herself on-screen. "Please," she scoffed. "There are far more incriminating images of Dr. Beaverman floating about the universe than that." By this, my favorite Ivy-by-the-Pacific alum could be referring to something as shocking as she once attended a videotaped orgy thrown by Poison at the Bonaventure Hotel or something as mundane as she sometimes picks her nose in front of the ATM machine. That's the thing about Dr. B.: You just never know.

As for the situation with Lauren, I'm pleased to report that she returned the third, or maybe it was the fourth, groveling message I left on her voice mail and assured me that the well-justified Shit Fit she began on the sidewalk at Oil Can Harry's was now over and forgotten. Though she was indeed spot-on in her assessment that her set in front of Roger, the TV talent booker, sucked serious ass, her manager is sticking by her and they'll continue to persevere. If Lauren's manager had bailed, I don't know how many groveling messages it would have taken to reestablish the peace, but I figure I was good for at least 20 more.

Though I still haven't found a new outlet for my Screening Party articles, the gang assures me they're still game to take part. When Ross couldn't make the first *Top Gun* party, we rescheduled it for last Wednesday, September 12, but last Wednesday was one day after September 11, 2001, the day we all thought the world was ending. Since that woeful morning, Tony and I haven't seen Lauren and Ross at all, face-to-face. Ross has been holed up in some postproduction facility somewhere, while Lauren has been sticking close to home, fielding calls from her family on Long Island. Compounding her anxiety is the fact that three days ago she threw her back out teaching a sculpt class and it's left her practically immobile.

Marcus has been over a few times. In fact, he came over the afternoon of the 11th to watch CNN with us and not be by himself. Full disclosure: We didn't just watch CNN. When reality got to be too harrowing, we popped in *Can't Stop the Music* and *Save the Last Dance,* which I thought was pretty good considering the world was ending.

As for Dr. Beaverman, she pops down almost nightly to watch *Entertainment Tonight* with us as it struggles to find its place in this strange new world. "Brooke Shields signed helmets at ground zero," she reiterated to Tony and me after one particularly hard-hitting story. "What the hell have *you two* done?"

"I repeated your Brooke Shields line to a journalist buddy of mine today at the *Shallow Hal* junket," I tell her, as the two of us pull into the Beverly Center parking structure.

"Did he think it was funny or sick?" she asks.

"Pretty much both," I reply. "The funny thing was, this kind of phony publicist guy overheard us talking and didn't get that we were being irreverent. He came over and he was like, 'Yeah, I was just at ground zero a couple of days ago with Scott Bakula. We signed.' His subtext was so like, 'My ass is covered. I've done *my* part.'"

While Dr. Beaverman and I search my dashboard and coat pockets for the parking stub I acquired 15 seconds ago, Tony, fresh from subbing a Trampolining for Tweens class at the Gym Dandy in Santa Monica, pulls up in the spot next to us. "I had to go to four different stores, but I found them," he reports, pointing to a large Toys "R" Us bag in his backseat.

"Found what?" asks Dr. Beaverman, getting out of the truck.

"Ross's birthday present," I say.

"Oh," she says. "I didn't realize."

"It was last Thursday," I tell her. "It's not a big deal. The gift can be from all of us. And I think Marcus might have made a cake."

"*Might* have?" says Tony.

"In other words, we're covered," I assure her.

The three of us walk together to the escalator, then take it down to street level so we can meet the rest of the posse for dinner at the Souplantation across the street. As we wait for the stoplight to change, I have to say that tonight feels like the first time in months that I've gone out with the express purpose of having a good time. It's a very strange sensation, and I'm not sure it'll take.

Still, if there's anything in this world that can put a smile on my face, a zing in my step, and a song in my heart, it's these six words: Now showing, *Glitter,* starring Mariah Carey. Though Marcus's "Countdown to *Glitter*" calendar became useless last month when Mariah's personal problems pushed back the film's release date, we all still managed to make it here on opening night. As the saying goes, wild horses—not unlike the one Mariah tamed and straddled in her "Butterfly" video—couldn't have kept me away.

"I just had a thought, you guys," I say, between spoonfuls of clam chowder at the Plantation. "What if it sells out? What if everyone in town decides they need a break from reality and says 'Hey, let's go see *Glitter*'?"

"Waiter," says Tony, "can you take this back? There's some crack in his soup."

"I know, it's unthinkable," I admit, "but what isn't?"

"Well, I got our tickets online," says Marcus, "so Perry and I are covered."

Yes, Marcus and Perry are an item, of sorts. A few days after *Cruising,* they had their first date and have had half a dozen or more since, though Marcus still isn't sure whether it's their slutty phases that have intersected or their nonslutty phases. I think he wouldn't mind it if it were both.

"I'll order the rest of the tickets now, then," says Ross, flipping open his cell phone. "How many do we need?"

I count around the table. Marcus and Perry are set, so that leaves me, Lauren and Barry, Tony, Ross, and Dr. Beaverman. "Six," I say.

"Who has a credit card I can use?" Ross asks. "Mine have been tapped out for months."

Barry whips out his wallet like George Jetson and hands over his Visa. While Ross dials 777-FILM and touch-tones his way to *Glitter* tix, Marcus withdraws his trusty cupcake-taker from the shopping bag he carried in, removes a glitter-covered cupcake, and places a single candle in it. "We're all set," Ross says, after hanging up. "I have to tell you guys, though, even the Moviefone guy was shocked. He was like 'You have requested...*Glitter*?' He literally said it like a question."

We all find Ross's deep-voiced and dubious Mr. Moviefone imitation hilarious. If the world doesn't stop turning later tonight, I'm sure I'll be nagging him to re-create it for years to come.

"This," Marcus says, placing the candlelit cupcake in front of Ross, "is a Gift I Made Myself. In honor of your birthday last week." Then, after being serenaded by our half-assed rendition of "Happy Birthday to You" Ross blows out his candle and says, "Thank you, all."

"We also have a little something for you in the car," Tony says. "It's *not* a Gift I Made Myself, although if you've got your heart set on that, I'll see what I can do."

"That won't be necessary," says Ross.

"To Ross's birthday...and Ross's movie...and these lemon muffins, which are *out of control,*" says Lauren, raising her soda glass.

"And to *Glitter,*" adds Tony, doing the same.

"And to Paul Verhoeven and Adrian Lyne," I say. "May they always get the financing they need and cast Denise Richards if at all possible."

"And make her make out with another girl," says Ross.

We leave the restaurant, divvy up the remaining *Glitter* cakes on the sidewalk out in front, then head back across the street to the Beverly Center. When we get to the cinemas on the top floor, we're told that our theater won't be open for another half an hour. So while Ross, Lauren, and Barry stand in line to get coffeed-up at the Starbucks kiosk, the rest of us wander into the Suncoast Motion Picture Company to check out the latest offerings in home video. We're scarcely in the door two seconds when the David LaChapelle–directed, drag race-themed music video for Mariah Carey's latest single, "Loverboy," starts playing on the store's wall of video monitors.

"You know what this is?" I ask as Mariah, in a bikini top, high heels, and Daisy Dukes that look as though they might get sucked up inside her at any moment, cavorts about waving a set of checkered flags.

"It's a cry for help, clearly," replies Dr. Beaverman.

"No, it's like when you go on a big theme park ride," I continue, as multiple images of Mariah swirl about the screens kaleidoscope-style, "and they show you a video *about* the ride to get you psyched up while you wait line."

"Totally," agrees Tony. "It's like, 'Settle in, folks, for this is just a small drop in the Big Bucket of Crazy you're going to be getting in…" Tony stops to take a quick look at his watch. "Forty-one minutes, assuming there's five minutes of trailers."

"I wonder if the movie's going to involve time travel," muses Marcus, "because it's supposedly set in 1983 and yet the Kameo song she's sampling in this video, "Candy," is from 1987."

"That's the least of our problems," groans Dr. Beaverman. "I mean, look at this. Every inch of her real estate is thrust in my face."

"The phrase, 'My eyes are up here' is clearly not in her vocabulary," concurs Tony.

"Ever since she divorced Tommy Mottola, Mariah cannot be naked enough," I remark. "I imagine her going to the wardrobe people on this video and being like, 'These pink plastic shorts are supercute, but is there any way we can make them chaps too but also still shorts?'"

"It is Dr. Beaverman's opinion that Ms. Carey could be diagnosed as a Freudian hysteric," says Dr. Beaverman. "Hysterics are women who like to flaunt their sexuality and present all of the trappings of sexual adventurousness and availability, the camel-toe hot pants, the low-cut tops, the coquettish poses, but in truth they're often sexually frigid. In spite of their shameless exhibitionism, they're actually very afraid of sex. At heart they're still little girls looking to be taken care of." Dr. Beaverman scrutinizes the video for another half a verse—although it could be a chorus, who can tell with this nonsong—then adds, "Although, God knows, Mariah could be the exception to Freud because she's practically getting it on with that traffic cone."

As Mariah continues to road-test the dexterity of her pink hot pants with a series of death-defying squats, Ross wanders in sucking on the straw of a caramel frappuccino. "Her knockers are totally asymmetrical," he remarks, staring at the screen. "The right one is larger than the left one. Anyone want a taste?"

"What should we call 'em?" poses Dr. Beaverman. "We need a famous duo where one person is bigger than the other." We consider Penn and Teller (too nerdy), Laurel and Hardy (too old-school), and Carnie and Wendy Wilson (no longer applicable) before settling on Farley and Spade.

"I don't begrudge Mariah her boobies or anything," asserts Perry, as a bikini-clad Mariah brings the clip to a climax by popping out of a giant cake. "She's here to entertain me, and she just totally did."

Before leaving the store, Tony, Ross, and I attempt to alter the title of the drag-racing film *The Fast and the Furious* to suit Mariah's road rally mini-movie, but we're just not nailing it. *The Crass at the Clitoris* is the best we can come up with, but we all know it ultimately won't do.

"*She's* fast and *I'm* furious," says Dr. Beaverman, before turning and striding purposefully out of the store.

The rest of us just genuflect, then follow Dr. Beaverman back to the theater lobby where Lauren and Barry are already waiting for our theater to open. "My boyfriend has a Fun Fact," Lauren boasts. "Tell them your Fun Fact, Barry."

"My girlfriend's a giant pain in the ass," says Barry, whose dry, jazz-cat monotone makes everything he says a good 50% funnier than it would normally be. "Oh, my *other* Fun Fact," he says after Lauren gives him a playful smack. "Well, a couple of muso friends of mine..."

"Muso means musician," Lauren explains.

"Got it," says Dr. Beaverman.

"See what I mean?" says Barry. "A couple of musicians I know worked on the *Glitter* soundtrack, and they said that because Mariah was afraid of piracy, the director—"

"Vondie Curtis-Hall, the actor," interjects Ross.

"—had to shoot the scenes with music, like club scenes and stuff, using *different* songs on the playback than what was ultimately going to be in the movie," continues Barry. "So it was a huge nightmare to edit because the beats that people were dancing to didn't necessarily match the beats of the new songs."

"What about the songs where Mariah sings?" wonders Marcus.

"Good question," says Lauren. "Barry?"

"From what I understand," says Barry, "Mariah had a sound-alike singer who recorded all her vocals. So when they were shooting, Mariah lip-synched to the sound-alike's voice, then her real vocals were added in later."

"Wow," I say. "That's really interesting."

"Everyone has better Fun Facts than me," whines Ross.

"Especially when you contrast that with, like, *A Star Is Born,*" I continue, "where Barbra and Kris recorded their stuff *live* while they were filming. It's like, 'Gee, I wonder what process is more organic?'"

"Do you think that's sort of standard procedure these days," Tony asks Barry, "or was Mariah being paranoid?"

"Probably the latter," says Barry, "but maybe she has good reason to. Who knows?"

"We have the same birthday, me and Mariah," remarks Marcus, getting a St. Olaf–style anecdote in just under the wire. "March 27. It's also the same day as Michael York and Quentin Tarantino. Every year on my birthday I buy something Mariah, like a CD single or a DVD."

"I can't shake this damn cold. I don't know if I should watch *Glitter* with compromised immunity." —Dr. Beaverman

"Some pasties," says Dr. Beaverman.

"Has that been getting harder and harder to do as the years go by and her songs all start to sound the same?" I ask. "Be honest."

"Totally," admits Marcus. "This year, I was standing in front of the CD single bin at Virgin, thinking, *I know you* used *to do a lot of nice things for me, Mariah, but what have you do for me* lately?"

Judging by the quizzical look on his face, I can tell Perry has no idea Marcus is quoting an old Janet Jackson song, but he seems charmed nonetheless.

"If I were you, Marcus," says Dr. Beaverman, "I'd look into becoming a Michael York aficionado, and quick." Dr. Beaverman punctuates her recommendation with a rafter-rattling sneeze. "I can't shake this damn cold," she laments. "I don't know if I should watch *Glitter* with compromised immunity."

"I hear you, sister," says Marcus.

"Or a fucked-up back," says Lauren, grimacing through an overhead stretch while Barry holds her latte.

"Perhaps *Glitter* will make us laugh," says Dr. Beaverman, putting an arm around Marcus's shoulder, "and help us build up those antibodies. A laughing body is a healthy body."

That's sort of what I've maintained all along, I think. Some folks take the edge off their workaday lives by hollering "Kill the ref!" during *Monday Night Football.* For others, it's a simple hobby, like knitting or entering their 5-year-old in beauty pageants, that tethers them to the earth and keeps them from spiraling completely into lunacy. For my mother, the sanity saver was yard work. For Matthew McConaughey, it's having a buddy over and playing the bongos with your nuts. My inner peacekeeper, it seems, is hanging out with these people in front of some screen or other and bringing Julia Roberts down a few notches. Hey, whatever works.

"*You are now entering* Glitter," Ross bellows, after the usher, Paul, opens the velvet rope and beckons us forward. "*Please stay seated and keep your arms and legs inside the star vehicle at all times.*"

"Theater 11," Paul says to me as he takes my ticket. "Down the hall and on your left."

"Wait, it's not in one of the big rooms upstairs?" I ask. "I mean, it's opening night."

Paul rolls his eyes at me in the kind of way that only a disenchanted minimum wager can, then punctuates his indifference by giving my ticket a violent tear.

"How may seats does 11 have?" I ask him.

"Like 50," he says.

"Good thing we called ahead," says Ross, as we dash to the shoebox-size theater like the land-rushing extras in *Far and Away.*

Once there, I take a seat in the center of the third row of the auditorium. Tony sits on my right, Ross on my left. Dr. Beaverman settles in to the left of Ross. "Within spitting distance of the exit," she points out, "and don't be surprised if I do start spitting."

Lauren sits behind me in the fourth row, with Barry behind Tony. Marcus and Perry take two seats in the front row. I'm not sure if this is so they can make out during the movie—they're quite big on the PDAs, it seems—or if they want there to be a row between them and the rest of us, in case we get beat up or asked to leave.

Over the next few minutes,a good 40 or so other brave and curious souls wander in and take seats. Among them, surprisingly, is the Accidental Boyfriend, along with his friend Carl and two dancer girls I recognize from his *Saturday Night Fever* tour. I swear to God, I didn't even know Shawn was in town.

"He must have implanted a homing device in my ass or something," I whisper to Tony as Shawn and his costars take seats in the last two rows. Though Shawn and I exchange happy-to-see-each-other waves, it's the shit-eating grin on his friend Carl's face that sort of takes me aback. I try to give him a "Thanks for letting us screw in your van" smile, but I don't know if I succeed. Who knows what one of those looks like, anyway?

"You didn't tell Endora we were going to be here?" Tony asks me.

"No," I say. "The last time I talked to him was like a week ago. They were in Denver. I think I mentioned we were going to try and do a Souplantation/*Glitter* thing, but I didn't think he was even going to be in town."

"We got two weeks off because of the attacks," explains Shawn, scooching into our row to give me a hug.

"Get this," he continues. "Remember that girl, Jillian? Well, she's convinced it was the fact that someone stole her Inner Peace Cards that brought all this shit on."

"I'm convinced of that too," I say.

"Did you tell him our Tivo message story?" asks Tony. I shake my head no. The Tivo message story is the lighter of our two Where-were-you-on-9/11 anecdotes. The heavier story involves him bursting into tears on the way home from our friendly neighborhood blood bank after being told that the Red Cross didn't want our homosexual blood but thanks anyway.

"Well, we had just gotten Tivo like the week before," Tony starts, "and it's amazing, P.S. So, the morning of the 11th, we're watching the live news coverage and freaking out when suddenly a message pops up on our screen that says, 'Tivo would like to change the channel and record *Mama's Family*.'"

"*Mama's Family*?!" repeats Shawn, laughing.

"I know," I say. "I was like, *That machine knows us better than we think.*"

Just then, Marcus rushes back and sneaks a mystery sack into Lauren's lap. "I shot my baking wad with the cupcakes," he explains, "but I did bring something to eat during the movie." Lauren opens the sack and withdraws the largest bag of Skittles I've ever seen in my life. Marcus spouts the candy's catch phrase, "Taste the rainbow," then both he and Shawn scurry back to their seats as the lights start to dim.

"I don't get it," says Lauren, ripping the Skittles bag open anyway.

"*Rainbow* was Mariah's last studio album before *Glitter*," says Barry.

"Jesus, are you *gay* now too?" Lauren says.

A minute or so later, during the trailer for, God help us, *Corky Romano,* Tony elbows me in the ribs and points frantically to the corner of the auditorium where three women have just taken the last empty seats in the place. "Tyra Banks just walked in," he whispers.

"*No?!*" I gasp.

I lean forward and steal a glance over to where Tony had pointed. Sure enough. There, in the far-left seat of the second row, sits my favorite *Coyote Ugly* actress who also happens to be a supermodel, Tyra Banks. On her right is another pretty young thing who I would guess is a friend. A row in front of them is a woman who looks like she could be Tyra's mother. After updating Dr. Beaverman and Ross about our special surprise celebrity guest, I turn around and tell Lauren and Barry. Then I start to panic, for there's no way short of a paper airplane or smoke signals to get the news to Marcus, as he's two rows away. The anxiety I feel over Marcus's Tyra ignorance is just this side of Chinese water torture, as Marcus and I discovered the joys of *Coyote Ugly* together at the El Capitan Theater. Three times, as a matter of fact.

By now you must be plenty confused as to who's where, so here is an overhead map of theater 11. A few of the people listed may seem mysterious to you now, but they won't for long.

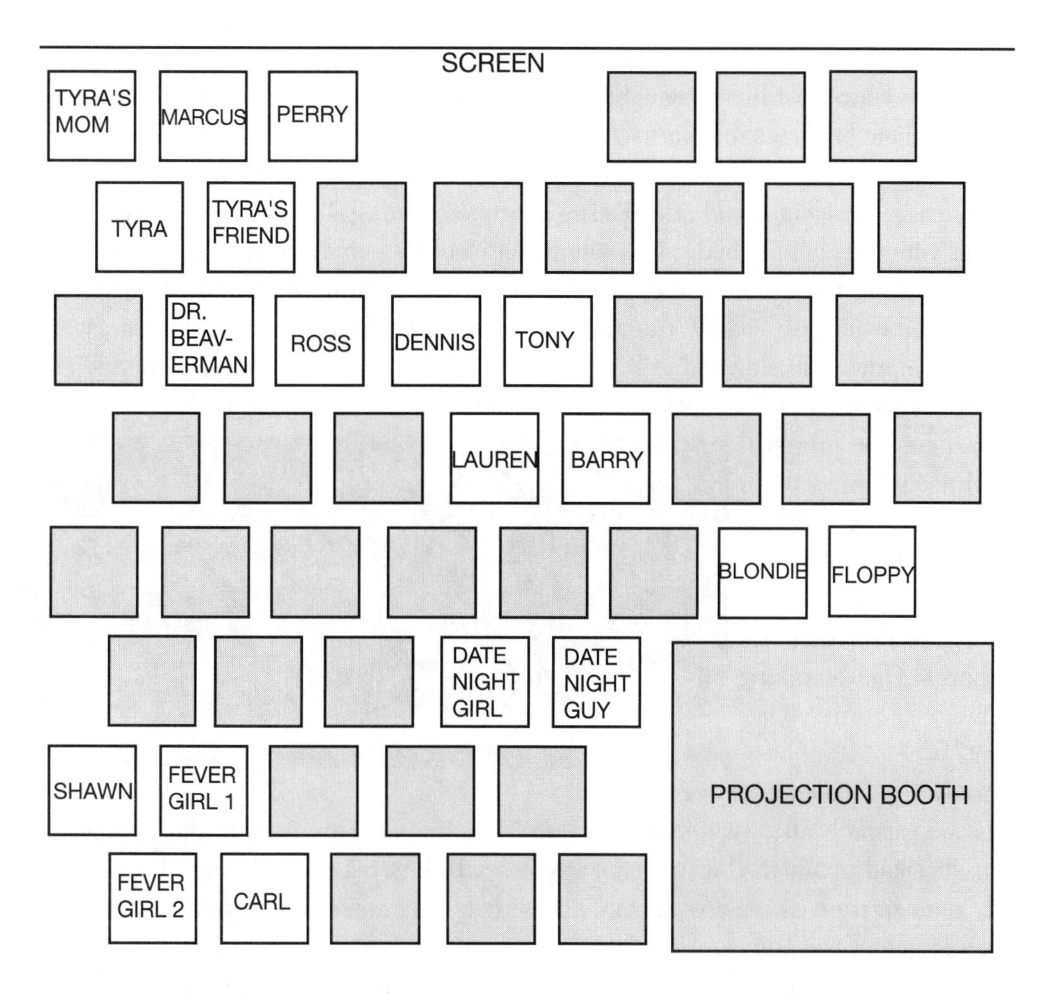

When the trailers finish, the Cineplex Odeon bumper plays and the screen goes black again. Then, finally, after months of anticipation, refrigerator reminders and tabloid cover stories, the Columbia woman comes and goes and *Glitter* begins. Hosanna.

The film opens in a sepia-drenched jazz club in the '70s, where we meet Lillian Frank (Valarie Pettiford), an orange headband–wearing, drunk-off-her-ass chanteuse, who's attempting to get through a bluesy ballad without passing out in a pool of her own boozy vomit.

While Lillian emotes her inebriated little heart out on the right side of the screen, the film's title suddenly fades in on the left, in a simple, sanserif, all-caps typeface. It's such a thrilling, long-awaited moment that the crowd can't help applauding. I don't clap, however, because my hands are busy lifting my trusty Canon Instamatic from my lap and snapping a picture of the screen. Though many in the house, friends and strangers alike, titter in disbelief, I'm confident that at least half of those folks are going to want copies later. They always do.

Soon we pan from the shit-faced and bumbling Lillian to the bar, where sits a pretty girl with wavy hair who's about 10 years too young to be tying one on in a joint like this. We come to learn it's Lillian's daughter, Billie, whom I like to refer to as Mini-Mariah. When her mom becomes too blotto to perform properly, she beckons Mini-Mariah to the stage to help her finish the song.

"Even as a child, she couldn't sing a straight tone," mutters Tony, as Mini-Mariah wakes the dogs with the high-pitched caterwauling that would become her signature sound.

After leaving the club, mother and daughter pay a surprise visit to Mini-Mariah's cold-hearted white baby-daddy, then head home to their dumpy clapboard house, which Lillian promptly burns down after falling asleep with a cigarette in her mouth. Soon the state decides she's an unfit mother, so it's off to the orphanage for Mini-Mariah.

The credits are still unfurling when Lillian tearfully puts Mini-Mariah and her tabby kitten, Whisper, into a social worker's sedan and blubbers, "They're taking you away just until I get better."

Though our sad young heroine is understandably apprehensive in this scary new environment, it must be said she's adjusting far better than her pet kitten, who is clearly feeling threatened by the boom mike.

"You'll like Thailand," says Lauren.

As the car pulls away, we hear grown-up Mariah's voice on the soundtrack singing a heartfelt ballad in which the superstar expresses Billie's need for closure. Though it's a pretty enough tune, there are certain words that I maintain should never be in a pop song, and one of them is *closure.*

"I could teach her to do a cartwheel," Tony offers as a tear-streaked Mini-Mariah arrives at the orphanage. "That'd cheer her up."

Though our sad young heroine is understandably apprehensive in this scary new environment, it must be said she's adjusting far better than her pet kitten, who is clearly feeling threatened by the boom mike.

I point out Whisper's bobbing and weaving to Tony, but by the time he turns his attention to the cat, the film has cut away to two of Mini-Mariah's fellow orphans, Roxanne and Louise. Tony's empty hands grasp for the air, searching for a remote that isn't there. "I'm having the Tivo shakes," he laments.

The three girls become fast friends, and then next thing you know it's 1983, and Mariah's all grown up and go-go dancing in a nightclub to Lime's "Babe We're Gonna Love Tonight," while wearing a skimpy leopard-print teddy. Theater 11 goes apeshit.

I don't know if it's the shock of Mariah's half-clad cavorting or the flash from my camera as I attempt to document Mariah's half-clad cavorting, but *something* about the moment causes Dr. Beaverman to lose her grip. And I'm not talking about her grip on reality. I'm talking about her grip on the Skittles bag.

Have you ever wondered why they call them Skittles? I'll tell you why. Because skittling is the sound that occurs when several hundred of those rainbow-tasting fuckers are dropped onto a raked cement floor. The ear-splitting skittling goes on for what seems like minutes, becoming increasingly hilarious as the seconds tick by. By the time the last Skittle has stopped skittling, the whole place is in hysterics.

Mariah, meanwhile, has finished go-go dancing and is now lounging backstage with her friends, the black and sassy Louise (played by real-life rapper Da Brat) and the Puerto Rican spitfire Roxanne (played by Tia Texada). The gal pals are chattering inanely about their outfits when a slimy record producer in a zoot suit—named Timothy Walker (Terrence Dashon Howard)—shows up and asks the ladies if they'd like to sing backup for his recording artist girlfriend, the gorgeously exotic but woefully tin-eared Sylk (Padma Lakshmi).

For some reason that makes nary a lick of sense, Mariah acts above it all and spurns Timothy's offer. Soon, however, reason wins out and Louise and Roxanne convince Mariah that backing up Sylk is at least as good a way to bring in some bling bling as shaking their half-naked asses to old Blondie songs.

The next thing you know, the trio are in a recording studio oohing and aahing the song "You and Only You" behind Sylk, who, dressed in a silver, fur-trimmed jumpsuit, looks like she came straight from the bus and truck company of *Cats*. "I'm so glad they gave Shimbleshanks a record deal," mutters Tony.

"Sylk is actually Salman Rushdie's girlfriend," whispers Ross, proving, once and for all, that his Fun Fact funk is all in his mind. "Don't you love the idea that the man who wrote *The Satanic Verses* is going to have to sit through this movie?"

"I love Sylk," I gush. And it's true. Lakshmi's haughty attitude and comically bad singing are the most intentionally entertaining things in the movie so far. Sylk rules.

Realizing that it might be a smart idea to release a record that's actually listenable, Timothy tells his engineer to bring Mariah way up in the mix and Sylk way down. His little trick works wonders, and in the next scene, when Sylk and the Sylkettes debut the song at a club, it's Mariah's voice we hear singing lead. I have to say, though, it's hard to focus on anyone's vocals given Mariah's crazy pigtails and Lance-Armstrong-in-drag wardrobe choice. As looks go, her bicycle messenger cap, horse-jockey top, and satiny short shorts are not so much '80s bad as just *bad* bad.

Backstage, after the show, Mariah has her first encounter with the DJ who might just save her life, a Bryan Adams–looking, Marky Mark–accented, sleeveless-T-shirt-and leather-pants-favoring disc spinner named Dice, played by British actor-musician Max Beesley. When Dice compliments Sylk on her new and improved sound, the talent-free superbitch thanks him, then tells a hovering photographer to shoot her alone because the back-up singers "don't matter." Miffed over being slighted, Mariah blows Sylk's cover by cooing a few bars of "You and Only You" within earshot of Dice.

"*That's* the girl you loved tonight, Kathy Selden!" shouts Ross, quoting *Singin' in the Rain,* the classic musical that, I believe is number 5 on his all time Top Ten.

After chatting up Mariah in the hallway, Dice drags the leg warmer–clad thrush out onto the dance floor, puts a "Rapper's Delight"–type tune on the turntable, then passes around the microphone, letting various club goers rap, riff, or what have you. As he starts bopping Mariah's way, the film cuts to Mariah's point of view. Then, thanks to some *Xanadu*-esque postproduction magic, everyone but Dice blurs into nothingness, showing us that she only has eyes for him. It's a deliriously cheesy, whoop-inducing, Skittles-dropping kind of moment, and we're all, even Tyra and her peeps, delirious with joy. It's official. We are now in heaven.

When Dice shoves the mike in Mariah's face, our songbird trots out a series of her trademark high-pitched riffs. It's impressive enough, but I would have preferred it if she'd launched into something really absurd, like "I Dreamed a Dream" from *Les Miz* and proven, once and for all, that underneath that bad Linda Ronstadt "Living in the U.S.A." outfit is a woman with a formidable Broadway belt.

Blown away by her talent, Dice takes Mariah outside and begs to produce her. Again, for no conceivable reason, Mariah acts suspicious and above it all. When she finally agrees to work with him, Dice asks how he can contact her, and Mariah replies, "You'll figure it out." Boy, this is one go-go dancing orphan who needs to work on networking skills.

Things are looking up for Mariah. As she walks down the street alone, all love-struck over Dice, the universe is so thrilled for her, fireworks spontaneously explode in the sky over her head. Again, we whoop. You would have too.

During a subsequent scene, in which Timothy tells Dice it will cost him $100,000 to buy Mariah out of her contract, I say right out loud that I think Dice is hot. Tony begs to differ. "His career is over," he says.

"She's singing 'I Didn't Mean to Turn You On,' yet she hasn't worn a bra this whole movie." —Lauren

Though I fear in my heart that Tony may be right, I like to imagine a sunnier scenario, one in which David Geffen, or some similar A-list power gay, gets Beesley a role in the next *Saving Private Ryan*–type all-boy picture, just as a thank-you for *Glitter.* The only condition is that the Diceman has to go to the mogul's Malibu mansion every night for a week, soak nude in the Jacuzzi, and regale his benefactor with stories about Mariah being unreasonable. We could get that career back on track in no time.

With Dice in her corner, Mariah soon finds herself in the studio laying down her first single, the Jimmy Jam and Terry Lewis–penned song "I Didn't Mean to Turn You On," which, as recorded by Cherelle, was the "Oops…I Did It Again" of the '80s.

"She's singing 'I Didn't Mean to Turn You On,' yet she hasn't worn a bra this whole movie," says Lauren.

"Hysteric," says Dr. Beaverman with an "I told you so" shrug.

Mariah is soon performing the song live to a club audience while sporting a metallic miniskirt and a glittery silver stripe on her right arm that is never mentioned or explained. Like homelessness, cancer, and the ratings success of *Becker,* it just *is.* Backing up Mariah are Louise and Roxanne, whose matching outfits are also rather skimpy. "Those three are like *Little Shop of Whores,*" says Tony.

While Mariah continues to cling to the fallacy that she didn't mean to turn us on, we cut to another club performance of that same song. In this one, Mariah wears a Farrah do, a slutty black French maid dress, and garters. The glitter stripe has moved up a few inches to her right shoulder.

The stripe migrates to her left side for the scene where she and Dice visit the offices of CMZ Records to toast Mariah's just-signed recording contract. This is a major moment in the life of her character, yet Ms. Carey has virtually no dialogue in the entire scene except for maybe one "Hello." Her eyebrows and boyfriend do all the talking, which causes me to wonder if she's not on some sort of Celine Dion vocal rest regimen. Say what you will about Whitney in *The Bodyguard*—and God knows, we did—at least she had lines.

Mariah's voicebox works better, it seems, when she's at home hanging out with her peeps. In fact, she's downright chatty in the scene where her roomies help her get ready for a night out with Dice that Mariah insists isn't a date. "Which panties do you think are hers?" I wonder, pointing to the several pairs of ladies' undies hanging in the bathroom.

"None of them," says Dr. Beaverman, as if I should have known better than to even ask the question. "She's never heard of panties."

I sense that things are about to get romantic between Mariah and Dice, because when he shows up at her place in a stretch limo, the '80s college-dorm-room-nooky favorite "Moments in Love" by Art of Noise starts playing on the soundtrack. Before long, Mariah, in a tight pink minidress, and Dice, in leather, natch, are sauntering into a fancy restaurant together. Mariah's glitter stripe is conspicuously missing in action, although maybe she painted it on Farley or Spade for Dice to discover later.

"I'm so hungry I could take off my top," I say as Mariah and Dice settle in at their table.

This quip seems to amuse Tyra, and I'll take that pride with me to my grave.

After sniffing at the single red rose Dice gave her like it's been dipped in Good Acting Sauce, Mariah gazes across the table and poses a question that I myself have uttered to more cocky, hard-to-read guys like Dice than I'd like to think about. "Is this a date?" she asks.

"Are you on your back?" says Tony.

The answer Dice gives her—"No, if this were a date, you would know it"—is in the same family as the "Yeah, right" replies I'm used to getting. Something tells me, however, that the DJ is blowing smoke up her dress, because after dinner, he takes Mariah back to his place and shows her his marimba. Yes, I said *shows her his marimba.*

Now, I have to admit here that I've never given the marimba the respect it deserves as an instrument. This is largely because the only time I've ever seen it played is in beauty pageants, and I've always, for no good reason really, wondered whether the marimba wasn't just a quick fix for an untalented girl. Though I have little evidence to support my theory, I've long suspected that any bimbo with operational limbs and a few months to practice could learn to play at least one crowd-pleasing up-tempo number on the marimba, like "Flight of the Bumblebee," for example. Again, I could be way off here. And if there's anyone who can make me rethink my stand on the marimba and those to tickle it, it's a tough-talking DJ leather stud like Dice.

"I want them to fuck on that thing until she has lines on her ass," decides Lauren, after Dice gives Mariah's buttocks a playful smack with his marimba sticks.

Though Mariah's done nothing all night but worry about the possibility that Dice might try to take advantage of her, in no time at all she's melting into his arms behind a wall of glass bricks. What's more, she suddenly has on a pair of white Bridget Jones panties that she couldn't have been wearing in the restaurant unless her panty lines were digitally removed in postproduction.

"Her hard-to-get shtick lasted about 3½ seconds," grumbles Dr. Beaverman as Mariah and Dice tumble onto the bed together.

After a little postcoital chitchat, Mariah's back in the studio, glitter stripe present and accounted for, recording what I think we're meant to believe is her first single, "Loverboy." Although if "Loverboy" is her first single, what was "I Didn't Mean to Turn You On," a demo? Is it just me or is Billie Frank's career trajectory foggier than the stage on a Doug Henning TV special?

One thing I'm not fuzzy on, however, is that Mariah is clearly counting on this movie to be her entrée into the Goofy Ponytail Hall of Fame. In the next scene, our songbird sports a side ponytail that even Suzanne Somers would veto as she canoodles with Dice in the back of a taxi. Before her boy toy can say, "Stop doing that shit with your hair or it's over," their musical love child, "Loverboy," comes on the car radio. Ecstatic, they make the driver stop, then dash together to a pay phone to spread the good news. "Mariah's calling her shift leader at Popeye's Chicken to say she's coming in late," Tony says.

Turns out she's calling Louise and Roxanne so they can squeal with her. The next thing you know, all three ladies, looking slutty in silver, are starring in the video for "Loverboy." This sequence opens with a close-up of Mariah, hair blown and extended Barbarella-style, cooing "Uh-huh, uh-huh, baby" as a hailstorm of glitter wafts over her. It's such a magically delicious, sugar rush of an image that the men and women of theater 11 have no choice but to whoop like banshees. I snap another photo.

Considerably less stoked about the image is the video's Eurotrashy director who stops the take and barks something so profound I'm surprised it's not the tag line on the movie's poster: "The glitter can't overpower the artist."

"Don't I know it," concurs Tony, who, throughout his years in that business they call show, has worn enough bedazzled ensembles to have authority on such matters.

Mr. Eurotrashy then proceeds to go off on another delightful rant that sounds as though it were pieced together from postings on Mariah.com. "We ask ourselves, is she white?" he says philosophically. "Is she black? We don't know. She's exotic. I need some more of her breasts."

More whooping.

At this point the movie gets a much-needed injection of comic relief and actual acting chops in the form of Ann Magnuson, who plays Kelly, Mariah's newly assigned, impossibly perky publicist. Sporting big shoulder pads, dangly earrings, and a Rosalind Chase from *L.A. Law* hairdo, it's as though all the '80s period detail that the rest of the film is vague on was incorporated into this one delightful character.

Unfortunately, Eurotrashy shoos Ms. Magnuson from the video set before she has time to literally hoist the movie onto her back and carry it to safety. Then the power-hungry auteur tries to take Mariah and her glitter stripe into creative directions they don't want to go, starting with her wardrobe. He wants Mariah in just the silver bikini. She prefers the more modest look of a see-through wrap *over* the silver bikini, because she's not particularly exhibitionistic.

Not surprisingly, Eurotrashy wins the bikini battle, and the wrap goes. However, when he brings in four muscle-bound studs in Speedos and body paint to cavort with Mariah on camera, Dice hits the ceiling and drags Mariah out of the studio in a huff. "I don't think we should have walked out," Mariah says to him later. "I don't want to get a bad reputation."

Some lines don't need color commentary from the likes of me to get a few whoops from the folks in theater 11. That line is one of them.

The next scene finds Mariah strutting down the sidewalk with Louise and Roxanne. It's total filler, save for the fact that the twin towers of the World Trade Center loom in the background, looking as majestic and invincible as they were two weeks ago. It's the first time in about an hour that I've thought of such matters, and like everyone else in the room, I can't help but sigh. Adding to the squirm factor is the fact that our heroine is sporting a shirt that says BOMBSHELLS, not to mention another goofy ponytail.

It would take a lot, at this point, for any film to drag me back into its neoreality, but *Glitter* does it in no time, when Mariah whips out her credit card and suggests the gal pals go shopping. A split second later the film cuts *Bewitched*-style to a shot of the trio walking down a different street, in new gold lamé outfits that are different in their individual elements but similar in their unmitigated hideousness. "It's Destiny's Aborted Children," says Tony, nailing it on the head as he so often does.

I come to a poignant realization during a subsequent scene, in which Timothy, the shifty music producer, tries to get Dice to cough up the $100K he owes him. "I miss Sylk," I whisper to Tony. "I want there to be a whole movie about Sylk."

"There is one," he replies. "It's called *Vanity: The E! True Hollywood Story.*"

Dice arrives home after his run-in with Timothy to discover a lovely gift from Mariah, a Yamaha DX-7 synthesizer. Overcome with gratitude, the DJ asks his mulatto muse if she'd like to move in with him. The next thing you know, a fresh-from-the-shower Mariah is unpacking her stuff in Dice's place and getting all misty-eyed.

"I found a box of my mom's things," she blubbers.

"While I was unpacking my tube tops," adds Lauren.

Mariah proceeds to regale her live-in lover with that long-winded fantasy she has in which her lush of a mom will see her perform on a big TV show and rue the day she sent her packing. While Dice listens sympathetically, Ross wonders aloud whether Beesley, the actor, had a bet going with the director during this scene that Mariah couldn't get all her lines out in one take. Though that scenario is not out of the realm of possibility, my Max Beesley fantasy is much more generous. In my version, Beesley considered himself Superactor to Mariah's Lois Lane, believing in his heart that if *he* were truer than a speeding bullet, more in the moment than a locomotive, able to leap awkward pauses in a single bound, then *she* would be convincing by association. He was going to be good enough for both of them.

In the next scene, while working on some lyrics at Dice's new keyboard, Mariah comes across some old photographs of her mother and Mini-Mariah. "Hey, Dennis, that's the picture you took at the beginning of the movie," Lauren says.

You know what? It actually looks like it could be.

Dice wanders in later to find Mariah, still bogarting the DX7, crooning a beautiful song she just wrote about her boozehound mother called "Reflections (Care Enough)." Mariah's pretty good here, and this could be well be one of the film's most affecting moments, but I'm too preoccupied with the mysterious square of red Plexiglas next to Dice's apartment door to surrender to it. "Is that like a hand sensor or what?" I ask Tony.

"I thought it was a kitty door," Tony replies.

"It's so you can tell from the street whether or not Mariah's on duty," Ross concludes.

By this point, you're probably thinking, *Those assholes aren't really saying that stuff in the movie theater and if they are, they must be whispering.* But I assure you, we're full-voiced and not the least bit timid. Nor are we alone. Other patrons are whooping and commenting right along with us.

I want to be clear about something here. I do not condone talking in movie theaters. In fact, I abhor it, even whispering. And the fact that, as a nation, our moviegoing manners are becoming more barbaric by the second is not lost on me. Tonight, however, seems to be some kind of special case, a national emergency, if you will, in which giving Mariah and Company a piece of your mind isn't just an entertaining diversion, it's a goddamn duty. And it's one I take seriously.

Luckily, the strangers in theater 11 seem to be on the same page with us. If they weren't, we would curtail our wagging tongues immediately. OK, maybe Tony wouldn't, but the rest of us would try our darnedest. Now back to the movie.

Having poured her heart out about it in song, Mariah's now determined to track down that missing mother of hers, even if she has to not dress like a hooker for 15 minutes to do it. Clad in a baby-blue sweater set that reveals nary a millimeter of Farley or Spade, Mariah visits a social services office to try and learn the whereabouts of one Lillian Frank. "I had to wear a *sweater,* you guys," I imagine Mariah complaining to Louise and Roxanne later. "It was clear up to *here* and then there was *another* layer on top of it. Oh my God. I thought I was going to *pass out*."

As a curt lady social worker riffles through the Lillian Frank file, Lauren can't help venture a guess as to what the woman's next words are going to be: "It seems your mother left special instructions that you're never to contact her," she says.

"The witness protection program bars us from telling you anything else," adds Ross.

"Except for that it's all your fault," Dr. Beaverman chimes in.

In actuality, the woman then tells Mariah she has "no current information" on Lillian Frank, then sends her on her way. To make matters worse, Mariah soon learns that her record company hates the songs she's been working on with Dice and wants her to collaborate with other producers.

But good news is just around the corner. It seems the producers of the prestigious USA Music Awards are just dying to have Billie Frank in their great big show. Though this strikes me as quite a coup for an artist with no album, Mariah behaves as though she can take or leave it.

At the show's rehearsal, Mariah meets Rafael, a sexy, dreadlocked R&B singer, played by Halle Berry's real-life squeeze, Eric Benet, and practically touches herself while she watches him run through his number at the piano. Hell, so do I. Then she takes the stage to rehearse her song, but it's not "Loverboy." It's "I Didn't Mean to Turn You On." What the hell, man? Billie Frank's discography consists of two songs and yet it continually leaves me flummoxed. Would it have killed Vondie Curtis-Hall to give us a couple of spinning *Billboard* Charts? A Casey Kasem cameo, perhaps?

After the awards, Mariah, wearing a pale pink minidress with fur trim, and Dice, in an open jacket and *no shirt,* share a limo ride home with Roxanne and Louise. In an exchange I suspect may have been ripped straight from Mariah's real-life divorce papers, a sloshed and supercilious Dice berates Mariah for dressing too provocatively. "Every bit is hanging out," he rants. The fact that he just attended an award show in *no shirt* doesn't strike him as the least bit hypocritical.

Mariah's friends try to stick up for their homegirl, but Dice slags them off too, calling Louise "fat ass" and Roxanne "roach bag." Livid, the backup girls demand to be let out of the car. When Roxanne turns back to Mariah and asks her to come with them, Mariah looks down forlornly and stays with her man. Later, at home, Mariah, still in her pink gown, dissolves into sobs while Dice assures her everything will be OK.

"It looked so good on Gwyneth!" wails a male mystery voice from the back of the house. I have no idea who this guy is, but he sounds sort of cute.

Mariah must have summoned up the will to go on living because in the next scene she's walking the streets again. Suddenly she spots a jabbering bag lady and decides, that since the woman's wearing a headband, it must be her long-lost mother. We know this because the "Closure" song starts playing in the background.

"I want the homeless lady to say, 'Soylent Green is people,'"says Ross.

The two women get closer, eyeing each other with an intensity bordering on cruising, then Mariah realizes it's not her mother after all and walks away despondently. No closure for her today, it seems.

"A woman usually becomes a hysteric as a result of being abandoned by one or both of her parents, more often the mother, according to Freud," Dr. Beaverman remarks. "So, believe it or not, this movie is right on the money, psychologically speaking."

Later, after being threatened and getting her cheeks squeezed by the menacing Timothy, Mariah has a big fight with Dice about the $100,000 deal he made behind her back. Though justifiably traumatized by the whole situation, she still has a career to think about and the show must go on. She's backstage about to perform on *Late Night Live* when she learns that Dice has been arrested for assaulting Timothy, so she leaves the studio immediately and runs to her lover's rescue. Apparently, the show doesn't have to go on after all.

Mariah bails Dice out of the slammer only to tell him how "over it" she is when they get home. "Since when has this been about you?" Dice hollers back. "This is about *us*."

"What movie are you in, Dice?" Tony has to ask.

"Don't blame me for your failure!" Mariah bellows.

"Hit 'er!" yells a mystery voice from the back row. I'm not sure if it's the same guy who shouted the Gwyneth line or not. Whoever it is, we just might be made for each other.

"You swing that ass around onstage and you hit a couple of high notes here and there and think that you're some colossal success!" Dice roars back.

"Hit 'er!" repeats the mystery voice.

OK, I have to see who this guy is. I turn around to see two men, my age or a little younger, pointing at each other, as if to say, "*He's* the one with the big mouth, not me." The fellow on the right has a friendly face and that floppy Tom Cruise in *Mission: Impossible 2* hair that I can't get enough of. The guy on the left is pretty fetching too, with a blond buzz cut and a matching soul patch, but it looks like he's got a ring on his finger. Maybe they're together.

Back on the screen, Mariah's had about all of Dice's emasculation rage she can handle without a change of hairdo, so she smacks him one and storms out. "I'll be at the Four Seasons!" spits Lauren.

It turns out Mariah doesn't need five-star pampering. What she needs is companionship and understanding, so she heads, kitty in tow, to the crappy apartment she used to share with Louise and Roxanne. "Roach Bag, Fat Ass, I'm home!" chirps Tony as Mariah knocks on the door.

I make a split-second decision to keep my eye on Whisper the Cat for the duration of the scene and I'm not disappointed. Even though that beast must be so old by now he has his own dialysis machine, there are still several priceless Whisper moments. One is the beleaguered look on Whisper's face when the door opens and Mariah says, "Hi." The other involves a bad bit of continuity where one moment Whisper is facing the camera and a split second later he's turned away in shame, clearly regretting the day he passed on that Nine Lives print ad to be a pawn in this undercooked domestic drama.

Mariah's old pals welcome her back to the land of hanging panties with open arms and soon our homegirl's hugging a pillow on a makeshift bed and experiencing more reflections. "Hey, Fat Ass!" I holler as Mariah. "What's the thread count on this shitty pillow, 50?"

"She's a huge star," marvels Lauren during the next scene in which Mariah's shown walking down a busy street, "yet she lives with her girlfriends, walks everywhere, and no one ever recognizes her."

"Welcome to Crazy Backwards Land," says Ross.

Then Mariah writes and records a song with Eric Benet. Though this whole subplot goes nowhere, there are a lot worse people to watch Mariah go nowhere with than the scrumptious Mr. Halle Berry in his tan, body-hugging YMLA shirt from the late 1990s.

Next, we learn via a radio DJ voice-over that Mariah not only has an album now, but it's shot to number 1 on the charts. What's more, she's going to perform songs from it at a concert at Madison Square Garden.

What happens next is sort of embarrassing to even write about, so I'll make it brief. Somehow, in their pain and longing, Mariah and Dice, in separate apartments, tap right into that collective unconscious we're always hearing about and write the exact same song without communicating with each other. Even Whisper is like *What the fuck?*

Though Mariah should be thrilled and grateful about her overnight success, her estrangement from Dice is turning her into an unreasonable diva before her time. While rehearsing "Loverboy" with her concert dancers, Mariah has a five-alarm Shit Fit, tossing the mike to the ground and crowing, "If I could *hear* myself it would be nice." I have to say, it's her most believable moment in the whole movie. "I'm not doing this shit anymore!" she adds, then storms out of the room. *Anymore,* I think. She's been a star for like 11 minutes.

"All along, her hairstyles have been a barometer for her level of drive," says Dr. Beaverman, pointing to Mariah's current ponytail, which is pure 1990 Madonna. "She's now in her Blond Ambition phase and showing more assertiveness. But underneath it all, she's still a wilting, hideous codependent."

Mariah flees the rehearsal and heads to Dice's place, but he's not at home. She lets herself in anyway and discovers that not only are she and Dice on the same page in terms of missing each other but they've been writing the same goddamn song. Mariah opts not to take legal action—this is Dice, not J. Lo, after all—and instead brings his sheet music to her lips and kisses it. Then she discovers a ticket to her Garden concert on top of the piano and decides Dice must still love her after all.

"*Mezzanine*?" says one of the back-row cuties disapprovingly. "What a cheap-ass."

Dice returns home a few minutes later, but Mariah's already gone. "That lip print is so big," observes Dr. Beaverman when Dice discovers the lipstick kiss on his sheet music. "Did she kiss it or sit on it?"

Looking closer, Dice sees there's a *B* written underneath the lip print.

"Bridget?" says Ross, racking his brain. "Betty?"

"Beyoncé," I declare.

My Beyoncé declaration brings down the house, and I'm not too modest to say so. My feeling of triumph is so delicious, it's all I can do not to say, "Thank you, good night, tip your flashdancers," and leave while I'm ahead.

We're all still tittering from Beyoncé when, a minute or so later, Timothy sneaks up to Dice on the sidewalk and deposits a bullet in his chest.

We then cut over to Madison Square Garden where the crowd is chanting "Billie! Billie! Billie!" But Ms. Frank is nowhere to be found. It turns out she's not late because of Dice's murder—she hasn't found out yet—she's just late because she's unprofessional. This part of her character nags at me, because it reminds of the way the real-life Mariah, in spite of being very hardworking, puts out this vibe that says *Infantalize me, please.* A healthy diva, I maintain, is a diva who has decided whether she wants to rule the world (see Madonna) or be taken care of (see Dion, Celine) because I don't think you can do both.

Everyone else, it seems, has made it to the Garden on time, from handlers to orphan friends alike. They're all hanging out in the green room worrying about Mariah and wondering if there's been some sort or hold-up with the glitter stripe. Suddenly they learn via the TV news that Dice the DJ has been shot dead. Mariah wanders in just in time to get the news, and she couldn't be more bummed out about it. She always figured the cat would go first.

Though the songbird blew off *Late Night Live* over a run-of-the-mill arrest, she decides that her Garden show is going to go on, dead DJ or no dead DJ. So, as her hardworking *Solid Gold*–style dancers Jazzercise their shapely asses off to "Loverboy," Mariah saunters nervously out onto the stage in a full-length, beaded, "Happy Birthday, Mr. President" gown, then puts a halt to the fancy footwork by doing a dramatic, sidelong

"Stop in the Name of Love" hand motion. She then tells the digitally enhanced crowd, "Everybody out there, don't ever take anybody for granted because you never know when you might lose them."

With that, she starts into "Never Too Far," the love theme from *Glitter* that she and Dice collaborated on but didn't know it. Is the Dice estate going to get a cut of the royalties, I wonder? Astonishingly, the band and lighting people also seem to have a psychic connection to the never-performed song and hit their marks perfectly. In another absurd twist, Mariah's dancers decide to stay onstage and hold each other while being moved by her performance instead of going into the alley to smoke.

As Mariah heads into the second verse, I have to admit that I sort of like this song. Screw it, I'm going start a grassroots campaign to get "Never Too Far" an Oscar nomination for Best Song because I want Mariah half-naked at the Oscars. I mean, if Lionel Richie can win a statue for "Say You, Say Me," I should, with a heartfelt mass E-mail, at least be able to get this fucker into the top five.

Just before the second chorus, director Hall serves up a shot of Mariah from the back that shows that our heroine was not so grief-stricken over Dice as to forget her trademark glitter stripe. There it is, in all its mysterious, metallic glory, beaming forth from the middle of her back.

Before going any further into what happens next, it's important that I explain something about my roommate, Tony. As you may have noticed, he has a way of saying out loud whatever pops into his demented, beautiful mind. I daresay my ass would be even saggier than it is were it not for the arduous clenching exercises I do every time he makes a pronouncement that, to my mind, crosses the line of propriety. For example, just a few weeks ago we met Debby Boone backstage at a regional production of *The King and I,* and within 10 seconds of saying hello, Tony told the "You Light Up My Life" singer she had a "phenomenal rack."

What's remarkable about this propensity of his is that it never results in hurt feelings, embarrassment, or fisticuffs. On the contrary, somehow everyone comes out smelling just like that rose Dice gave Mariah back when he was trying to get in her pants. Debby Boone loved him.

These incidents, let's call them Tony Moments, usually play out in the following sequence:

Step One: Something absurd in the universe provokes a response in Tony.

Step Two: Tony makes a pronouncement about it to or in front of innocent civilians that I find shocking, presumptuous, profane, or all three.

Step Three: The civilians take a moment to truly experience their disgust and incredulity.

Step Four: The uncomfortable moment passes and the civilians fall in love with Tony and his irrepressible, un-PC mouthiness. Then the heavens open and joy juice rains down, drenching everyone within a 50-foot radius with love, light, and laughter.

This chain of events is about to unfold tonight here in theater 11 of the Beverly Center. Having spent the last hour and a half trying to come up with a logical explanation for Mariah's magical mystery stripe, and failing miserably, Tony decides to discuss it with an expert, someone who knows a little more than he does about the fashion and beauty business.

"Tyra!" he shouts, stopping my heartbeat in its tracks. "What is *up* with that glitter stripe on her back?"

Oh, my God, he said her name. Out loud. He addressed supermodel-turned-actress Tyra Banks. He asked for her thoughts on the glitter stripe. And now there's no turning back.

I want to be dead. My cheeks are so tightly clenched I'm surprised I haven't inhaled the seat cushion. There's a hush over the theater as everyone's waiting for the shit to hit the fan and wondering if they're in the line of fire. I don't have to wonder. I know I am.

Tyra rises from her seat rather quickly, though in my mind it seems more like that slow-motion effect we saw earlier when everyone on the dance floor got blurry but Dice. Then she turns back to face us and, in a voice that's sassy and not the least bit modelish, says the 10 words I'm going to be dining out on for the next 10 years: "*Thank you.* I've been trying to figure that out *myself.*"

The crowd erupts. If my "Beyoncé" quip was a 7.5 on the hysteria meter, Tyra's retort is a solid 11. Mixed in with the laughter is a big dollop of relief as well as this odd "Whaddaya know?" feeling brought about by the exhilarating discovery that at least one glamorous Hollywood celeb is actually *game.* Maybe they really are just like the rest of us.

I'm delirious with joy. Tony has, once again, made the sun shine out of his ass, and I have an excellent view.

After getting teary-eyed and doing a swivel move that makes Ross wonder aloud if her stilettos have been glued to a lazy Susan, Mariah brings her song to a high-pitched, poignant finish. As the lights fade on her devastated face, one of the back-row cuties tosses out another "Hit 'er!" For some reason, this one falls flat, perhaps because it smacks of kicking Mariah while she's down, although, let's face it, that's pretty much the theme of this whole evening.

I turn and steal a glance at the back row. Floppy has one hand up at his temple and is looking into lap like he wants to disappear. Blondie, meanwhile, is trying to look nonchalant. This must mean that Blondie's the domestic violence enthusiast and Floppy's currently clenching his ass over a "bring it up again" that just didn't fly. Floppy's my guy, I decide.

After her performance, Mariah discovers a note in her dressing room from Dice. I assume he penned it before he was shot, but who can be sure with this movie? She takes the letter, hops into a limo, and pulls away from Madison Square Garden, while the marquee flashes behind her, BILLIE FRANK SOLD OUT. She sure as fuck did.

As Billie rides, via voice-over we hear the contents of Dice's letter, but counter to logic, it's not Dice's voice reading his words. It's Mariah's voice reading Dice's words. "Only in Crazy Backwards Land," mutters Ross.

The limo pulls up to a farmhouse straight out of *Green Acres,* and soon Mariah's mother, Lillian, appears on the porch, looking rested and far younger than she did 15 years ago when she was saddled with Mini-Mariah and her cavalcade of needs.

Well, it looks like the claustrophobic blue sweater set did the trick, because, according to Dice's letter, the woman at social services has tracked down Mariah's mother. Turns out she's not sharing bunk beds with Paula Poundstone at Promises Malibu or heading up her own harem of crack whores. She's living off the fat of the land on a farm in Maryland. Mariah tells the limo driver to take her directly there. Home, James, indeed.

Soon it's daylight and they're still driving. *"Wait a second, this is where I shot the 'Dreamlover' video,"* says Tony when the limo passes a rolling field of grass. *"It's always the last place you look."*

The limo pulls up to a farmhouse straight out of *Green Acres,* and soon Mariah's mother, Lillian, appears on the porch, looking rested and far younger than she did 15 years ago when she was saddled with Mini-Mariah and her cavalcade of needs.

"Git off my propitty!" hollers Lauren.

"Could you guys be *quiet*?" shouts someone from the last row, someone we haven't heard from before. It sounds like a teenage girl, perhaps a diehard Mariah fan on date night, who has waited until the last scene of the film to give our loudmouthed asses a piece of her mind. I'm a little mortified because I don't like to upset anyone, ever. I thought we were all on the same page here, all 50 of us.

Tony decides he'll be the one to answer her question for all of us. "I kind of doubt it," he says.

Oh, shit. Her boyfriend, who I imagine to be an aspiring pugilist who's already cranky from having to sit through *Glitter,* is going to *beat my ass.*

I'm about rush out to Hallmark to buy a "Sorry we shit all over *Glitter*" card, from their more subversive Shoebox line, when an image appears on screen that stops me in my tracks. It's a moment that needs no comment from any of us to merit whooping: As

Mariah slinks through the yard to greet her mother, her heels sink into the grass. This is why the *Hee Haw* Honeys always wore flats.

We're helpless with laughter when Mariah dissolves, rather convincingly, into tears and falls into her mother's arms.

"I want her to look up and go, 'Mom, still with the *headbands*?' " says Tony, as the camera does a 360 around them.

"I'm so glad you're here, Billie," says Ross as Mama Frank. *"You can help me harvest the sorghum crop."*

And then the credits start to roll. Date Night Girl and her Guy leave first. A few assorted strangers follow, but none of our posse can seem to move. It's obvious no one wants to leave this room, let alone go back to reality, or what passes for reality on September 21, 2001.

Shawn sneaks up behind me, pulls my head back, and kisses me on the forehead. "We have to go," he says. "We're driving back to San Diego tonight. I'll call you later." And then he's gone. What, no puff of smoke?

Marcus and Perry then leave their seats in the front row and slide, facing us on their knees, into the just-vacated chairs in row two.

"So many junkies end up on farms in Maryland," remarks Perry.

"Why, old Richard Pryor's got a place right up the road," says Tony in his best Country Time Lemonade twang. "Used to freebase heroin. Now he's got the best tomaters in the whole county."

"And that little cottage by the feed store is Courtney Love's," I say, getting in on the act. "She makes her own jam."

"Her Frances Bean just won the 4-H biggest pumpkin award for the second year running," adds Ross.

"Mariah couldn't even bother to go pick out a casket for her dead lover," grumbles Dr. Beaverman, who obviously still has a few bones to pick with *Glitter,* "or take a new, clean sleeveless black T-shirt to the funeral home so he could be laid out in it. No, she has to sing at Madison Square Garden, then zip off to her mother's place in Maryland. Meanwhile, the love of her life's in a drawer in the morgue with a toe tag on. Deplorable."

As Dr. B. rants on, we pretend not to stare as Tyra and Friends head for the exit. "Well, they can't all be *Coyote Ugly,*" Tony calls out to her.

"Oh, I *know,*" says Tyra playfully.

"I'm sorry if we ruined the movie for you," says Tony.

"Please, you *made* the movie," she says. "I just have to know one thing: Do you guys love her or hate her?"

Again we let Tony answer for all of us. "Yes," he says.

Once they're gone, Marcus leans into me and gasps, "I didn't know Tyra was here until Tony said her name. I nearly peed my pants. Her mom—I think it was her mom—

was next to me, and all I knew was that these pretty hands would reach over and grab her whenever something ridiculous would happen."

"You must have seen a lot of those hands," says Barry.

"Hey, the last name of the actress who played the homeless woman is Hensley," says Ross, pointing at the screen.

"Maybe she's *my* mother," I say.

When the credits finish, the only people left in the theater are the eight of us and Floppy and Blondie. I take another look back at them as they get up and leave. I think Floppy smiles at me, but I'm not sure.

We follow them out then loiter in the hallway outside the theater while everyone except Ross, Lauren, and I hit the rest room. Across the hall, Floppy waits for his friend to do the same.

"The only thing that would have made that movie better," I remark, "was if her character was actually named Glitter, like 'Your turn to feed the cat, Glitter,' or 'Doesn't Glitter have an amazing voice'?"

"See, *that's* what I don't get," says Lauren. "Everyone's always telling Mariah's character what amazing voice she has, yet all she ever sang were these dance songs that anyone could sing."

"Anyone except Sylk," I remind her. "*That's* what I want to see: *Glitter 2: Sylk's Revenge.*"

"I want Ann Magnuson and Sylk to solve mysteries together," says Ross.

Suddenly, Lauren moves in and under her breath says to me, "That guy over there's totally checking you out." She's referring to Floppy.

"You think?" I say.

"Well, he's not checking *me* out," she says.

"He's not checking *me* out," echoes Ross.

When I look back to Floppy, he's going into the bathroom just as Marcus, Tony, and Blondie are coming out.

"Go talk to him," says Lauren.

"I don't know," I say. "I think he might be too sexy."

"Oh, Dennis," she says impatiently. "Remember what you said to me that first night I went to open mike night at the Comedy Store?"

"Where the fuck are we supposed to park?" I guess.

"I wanted to turn around and go home," she says, "and you said something like, 'It's not about *getting* what you want, it's about going after it.' "

"Damn, that's *good.* I said that?"

Lauren nods.

"Don't make me get out the sugars and Equals again, young man," Ross threatens.

Barry and Perry are just leaving when I head into the men's room, leaving me alone with Floppy. He's standing at a urinal with his back to me. I try to listen for a stream, thinking that if there *isn't* one, I'm totally in. My plan is to pretend to fiddle with a pesky contact lens in the mirror, then try to say something clever to his reflection as he comes up to wash his hands, but there are no mirrors. No mirrors in the Beverly Center Cineplex Odeon men's room. Don't they know who their clientele is?

"I'll give you 20 bucks cash money right now for your T- shirt," Floppy says to me as I inexplicably dry my hands, which were never wet to begin with.

When I turn to face him, he's got a sexy "Let's make a deal" look on his face, and I must say, it's a pretty doggone handsome face, even in this bad fluorescent lighting.

"You can have my shirt in exchange," he offers, sticking out his chest so I can read the slogan that's printed across his sleeveless powder-blue T-shirt: SOMETIMES GOD JUST CLOSES A DOOR.

"That's pretty funny," I say, laughing, "and totally true."

"Thanks," he says. "I designed it myself. I have a little T-shirt company on the side."

"Cool," I say. Well, it *is* cool. Shut up.

"So?" he says, pulling a $20 bill from his Velcro wallet and holding it out to me. I pull the bottom of my T-shirt away from my waist and gaze down at my beloved, shirtless Gregory Harrison, who is still sexy as hell, even upside down.

"I don't know if I can part with this," I hedge. "I got the iron-on off eBay and spent months trying to find the perfect shirt to put it on. It was kind of a big deal." Floppy shrugs and tucks his 20 back into his pocket. "You know what?" I say excitedly. "I still have the E-mail address of the guy I bought it from. I bet we could get you one. Write down your info."

"*For Ladies Only,*" says Floppy wistfully while I dig out a pen and something to write on. "I discovered some interesting things about myself watching that movie."

"Same here," I say, then watch as he writes down his name and phone number. "Aaron," I say, reading from the slip of paper. "I'm Dennis."

"Nice to meet you," he says.

"I just gotta know," I say, putting the pen and paper back in my pocket, "Were you the one who made that genius mezzanine comment?"

"Uh-huh," he says, laughing. "You were Beyoncé, right?"

"Uh-huh," I say.

We bask together in the *Glitter* afterglow for a few seconds, during which time I'm overcome with the desire to see him without a shirt on. "Fuck it, let's switch," I say, then toss off my coat and strip off my stripper shirt as fast as possible so I can be done before he starts. I don't want to miss a thing.

"It looks better on you," I say afterward, giving him the once-over.

"Nah, it doesn't," he says, reaching back into his pocket for the 20.

"You can keep your money," I tell him.

He smiles, then shifts his gaze down to my front pants pocket. "You can keep my phone number."

Before we leave the bathroom, I take my camera from my coat, open the lens, and hold it down by my waist. I want to capture the look on everyone's faces when Aaron and I emerge from the can with each other's shirts on. I'm not disappointed.

I introduce Aaron and Johnny—that's his blond friend's name—to everyone except Dr. Beaverman, who is just now emerging from the ladies' room.

"I'm sorry, kids," she says. "I just ran into the girl who told us to be quiet in there. She had a fight with her fella."

"Did you apologize for us?" I ask.

"Not so much," says Dr. Beaverman, "although I did tell her I think the message Mariah's sending to young girls with this movie is a travesty."

"What message is that?" asks Marcus.

"That it's OK to sacrifice yourself and your career for some no-account boyfriend as long as he's willing to stick it to you every night," she says.

"Oh, that message," says Perry.

"What did she say when you said that?" I ask.

"Something in Spanish," says Dr. Beaverman, "that I believe was derogatory toward *moi,* but what are you gonna do? I try to help where I can."

As we make our way out of the multiplex and into the mall proper, Dr. Beaverman gives Aaron and Johnny a quick hello then starts back in on *Glitter.* "There is a common archetypal Jungian theme in these women-on-top, *Star Is Born* kind of movies," she asserts. "The woman on top, in this case Mariah, will stick with the albatross boyfriend no matter how untalented or how much of a fashion emergency he is. A man on top would think nothing of discarding the woman who helped him, but the woman on top will stand by her man to the bitter end, until outside forces—i.e., death or suicide, separate them. I knew as soon as we met Dice that he was a goner. I was just hoping he'd take her with him and it would turn into *Star 80.*"

"Johnny and I need to catch this," says Aaron, pointing to the bank of elevators in the center of the mall. "But I've enjoyed listening to you," he adds, looking to Dr. Beaverman. "You have great insights."

"Try telling that that to the crying Latina in the bathroom," says Dr. Beaverman.

While Aaron and Johnny wait for the lift, Dr. Beaverman gives them one final insight for the road. "I'm hoping now that Mariah's found her mother she'll actually dress in something that doesn't reveal her tits, ass, or pubic area," she says, as our new friends step into the elevator. "So *Glitter* is actually an uplifting movie in the end. Now that her mother is back in her life, Mariah's going to put a bra on and cover up that body."

As the elevator doors close, Johnny says, "Good night," while Aaron gives me the international hand signal for "Call me." "That guy has the same shirt as you," Dr. Beaverman observes. I decide to save the story of Aaron and the Magical Shirt Switch for the ride home.

No one speaks for a while as we amble through the empty mall. We're spent, it seems, sated, apprehensive about the future but grateful that a good time like tonight can still be had.

When I'm feeling frustrated in life, it's usually because I feel like there's a sizable gulf between what I have and what I *should* have, in terms of career, love life, square footage, those sorts of things. This sensation is likely to come over me when yet another magazine has gone under without paying me or when I find myself at a party at a gorgeous Mediterranean house in the hills belonging to someone my age or younger who writes for television. I'm not saying these feelings are justified or healthy or even that frequent, I'm just saying I have them.

The point I'm trying to get to is that I never have those kinds of feelings about my friends. And I can't imagine any success-driven scenario—like, say, me celebrating my Oscar win with my naked husband, Viggo, in our Malibu hot tub—that would leave me feeling as happy to be alive as a night out at *Glitter* with these people.

"Poor Mariah," says Marcus, finally breaking the silence, as we take the first of several escalators down to the parking garage.

"She'll bounce back," I say.

"This will be a good lesson for Mariah Carey," argues our resident tough-love proponent, Dr. Beaverman, "because damn her ass for thinking whatever she put down in the recording studio was going to be a hit. A little soul searching will do her good."

We hug good night at the bottom of the level 3 escalator, vow to take on *Top Gun* soon, then head to our respective vehicles. I'm about to start the truck when I notice Lauren, across the parking lot, smiling beatifically while Barry kneels in front of her. "Oh my God, is he *proposing*?" I say, then look a closer. "No, just tying her shoe because she can't do it herself."

"That's love," says Dr. Beaverman.

I start the truck, flip a U, and head toward the exit ramp, passing Marcus and Perry, who are making out next to Perry's Jeep like there's no tomorrow. And guess what? Maybe there's not. Just as I'm about pull onto the circular ramp down, I see a flash of light in my rearview mirror. I hit the brake and look back over my shoulder. "Ross's birthday gift," I say to Dr. Beaverman. "I totally forgot about it."

I shift into park, and the two of us watch as Ross and Tony, positioned between two massive cement pillars, engage in a light-saber duel while the lights of the city flicker behind them like stars. If George Lucas were here, he'd put the camera right where we are now, assuming he still uses cameras. Who can keep up?

Because she knows from such highbrow things, Dr. Beaverman has no trouble tuning into a classical radio station. She cranks the volume, and for several minutes we watch raptly as our weekend Jedi warriors, accompanied by Mozart, advance and retreat, parry and lunge, fumble their weapons and laugh about it. I'm not sure if it's the Force, but something is definitely with them.

"Six dollars," says the parking attendant, a minute or so later, when we finally drive up to the exit. *Six dollars?* I think. Wow, we've been here a long time. Any other night I'd feel a bit guilty blowing so much money on parking, but tonight it feels like a bargain.

"I got it," says Dr. Beaverman, handing me a 10. "You drove."

Greg Henry

About the Author

Dennis Hensley is the author of the best-selling novel *Misadventures in the (213)*. As a journalist, he has published articles in *Movieline, Cosmopolitan, TV Guide, The Advocate, Out, In Style, Us Weekly, Detour*, and *British Premier*. An accomplished performer and musician, he has also recorded a CD of his own songs, *The Water's Fine.* He lives in the (818).

To contact Dennis with your *Screening Party*-related rants, raves, and remembrances, send an E-mail to ScreeningParty@aol.com or visit his Web site: www.dennishensley.com.